I0605083

SCREAMING AND CONJURING

SCREAMING AND CONJURING

THE RESURRECTION AND UNSTOPPABLE RISE OF THE MODERN HORROR MOVIE

CLARK COLLIS

1984

SCREAMING AND CONJURING

This is a work of nonfiction. The events and experiences detailed herein have been faithfully rendered as remembered by the author and interviewees, to the best of their ability.

COVER ILLUSTRATION: Gary Pullin
EDITOR: Dan Lockwood
LAYOUT: Arkadii Pankevich
INDEX: Nick de Somogyi
Image credits appear in the back of the book.

LIBRARY OF CONGRESS CONTROL NUMBER: 2025936623

LC record available at https://lccn.loc.gov/2025936623

ISBNs: 9781948221351 (hardbound), 9781948221368 (ebook)

Printed and bound in PRC.

1984 PUBLISHING
Cleveland, Ohio / USA
1984Publishing.com
info@1984publishing.com

FIRST EDITION / FIRST PRINTING

9 8 7 6 5 4 3 2 1

For my father, Bernard,
who loved Westerns but came with me
to see Hellraiser *anyway.*

CONTENTS

INTRODUCTION

Don Coscarelli is a filmmaker famous in the horror community for his often-terrifying movies and routinely amiable nature. While only in his mid-twenties, Coscarelli wrote and directed 1979's independently financed *Phantasm*, about an otherworldly undertaker who goes about his evil business with help from a lethal flying sphere. The film was a franchise-inaugurating hit which so impressed a young J. J. Abrams that the director later referenced the movie by giving the name Captain Phasma to Gwendoline Christie's character in 2015's *Star Wars: The Force Awakens*. More than two decades after making *Phantasm*, Coscarelli directed 2002's *Bubba Ho-Tep*. Another low-budget movie, the horror-comedy starred Bruce Campbell as a mummy-battling Elvis Presley and, like *Phantasm*, would go on to be hailed by horror fans as a cult classic. A few years later, Coscarelli confirmed his reputation as a maestro of the genre by directing the first episode of the horror anthology TV show *Masters of Horror*, "Incident On and Off a Mountain Road."

Coscarelli tends to recall his professional setbacks and battles with a smile. Even so, when the filmmaker spoke over Zoom for this book, his mood darkened as he talked about the state of his career, and of the horror genre as a whole, during the early 1990s. The director illustrated the parlous state of the horror movie at that time by relating what he described as a "funny story," although the humorous nature of the anecdote would only have become apparent retrospectively.

After directing 1989's wilderness-set adventure-thriller *Survival Quest*, Coscarelli thought he had found his next film when he read the horror novel *Dead in the West*. The book was written by prolific Texan author Joe R. Lansdale, whose many tales include the stories that Coscarelli would later adapt for *Bubba Ho-Tep* and his *Masters of Horror* episode. "I seized on *Dead in the West*, which is sort of a Clint Eastwood western with zombies, okay?" said Coscarelli. "It's a great book; it would make a great movie."

In search of finance, the director approached New Line Cinema. This independent studio had enjoyed so much success with 1984's *A Nightmare on Elm Street* and its sequels that New Line was nicknamed 'The House that Freddy Built,' a reference to the franchise's supernatural killer, Freddy Krueger. Surely, Coscarelli thought, the company would see the potential in the project. "I distinctly remember sending it over to New Line, which had made all this money off of the Freddy stuff," said Coscarelli. "I can remember getting a call back from the New Line guy and he goes, 'Don, this is a zombie movie. We would *never* make a zombie movie.' Of course, this was before the rise of the zombie stuff. You couldn't sell a zombie film back then. I literally took the script, and every time the 'z' word was in it, I changed it to 'creature'." The director was still unable to secure financing. "It was a tough period," he concluded. "I was in the wastelands from '91 to '95."

Coscarelli is not alone in looking back at the period as a rough one for horror movies. Although some significant genre films were released during the early '90s, including 1992's Tony Todd-starring *Candyman* and the same year's Francis Ford Coppola-directed *Bram Stoker's Dracula*, there is no doubt that the genre had reached something of a nadir, with even hardcore fans wearying of being served sequels from fading franchises and other cash-grab releases. As *Scream* screenwriter Kevin Williamson explained to me, "We were going through that era where people were just throwing five dollars at a movie, making a horror film, getting a return on their investment, and moving on. No one cared about quality."

Several decades on, however, the horror genre is in unarguably robust health. As I write this introduction in the spring of 2025, horror movie fans can look back at a remarkably fecund period. The list of notable genre movies released over the last 12 months alone boasts *Longlegs*, *Heretic*, *Alien: Romulus*, *A Quiet Place: Day One*, *Late Night with the Devil*, *The First Omen*, *Strange Darling*, *Abigail*, *V/H/S Beyond*, *Immaculate*, *Smile 2*, *Sting*, *Cuckoo*, *Oddity*, *Terrifier 3*, *The Substance*, *MaXXXine*, the English-language remake of *Speak No Evil*, *I Saw the TV Glow*, *Blink Twice*, *In a Violent Nature,* Japanese director Kiyoshi Kurosawa's *Chime*, the South Korean film *Exhuma*, *Nosferatu*, *Wolf Man*, Steven Soderbergh's *Presence*, *The Dead Thing*, *Heart Eyes*, and Stephen King adaptation *The Monkey*. Filmmaker Michael Dougherty is a lifelong fan of the genre who directed the beloved 2009 horror anthology *Trick 'r Treat* as well as the 2019 blockbuster *Godzilla: King of the Monsters*. When I spoke with him in the summer of 2024, Dougherty admitted to feeling a little daunted by the sheer quantity of new horror movies being released. "It's almost so overwhelming that I can't keep up," the director said. "It's a golden age, but it's kind of what you make it, right? Between streaming and theatrical, it's up to you to pick and choose and navigate your way through all these different horror films."

At a time when entertainment industry experts are expressing fears about the future of the big-screen experience on a seemingly daily basis, the horror genre is a reliable generator of profits for cinemas, outperforming expectations again and again. When *The Hollywood Reporter* revealed in March 2022 that filmmaker Fede Álvarez was set to direct a new movie in the *Alien* series for 20th Century Studios, the article noted that the project was "intended to be made for Hulu as part of 20th Century's ambitions to make more than 10 movies a year for the Disney-operated streaming service." The studio later changed tack and released Álvarez's film, *Alien: Romulus*, to cinemas in the late summer of 2024. The movie was a worldwide theatrical hit, earning $105 million at the US box office and another $245 million internationally.[1]

The Substance, too, endured a circuitous route to the screen. French filmmaker Coralie Fargeat's movie stars Demi Moore as a middle-aged celebrity whose attempt to recapture the physical attributes of youth results in grotesque disaster. The film was produced by the UK-based Working Title, but their parent company, Universal Pictures, decided not to distribute Fargeat's body-horror story. *The Substance* was instead put into cinemas by streaming service MUBI and went on to become a critical and commercial hit. The film earned $77 million worldwide and was nominated for Academy Awards in the categories of Best Picture, Actress, Director, Original Screenplay, and Makeup and Hairstyling. Although the film would win just the latter trophy, Moore's defeat in the Best Actress race by *Anora* star Mikey Madison still represented a victory for horror. Madison's handful of previous significant film roles included playing a murderer in 2022's *Scream*, the fifth film in the slasher series. The actress became the first of the franchise's 'Ghostface' killers to win an Oscar.

Terrifier 3 is yet another 2024 horror movie that confounded expectations, this one spectacularly so. Director Damien Leone's gruesome and unrated slasher movie, starring David Howard Thornton as the homicidal Art the Clown, cost just $2 million to make. When the boutique entertainment

---

[1] Most of the box office information in this book comes from the website boxofficemojo.com. Box Office Mojo combines revenue from US and Canadian theaters into a single "domestic" figure. References to "domestic" or "US" grosses also include revenues from Canada; references to "foreign" or "international" territories include all countries other than the USA and Canada.

company Cineverse released the film in the US a couple of weeks before Halloween, Leone's movie replaced the much-hyped and much more expensive superhero sequel *Joker: Folie à Deux* as the biggest film in the country, with weekend earnings in excess of $18 million. "David beat Goliath," Cineverse CEO Chris McGurk told media outlet *The Wrap* on the Sunday following the release of *Terrifier 3*. "Even if we had just made $5 million, we would have had a home run. $10 million would be the grand slam of grand slams. But to actually do over $18 million and to win the weekend amongst all those studio tentpoles is just really unbelievable." *Terrifier 3* would ultimately gross $53 million at the domestic box office alone.

In December 2024, *Time* posted an article of the following year's "most anticipated movies." Of the 41 films written up by the outlet's Ben Rosenstock, an impressive ten were horror movies. Several of those projects were the work of acclaimed directors, with *Black Panther* filmmaker Ryan Coogler releasing his first genre movie *Sinners*, Guillermo del Toro delivering his long-in-the-works version of *Frankenstein*, and del Toro's fellow Best Director Oscar-winner Danny Boyle overseeing franchise reboot *28 Years Later*, the first in a planned new trilogy for the rage-virus series.

The business model of movie studios is now firmly centered around big-budget productions based on globally recognized intellectual properties. From *Inside Out 2* to *Deadpool & Wolverine*, nearly all of 2024's biggest box office successes were franchise continuations. Horror movies tend to be relatively cheap to make, and the genre is one of the few remaining ways filmmakers can tell fresh, even personal, stories and still stand a chance of securing a significant theatrical release. Although many recent horror hits have been entries in established franchises, the genre also produced an array of original movies, often from fresh talents like *In a Violent Nature* director Chris Nash and *I Saw the TV Glow* filmmaker Jane Schoenbrun. "I love the splattery horror movies, I love the Sam Raimi movies that almost feel like comedies, but I also love the serious horror movies that are subtle and artful," says Schoenbrun. "I always sort of joke that David Lynch and David Cronenberg were my two dads. *I Saw the TV Glow* is very much threading the needle between coming-of-age, and horror, and a really personal investigation of a queer sense of self."

Screaming and Conjuring tracks the roots and early years of this extraordinary renaissance, starting with the release of the ground-breaking and influential *Scream* in 1996 and concluding with the arrival of 2013's *The Conjuring*, which spawned the horror genre's most successful franchise of all time. The 17-year period between the theatrical debuts of these two movies found audiences enjoying an incredible volume and variety of films. Many would be recognized, either when released or later, as horror classics, with the likes of *Pan's Labyrinth*, *The Others*, *The Strangers*, *The Descent*, *Sinister*, *The Mist*, *Jennifer's Body*, and Michael Dougherty's *Trick 'r Treat* now firmly established in the upper reaches of the horror canon. Several of the era's films, including *28 Days Later*, *Saw*, *The Ring*, *Hostel*, *Resident Evil*, and *Final Destination*, would birth franchises, a large number of which are going concerns today.

The period would see different types of horror films going in and out of vogue. The wave of slashers populated by TV stars that followed the release of *Scream* would cede ground to a craze for remakes and for more visceral and violent tougher material, so-called "torture porn." Don Coscarelli never got to adapt *Dead in the West*—at least not yet—but through the 2000s, zombies were stumbling about, or running like Olympic sprinters, in films like Zack Snyder's *Dawn of the Dead* remake and *Shaun of the Dead*, as well as *The Walking Dead*, the hugely popular TV show developed by *The Mist* director Frank Darabont. Supernatural tales proved similarly popular, with the success of 2009's *Paranormal Activity* ushering in a wave of ghost stories like *Insidious* and, ultimately, *The Conjuring*.

Horror fans would be introduced to new onscreen genre icons, from Neve Campbell to Tobin Bell to *Conjuring* stars Patrick Wilson and Vera Farmiga, as well as thrilling to performances from familiar favorites like Robert Englund, Kane Hodder, and Barbara Crampton. The genre would also act as a launchpad for future A-list talent like Rachel Weisz, Vin Diesel, Christian Bale, Naomi Watts, Dwayne Johnson, and Cillian Murphy.

While established filmmakers such as Coscarelli, Wes Craven, Sam Raimi, George A. Romero, John Carpenter, and Mick Garris continued to work in the genre, such horror luminaries were joined by a new group of creatives, which included Kevin Williamson, James Wan, Leigh Whannell, James Gunn, Eli Roth, Edgar Wright, Diablo Cody, and Scott Derrickson. Many of these younger talents would leave horror—if only temporarily—to become architects of much more lavishly budgeted ventures, helping to build an industry reliant on superheroes and other IP, for better or worse.

Gremlins and *Piranha* filmmaker Joe Dante once told me that "the horror movie is inherently a political genre." That statement was proved in the years following the release of *Scream*, as writers and directors were affected by, and dealt with, current events. Some incidents, like the 1999 massacre at Columbine High School, would have a cooling effect on horror as politicians scrambled to apportion blame for the tragedy and found an easy scapegoat in the entertainment industry. Other events, such as the 9/11 attacks in 2001 and the Bush administration's subsequent War on Terror, would inspire filmmakers working in horror as much as, if not more than, those creating in other genres.

More than ever, horror would show itself to be a community, one linked by multitudinous bonds. Directors, writers, producers, and special effects artists inspired each other to achieve greater artistic heights. Filmmakers worked together on projects and recommended collaborators to their peers. Sometimes, iconic genre directors would even meet up *en masse* to complain, commiserate, and make plans over burgers and drinks. The story of the era is also the tale of the companies who made it their business to *make* a business from terror, such as New Line, Dimension Films, Lionsgate, Screen Gems, and Blumhouse.

Screaming and Conjuring is told from the perspective of the American film business, but that industry was greatly influenced by what was happening in the genre abroad. Filmmakers in the US watched, and were inspired by, the movies coming out of the United Kingdom, Japan, South Korea, France, Spain, and elsewhere at the same time that producers were hiring foreign filmmakers like Guillermo del Toro, Alexandre Aja, and Andy Muschietti.

The post-*Scream* period would set the table for the era that followed. Filmmakers who established themselves in Ghostface's wake have continued to unleash new terrors. They have been joined by other auteurs like Jordan Peele, Ari Aster, Robert Eggers, and Julia Ducournau, who have all benefited from, and further enriched, a thriving horror scene.

Screaming and Conjuring is a love letter to the genre and to the artists who overcame often seemingly insurmountable odds to bring their visions to the screen. Hopefully, it is also a love letter for fans of the genre—of which I am most definitely one—who have kept their faith with the notion that there are few things more fun than having the hell scared out of you by a movie. As Adam Green, director of the 2007 slasher film *Hatchet*, told me, "Doing horror conventions, you get to travel all over the place, and all of a sudden there's a line of people that want to tell you stories. 'This was the last movie I watched with my dad before they died.' 'This was our first date.' Whatever it might be. All of a sudden, the industry bullshit, it just becomes noise, because you look people in the eyes, and shake their hands, and [they] care so much about what it is you do. Not a lot of genres are like that. I highly doubt romantic comedy fans give a shit about the filmmakers. I'm very lucky to have these people in my life. I know everybody thinks they have the best fans. *I* have the best fans."

CHAPTER 1

"WHAT'S YOUR FAVORITE SCARY MOVIE?"

The world premiere of director Wes Craven's horror-comedy *Scream* took place on December 18, 1996, at the AMC Avco Center in Los Angeles' Westwood neighborhood. The event was attended in force by Hollywood's contingent of young and famous actors. *Scream* cast members Neve Campbell, David Arquette, Matthew Lillard, Skeet Ulrich, Rose McGowan, and Courteney Cox were all present. So, too, were Cox's *Friends* co-stars David Schwimmer, Matt LeBlanc, Matthew Perry, and Jennifer Aniston. The guests also included Famke Janssen, Patrick Dempsey, Reese Witherspoon, and the relatives of another attending *Scream* star, Jamie Kennedy. "My family came, and I had a limo, but I could only put X amount of people in it," says the Philadelphia-raised actor. "We had to rent another car—it was like the Clampetts." Kennedy recalls the audience enjoying the film. "There was so many people that we were in the overflow theater," he says. "People liked it a lot. I remember sitting there and my mom's like, 'That's you!' We went to this cool place in West Hollywood afterwards, and my dad was eating hummus by Steven Seagal. I was like, 'Dad, just make sure Steven Seagal gets the hummus!'"

Photos from the premiere show Skeet Ulrich looking a little worse for wear, and the actor admits to imbibing some Dutch courage before his arrival at the screening. "I remember getting there," he says. "I took my stepbrother, and we had a couple of drinks before, and I don't remember a whole lot, to be honest. I don't remember if we watched the film or we all just went in and bailed."

Any buzz around the commercial potential of *Scream* following the premiere lasted not much longer than the one enjoyed by Ulrich. Craven's tale of high schoolers menaced by a masked killer—or *killers*, as the movie's climax reveals—in the fictional California town of Woodsboro was released

Someone has taken their love of scary movies one step too far.
Solving this mystery is going to be murder.
SCREAM
DAVID ARQUETTE
NEVE CAMPBELL
COURTENEY COX
MATTHEW LILLARD
ROSE McGOWAN
SKEET ULRICH
and DREW BARRYMORE
SOUNDTRACK AVAILABLE ON
Visit DIMENSION FILMS on the web at: http://www.dimensionfilms.com
THE HIGHLY ACCLAIMED NEW THRILLER FROM WES CRAVEN

two days later, on December 20.[2] The R-rated film initially proved a box office failure despite the best efforts of its creators and financiers.

Scream was distributed by the relatively new Dimension Films, the genre arm of the New York-based Miramax Films. Miramax had been founded in 1979 by producers Bob Weinstein and his older brother Harvey, decades before the public revelations that the latter was a sexual predator and rapist. Miramax had established a reputation for releasing critically acclaimed films like 1989's *My Left Foot* and 1992's *The Crying Game*, Oscar-winners both. Through Dimension, which was overseen by Bob Weinstein, the brothers hoped to attract the teenagers and twentysomethings who made up the bulk of cinemagoers with thrillers, action films, and, in particular, horror movies.

For *Scream*, the Weinsteins had signed off on a cast with plenty of appeal to youthful movie fans. In addition to the very famous Courteney Cox, the film featured a bona fide Hollywood icon in *E.T. the Extra-Terrestrial* actress Drew Barrymore, whose character Casey Becker is surprisingly killed off in the movie's opening sequence. Neve Campbell was also a well-known face thanks to her role on the popular teen drama *Party of Five* and, earlier in the year, had starred alongside Ulrich in horror film *The Craft*, a tale of high school witches. "Bob just wanted people that he could get on chat shows," says *Scream* editor Patrick Lussier, of Weinstein's attitude to casting. "He wanted people who could promote the movie, which is why he mined so many people from TV, because they could get on talk shows, they could chat up the movie, and it wouldn't cost him anything."

Dimension was giving *Scream* a wide release in around 1,400 cinemas, an ambitious number for a film about the slaying of teenagers coming out just ahead of Christmas. The movie would face stiff competition at the box office from the simultaneously released TV show spin-off *Beavis and Butt-Head Do America* and the Tom Cruise romantic comedy *Jerry Maguire*, which had arrived on screens the previous week and already established itself as one of the holiday season's hit films. "I'm holding my breath, you know," Craven said in an interview with the monthly horror magazine *Fangoria* prior to the release of *Scream*. "I rely on the expertise and the genius of Bob Weinstein, who has a knack for marketing things. It is a very, very competitive time and we're all, I wouldn't say worried, but holding our breath."

---

2 Unless otherwise noted, release dates refer to a film's theatrical debut in the US.

Scream placed fourth at the US box office over its opening weekend. The film trailed not just *Beavis and Butt-Head Do America* and *Jerry Maguire* but also Walt Disney Pictures' live-action remake *101 Dalmatians.* Craven's film grossed $6 million, a moderate-to-poor return for a film with a budget of around $14 million and a figure that was dwarfed by the $20 million earned by the Beavis and Butt-Head film. Matthew Lillard remembers being sad but not surprised by the film's disappointing commercial performance. "We had all seen the movie, and loved the movie, but I don't think anyone expected it to be successful," he says.

Lillard's reaction was informed by recent history. During the mid-'90s, the horror film seemed to have fallen out of favor with audiences. In terms of box office returns during the calendar year, the only horror movie to crack the US top 50 in 1995 was *Species*, which starred Natasha Henstridge as a half-human, half-alien creature and grossed $60 million. Prior to the arrival of *Scream* in cinemas, 1996 had seen a couple of moderately successful horror releases, the Neve Campbell-starring *The Craft* and the Robert Rodriguez-directed *From Dusk Till Dawn.* Rodriguez's vampire film was financed by Dimension and written by Quentin Tarantino, who also starred in the movie alongside George Clooney, Juliette Lewis, and Harvey Keitel. *The Craft* and *From Dusk Till Dawn* both opened at number one on the US box office chart, but neither movie's domestic gross broke the $30 million mark. In comparison, the year's most popular film, the Will Smith science fiction movie *Independence Day*, earned $306 million in total at the domestic box office and an even greater amount in foreign territories. 1996 had also seen a clutch of expensive horror productions, notably *The Island of Dr. Moreau*, the Julia Roberts vehicle *Mary Reilly*, and the Peter Jackson-directed *The Frighteners*, flop on release.

The horror movie had been a staple of the film industry's output since Universal Pictures released *Dracula* and *Frankenstein* in 1931. Those two films effectively launched an ultimately interlinked franchise showcasing the so-called Universal Classic Monsters, a line-up that would come to include the Mummy, the Invisible Man, the Bride of Frankenstein, and the Wolf Man, among others. With Universal's interest in horror waning in the '50s, the studio's monster mantle was picked up by the British company Hammer, with releases like 1957's *The Curse of Frankenstein*, 1958's *Dracula* (a.k.a. *Horror of Dracula*), and 1959's *The Mummy.*

In the '60s, '70s, and '80s, the major Hollywood studios unleashed a string of horror hits from *Rosemary's Baby* to *The Exorcist* to *Carrie* to *The Omen* to

Alien to *Poltergeist*. Simultaneously, the genre was further bolstered by independently produced successes, including *Night of the Living Dead*, *The Texas Chain Saw Massacre*, *Phantasm*, *Halloween*, *The Evil Dead*, *Re-Animator*, *Hellraiser*, and the Wes Craven-directed *A Nightmare on Elm Street*.

Horror could therefore claim decades of residency at the heart of the Hollywood ecosystem, but there was no guarantee of that situation continuing. The western, the musical, and the war movie had enjoyed similarly successful runs as box office mainstays. By the mid-'90s, all three genres were approaching obsolescence. The box office failure of *Scream* offered more evidence that the horror film was headed in the same direction. "When it tanked, you were like, 'Oh well, we move on,'" says Lillard.

What happened next meant that Lillard and his co-stars would never be able to entirely move on from *Scream*, no matter how many film and TV credits they acquired. By 1996, movie studios customarily oriented a film's marketing strategy around its hopefully lucrative opening weekend, and executives were accustomed to seeing grosses fall sharply after that initial release frame. Thanks to strong word of mouth, *Scream* bucked this trend. Craven's film earned $9 million over the movie's second weekend in cinemas—an increase of 42 percent from its first three days on release—and $10 million the weekend after that. "Word got around that Wes wanted to do a celebration for it being a hit," says Skeet Ulrich. "Everybody was like, 'Well, it's not.' I guess the word of mouth just kept steamrolling and steamrolling."

Scream was released before box office returns could be easily tracked on the internet. Neve Campbell, who played the film's lead role, high school student Sidney Prescott, was another cast member unaware that the movie had become a success. "I didn't know anything about box office," says the actress. "My team called; I think it was week three. They're like, 'So we just want you to know that it made $30 million.' I went, 'Oh, is that bad?' They went, 'No! That is a good thing! A really good thing!'"

The movie's grosses started to fall after its third week on release, but *Scream* continued to rack up impressive earnings through March. The film grossed around $100 million before it finally departed cinemas at the end of May to make way for a home video release in June. The movie also performed well abroad, with a total global take of $173 million. The quality and success of the film were noted by *Fangoria* editor Tony Timpone in his letter to readers for the magazine's May 1997 issue. "As I write these words in mid-February, *Scream* is closing in on an $80 million box office take, making it one of the most successful horror films of all time," Timpone wrote. "After a lengthy genre decline, savvy audiences were ready to be scared again, and *Scream* delivered in spades... The studios are all searching for new horror projects now, and a boom may be on the horizon."

Timpone's dream of a genre renaissance swiftly became a reality. *Scream* would launch one of horror's most successful movie series and inspired others to apply their skills to the terror tale arena. In the decade and a half following the release of the movie, filmmakers introduced cinemagoers to a flood of fresh heroes and, more importantly, villains. By the time director James Wan released his own wildly successful and franchise-inaugurating horror film *The Conjuring* in 2013, the genre had changed almost beyond recognition, just as the world itself had become a dramatically altered place. All of which would have come as a surprise to Skeet Ulrich as he made his blurry way along the red carpet at that Westwood premiere and to Jamie Kennedy as he tried to ensure that Steven Seagal got to eat hummus at the after-party.

"They turned our little movie into a juggernaut," says Matthew Lillard. "At the premiere, nobody had a sense of that. Nobody had a sense of the tidal wave that was coming."

Scream was the brainchild of screenwriter Kevin Williamson. Born in 1965, Williamson grew up in Oriental, North Carolina, loving horror movies, the genre dovetailing with the queer teenager's sense of being an outsider. Writing in his introduction to the published version of the *Scream* script, Williamson would recall how his world was turned upside down by 1978's *Halloween*, which starred Jamie Lee Curtis as an awkward high schooler named Laurie Strode who is menaced by the masked killer Michael Myers. "The movie frightened me beyond belief," recalled Williamson. "There were moments when I would forget to breathe because I was so wrapped up in the moment. When Jamie Lee Curtis screamed, I screamed. When she ran, I ran. I can vividly remember pounding my feet on the floor as she raced across the street trying to escape the clutches of Michael."

Williamson borrowed his parents' 8mm camera, ordered a film splicer from the Sears catalog, and started making movies in the backyard of his house. These early efforts included a film about a hooded figure in a fisherman's slicker who kills off a group of friends. Williamson won a scholarship to study acting at East Carolina University. Later, he moved to New

York and then Los Angeles, where he enrolled on a UCLA screenwriting course while trying to find work onscreen. Williamson wrote the script for a film called *Killing Mrs. Tingle*, about high school students who take a teacher hostage. His agent sold the screenplay to Interscope Communications, which produced the 1992 thriller *The Hand That Rocks the Cradle*, but the project failed to get off the ground. Having spent the money he had received for the script, Williamson was forced to start borrowing cash from friends.

A year after the sale of *Killing Mrs. Tingle*, Williamson was housesitting in Westwood, watching a TV show about Daniel Rolling, a.k.a. 'The Gainesville Ripper,' who had murdered five students in Florida during August 1990. Unnerved, Williamson called a friend as he checked that the house was secure. While the writer looked in closets and under beds, a butcher knife in one hand and a cordless phone in the other, Williamson and his friend started talking about horror movies and the genre's most terrifying killers. The incident would provide the inspiration for *Scream*, or *Scary Movie* as the writer titled his screenplay. "I wrote an outline in about two weeks," Williamson says. "Then I took that outline, and I went to the desert, and I hid in this little biddy hole, and I wrote. Three days later, I had a script."

With his screenplay, Williamson paid homage to, and lovingly poked fun at, the slasher movie. The central trope of this horror subgenre finds a group of friends being whittled down by a killer until the murderer is defeated by the movie's so-called 'final girl' (defeated, that is, until the killer inevitably returns in the franchise's next entry). The slasher film had proved popular in the late '70s through the '80s, with multiple flourishing franchises.

The craze had been kicked off by director John Carpenter and his co-writer, producer, and girlfriend Debra Hill with *Halloween*, the film which had so affected the young Williamson. "The idea was to write something about babysitter murders," says Carpenter. The director recalls that Hill "wrote the first draft, and I polished it, wrote the second draft, the shooting script, and then off we went." Hill, who passed away in 2005, was responsible for casting Jamie Lee Curtis as the film's final girl, Laurie Strode. "Debra got excited because she was the daughter of Janet Leigh and that was *Psycho*," says Carpenter. "Jamie came in and read for it. She was just great." The daughter of Leigh and *Some Like It Hot* star Tony Curtis, the actress had recently been let go from the submarine-set sitcom *Operation Petticoat*. "I thought that was the end of my entire life," says Curtis. "I was 19 years old, I'd been on a TV series, and now I was fired and I was devastated. The reason that I bring it up is, had I not been fired, I would not have been available to audition for *Halloween*. So the irony is that a really sad thing happened to me and then this amazing thing happened."

Carpenter's first movie, 1975's science fiction-comedy *Dark Star*, began life as a student film he directed while attending college at Los Angeles' USC. His second feature, 1976's low-budget action-thriller *Assault on Precinct 13*, screened at the London Film Festival, but the Kentucky-raised filmmaker remained a mostly unknown quantity in Hollywood.

Jamie Lee Curtis and director John Carpenter on the set of *Halloween* (1978).

Carpenter shot *Halloween* for a meagre budget of $300,000. The film's visuals were enhanced by the movie's synthesizer score, which was composed and performed by the director. The soundtrack included an unforgettable main theme, written in the 5/4 time signature, to which the director had been introduced by his violinist father. "When I was 13, my dad taught me how to do 5/4 time," says Carpenter. "Pah-pah-pah. Pah-pah-pah. Pah-pah. Pah-pah. *Halloween* theme! It's pretty simple." Simple, but effective in terms of amping up the film's tension. "That was amazing," says Nick Castle, who attended USC with Carpenter and played the murderous Michael Myers in the film. "Tommy Wallace, who was the editor and production designer, he said, 'We screened the picture once without music and went, 'Hey, okay, that worked.' Then we screened it again with music and went, 'Oh my God, it *works*.'"

Halloween was released at the end of October 1978. The movie earned a then-impressive $1.2 million during its first week in cinemas and continued to attract audiences through the winter, eventually becoming the most successful independent film of all time, with a domestic gross of around $46 million.

Horror had always been regarded as one of Hollywood's more disreputable genres. Rarely honored by the Academy Awards, frightening films were a source of revenue but little pride as far as many studio executives were concerned. Despite Curtis having played the lead role in a record-breakingly successful film, the actress discovered that *Halloween* did not lead to other acting jobs. "I didn't get any work after I finished *Halloween*," she says. "The only work I got was a *Charlie's Angels* episode where I'm Cheryl Ladd's best friend, and a pro-golfer, and we wrestle alligators, and an episode of *Love Boat* where my mother plays my mother." Curtis' first movie role after *Halloween* would be in 1980's Carpenter-directed ghost story *The Fog*. "Because I wasn't getting any work, John Carpenter wrote the part in *The Fog* for me," says Curtis. "Then, once I did *The Fog*, I was able to get a couple of horror movies, *Prom Night* and *Terror Train*."

Carpenter and Hill co-wrote a *Halloween* sequel, *Halloween II*, which featured Michael Myers hunting Curtis' Laurie Strode in a hospital. Directed by Rick Rosenthal and released in October 1981, the sequel grossed ten times its $2.5 million budget at the US box office. Michael Myers was seemingly burned to death at the end of the film, and Carpenter and Hill believed they had concluded the saga of the masked killer. *Halloween* executive producer Irwin Yablans and financier Moustapha Akkad were interested in making a third film. Carpenter and Hill only agreed to participate if the movie was Michael Myers-free, in effect turning the franchise into an anthology series. The result, 1982's *Halloween III: Season of the Witch*, was directed by *Halloween* production designer Tommy Lee Wallace. The film starred Tom Atkins as a doctor who uncovers a plot to kill children with Halloween masks and was greeted unfavorably by cinemagoers keen to see more Michael Myers mayhem. Like so many horror movies that commercially underwhelm when originally released, *Halloween III* would eventually garner an army of fans in the genre community. At the time, negative reaction to the threequel meant that the franchise's masked killer returned in 1988's *Halloween 4: The Return of Michael Myers*, which was made without the involvement of Carpenter and Hill.

The success of *Halloween* prompted a slew of copycat movies, notably 1980's *Friday the 13th*, about a group of counselors being murdered at a summer camp. Director Sean S. Cunningham's low-budget film benefited from the talents of special effects makeup artist Tom Savini, a former Vietnam War combat photographer intent on bringing a new kind of realistic gruesomeness to the big screen. The *Friday the 13th* cast included Adrienne King, who portrayed the film's final girl Alice, and Kevin Bacon, who played

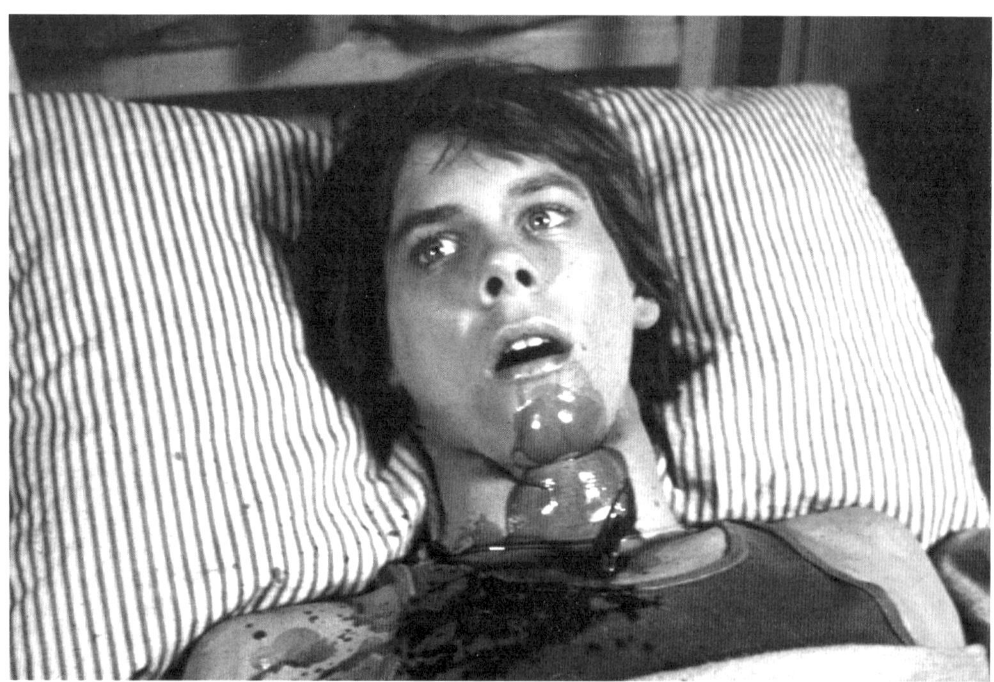

Kevin Bacon in *Friday the 13th* (1980).

a doomed counselor. "Some of the movies that I've been in were by choice," says the *Footloose* and *JFK* actor. "*Friday the 13th*, that's just because I needed to pay the rent, really. Tom Savini, I guess that's probably the movie that put him on the map. What I remember was that I have sex with the girl, and then smoke a joint, which means in horror language that they're dead." The actor's character, Jack, is killed when an unseen assailant pushes an arrow up through the mattress of his bed and into his throat. "I was on my knees underneath the bed with my head tilted back and this fake neck and chest," says Bacon. "I got under the bed, and they lit it, and they applied the makeup. I mean, it was a really long time in a tortuous kind of position. They also said, 'Just know we only have one of these necks.' So there really was no take two."

Distributed in the US by Paramount, *Friday the 13th* earned almost $40 million at the US box office. A swiftly produced sequel, 1981's *Friday the 13th Part 2*, was another hit, and six more franchise entries arrived on screens over the next eight years. In the original film's twist ending, the killer is revealed to be actress Betsy Palmer's Mrs. Voorhees. Subsequent movies showcased the homicidal activities of her son, Jason Voorhees, as evidenced by the titles of 1986's *Friday the 13th Part VI: Jason Lives* and 1993's *Jason Goes to Hell: The Final Friday*.

Wes Craven introduced his own iconic slasher villain with 1984's *A Nightmare on Elm Street*. Written and directed by the future *Scream* filmmaker, the movie starred Heather Langenkamp as teenager Nancy Thompson, whose dreams are invaded by Robert Englund's supernatural maniac Freddy Krueger. Craven was raised in a strict Baptist household and saw only a few films until he was a senior in college. The student fell in love with movies and began to make short films while teaching humanities at Clarkson College of Technology in Potsdam, New York. "I was teaching college and felt a sort of malaise, and I was actually trying to write a novel, and sort of became fascinated with film," Craven recalled at a 1999 Writers Guild Foundation panel titled 'I Know What You Screamed Last Summer.' "Very quickly, a bunch of the French New Wave and European New Wave films were coming to the college campus. I saw those and fell in love with them. So I quit my job and went to New York to get into film."

After arriving in the city, Craven saw director George A. Romero's 1968 movie *Night of the Living Dead*. The black and white film found a group of people fending off undead flesh-eating ghouls—or 'zombies' as they would come to be named in the years that followed—at a remote farmhouse. A box office hit, the film was subsequently acclaimed for its casting of Black actor Duane Jones as the movie's hero and for Romero's subtextual assessment of American citizenry as mindless monsters. "I was still an ex-college professor just sort of sweeping floors in New York," Craven said at the 'I Know What You Screamed Last Summer' panel. "I just saw that incredible vitality and that George was making social comment at the same time that he was scaring shit out of you."

Craven gained notoriety with his brutal 1972 rape-revenge movie *The Last House on the Left*—a reworking of Ingmar Bergman's Oscar-winning 1960 film *The Virgin Spring*—and scored a hit with 1977's *The Hills Have Eyes*, about a vacationing family who battle a desert-dwelling cannibal clan. Craven's next assignment was 1978's *Stranger in Our House* (a.k.a. *Summer of Fear*), a TV movie starring *The Exorcist* actress Linda Blair. "They brought me Wes as a potential director," says Blair. "They explained to me who Wes was, up-and-coming, and would I consider him as the director. And Wes is incredible. He's funny, he's precise, he's probably one of my favorite directors."

Craven was unable to find work outside the horror genre and his career began to falter. The director's next film, 1981's *Deadly Blessing*, performed poorly in comparison to *The Hills Have Eyes*, and 1982's comic-book adaptation *Swamp Thing* struck out with both critics and cinemagoers.

Craven spent years working on the script for *A Nightmare on Elm Street.* The screenplay was inspired by an article in the *Los Angeles Times* about some relatively young men who had mysteriously died in their sleep. The character of Freddy Krueger, meanwhile, was partly based on Craven's childhood experience of seeing a fedora-wearing stranger outside his house who sensed that the boy was watching him and turned to meet his gaze. But the director could not interest anyone in backing the movie. Craven was forced to seek financial assistance from *Friday the 13th* director Sean S. Cunningham—who had produced *The Last House on the Left*—just to pay his bills. "I was absolutely broke," Craven recalled to the outlet *Vulture* in 2014. "I think I wrote the first draft of *Nightmare on Elm Street* in '79. No one wanted to buy it. Nobody. I felt very strongly about it, so I stayed with it. At a certain point, I was literally flat broke. I had to borrow five grand from Sean Cunningham to pay my taxes for that year. So I was $5,000 in debt, and had no job, and I'm broke."

Craven eventually struck a deal with New Line Cinema, a New York-based independent production and distribution company founded in 1967 by the then 27-year-old Robert Shaye. "He was always interested in filmmaking," says the New Line founder's actress sister Lin Shaye about her sibling. "At one point, he played around with being an actor. And he was terrible! He decided to start a distribution company. I actually was sharing an apartment with him in New York when he brought home the first stationery that had 'New Line Cinema' on it."

New Line's early successes included a re-release of 1936's anti-drug exploitation film *Reefer Madness*—which, decades on, played well to stoned college kids—and 1972's trash classic *Pink Flamingos* from writer-director John Waters. "*Pink Flamingos*, when we had the premiere, I still sort of distributed the film," says Waters. "But then I needed to get a real distributor, and I went to New Line, because I liked what they had done. They were putting exploitation and art films together at the same time, which were my influences."

Starting in the early '80s, New Line began betting heavily on horror. The company produced the 1982 slasher film *Alone in the Dark* and distributed director Sam Raimi's 1983 movie *The Evil Dead*, about a group of friends beset by demonic ghouls at a remote cabin. The film starred Raimi's friend Bruce Campbell, who over the years has delighted interviewers and fans with his good-natured complaining about the physical torments he endured shooting the movie and its two sequels, 1987's *Evil Dead II* and 1993's *Army of Darkness*. "Bruce is right to be complaining," says Raimi. "Sometimes I'd have to hurt him with a two-by-four for the good of the audience. I'd have to explain to him: 'It's really what the audience wants.' He had to live the character, and I was the one that was going to help him get there." Seeking distribution for *The Evil Dead*, Raimi, Campbell, and producer Rob Tapert showed the film at the 1982 Cannes Film Festival. The movie attracted the attention of Stephen King, the bestselling author of horror novels *Carrie*, *The Shining*, and *'Salem's Lot*. King wrote an appreciative article for *Twilight Zone* magazine, hailing Raimi's tale as "the most ferociously original horror film of 1982." New Line subsequently picked up the movie's US distribution rights. Although *The Evil Dead* was only a minor hit in the States, the film was swiftly acknowledged as a classic by horror fans and encouraged Shaye to pursue more genre projects, including *A Nightmare on Elm Street*.

Robert Englund first met Craven at his audition for the role of *A Nightmare on Elm Street* villain Freddy Krueger. The actor recalls that he "half-expected this guy [to be] all dressed in black, rather goth. I walk in the office,

Promotional image for *The Evil Dead* (1983) with Bruce Campbell and Theresa Tilly.

and he's resplendent in Ralph Lauren. He's got tortoiseshell reading glasses; a trimmed, immaculate beard; and he's this erudite raconteur." After casting Englund as Krueger, Craven was delighted with what the actor contributed on set. "Robert Englund played it to the stars," the director said. "I mean, I had it on the page, but he took it, and ran with it, and made it something entirely his own." Craven would recall that Englund's co-star Heather Langenkamp was an equally enthusiastic participant during the film's shoot. "Heather was incredibly game," he said. "I remember the bathtub scene, where Freddy's claw comes up between her legs. She just laughed and good-naturedly did it, and was sitting on a bathtub that literally had no bottom, because they had a guy down below her in a big tank in a frogman's suit, and she was literally holding herself up by sitting on the rim of this otherwise bottomless tub." As part of New Line's deal to finance Craven's film, Robert Shaye insisted that the director cast his sister Lin, who played a teacher in the film. "Bob was very instrumental in me getting opportunities," she says. "I'm more than grateful that I was able to roll it off into success. If you fucked it up, then you were done, and I didn't. I made Bob look good."

New Line released *A Nightmare on Elm Street* on November 9, 1984, even if many potential cinemagoers could have been forgiven for not realizing it existed at all. "The whole culture was so different toward horror," says Langenkamp. "We really were a whispered-in-the-dark-alleyway [thing] back then." *A Nightmare on Elm Street* was a career-reviving hit for Craven, earning $25 million in the US. But, like Jamie Lee Curtis before her, Langenkamp realized that starring in a successful horror film was not as useful professionally as she might have hoped. "No one in Hollywood saw *Nightmare on Elm Street* when it came out," she says. "I would go into auditions and mention it, and people would nod politely. It was not a big hit in the halls of power."

Robert Shaye greenlit a sequel, the Jack Sholder-directed *A Nightmare on Elm Street 2: Freddy's Revenge*, which was released in 1985 and grossed $30 million

UK poster for *A Nightmare on Elm Street* (1984) by artist Graham Humphreys.

in the US. A third movie, Chuck Russell's *A Nightmare on Elm Street 3: Dream Warriors*, followed in 1987 and performed even better, earning $44 million at the domestic box office. Langenkamp and Craven returned to the franchise for *A Nightmare on Elm Street 3,* the actress to reprise the role of Nancy, and the director to co-write the script. By then, Englund's homicidal ghoul had emerged as the franchise's unique selling point. The importance of the character was evidenced by the title of a spin-off TV show, *Freddy's Nightmares*, which started screening in syndication from October 1988.

Craven went on to direct several more horror movies, including 1988's voodoo-oriented *The Serpent and the Rainbow* and 1989's *Shocker*. The director stayed away from Freddy Krueger, though, and from Shaye's New Line, believing that he had not been suitably remunerated for creating the *Elm Street* franchise. "I can't remember us ever having any kind of a shouting match or anything like that," said Craven of his relationship with Shaye. "Bob just profited from it immensely more than I did."

1988's *A Nightmare on Elm Street 4: The Dream Master* was directed by Finnish filmmaker Renny Harlin and earned $49 million at the US box office. The movie proved to be a commercial high point for the franchise, with the following year's *A Nightmare on Elm Street 5: The Dream Child* grossing half as much as its predecessor. "I imagine that was tricky," said Craven of the sequels produced without his participation. "I think some of the directors did really, really good jobs. I know there was a big pressure to have one come out every year. So that's always kind of a recipe for semi-disaster. It's just a little bit too short of a time to have somebody get inspired with some genius idea, and get that written, and get that shot, and edited, and out in the theaters. I've been under the gun several times and it's very difficult." Producer and New Line veteran Rachel Talalay directed 1991's *Freddy's Dead: The Final Nightmare*, guided by the company's decision to emphasize the franchise's more comedic side. "If I were to remake it, I would make a scarier version," says Talalay. "That wasn't the directive at that point."

Talalay's film earned more than *A Nightmare on Elm Street 5*, but Shaye was keen for Craven to become involved with the franchise again and struck a new financial deal benefiting the director. "Ten years later, he did come to me and make some amends," said Craven. The director pitched New Line a movie that would be released with the title *Wes Craven's New Nightmare*. The film featured Craven, Langenkamp, Englund, and even Shaye playing versions of themselves, while Englund also portrayed a new iteration of Freddy Krueger who breaks through into the 'real world' to torment his creators.

New Nightmare was the first of the director's films to be edited by Patrick Lussier. The Canadian had previously worked with Craven on a short-lived science fiction TV show called *Nightmare Cafe*, which starred Robert Englund and premiered on NBC in 1992. Like Englund, Lussier was impressed by Craven's professorial air. "He was very much an intellectual, with a really sly wit and a very educated approach to horror," the editor recalls. After *Nightmare Cafe*, Lussier worked with Craven for much of the next decade and a half. "We would spend hours in the cutting room talking about everything from giant squids to politics to birds," says the editor. "Wes was a huge birder. All the bird sounds in the movies had to be very specific for the time of day. If we had the wrong bird call for the time of day, we'd all get in trouble."

New Nightmare was released in October 1994 and grossed $18 million at the domestic box office, making the movie the least successful entry in the franchise to date. The disappointing performance of the film confirmed that the slasher boom launched 16 years earlier by John Carpenter and Debra Hill with *Halloween* was over. The fifth entry in the franchise the pair had created, *Halloween 5: The Revenge of Michael Myers,* had grossed just $11 million in the US when the film hit cinemas in 1989. The same year saw the release of *Friday the 13th Part VIII: Jason Takes Manhattan*. The film earned $14 million domestically, the lowest gross for the series. Four years later, 1993's *Jason Goes to Hell: The Final Friday* raked in just a little more than its predecessor. The *Child's Play* series, about the Brad Dourif-voiced killer doll Chucky, was another slasher franchise in commercial decline. 1988's *Child's Play* and 1990's *Child's Play 2* were both fair-sized hits. 1991's *Child's Play 3* earned roughly half that accrued by the first two entries.

By now even the horror magazine *Fangoria* seemed to have lost patience with the state of the slasher genre. In the early '90s, Dimension had acquired the distribution rights to the *Halloween* franchise, outbidding New Line, which had planned on partnering with John Carpenter on a sequel. Directed by Joe Chappelle, *Halloween: The Curse of Michael Myers* performed modestly after the film was released in September 1995. *Fangoria* contributor Chas Balun subsequently wrote an article rounding up "The Year in Fear," in which he described Chappelle's film as "a useless and unwelcome" entry in the *Halloween* series. "It's time to move on," he wrote, referring to the slasher sequels that had clotted the release schedules over the previous decade and a half.

The future looked no rosier for horror franchises outside of the slasher realm, with the respective series inaugurated by *Night of the Living Dead,*

The Exorcist, *The Texas Chain Saw Massacre*, *The Omen*, *Alien*, *Poltergeist*, and *Phantasm* either on hiatus or falling out of favor with audiences.

The first half of the '90s saw a clutch of big-budget horror releases, including 1992's Francis Ford Coppola-directed *Bram Stoker's Dracula* and 1994's *Interview with the Vampire* with Tom Cruise and Brad Pitt. Both sumptuous films mined the literary-minded gothic horror genre and both were box office hits. This mini-trend would end with the commercial failure of 1996's Julia Roberts-starring *Mary Reilly*, which retold Robert Louis Stevenson's novel *Strange Case of Dr Jekyll and Mr Hyde* from the perspective of Jekyll's maid.

In April 1994, the film industry trade magazine *Variety* devoted an article to the parlous state of the genre headlined "Scary Future For Horror Pix." "Director David Cronenberg said the underlying theme of all horror films was death," wrote reporter Leonard Klady at the start of the article. "But now that once-vigorous genre is raising its own questions of mortality." Klady's decision to open the article with a quote from Cronenberg was appropriate. The Canadian filmmaker had established himself as an important horror auteur with films like 1981's *Scanners*, 1983's James Woods-starring *Videodrome*, and his 1986 remake of *The Fly* with Jeff Goldblum and Geena Davis. More recently, Cronenberg had moved away from the genre, directing a 1991 adaptation of William Burroughs' novel *The Naked Lunch* and 1993's drama *M. Butterfly*. Klady's article made clear that there were plenty of reasons to fear for the health of horror beyond Cronenberg's departure. "The grim reapers point to recent lackluster box office and dwindling video sales for horror as an ill wind," the *Variety* writer continued. "Many in the business say it's a tired genre and that even diehard fans have been turned off by a glut of mediocre products."

Yet cinemagoers were still lining up for films that featured horrifying or otherwise outré material. As veteran franchises were failing to recapture the magic of their earliest years, the interest of many potential audience members was being piqued by a group of young filmmakers who, though mostly working outside the horror arena, would have a dramatic impact on the genre. The early '90s saw a sea change in pop culture as a fresh wave of artists reacted against what had come before. In the realm of music, bands like Nirvana, Pearl Jam, Soundgarden, and Nine Inch Nails made so much of '80s music seem suddenly out of fashion. In film, directors such as Steven Soderbergh, Robert Rodriguez, Kevin Smith, and Quentin Tarantino represented a new generation of hip filmmakers.

Tarantino's directorial debut, the crime-thriller *Reservoir Dogs*, premiered at the Sundance Film Festival in 1992. The film was packed with snappy dialog, including a conversation about the meaning of Madonna's hit single "Like a Virgin," and was short on neither blood nor violence. Wes Craven attended the 1992 Sitges Film Festival and left a screening of *Reservoir Dogs* before the end of the movie. "Five people walked out of that audience, including Wes Craven," Tarantino would recall at a 25th anniversary screening of his film at the Tribeca Film Festival in 2017. "The fucking guy who did *Last House on the Left* walked out? The guy who did *Last House on the Left*, my movie's too tough for him." *Reservoir Dogs* was a minor hit in the US and played well around the world. The garrulous Tarantino swiftly achieved star status among cine-literate movie fans with interviews in which he detailed his rise from video store clerk to fêted filmmaker.

After the release of *Reservoir Dogs*, Tarantino decamped to Amsterdam, where he and his friend Roger Avary worked on the script for what would become *Pulp Fiction*. The film was financed by Miramax, and Tarantino shot the movie with a cast full of famous faces including John Travolta, Samuel L. Jackson, Uma Thurman, and Bruce Willis. As with his first film, *Pulp Fiction* contained horrific moments, from Willis' boxer and Ving Rhames' crime boss being threatened by rapists to Travolta's hitman ramming a hypodermic needle full of adrenaline directly into the heart of Thurman's overdosing character. *Pulp Fiction* premiered in May 1994 at the Cannes Film Festival, where it won the Palme d'Or.

Pulp Fiction was released on October 14, 1994, the same weekend as *New Nightmare*. Tarantino's film topped the box office chart; Craven had to settle for third place, behind *Pulp Fiction* and the Sylvester Stallone-Sharon Stone action-thriller *The Specialist*. *New Nightmare* rapidly disappeared from cinemas; *Pulp Fiction* became a worldwide hit—earning over $100 million in the US alone—and a pop culture phenomenon. The film was nominated for seven Academy Awards, including Best Picture, with Tarantino and Avary winning in the category of Best Original Screenplay.

Kevin Williamson wasn't interested in writing just another slasher movie. He used his familiarity with the subgenre to craft a whodunnit plot with genuine scares and laughs. His high school characters, like real-life teenagers, had seen genre movies and referenced those films as actual people would surely do. In the finished movie's very first sequence, Drew Barrymore's

Casey Becker is quizzed over the phone about horror films by a seeming stranger—voiced by Roger L. Jackson, but later revealed to be one of the movie's Ghostface killers—and tells him that her favorite is *Halloween*.

"What's yours?" asks Becker.

"Guess," comes the reply.

"Um, *Nightmare on Elm Street*," Barrymore's character responds.

"Is that the one where the guy had knives for fingers?" asks the mysterious caller.

"Yeah, Freddy Krueger," says Becker.

"Freddy, that's right," the caller agrees. "I like that movie. It was scary."

"Well, the first one was, but the rest sucked," Becker replies.

Director Wes Craven and Drew Barrymore on the set of *Scream* (1996).

Such post-modernist joking about the sequels that had followed Wes Craven's original *A Nightmare on Elm Street* was one way Kevin Williamson hoped to set his movie apart from the previous decade's torrent of slasher films. "I thought the horror genre was just in the toilet and no one cared," says the screenwriter. "I sat down and wrote a movie I wanted to see." The result was a satire of horror films that also seemed far more realistic than many of the form's recent examples.

The notion of planning to tell a story over multiple films was still very much a Hollywood rarity. George Lucas' original three *Star Wars* films and the second and third *Back to the Future* movies—which had been shot in quick succession by director Robert Zemeckis—were among the few examples of that successfully coming to pass. Regardless, Williamson had plans to continue the story of *Scary Movie* in two more films should the first one prove a success. "I had a treatment [for *Scream 2*]," he says. "And as soon as I had that, I had an idea for the third one. And so I said, 'Oh, it's a trilogy.'"

Williamson's agent sent out his script to possible purchasers, including Dimension, in the summer of 1995. The Weinsteins had founded the label three years earlier. The brothers hoped to emulate the success New Line had enjoyed with the *Nightmare on Elm Street* franchise, as well as 1986's *Critters*, a horror-comedy about diminutive aliens which had spawned three sequels. They were also irritated by Robert Shaye having established a New Line subsidiary called Fine Line with the plan of making the kind of awards-attracting movies in which Miramax specialized. The Weinsteins' ability to greenlight projects, rather than pick up the distribution rights for already produced films, was enhanced after Miramax was bought by Disney at the end of June 1993, in a deal that left the brothers in charge of their company.

The Weinsteins had a history with horror. Among the brothers' earliest movie projects was 1981's *The Burning*, a summer camp-set slasher film 'created and produced' by Harvey Weinstein and co-written by his brother. The film featured early-career appearances by Jason Alexander and Holly Hunter and effects by Tom Savini. *The Burning* was directed by Tony Maylam, who had made a concert film starring the band Genesis that was distributed by the Weinsteins. In an interview conducted for a DVD release of *The Burning*, Savini recalled that Maylam fell out with the Weinsteins—by no means the last occasion a filmmaker would wind up at loggerheads with the siblings. "They eventually re-edited the film at the end to do what they wanted to do and not what was in the script or what Tony had in mind," said Savini.

A decade on, Bob Weinstein re-applied himself to the horror genre after the establishment of Dimension. In 1992, the label distributed *Hellraiser III: Hell on Earth*, and in 1993 *Children of the Corn II: The Final Sacrifice* and *Re-Animator* director Stuart Gordon's science fiction-thriller *Fortress*. The company's first substantial hit was filmmaker Alex Proyas' 1994 comic-book adaptation *The Crow*. Paramount was set to distribute the film but Dimension acquired the movie following the tragic on-set death of its star Brandon Lee. Made for $23 million, *The Crow* was released in May 1994 and grossed $50 million at the US box office. In 1995, Dimension put out *Halloween: The*

Curse of Michael Myers, *Children of the Corn III: Urban Harvest*, and *The Prophecy*, a franchise-birthing horror-fantasy starring Christopher Walken as the archangel Gabriel.

The Weinsteins offered $400,000 for Williamson's script and were outbid by *Platoon* director Oliver Stone's Ixtlan Productions. Williamson decided to sell the screenplay to Dimension after his lawyer told him that Bob Weinstein was keen for his new company to make a mark in the horror genre and was more likely to make the film than Stone.

When Dimension went looking for someone to direct *Scary Movie*, Craven was at the top of the list. The director had followed *New Nightmare* with 1995's Paramount-produced *Vampire in Brooklyn*, a horror-comedy starring Eddie Murphy. The movie was ill-fated, with the film's principals pushing the tone in different directions. Worse, the shoot featured a genuine tragedy when stuntwoman Sonja Davis was fatally injured executing a 42-foot fall. *Vampire in Brooklyn* was excoriated by reviewers. Released in October 1995, the film was another commercial disappointment for Craven.

Still, despite the cooling of his career, he was reluctant to direct Williamson's script. "He turned it down several times," says editor Patrick Lussier. "He didn't want to do something that was so extreme, although I know he was a fan of the script. I remember him telling me, 'Just read the opening,' what became the Drew Barrymore sequence. It was like, holy shit!"

Julie Plec was someone else in Craven's circle who recognized the quality of Williamson's screenplay. Years later, Plec would become a successful TV writer-producer, developing, with Williamson, the hit series *The Vampire Diaries*. In 1995, the recent Northwestern University graduate was working as Craven's assistant. "Everybody always asks, 'Was he scary?'" she says. "No, he was a very kind, gentle, very intelligent man. Loved his bird books, loved his crosswords. He was very passionate about not just telling stories but the act of making the movie itself. He really enjoyed building a community around him of partners that he would take from movie to movie. In a way, he built his own traveling troupe."

Plec was given a copy of Williamson's screenplay by a development executive at Craven's company named Lisa Harrison. "I loved it so much because it was a movie I felt was written for people like me," she says. "All the Jason movies, the Michael Myers movies, the Freddy movies, that was my adolescence. I was one of the people screaming at the screen, 'Don't go upstairs! Why are you so stupid?'" Plec's enthusiasm for Williamson's script did not convince Craven that he should direct the film, though. "Wes was like, 'I made the movies that this movie is sending up, why would I do this?'" says Plec. "He appreciated that the giggling assistant in the front office was saying it's the best script she'd ever read, but he was looking to do something that felt more like an auteur piece."

Craven had already agreed to direct a very different kind of horror movie for Dimension. In January 1994, Bob Weinstein confirmed to *Variety* that Miramax had acquired the film rights to Shirley Jackson's 1959 supernatural tale *The Haunting of Hill House*. *West Side Story* director Robert Wise had previously adapted the novel as 1963's *The Haunting*, widely regarded as a horror classic. In the summer of 1994, Weinstein hired Craven to direct a new film version of Jackson's story.

With Craven out of the frame for *Scary Movie*, Bob Weinstein pursued Robert Rodriguez, whose film *Desperado* was a hit for Sony Pictures after the company distributed the Antonio Banderas-starring action movie in August 1995. Rodriguez demurred, opting to make *From Dusk Till Dawn* for Dimension instead. "About 500 people were considered for the director's spot!" Williamson told *Fangoria*, following the release of *Scream*. According to the screenwriter, the candidates included *Shallow Grave* and *Trainspotting* filmmaker Danny Boyle and Anthony Waller, director of the 1995 horror movie *Mute Witness*. "They were looking for the new Wes Craven," Williamson explained to *Fangoria*. "And finally, Bob Weinstein said, 'Well, what about the old Wes Craven?'"

Before the end of 1995, the Weinsteins had shelved their new version of *The Haunting*. Julie Plec was still convinced that Craven should tackle Williamson's screenplay and pushed him in that direction. "I said, 'They can't find a director for this, and they really want you,'" says Plec. "He joked, 'Well, tell them to make me an offer I can't refuse.' I took the joke out of it, and told Lisa Harrison to tell Dimension to make him an offer he couldn't refuse. And they did. And he took it."

Drew Barrymore was initially enthusiastic about playing the film's heroine and final girl Sidney Prescott. The actress' track record at the box office had been spotty since her days as a child star, but she had remained in the public eye, playing the lead role in the 1993 true crime TV movie *The Amy Fisher Story* and appearing in 1995's *Batman Forever*.

Skeet Ulrich successfully auditioned for the role of Sidney's boyfriend Billy Loomis, who at the end of the film is revealed to be one of the movie's killers. "Thought it was the coolest thing I'd read at that point in my career," says Ulrich of Williamson's script. "At that point, I hadn't really played any dark characters *per se*, so it was really exciting for me to possibly be able to do that."

Matthew Lillard was similarly impressed by the script. "I thought it was terrifying," says the actor. Lillard particularly enjoyed the screenplay's referencing of previous horror films. "Before *Scream* came along, everyone was trying to make movies that were non-referential, right?" he says. "You were trying to make a movie that, if you turned it on ten years later, that it would still be relevant. Kevin Williamson was like, 'Screw it, we're going to go the exact opposite way.'"

Lillard initially auditioned for the role of Billy Loomis and was then asked to try out for the role of Loomis' friend, and the film's other killer, Stu Macher. "They said, 'Why don't you come back and come in for the best friend?'" Lillard recalls. "I had two hours to review the material and then audition with Wes. So Wes walked in and he actually gave me the part in the room, which was kind of crazy. He was like, 'Yeah, you're the guy.'"

(*Left to right*) Skeet Ulrich, Jamie Kennedy, and Matthew Lillard in *Scream*.

The search for someone to play the lead role of Sidney Prescott began again once Barrymore announced that she would rather take the smaller part of Casey Becker. The actress argued that having her play the doomed Casey would confound the expectations of cinemagoers who assumed she was portraying the film's final girl, not an early victim. Plec recalls Craven being saddened by Barrymore's decision, believing that her choice had been prompted by his low status as a director of horror films. "One of the nicest things about Wes was that he was very humble and didn't have a raging ego, but with that also came an insecurity," she says. "Drew said she wanted to play Casey instead of Sidney, and he thought it was because he wasn't elite enough of a filmmaker for her to be excited about him. He was really disappointed. She made a really good case for it, which is the Janet Leigh [in *Psycho*] case, which turned out to be incredibly the right move, and Wes obviously recognized it eventually as the right move. At the time, I think he felt a little wounded that maybe he wasn't cool enough in her eyes. Then they went on to have a beautiful relationship and a great experience with each other, and I think he never looked back, but I remember that moment pretty clearly."

The shortlist of actresses in the frame to replace Barrymore was comprised of Alicia Witt, Brittany Murphy, and Neve Campbell. The trio all screen-tested opposite Ulrich, with the *Party of Five* actress finally being offered the role. Campbell had reservations about accepting the part, not being a fan of slasher movies or the genre as a whole. Asked to name her favorite horror movie, Campbell would routinely choose *The Changeling*, director Peter Medak's 1980 ghost story. "It was the first horror movie I ever saw," she says. "It was one of the last horror movies I ever saw." Having already appeared in *The Craft*, Campbell was worried that her movie career would be circumscribed if she received the tag of 'scream queen.' "I was like, I don't know what the response is going to be, I don't know how people are going to react to that," she says. Campbell eventually overcame her reservations and agreed to play Sidney.

Craven filled out his cast with Courteney Cox, *Happy Days* actor Henry Winkler, and several more young newcomers: Rose McGowan, David Arquette, and Jamie Kennedy. "I know the studio wasn't exactly excited to have me, because I didn't have any credits," says Kennedy, who played the film's high school horror movie expert Randy Meeks. "It was really Wes and the team who pushed for me to get the part. Without them, I wouldn't be talking to you."

Neve Campbell and Rose McGowan in *Scream*.

Craven shot *Scream* in the city of Santa Rosa during the spring of 1996. The principal cast stayed at the DoubleTree hotel, where David Arquette, who was playing Woodsboro deputy sheriff Dwight 'Dewey' Riley, turned his room into a hang-out zone. "I have the distinct memory of us getting out of the van covered in blood and all these happy-go-lucky tourists going off into the Napa countryside to drink wine," says Lillard. "We would all go to David Arquette's room at six in the morning, covered in blood, and have a couple of beers and unwind."

Craven gave his *Stranger in Our House* star Linda Blair the cameo role of a reporter who at one point in the film bluntly asks Campbell's character, "How does it feel to be almost brutally butchered?" Blair recalls that "Wes called me and said, 'Everybody's driving me crazy, everybody wants you to be part of this, but I didn't write anything for you. If I write a little something-something, will you come up and play?' 'Sure!' And that is how I became the obnoxious reporter."

The production's fake blood and gore was provided by the special effects company KNB EFX Group, which had been founded in 1988 by

Courteney Cox and David Arquette in *Scream.*

Robert Kurtzman, Greg Nicotero, and Howard Berger. Berger and the Pittsburgh-raised Nicotero had both worked on George Romero's 1985 zombie film *Day of the Dead*, and all three were hired for Sam Raimi's *Evil Dead II*. The trio established KNB when they collaborated again on the 1989 slasher film *Intruder*. "I started in 1984 in Pittsburgh with George Romero on *Day of the Dead* and moved to LA in the fall of 1985," says Nicotero. "We got a house, and it was me, Howard, and Bob Kurtzman, and we were all working at different places. When *Evil Dead II* came around, between me interfacing with production, and Howard applying Bruce's makeups, and Kurtzman applying a lot of the stuff, we covered all aspects of a prosthetics company." KNB swiftly established itself as a leader in the arena of practical special effects. The company worked on director Rob Reiner's 1990 Stephen King adaptation *Misery* and the same year's Kevin Costner western epic *Dances with Wolves*, for which the company created two dozen buffaloes.

Wes Craven had first worked with KNB on his 1991 horror film *The People Under the Stairs* and continued to employ the company's services on *New*

Nightmare, *Vampire in Brooklyn*, and then *Scream*. Nicotero describes the 1996 film as, "probably the most prosthetics-heavy of all the *Scream* movies. The first *Scream*, we did the body of Drew Barrymore that's hanging, gutted, we did Rose McGowan's head that gets crushed in the garage. It was really Wes spreading his wings a little bit and being a little more gory and a little more gruesome. I don't think the rules of the world had been really solidified in regards to what the tone was going to be. When we did *Scream 2* and *Scream 3*, there was less and less. It ended up being a lot of blood and stab wounds as those movies progressed, because there was a certain sense of humor to them. Wes felt that the excessive gore didn't necessarily play into what *Scream* was about."

Craven asked KNB to design the mask that would be worn by the movie's killers. "Those things are so challenging to nail," says Nicotero. "We had

Prop Ghostface mask at BFI IMAX film memorabilia exhibition in London, 2018.

done some preliminary sculptures, like, 'What do you think about this or that?' Ultimately, they found a commercially produced mask that they liked and they're like, well, we'll just license that." The white, open-mouthed Ghostface mask worn by the killers in the film was found by *Scream* executive producer Marianne Maddalena as she was searching for locations in northern California. "We were scouting in Santa Rosa and couldn't figure out the killer's look," Maddalena would recall to *Fangoria*. "We had all our special FX guys trying out ideas, and Wes didn't like any of them. One day, I was scouting out this lady's house that we didn't end up using—the same one where Hitchcock's *Shadow of a Doubt* was shot. We were upstairs in the bedroom, and I saw this ghost mask there. I said to everybody, 'We could use this, it's perfect.' [...] The only thing different was that it had a white shroud instead of a black one. Then we got the rights, and the rest is history."

Craven spent the early part of the shoot filming the movie's opening sequence, in which Barrymore's character is murdered. When executives at Dimension saw the footage, they were appalled. "They were very unhappy with Wes' first week of dailies and were threatening to fire him, and saying he was like a journeyman, and a hack, and all that sort of stuff," says Patrick Lussier. "They were sending him dailies of other movies and said, 'This is how you do scary movies.' And that was the Drew Barrymore sequence!"

In an attempt to keep the project on track, Lussier edited together the footage to show Bob Weinstein the quality of the material. "I cut it together, and Wes had a temp music note, and we sent it off to New York," he says. "They were not just apologetic, but literally like, 'Oh my God, we had no idea that this was going to work so well.' They proceeded to do a total 180 and completely support Wes and his vision. The fact that Bob Weinstein admitted he was wrong to Wes, I think is a big deal. For all the chaos and everything that he can create—which he definitely could—that's not insignificant in my mind."

Scream was shot mostly in sequence, with the concluding chunk of production capturing the film's third act party sequence. "The last month of the movie, we shot the final scene," says Julie Plec. "We called it scene 114, even though it had 97 parts. We shot it for a month [of] night shoots. We'd get to work at five o'clock, we'd wrap at seven in the morning. On Saturday mornings, we'd all go back to the hotel and get drunk in either the teamsters' office suite—the teamsters had a full bar—or the dolly grip's hotel room, because he had a margarita blender."

Matthew Lillard has fond memories of working with Craven. "He was really the best," says the actor. "He became this father figure for all of us. He was this director who was very sweet, and soft-spoken, and very clear what he wanted. He wasn't like this control freak where he was crafting this performance. You'd have to do takes as written and then he'd be like, 'Hey, try something different.' It was an introduction into the world of Hollywood in a way that none of us ever expected, and over the years I think that we became special to him, because I don't think every *Scream* experience was that. I mean, every *Scream* experience past the first was this huge weight of expectation. For us, nobody cared. So I think that he looked at our cast and our experience as a gift."

Bob Weinstein would ultimately decide to retitle the project from *Scary Movie* to *Scream*, much to Craven's annoyance. "I was very upset about it," the director told *Entertainment Weekly* writer Tim Stack years later. "When we started, [I got] a robe as a gift that said '*Scary Movie*' on it. Then toward the end [Bob Weinstein] said, 'I'm going to change the title to *Scream*.' And I was like, 'That sucks!' I told my assistant to take the robe and cut it up into three-inch squares and mail it back to him. She didn't do it, so I still have it."

At the end of the shoot, Neve Campbell and the rest of the core cast had an emotional meal with the director. "We all sat around and had a dinner, after we wrapped, in this little Italian restaurant in Santa Rosa," says the actress. "Everyone stood up, and made a toast, and expressed how meaningful the experience was in some way, and how life-changing it was in some way for each of us. It meant a lot, for some reason. It meant a lot, that film."

Scream would mean a lot to the horror genre as a whole. It re-proved the commercial appeal of scary movies and ushered in a wave of films that found casts of young, easy-on-the eye actors—often the stars of TV shows—being menaced and murdered by mysterious forces. Several of those films would be written by Kevin Williamson himself.

CHAPTER 2

"THE WAY I SEE IT, SOMEONE'S OUT TO MAKE A SEQUEL."

Scream was of massive importance to Dimension and to Miramax, whose releases tended to generate good reviews and awards rather than huge profits. Following the release of Wes Craven's film, Dimension signed a deal with Kevin Williamson, which the *Los Angeles Times* reported "could earn him as much as $20 million," and set him to work writing a sequel, *Scream 2*. "The last time we saw anyone like him, it was Quentin Tarantino," Bob Weinstein told *Entertainment Weekly* writer David Hochman.

Tarantino gave his thumbs-up to Williamson in the course of an interview with *Fangoria* to promote his Rolling Thunder company's re-release of Italian director Lucio Fulci's 1981 film *The Beyond*. "Williamson did with *Scream* what I did with gangster films," Tarantino told the magazine's editor Tony Timpone. "Horror was pretty much fucking dead when he did that. Not only did he revitalize it and kind of give some respect to the slasher genre, but he even commented on why all these other horror films have been so crappy."

Prior to the release of *Scream*, the Weinstein brothers had wanted Craven's next movie for them to be a werewolf film called *Bad Moon Rising*. The script was by Scott Rosenberg, who had written the screenplays for two Miramax productions, 1995's *Things to Do in Denver When You're Dead* and 1996's *Beautiful Girls*. "Scott Rosenberg had a script called *Bad Moon Rising*, which was a motorcycle biker-werewolf movie," says Julie Plec. "Harvey and Bob wanted Wes to make that movie so badly, and Wes did not want to make it. After a test screening of [what was] still called *Scary Movie* in New Jersey, Harvey took us all to Cipriani. He said to Wes, 'If you agree to make *Bad Moon Rising*, I will give you any movie on the Miramax slate that you want.' Wes really wanted his next movie to be not horror and so he agreed." In exchange for Craven consenting to make *Bad Moon Rising*,

Miramax agreed to finance the film *Music of the Heart*, about violinist and educator Roberta Guaspari. After *Scream* struck gold, though, Craven signed on to direct *Scream 2*. As Plec recalls, "When *Scream* was such a hit, and they fast-tracked *Scream 2*, then *Bad Moon Rising* went away, and he still got to make his violin movie."

Bob Weinstein wanted to release *Scream 2* in December 2007, just a year after the first movie. That resulted in an overly full schedule for Williamson. The *Scream* creator was already occupied writing and producing his teen drama TV show *Dawson's Creek*, which would premiere on The WB network in January 1998. "I was down in North Carolina, working on *Dawson's Creek*, and I remember just sitting, panicked and frantic, trying to write *Scream 2*," he says.

After two years as Craven's assistant, Plec was promoted to the position of development executive in 1997 and would receive an associate producer credit on *Scream 2*. She describes the rushed development of the sequel as "a crazy process. The movie was greenlit before there was even a page of the script. Bob Weinstein says, 'We're shooting a movie in June, when Neve and Courteney are on hiatus, go write a script.' If you're shooting in June, that means you're prepping in March. It is *January*. It became a race against time to get that done. Kevin was doing the *Dawson's Creek* pilot at the same time. When you are the creator of a TV show, and you're shooting the pilot, that pilot needs you 24 hours a day, seven days a week, for about six weeks. And he was trying to write the draft for *Scream 2* at the same time. It was not easy." Plec recalls that she and *Scream 2* producer Marianne Maddalena visited Wilmington in North Carolina, where Williamson was working on *Dawson's Creek*, "to basically sit and get any moment he was available—*any* moment, like, five minutes here, ten minutes there, to just get him to put a few words on the page."

In fact, Williamson's first box office hit after *Scream* would not be a Dimension release. Even before Craven had started shooting *Scream*, the screenwriter was crafting an adaptation of the 1973 book *I Know What You Did Last Summer*. Written by young adult author Lois Duncan, the novel concerns four teenage friends who accidentally run down and kill a cyclist and cover up their involvement in the crime. A year on from the incident, the quartet is menaced by someone who seems to have knowledge of the event.

The rights to the book were owned by Mandalay Pictures, a production company recently founded by ex-Sony Pictures boss Peter Guber. Williamson was approached about the project after selling his *Scream* script to Dimension, and the suddenly hot screenwriter was given *carte blanche* to change Duncan's source material. The writer revived the character of the fisherman from his backyard horror movie and turned the character into his script's mysterious antagonist.

Williamson's new villain was inspired and informed by the writer's background. "I come from a fishing community in North Carolina," he says. "My dad was a fisherman, his dad was a fisherman. It's a fishing family. In the book *I Know What You Did Last Summer*, there was no fishing, there was no boat, there was nothing. They wanted an iconic killer, *à la* Jason and Michael Myers, and so [I thought] why don't I create the Fisherman? I went to my dad, and he walked me around the boat, and he showed me the A-frame, and how someone would be jerked up to the top. Then I wrote it, and he went, 'Kevin, that would never happen.' I said, 'Yes, but it's in the movie, Dad.'"

The cast of *I Know What You Did Last Summer* included Neve Campbell's *Party of Five* co-star Jennifer Love Hewitt as the final girl Julie, along with Ryan Philippe, Freddie Prinze Jr., Sarah Michelle Gellar, and Johnny Galecki. "I wrote that movie, I did a set of rewrites, and then I came back after they shot the film, and I did a reshoot," says Williamson. "We added Johnny Galecki's death scene on camera, and we changed the ending. The good news was, we were filming *Dawson's Creek* in the exact same studio where they were filming *I Know What You Did Last Summer*, so I could kind of bounce back and forth."

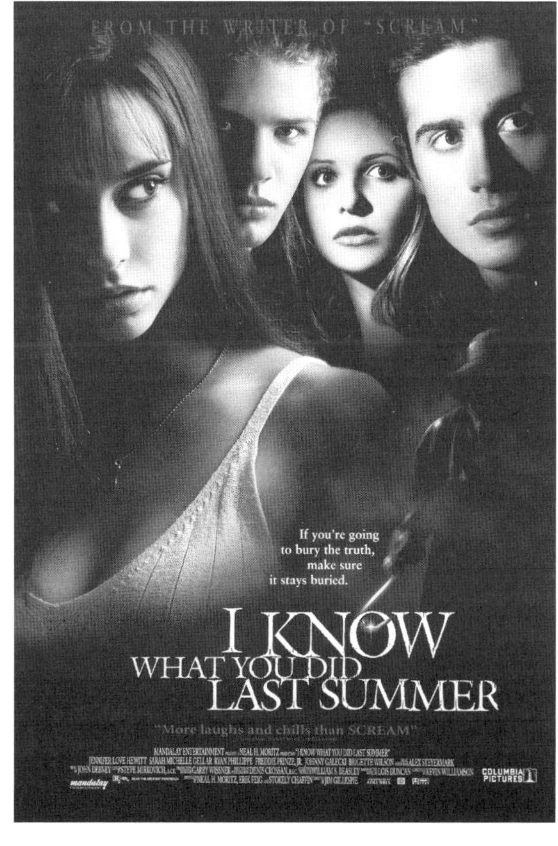

Novelist Lois Duncan was unaware of the changes Williamson had made to her story. In a Q&A with fellow young adult author Barry Lyga published in the 2010 edition of *I Know What You Did Last Summer*, the writer revealed that she first learned about the character of the Fisherman when she saw the finished movie. "It was my characters and my plot gimmick, but then it went in all directions," she said. "I was quite horrified by the sensationalized violence. Several years earlier, my own teenage daughter, Kait, had been chased down in her car and shot to death, and I had seen, right in front of my eyes, what real violence is. To have people screaming and laughing about it did not go down well... So I was not happy with the movie, but I have to admit I was happy with the fact that the book had been made into a movie, because that made all my backlist suddenly very popular. It was like getting a rebirth, but in a very strange way."

Directed by Scottish filmmaker Jim Gillespie, *I Know What You Did Last Summer* cost $17 million and earned almost that amount at the domestic box office over its opening weekend in October 1997. The film was the number one movie in the US for three weeks in a row and grossed $126 million around the world. A sequel, *I Still Know What You Did Last Summer*, directed by *Judge Dredd* filmmaker Danny Cannon and written by Trey Callaway, arrived on cinema screens in November 1998.

As Craven assembled his cast for *Scream 2*, it became clear that Neve Campbell's fears about the first film having an adverse effect on her career were unfounded. *Scream* burnished the reputations of actors like Campbell and Courteney Cox, who were already familiar to young TV watchers, and positively introduced the public to lesser-known talents like Jamie Kennedy and Matthew Lillard. As *Entertainment Weekly* writers Judy Brennan and Chris Nashawaty noted in an article announcing the start of shooting on *Scream 2*, "Perhaps the most intriguing aspect of the *Scream* phenomenon is the feeding frenzy the sequel has sparked among Hollywood agents, all of whom are itching to get their rising stars the same hip exposure that Barrymore, Campbell, Cox, Arquette, and Skeet Ulrich garnered from the first film." Appearing in the sequel, which found Campbell's heroine being stalked by Ghostface while attending college, suddenly seemed like a good idea to many young Hollywood actors and their representatives. "I hoped it elevated the genre," says Williamson of the first *Scream*. "It certainly helped the genre in terms of maybe giving a kick in the butt."

Scream stars Campbell, Cox, Arquette, and Kennedy were joined on the production by Sarah Michelle Gellar, Heather Graham, Timothy Olyphant, and Jerry O'Connell. Where the first film had effectively featured an all-white cast, several Black actors appeared in *Scream 2.* Jada Pinkett Smith and Omar Epps portrayed a couple who are murdered in the opening scene; Elise Neal played Sidney's college friend Hallie and Duane Martin took the role of a cameraman working with Cox's TV reporter Gale Weathers. "Well, it came from an all-white cast of *Scream 1*, to be absolutely honest," says Williamson of the sequel's comparatively diverse onscreen line-up. "You know, you start casting one role individually, and you cast the next one, and the next one, and before you know it, you have an entire cast of white people, and that was a big mistake. We all recognized it, and we all wanted to change that."

In the film's opening sequence, the characters played by Pinkett Smith and Epps attend a crowded screening of a slasher film called *Stab*, which is based on the events of *Scream.* The notion of this horror-movie-within-a-horror-movie had been foreshadowed in the first film when Campbell's character said, "With my luck, they'd cast Tori Spelling" as her in any subsequent movie about the killings. Spelling did indeed appear in *Stab*, portraying the *Scream* heroine. "I wrote that opening scene right away," says Williamson.

Omar Epps and Jada Pinkett Smith in *Scream 2* (1997).

"I knew I wanted to do total meta and I wanted to have a film version of the opening scene [from the original *Scream*] onscreen while we were watching someone else get killed. I thought Wes did that so beautifully. I loved the way he filmed *Stab* and I thought it worked really great. It was just what I wanted in that scene. And then it became the whole spine of *Scream 2*, which is that *Stab* has come out and created a copycat killer, and has put all the attention right back on Sidney, and all she wants to do is disappear. It was a great conflict for this character."

During the production of the first *Scream*, no one had worried about plot details becoming public. In the wake of that movie's success, though, information about the sequel was closely guarded. As Jerry O'Connell joked to *Entertainment Weekly* writer David Hochman in the journalist's cover story about the movie, "When I first got the script, two men with Uzis delivered it and stayed with me until I was done reading it."

The *Entertainment Weekly* article related how, despite the production's precautions, a big chunk of Williamson's script wound up on that comparatively new technological development, the internet. "As soon as Kevin's first 40 pages came in, they went out almost immediately onto the internet," Craven told the magazine. "So all that was blown, and we had to go into rewrites."

According to Williamson, he never actually rewrote the script for *Scream 2*. Rather, the writer oversaw the deliberate leaking of fake pages, so that it would not matter if details from the real screenplay appeared online. "Here's what happened," he says. "I knew the script was going to get leaked, because everyone was talking about it, there was press, press, press: 'What's going to happen in *Scream 2*?' Luckily, we had caught the zeitgeist, and everyone wanted to know about *Scream 2*. So I knew it was going to leak eventually—there was no way we could hold on to it. We were sending the script out without the last 75 pages to do our best, but we knew it would come out. My assistant wrote a dummy script with Dewey as the killer, and we leaked the fake one. So by the time the real one got out there, there was no fuss, no one cared."

Williamson continued working on the script during the production of *Scream 2*, which was shot in Atlanta and Los Angeles. "I was there in Atlanta, because I was still writing the script on the set," he says. "The other day, I was looking at these pictures, there's a picture of David Arquette passed out on the grass and me passed out on the grass. Everyone was doing a hundred different things by then. I was flying back from *Dawson's Creek*. A lot was going on. Yeah, it was a blur."

Williamson planned for the film's finale to take place at a theater on the campus where Campbell's character is studying. The writer was still reworking the sequence until the last possible moment. "We were writing *Scream 2* until we were done shooting *Scream 2*," says Plec. "We were in the trailer, outside where we were shooting the big theater-spectacle scene, sitting in a trailer with Liev Schreiber, trying to crack the last act of the movie. Write, rewrite, rewrite again. Never stopped rewriting that one. It was insane."

Hochman's *Entertainment Weekly* cover story highlighted how the original *Scream* had helped revive the horror genre. On the night the journalist visited the *Scream 2* set in Pasadena, Wes Craven was joined by his fellow horror auteur George A. Romero. In the years since *Night of the Living Dead*, Romero had unleashed several more gore-drenched horror movies, from 1979's Tom Savini-assisted *Dawn of the Dead* to 1982's Stephen King-written *Creepshow* to 1985's *Day of the Dead*, which completed his original zombie trilogy. The filmmaker spent much of the '90s in development hell, fruitlessly attempting to get a slew of projects off the ground. Romero was one of the directors Dimension had approached about making the first *Scream*, but the filmmaker had passed. "I think they were offering it to everybody, but it was different, they didn't know what it was, and they didn't know whether it was meant to be campy, funny, or what," Romero told the magazine *Stuck*. "Miramax at that time were thinking of it as a flat-out horror and I said to them, 'Who wants to rehash an old genre?'"

When Romero visited the *Scream 2* set, he had only completed one film in the previous nine years, a 1993 adaptation of Stephen King's novel *The Dark Half*. Romero seemed in good spirits, partly because of how the popularity of Craven's original *Scream* might help his own career. "The genre was dying and *Scream* saved it," the director told Hochman. "It's great for all of us horror guys. Even my phone is starting to ring again."

Craven and editor Patrick Lussier were worried about securing an R rating for *Scream 2* from the Motion Picture Association of America (MPAA) ratings board, a quest which had proved difficult with the first film. The two years prior to the release of *Scream* had seen an extended attack on the entertainment industry, or at least its more explicit output, by Bob Dole, the Republican nominee in the 1996 presidential election. Dole criticized TV networks, film studios, and record companies for what he claimed was the entertainment industry's lax and profit-minded approach to featuring sex and violence in their output. In July 1996, Dole visited the 20th Century

Fox studio in Los Angeles and gave a speech praising *Apollo 13*, *Babe*, and even *Braveheart*, whose violence the politician said was "true to the story… not just brutality thrown in there for the shock and thrill of it." Still, Dole argued that TV networks and studios should make family-friendly product for both commercial and moral reasons. "You can watch your ratings rise and your box office receipts go up and still look at yourself in the mirror," the politician said.

The controversy over violence in movies had been referenced by Williamson in his first *Scream* script. Toward the end of the film, Campbell's Sidney Prescott accuses the movie's killers of being "sick fucks" who have seen "one too many movies." "Now, Sid, don't you blame the movies," responds Ulrich's Billy Loomis. "Movies don't create psychos; movies make psychos more creative!"

On the original *Scream*, the MPAA had sided with Bob Dole rather than Ulrich's blood-spattered killer. *Scream* was originally given a rating of NC-17, which would have doomed the movie at the box office. "The MPAA flatly announced, 'You're miles from it, you'll probably never be able to get an R rating,'" Craven had told *Fangoria* before the film was released. "Well, we did, but it took endless screaming and crying, and writing letters, and paring it back somewhat."

Craven and Lussier assumed they would have a similar battle on *Scream 2*. But with the presidential election now in the past (Dole having lost to incumbent Bill Clinton), that proved not to be the case. "Our biggest fear [on] *Scream 2* was the ratings board," says Lussier. "Wes shot variations of scenes that were more violent, especially Omar's death and Jamie Kennedy's death. We cut those in to send to the MPAA, thinking that they would reject it and then we could cut it back to the way Wes wanted. They gave us an R rating the first time, and we still cut it back to the way we wanted it. People say, 'Well, can we see the more violent versions?' No. It wasn't better, it was just more extreme for a specific purpose, it was never designed to be part of the movie."

Scream 2 opened on December 12, 1997, and earned $32 million over its opening weekend. The second film's final US gross was just $2 million short of the original, further enhancing Kevin Williamson's reputation. A profile of the writer published on CNN.com in August 1998 claimed that Williamson "has single-handedly resuscitated the lost art of horror, penning the screenplays to *Scream*, *Scream 2*, and *I Know What You Did Last Summer*, which together grossed $500 million at the box office."

Audiences would have to wait longer for *Scream 3* than they had for the second film, as Wes Craven was occupied directing his non-horror movie, *Music of the Heart*, which starred Meryl Streep. Patrick Lussier worked on the film and recalls Harvey Weinstein asking his own people to edit a different version of Craven's movie. "Harvey had this whole room where he would be cutting your movie behind your back," says Lussier. "I remember Wes getting a tape of it, and he looked at two minutes of it, and popped it out, and threw it in the trash." Released in October 1999, *Music of the Heart* earned just $14 million at the US box office. To Craven's satisfaction, the film would secure two Oscar nominations, for Streep's performance and the Diane Warren-written song "Music of My Heart."

After the release of *Scream*, Dimension paid $225,000 for another original horror script, *The Faculty*, about a high school invaded by aliens, from writers David Wechter and Bruce Kimmel. Bob Weinstein asked Kevin Williamson to rewrite the screenplay, telling him that he could do what he wanted with the script as long as the finished film involved extraterrestrials. Williamson originally intended to make *The Faculty* his directorial debut, but Weinstein ultimately hired Robert Rodriguez to oversee the special effects-packed project. The *Desperado* filmmaker filled the cast with up-and-coming actors like Josh Hartnett, Jordana Brewster, and Elijah Wood. A diehard horror fan, Wood was apprehensive about appearing in *The Faculty*, which Dimension so clearly hoped would become another *Scream*. "The movie was coming at what was the tail end of that *Scream*-inspired revisit to teenage horror films," he says. "Kevin Williamson started a great thing and then started a bad thing at the same time. When something really great comes out, there are a million imitators. I remember getting the script, and being aware of that and a little bit wary of jumping into what was such a popular genre." *The Faculty* was released on Christmas Day, 1998, and earned $11 million in the US over its opening weekend. *Los Angeles Times* writer Patrick Goldstein described that figure as "a modest showing considering that Miramax spent a record $30 million marketing the film."

The Faculty was beaten into cinemas by *Urban Legend*, another film clearly designed to attract the teenage and twentysomething cinemagoing audience. Directed by Australian filmmaker Jamie Blanks and distributed by Sony Pictures, the movie had an intriguing hook about characters being murdered in ways inspired by modern folklore. The film starred Jared Leto from the TV show *My So-Called Life*, Rebecca Gayheart from *Beverly Hills, 90210*, and Joshua Jackson, who played the character of Pacey on *Dawson's*

Creek. Blanks cast Robert Englund in the role of a college professor. "After I took the makeup off in '94, when we'd done the first battery of *Nightmare on Elm Street* movies, I had aged, and my face was turning into an interesting character," says Englund. "I could segue into Vincent Price/Christopher Lee parts, and that was just this great thing." Released in September 1998, *Urban Legend* earned $38 million at the domestic box office, and a sequel, *Urban Legends: Final Cut*, followed two years later.

The in-demand Kevin Williamson also helped relaunch the *Halloween* series following the disappointment of 1995's *Halloween: The Curse of Michael Myers*, which had grossed just $15 million in the US. The franchise's commercial appeal had fallen so far since the spectacular earnings of Carpenter's original film that Dimension, which still held the distribution rights to the series, planned on making the next entry a straight-to-video release. Then Jamie Lee Curtis revealed her willingness to reprise the role of Laurie Strode.

Jamie Lee Curtis and Chris Durand in *Halloween H20: Twenty Years Later* (1998).

In the years since starring in *Halloween II*, the actress had established herself outside horror with her performances in films like 1983's *Trading Places* and James Cameron's 1994 action blockbuster *True Lies*. As the 20th anniversary of *Halloween* approached, Curtis suggested to John Carpenter and Debra Hill that the trio reunite for a new film. "I said to them, 'Guys, the movie's going to be 20 years old next year, why don't we revisit it?'" she says. "But then everybody was busy, and, by the end, I was the only one involved with it. To this day, I regret that I didn't say, 'If Debra's not the one producing this movie, I'm not doing it.' But what ended up happening was, she wasn't part of it, John wasn't part of it, and I was still part of it. It was a machine going down the road, and I was excited about it, and honestly, it was also I was going to be paid well."

The awkwardly titled *Halloween H20: Twenty Years Later* was directed by Steve Miner, whose credits included *Friday the 13th Part 2* and the pilot of Williamson's *Dawson's Creek*. Williamson himself wrote a treatment for the film and later polished the script, which was credited to Robert Zappia and Matt Greenberg. With *Dawson's Creek* actress Michelle Williams, Josh Hartnett, and rapper LL Cool J cast in supporting roles, *Halloween H20* had obvious appeal to horror fans keen to see more releases like *Scream* and its sequel. Director Miner even re-used some of composer Marco Beltrami's score for *Scream* and included a sequence in which footage from *Scream 2* plays on a television. Released in August 1998, the film grossed $55 million at the US box office, a more-than-healthy return for a film with a $17 million budget. Curtis would play Laurie Strode yet again in 2002's Dimension-distributed *Halloween: Resurrection* with her character definitively perishing (at least in this timeline) at the hands of Michael Myers in the film's opening sequence.

Two months after Michael Myers had returned to screens with *Halloween H20*, a more diminutive slasher icon showed that he could successfully pivot in a post-*Scream* world when *Bride of Chucky* became a box office hit. The

Chucky and Tiffany in *Bride of Chucky* (1998).

screenplay for the fourth *Child's Play* film was written by Chucky creator Don Mancini, inspired by the brainwave of franchise producer David Kirschner. "There used to be a place called Rocket Video in LA, and I was there on a Friday night with my wife," says Kirschner. "I see *Bride of Frankenstein*, and I called Don from the store, and I said, 'Let's give Chucky a bride.' From there, he just created that whole thing."

Mancini gave the film a broader, and more knowing, comedic streak than previous entries in the *Child's Play* series. He also decided to write a movie that better reflected his sexual identity. "When we did *Bride of Chucky* in '98, that is when I started injecting specific queer content," he says. "I was at a point in my life as a gay guy where I was fully out and, at the same time, I was tasked with reinventing my franchise. How do you keep it fresh? Well, how about having some gay characters!"

The movie's cast included Oscar nominee Jennifer Tilly (who portrayed the titular bride), David Arquette's sibling Alexis, and a teenage Katherine Heigl. Directed by Hong Kong filmmaker Ronny Yu, *Bride of Chucky* grossed $32 million at the US box office, returning the franchise to the commercial heights of its first two entries.

If the period immediately following the release of *Scream* represented a second golden age for the slasher genre, not every horror director was in thrall to the form. As Craven and Williamson paid homage to John Carpenter with their Ghostface tales, and other franchises rode the wave they had created, some filmmakers—including Carpenter himself—looked elsewhere for a more vintage vein of inspiration.

In the decades since Universal had released 1931's Bela Lugosi-starring *Dracula*, the vampire film had become firmly associated with lushly presented gothic horror, a tradition continued by 1992's *Bram Stoker's Dracula* and 1994's *Interview with the Vampire*. But the second half of the '90s would find the Transylvanian Count's onscreen descendants ditching capes and castles for more modern accoutrements in movies which gave bloodsuckers new cinematic life. Among these was writer-director Larry Fessenden's low-budget 1997 film *Habit*. A contemporary reworking of the vampire myth, the movie was set not in Europe's picturesque Carpathian Mountains but in Manhattan's then-scuzzy downtown area.

The New York-raised Fessenden began a lifelong love affair with the Universal monster films of the '30s and '40s when he saw them on television as a child. "I grew up with the old black and white horror movies," says the writer-director. "There was a movie dump in the '60s, TV just bought a whole package, so they fed them to my generation. If you liked horror, you watched *Chiller Theatre*. I couldn't wait for my parents to go out on a Saturday, so I could watch these movies—*Frankenstein*, and *Bride of Frankenstein*, and *Wolf Man*."

Fessenden became obsessed with the metaphorical qualities of the Universal movies and their much-tormented monsters. "I really do think horror is owned by this idea of psychology; it's a great way to talk about identity, because the whole monster thing is [about] otherness," he continues. "It's always had that fear of the other and the feeling of *being* the other. If you felt you were losing your grip on reality, you had a place in horror, and the power of the metaphor is what made it beautiful." Fessenden was also drawn to more modern films like George Romero's *Night of the Living Dead* and the movies being made by the directors of the so-called New Hollywood. "In the '70s, I loved more character-driven pieces," he says. "I loved Scorsese, the work of De Niro, Pacino, Nicholson." Fessenden found less to enjoy in *Halloween* and the cycle of slasher films that followed. "So dedicated was I to *Night of the Living Dead*, Roman Polanski's early films, and a kind of independent edginess, that when *Halloween* came out, I was resistant," he says. "It seemed like horror for horror's sake. Now I watch them with great coziness. In October, I'll watch Freddy Krueger. But I never liked the commodification of this essential emotion that happened in the '80s."

Fessenden studied film at NYU and made his feature debut with 1991's *No Telling* (a.k.a. *The Frankenstein Complex*), about a scientist who moves to the country so he can perform experiments on animals. "I always joke that animal rights, vivisection, are not the topics to make your first film [about]," he says. The movie cost around $500,000 and "was a bit of a bust," according to the director. The filmmaker reassessed his approach to production after collaborating with director Kelly Reichardt on her own feature debut, the 1995 independent drama *River of Grass*. Fessenden starred in and edited the movie, which cost just $60,000 and was nominated for prizes at the Sundance Film Festival and the Independent Spirit Awards. Working on Reichardt's film inspired Fessenden to make his own micro-budgeted tale, *Habit*. "That was an essential lesson," he says. "I was done with the *No Telling* model, I wanted to do something more hands-on that cost less."

Meredith Snaider and Larry Fessenden in *Habit* (1997).

Fessenden wrote, directed, and edited *Habit*, which was produced by his company Glass Eye Pix. "I determined to make *Habit* my way," he says. "Very small production—we had five crew members, shooting in 16mm, all around New York." The wolfish-looking filmmaker cast himself in the lead role of Sam, an alcoholic New York bartender, who starts to believe that his new girlfriend, played by Meredith Snaider, is a supernatural entity. "The premise was, what would it be really like to meet a vampire?" says Fessenden. While the film featured enough genre tropes to qualify as a horror movie, it was, at heart, a semi-autobiographical and decidedly uncommercial character study. "It never really occurred to me to think about what people wanted to see, but it was a yearning inside myself," he explains. "There was the idea of the sexual addiction, and my contemplations of alcohol and self-destruction. I wanted to show that some of us live with horror tropes every day, we wake up wondering if we're going to have a heart attack or if we're going to be attacked."

Fessenden had shot a primitive version of *Habit* on video in the early '80s. "The movie had a vibe and it was utterly unique," he says of the initial iteration of the tale. "This was 1981, the last vampire movie had been *Dracula* with Frank Langella, which is fantastic, but Hollywood was concerned with the old monster tropes. I was eager to make a Scorsese movie with a monster in it." The mid-'80s saw the release of several contemporary vampire movies, including 1985's *Fright Night*, 1987's *The Lost Boys*, and the same year's Kathryn Bigelow-directed *Near Dark*, but all were wildly dissimilar to Fessenden's feature.

Yet Fessenden was not the only New York-based independent auteur making an untraditional vampire film. 1995 saw the release of arthouse director Michael Almereyda's low-budget film *Nadja*. Financed by *Blue Velvet* filmmaker David Lynch, the moody bloodsucker tale starred Elina Löwensohn as Dracula's daughter, a creature of the night and of Manhattan's nightlife. Nadja was followed into cinemas by *The Addiction* from Abel Ferrara, director of notorious 1979 slasher movie *The Driller Killer*. Ferrara's new film was a metaphorical rumination on drug addiction and AIDS starring Lili Taylor and Christopher Walken as New York-dwelling vampires.

While Wes Craven's *Vampire in Brooklyn* and Robert Rodriguez's starry, action-packed *From Dusk Till Dawn* were far removed from Fessenden's scrappy New York tale, the arrival of *Nadja* and *The Addiction* ahead of his movie's unveiling was a different matter. "I remember being annoyed, because I had made the first East Village vampire movie, but those got a lot of attention," says the director. "Obviously Abel is of note, and so indeed is Michael Almereyda. I feel like [by] the next year, *Habit* was already old news."

Fessenden's fears seemed to be confirmed by the problems he encountered getting his film seen. The director had hoped to premiere *Habit* at the Sundance Film Festival. When the event failed to accept the movie in a timely fashion, Fessenden instead launched his vampire tale at the Chicago Film Festival in October 1995. After *Habit* was turned down by dozens of distributors, Fessenden put the movie on screens himself. "I ended up distributing it in about forty theaters," says the director. "I basically built the model of Glass Eye Pix through this film, which is to defend good work, not listen to the powers that be, fuck Sundance. [You] have to make your own way, especially in the horror space. I was proposing that you can make personal, character-driven horror films, because horror is a way to talk about everything from identity to loneliness to alcoholism to social disorders, and so on."

Habit received a rave write-up from Roger Ebert, who recommended the film over David Lynch's recently released *Lost Highway* in his review for the *Chicago Sun-Times*, and Fessenden won the 'Someone to Watch' trophy at the 1997 Independent Spirit Awards. The following year, the *Habit* auteur was nominated by the same awards body in the Best Director category alongside Paul Schrader, Wim Wenders, and Robert Duvall, who won for his work on *The Apostle.*

Fessenden would go on to write and direct 2001's Glass Eye Pix-produced *Wendigo*, a psychological thriller-cum-creature feature starring Patricia Clarkson and Jake Weber. He also secured small roles in 1999's *Bringing Out the Dead*—directed by his beloved Martin Scorsese—and Michael Almereyda's 2000 version of *Hamlet*, starring Ethan Hawke in the title role.

Habit remained an obscure title even to many genre fans, but Fessenden's movie—and his fiercely independent attitude—had an outsized influence on a younger generation of filmmakers. Several would enlist the help of the movie's creator when they embarked on their own careers in horror.

Arguably, the most influential horror release of the '90s—in terms of influencing the film industry at large—was not *Scream* at all, but 1998's *Blade.* The movie starred Wesley Snipes as the vampire-hunting Marvel comics character and helped launch a wave of superhero movies that would come to dominate pop culture over the next two decades.

Director Richard Donner had made a hit out of a DC superhero character with 1978's *Superman* and Tim Burton had repeated the trick with 1989's *Batman.* Both films inaugurated franchises, but the box office potential of comic-book superheroes remained largely untapped by the early '90s. Marvel had enjoyed much less cinematic success than DC despite being the home of Spider-Man, Iron Man, the X-Men, Captain America *et al.* 1986's *Howard the Duck* was a commercial catastrophe and 1989's Dolph Lundgren-starring *The Punisher* essentially went straight to video in the US. Over the years, Marvel had sold the rights to the company's characters to an array of studios. New Line wound up with the option to make a movie based on Blade. "It was a convention in Hollywood that you could only make a comic-book film if it was based on the top tier characters: Batman, Superman, maybe Spider-Man," *Blade* screenwriter David S. Goyer recalled during a lecture he gave at BAFTA in 2013. "*X-Men* hadn't even been made. There was no thought that you could make a film out of a secondary or tertiary character… Marvel thought so little of this character that they optioned it to New Line for $125,000. That was all they made on that film."

As a kid growing up in Michigan, Goyer loved comic books and horror movies, interests which earned him the nickname 'The Prince of Darkness.' Goyer studied screenwriting at USC and when he was just 22 sold a script called *Dusted*, about a cop who goes undercover in a prison. Retitled *Death Warrant*, the screenplay became a 1990 vehicle for rising action star Jean-Claude Van Damme. Goyer also wrote a film called *Demonic Toys* for Charles Band, a prolific director and producer of low-budget horror films. According to Goyer, Band showed him the poster that had already been designed for *Demonic Toys* and told him he had eight days to come up with a script to go with it.

Goyer developed the screenplay for *Blade* with director of photography-turned-filmmaker Ernest Dickerson. The New Jersey native had worked as cinematographer on Spike Lee's early movies—including 1989's *Do the Right Thing* and 1992's *Malcolm X*—and made his directorial debut with 1992's crime drama *Juice*, starring future *Scream 2* actor Omar Epps and rapper Tupac Shakur.

Like Goyer, Dickerson had a longstanding love for the horror genre. "Growing up in Newark, New Jersey, whenever there was a new horror film coming out, it was a big thing in my neighborhood," he says. "As a kid, [I] saw horror films like the original *House on Haunted Hill*, *The Tingler*, *I Was a Teenage Werewolf*, *Day of the Triffids*. Then I started reading horror literature, I learned about H. P. Lovecraft, and [I've] been a fan of it ever since."

After studying cinematography at NYU in the early '80s, Dickerson was hired as a DP on the George Romero-produced horror anthology TV show *Tales from the Darkside* and then as a second unit cameraman for Romero's *Day of the Dead*. During the shoot, Dickerson encountered a young Greg Nicotero, who was still several years away from co-founding KNB. "Nicotero was mass-producing zombies," says Dickerson. "When we started shooting at 7 am, they started feeding us one zombie here, two here, five here, ten here. By the end of the day, we had this big shot where the full zombie horde is marching up the street."

With *Juice*, Dickerson joined a new wave of young Black auteurs that also included Spike Lee, John Singleton, and *Menace II Society* directors Albert and Allen Hughes. For his second film, Dickerson wanted to make a thriller or a horror movie. Like many of his peers, the filmmaker found himself pigeonholed by studio executives as a director of what was then known as 'urban' cinema, movies aimed principally at an African-American audience. "I remember one time I was sent a rap version of *Alice in Wonderland* called *Yo, Alice*," he says. "I was like, no way."

Dickerson signed on to direct 1994's *Surviving the Game*, which starred Ice-T as an unhoused man hunted for sport by characters played by Rutger Hauer, Charles S. Dutton, and Gary Busey. The action thriller was financed by New Line, which was looking for someone to make *Blade*. "I'm doing *Surviving the Game* and Bob Shaye tried to get me thinking about *Blade*," says Dickerson. "They had this comic, *Tomb of Dracula*, about a team of vampire hunters, and Dracula was their main villain. Blade was kind of old school, from the '70s, he had an afro. I said, 'Well, I'm not really feeling this.'"

Dickerson found inspiration in Richard Matheson's science fiction-horror novel *I Am Legend*. Originally published in 1954, the book was set in a post-apocalyptic world where a pandemic has turned nearly all the world's surviving population into vampires. "At first, I didn't know what to do with the character [of Blade]," says Dickerson. "But I had read again *I Am Legend*, and the thing that I loved about *I Am Legend* is that there was a scientific rationale for vampirism." The director was further inspired by his knowledge of world cinema. "I was looking at a lot of Hong Kong films at the time," he says. "I was looking at *A Chinese Ghost Story*, *A Chinese Ghost Story II*, *A Chinese Ghost Story III*. I was really interested in the wire work, and the swordplay, and everything else." Dickerson pitched New Line on a fresh approach to the Blade character. "I said, 'We can have a scientific rationale for vampirism, and Blade should almost be like a ninja, he should be adept at using a samurai sword,'" says the director. "They liked that idea, and I interviewed some writers, and I hung out with David Goyer a couple of times, and we had similar likes. I said, 'Okay, let's bring Goyer on to write the screenplay.'" Dickerson recalls that he was responsible for recruiting Wesley Snipes to the project. "I had already worked with Wesley a couple of times," he says. "I said, 'Wesley should be Blade. He's a martial artist, he looks great, and he can play the character.' I brought him into the fold."

Goyer's script for *Blade* featured elaborate and potentially expensive sequences, including a 'blood rave' scene, which found vampires being doused in gore at a nightclub. According to Dickerson, New Line claimed that the project was too pricey, leading to the filmmaker's departure from the project. "They said that the script Goyer and I had crafted was a $50 million Wesley Snipes movie, and there was no way that they were going to spend $50 million on a Wesley Snipes movie," recalls Dickerson. "I said I could do it for 25, with rigorous planning, because I was used to shooting on lower budgets, [but] they shelved the project. I was told it was dead, that they didn't want to spend the money on it. And life goes on."

The development of *Blade* would also go on, turning into a four-year-long odyssey for Goyer. For a period, director David Fincher circled the project, but the job was eventually given to a young filmmaker named Stephen Norrington. The British Norrington had helped craft the creature effects on James Cameron's *Aliens* and Fincher's *Alien 3*. Norrington had made his directorial debut with the low-budget 1994 British horror movie *Death Machine*, which starred Brad Dourif and featured Rachel Weisz in her first film appearance. Ernest Dickerson was displeased to learn that New Line had continued to develop *Blade* without his involvement. "I was in my agent's office, and I saw that *Blade* was in production as a Wesley Snipes movie directed by some guy called Stephen Norrington, who I'd never heard of," says the director. "I was kind of pissed off."

New Line was able to attract an impressive supporting cast for the project. Stephen Dorff played the film's main villain Deacon Frost, horror veteran Udo Kier agreed to portray a vampire named Lord Dragonetti, Sanaa Lathan was cast as Blade's mother, and singer-songwriter Kris Kristofferson signed on for the role of Blade's mentor Whistler. The blood rave scene was shot at a meatpacking factory, where the film's production designer Kirk M. Petruccelli added a sprinkler system capable of raining down fake gore on the dancers. A relative of Ernest Dickerson was among the extras who worked on this sequence. The director was aggrieved to discover how closely Norrington's film was following the version of the movie he had developed with Goyer. "My brother-in-law did some day work as an extra on *Blade*," he says. "He came home one day telling me how he had spent the whole day in this nightclub scene where blood was dripping from the pipes. I said, 'Are you serious?' It's one of my Hollywood horror stories."

Blade opened on August 21, 1998. Norrington's movie earned a healthy $17 million over its first weekend in cinemas, enough to replace Steven Spielberg's *Saving Private Ryan* at the top of the box office chart. The film went on to gross $70 million in the US and another $61 million around the globe. In financial terms, *Blade* would be overshadowed by several of the year's other hits, like filmmaker Michael Bay's *Armageddon*, which grossed $201 million in the US, as well as the James Cameron-directed 1997 hold-over *Titanic*, the first film to earn over $1 billion globally. Even so, Norrington's movie demonstrated the appeal of Marvel characters and suggested the potential for further comic-book adaptations. The year after the release of *Blade*, 20th Century Fox put the long-gestating *X-Men* before cameras. Released in July 2000, the film earned $296 million worldwide. In 1999, Sony licensed the rights to Spider-Man and hired *Evil Dead* trilogy director Sam Raimi to direct a big-budget Peter Parker adventure.

New Line asked David Goyer to start writing a *Blade* sequel. Inspired by *The Dirty Dozen*, Goyer's script had his Daywalker hero cooperating with vampires to take on a new breed of bloodsuckers called Reapers. To direct *Blade II*, New Line hired Guillermo del Toro. The Mexican filmmaker's first film, 1992's *Cronos*, starred Federico Luppi as an antiques dealer who succumbs to vampirism via a centuries-old mechanical device. The movie had put del Toro on the international filmmaking map after screening at the Cannes Film Festival in the spring of 1993.

Bob Weinstein's Dimension produced the director's second film, 1997's *Mimic*, about giant insects masquerading as humans in New York. The movie was edited by Patrick Lussier, his first job after *Scream*. "Del Toro was fascinating," says Lussier. "He is truly a visionary. He is an amazing artist and visualist. That was his first big American feature, so there was a lot to wrangle, including the insanity of Dimension Films at the time." During the production, relations between the director and Dimension became strained. "*Mimic* was not a good experience for anybody," Lussier remembers. "The studio thought they were making one movie, and Guillermo was making a different movie. It's that thing when you see 'Day 75 of 50' on the call sheet, you know you're in trouble." At one point during the shoot, Bob Weinstein actually fired del Toro and approached Danish filmmaker Ole Bornedal—who directed 1997's Dimension-distributed horror-thriller *Nightwatch*—about taking over the project. The Mexican was reinstated as director after the film's star, Mira Sorvino, told the Dimension boss that she would walk if the director left the project. "That was a bad day," says

Lussier. "They fired him on a Friday and rehired him on the Monday. Ole Bornedal flew in, and, by Monday, he was no longer going to take over the movie. Then Ole stayed on as a producer and just became really supportive of Guillermo."

Doug Jones played one of the film's human-sized insects during re-shoots that took place in Los Angeles. The tall, thin actor had previously portrayed a zombie in 1993's *Hocus Pocus* and a mutant kangaroo in 1995's Rachel Talalay-directed *Tank Girl.* "I was brought in three weeks before the movie opened in theaters," Jones says of *Mimic.* "We were under the gun to get this done. I went downtown, stood on top of a four-story building with a rain machine hitting me, bug mask on. Then I stayed for three days, because Guillermo del Toro liked me. Our second day of filming, he sat down across the lunch table from me and said, 'So, tell me everything you've done before!'" The actor's brief stint on *Mimic* would lead del Toro to repeatedly cast Jones in his movies over the years ahead. "Guillermo del Toro understands humanity and human beings more than any psychologist I've ever met," says the actor. "When he meets you, he'll sum up your behaviors, your postures, your speech patterns, and he'll have a control panel that he's developing as he gets to know you, and he knows how to push all the buttons to get a performance out of us. He's brilliant that way, he really is."

Del Toro's brilliance could not save *Mimic* at the box office, however. The pricey venture was released in August 1997, and grossed a disappointing $25 million in the US. The always franchise-hungry Dimension would still greenlight two straight-to-video sequels directed by other filmmakers, 2001's *Mimic 2* and 2003's *Mimic 3: Sentinel.*

Following the *Mimic* shoot, del Toro suffered a personal trauma when his father, Frederico, was kidnapped in Mexico and held for ransom before being released after 72 days. "Two horrible things happened in the late '90s," del Toro recalled, speaking at the London Film Festival in 2017. "My father was kidnapped, and I worked with the Weinsteins, and I don't know which one was worse. Actually, the kidnapping made more sense, because I knew what they wanted."

To save family members from further danger, del Toro moved away from Mexico and decamped to Madrid to shoot his third film, 2001's Spanish Civil War ghost story *The Devil's Backbone.* Backed by Pedro Almodovar's production company, the result was well received by critics and reinvigorated the director's love for the filmmaking process.

Del Toro was intrigued by the opportunity that Goyer's *Blade II* script offered to create a new kind of monster. The filmmaker redirected the franchise toward pure horror with the design of the Reapers, whose lower jaw split at the chin to reveal a terrifying proboscis. "Guillermo said, 'I want this to be the best vampire ever!'" explains makeup effects artist Steve Johnson, whose company Edge FX worked on the film. Johnson recalls that the director put together a brain trust to come up with the design of the creature, whose members included comic-book writer Mike Mignola, creator of the superhero Hellboy. "He brought Mike Mignola, and he brought Constantine Sekeris from my company, and he brought me, himself, and I believe there were one or two other artists," says Johnson. "We had a round table discussion, and we all brought our work to the table. Guillermo was saying, 'This is going to be'—pounding his fist on the table—'the best vampire.' We sat there and beat our heads on the table for months. What does this vampire look like? Guillermo had given us a few design points like, 'We want this vampire to be very different, we want it to not just be the fangs.' Some of the ideas were even a little bit nuttier, like [having] the vampire fang, the vampire orifice, in the palm, so you could use it as a weapon. But the bifurcation of the face seemed to be more striking."

The finished film would feature a memorably grotesque sequence in which Blade's vampire ally Nyssa, played by Leonor Varela, performs an autopsy on a Reaper. This makeup effect was designed by Johnson, who had experience depicting posthumous procedures. In 1995, Fox had broadcast a documentary special called *Alien Autopsy: Fact or Fiction?* about footage which purportedly showed a real dead extraterrestrial. Johnson was subsequently asked by ABC's *20/20* show to demonstrate how the film could have been faked. "Guillermo knew that I had done this alien autopsy thing," says Johnson. "I think that had a little bit to do with him putting that scene in. It's not an easy thing to do, to

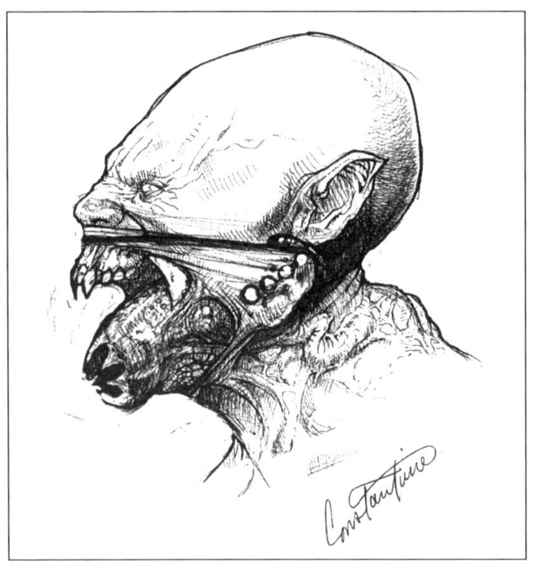

Concept sketch for *Blade II* (2002).

cut something open in layers and make it look real. If it's going to bleed, or if it's going to ooze, all that stuff's got to be figured out, and then it's sealed inside the next layer. It really has to work like a real body. I put the same people in charge [for the *Blade II* scene] that had done my alien autopsy, it was just a Reaper instead of an alien."

In 1998, New Line had embarked on the company's biggest gamble to date, agreeing to bank roll director Peter Jackson's three-film adaption of J. R. R. Tolkien's fantasy novel *The Lord of the Rings*. The first movie, *The Lord of the Rings: The Fellowship of the Ring*, was released in December 2001, with the two remaining films following over the next couple of years. Del Toro believes that New Line's resources being so concentrated on Jackson's films helped *Blade II* arrive on screens unscathed. "*Blade II*, everybody at New Line was watching *Lord of the Rings* being made, so we were left alone by default," he recalled to the BBC in 2010. "I remember, we showed the movie to Bob Shaye, and Bob Shaye said, 'It's vile, it's violent, it's disgusting, it's repulsive. But if that's the movie you want to release, that's the movie we'll release.'"

Luke Goss and director Guillermo del Toro on the set of *Blade II*.

New Line opened *Blade II* on March 22, 2002. Del Toro's film earned $32 million over its first weekend on release, almost twice as much as the first movie. The film would gross $82 million in the US and another $72 million in foreign territories, making the movie a satisfyingly large hit for both the studio and del Toro.

Goyer had made his directorial debut with 2002's John Leguizamo-starring drama *Zig Zag* and successfully lobbied to take the reins of the third *Blade* film, *Blade: Trinity*. Goyer's script for the movie featured Blade reluctantly teaming up with the Nightstalkers, a team of vampire hunters played by Jessica Biel, Ryan Reynolds, Patton Oswalt, and Natasha Lyonne.

The *Blade: Trinity* shoot was a notably testing one. Speaking to The A.V. Club in 2012, Patton Oswalt described how Snipes attempted to strangle Goyer, an allegation the *Blade* star denied. "If I had tried to strangle David Goyer, you probably wouldn't be talking to me now," Snipes told *The Guardian* in 2020. "A Black guy with muscles strangling the director of a movie is going to jail, I guarantee you."

Any hopes of *Blade: Trinity* continuing the franchise's upward commercial trajectory were crushed by New Line's decision to open the movie on December 10, 2004, the same day as Warner Bros.' *Ocean's Twelve*. Steven Soderbergh's heist sequel easily won the weekend with a gross of $39 million. *Blade: Trinity*, which cost around $65 million, had to settle for a distant second place, earning $16 million. Goyer's film took in $131 million at the global box office, roughly the same as the much cheaper *Blade* and $24 million less than *Blade II*.

In October 2006, Wesley Snipes was charged with multiple crimes related to his taxes. Starting in December 2010, the actor served 28 months in jail. By the time Snipes was released in April 2013, the superhero genre which he had done so much to relaunch with *Blade* had firmly established itself as a central pillar of Hollywood output. Sam Raimi's Sony-backed *Spider-Man* was released in 2002 and became the biggest-grossing film of the year in the US. The movie was followed by two, also lucrative, Raimi-directed sequels, in 2004 and 2007. In 2008, Marvel Studios released the Robert Downey Jr.-starring *Iron Man*, setting the table for a record-breaking series of hits told in the Marvel Cinematic Universe, which would not crest until 2019's *Avengers: Endgame*.

Movies based on DC Comics characters would also proliferate. In 2005, Warner Bros. released *Batman Begins*, which was directed by Christopher

Nolan and co-written by the director and Goyer. Nolan would direct two sequels, re-establishing the commercial credentials of Batman and DC as a cinematic force. "I got a lot of jobs because of it," Goyer would say of *Blade*, speaking to *Entertainment Weekly* writer Leah Greenblatt in 2018. "It was one of the primary reasons why Chris Nolan wanted me to write *Batman Begins*."

Two months after New Line released 1998's *Blade*, Columbia Pictures unveiled John Carpenter's contemporary take on the bloodsucker genre. *Vampires* starred *Videodrome* actor James Woods as the cigar-chomping Jack Crow, who leads a Vatican-backed team that tracks down and kills the titular monsters.

Professionally, Carpenter had endured a rough '90s, starting with 1992's *Memoirs of an Invisible Man*, a misbegotten science fiction-comedy and box office bomb starring Chevy Chase. 1994's *In the Mouth of Madness*, a 1995 remake of *Village of the Damned*, and 1996's *Escape From L.A.*—an expensive sequel to the director's 1981 film *Escape From New York*—were three more commercial failures.

In May 1997, *Variety* revealed that Woods had "signed a seven-figure deal" to star in *Vampires*, which was adapted from a 1990 novel by John Steakley. The outlet noted that the actor was hot off his Oscar-nominated performance as a white supremacist in director Rob Reiner's courtroom drama *Ghosts of Mississippi*. The *Vampires* cast also included Daniel Baldwin, Maximilian Schell, and *Twin Peaks* actress Sheryl Lee.

Carpenter chose Sante Fe to shoot the film, which turned out to be one of the director's more violent and bloody affairs. "This film has some old-fashioned stuff in it, like decapitations, slashed throats, and ripped bodies," Carpenter told *Fangoria*. "We took vampires, the myth, and the action seriously. We wanted to make it very realistic, which either works or it doesn't. But we weren't going to make it a comedy, even though this is the day of the parody where you can wink at the audience."

KNB co-founder Greg Nicotero had worked on the effects for *In the Mouth of Madness* and reteamed with Carpenter for *Vampires*. "It was this kind of vampire-western, it was really unique," says the special effects artist. In the finished film, viewers would see the movie's vampires erupt in flames when they encountered daylight. Nicotero and special effects supervisor Darrell Pritchett were inspired by Carpenter's *The Thing*, the director's

1982 remake of 1951's *The Thing from Another World*. In particular, the pair looked at the scene in which Kurt Russell's hero R. J. MacReady incinerates Thomas G. Waites' character Windows. "The vampires themselves were pretty standard—contact lenses, and dentures, and they all had the sort of goth look," says Nicotero. "But myself and Darrell Pritchett, we really wanted to do something different when the vampires hit sunlight. I always loved the gag that John did in *The Thing* when Windows is transforming, and they hit it with the flamethrower, and you see the legs moving." He recalls that he and Pritchett "spent a lot of time developing these shriveled husks and corpses, and we would bury all the rods and stuff so they could be puppeteered. When they would grab them and drag them into the sun, we could light them on fire and you would see them moving."

Vampires was released on October 30, 1998. The film became the first Carpenter-directed movie to top the box office since 1988's *They Live*, winning the weekend with a gross of $9 million. The film's final domestic tally of $20 million was enough for fans of Carpenter to call the movie a comeback.

Concept sketch for John Carpenter's *Vampires* (1998).

Vampires was released at a moment when audiences were showing their appreciation for horror with a lighter, more knowing touch than was found in John Carpenter's tale. The movie followed not just the first two *Scream* films but also the TV show *Buffy the Vampire Slayer*, which had premiered on The WB network in March 1997. Created by Joss Whedon and starring Sarah Michelle Gellar as reluctant high school heroine Buffy Summers, the series' young cast and irreverent approach to genre tropes undoubtedly appealed more to many teenagers than the grisly mayhem of *Vampires*.

Carpenter himself believed that his film's serious tone hurt the movie's profitability. "It wasn't a massive hit, and we always want it to be bigger," Carpenter later told *Fangoria*. "But it was a straight movie, which is a problem nowadays. If you do a straight movie, a lot of the audience doesn't want to see it. Maybe it's old-fashioned, I don't know."

While New Line and Columbia were exploring various types of vampires, Trimark Pictures was finding success with a wildly different creature from myth and legend.

The 1993 horror movie *Leprechaun* was written and directed by first-time filmmaker Mark Jones and starred British actor Warwick Davis as the tale's murderous creature. "I was watching the Lucky Charms commercials, and they had the cute little leprechaun advertising cereal," says Jones. "They'd done all the holidays, *Friday the 13th* and *Halloween*, and I figured, no one's done *St. Paddy's Day*, and no one's done an evil leprechaun. I wrote a script, and made the rounds, and then Trimark picked it up."

Trimark was founded by Iran-born businessman Mark Amin, a co-owner of the successful 20/20 Video chain of rental stores. The company was initially called Vidmark, the name reflecting Amin's original plan to produce and distribute straight-to-video product. "I founded Vidmark in 1985, and it was basically a pure video company," says Amin. "We decided to expand into theatrical and were looking for movies that had theatrical potential, and could be made for a low budget, and would have a target audience." Jones' pitch fitted the bill. "The concept of a killer leprechaun, nobody had ever done it, and we thought it would have an audience," says Amin.

Warwick Davis had struggled to find movie work after starring in the 1988 fantasy film *Willow* and saw *Leprechaun* as a chance to both pay some bills and play a very different character. "At that point, I think everyone was seeing me as playing a good guy, having seen films like *Willow*," says the actor. "The script arrived, and after a couple of pages, I was like, I want to do this."

The cast of *Leprechaun* also included Courteney Cox's future *Friends* co-star Jennifer Aniston in her first significant film role. Amin recalls casting Aniston as an easy decision. "It was about, can we have somebody that's right for the role, that has the right energy," he says. "And she fulfilled both."

Leprechaun cost $1 million and grossed $8 million in US cinemas, encouraging Amin to pursue more theatrical product and more horror movies. In addition to greenlighting 1994's *Leprechaun 2*, Amin signed a deal to distribute director Peter Jackson's early, and famously blood-drenched, film *Braindead*, which was retitled *Dead Alive* for the US market.

The expanding company's new employees included a young executive named Peter Block. The Connecticut-raised Block had first connected with the horror genre when he was around 12 and saw a girl reading a Stephen King book. "I was interested in her, so I became interested in the book, and the book was *'Salem's Lot*," he says. "I never got the girl, but I got the author, and from then on I was reading King."

Block became enthusiastic about working for Trimark after he was given a preview of their upcoming projects. "I didn't know anything about the company," he recalls. "I said, 'Well, show me what you're working on.' They showed me *Braindead*, and I was like, *that* I want to work on." After joining Trimark, Block agitated for the company to invest more in horror. "I knew the horror audience was never satisfied," he says. "People who were renting arthouse titles would rent one title a month. The horror audience would rent six movies at the weekend."

Through the '90s, Trimark bulked up its release schedule with horror films like director Kasi Lemmons' supernatural thriller *Eve's Bayou* and Brian Yuzna's straight-to-video slasher film *The Dentist*. Several of the company's acquisitions reflected Block's adventurous taste. "I loved foreign horror like nobody's business, and I liked indie horror," he says. "I liked the things that just didn't look like what other people were doing."

In 1998, Trimark released Canadian filmmaker Vincenzo Natali's *Cube*, about a group of strangers trapped in a vast construction made up of interlinked, and booby-trapped, cells. Block had seen the movie at the Toronto International Film Festival the previous year and remembers being "blown away by how much I liked the movie. It was one of the first acquisitions I made for the company and that was a tremendous success for Trimark." Trimark also released Guillermo del Toro's debut *Cronos* on video. "I loved *Cronos* from the time I saw it, worked really hard on it," says Block.

The *Leprechaun* film series would outlast the company that gave birth to Davis' monster. Although 1994's Rodman Flender-directed *Leprechaun 2* earned just $2 million in the US during its theatrical run, 1995's *Leprechaun 3* and 1997's *Leprechaun 4: In Space* were popular straight-to-video releases. The latter two films were directed by English-Australian filmmaker Brian Trenchard-Smith, who deliberately spoofed James Cameron's *Aliens* for the Leprechaun's fourth adventure. "I did propose a further Leprechaun film, *Leprechaun in the White House*," says the filmmaker. "But they said, 'No, you're getting too wacky.' I left a voicemail on the relevant executive's directed line after the Monica Lewinsky scandal broke 18 months later and said, 'Hi, remember me and my *Leprechaun in the White House* idea? Wouldn't you like to have 1,200 prints ready *right now*?' I never got a reply."

Instead of having the Leprechaun visit the Oval Office, Trimark sent Davis' character to the inner city for 2000's *Leprechaun in the Hood*, which was directed by Rob Spera. The movie included the sight—and sound—of Davis' character rapping in a nightclub. The fifth *Leprechaun* film was another successful straight-to-video hit. "Every time we made one, it surprised us that there was an audience and people kept asking for it," says Amin.

In 2000, the rival production and distribution entity Lions Gate Entertainment (later Lionsgate) bought Trimark for around $50 million, and Amin's company was folded into the studio the following year. Soon after, the company greenlit 2003's *Leprechaun: Back 2 tha Hood*. In 2007, *Entertainment Weekly* would put the movie in third place on a list of 'The worst

Warwick Davis in *Leprechaun* (1993).

movie sequels.' "If a movie could spark a race riot, this is it," wrote the outlet's Chris Nashawaty.

Lions Gate put a pause on the *Leprechaun* franchise after its initial six-movie run but continued to maintain an interest in horror. That investment would pay off in unexpected and unprecedentedly lucrative ways with films featuring acts much darker and more visceral than the malicious hijinks of Davis' Irish gremlin.

CHAPTER 3

"I SEE DEAD PEOPLE."

Brendan Fraser was in Morocco, shooting 1999's *The Mummy* and pretending to choke on a hangman's noose, when he started to asphyxiate for real. Fraser had been cast by writer-director Stephen Sommers as adventurer Rick O'Connell, who, in the course of the film, is sentenced to death by hanging at a prison in Cairo. "I figured, before the camera lands on me, I will take three really deep breaths, so my face turns purple and my veins pop out of my neck," says the actor. "The stuntman took up the tension on the rope, and I went up on the balls of my feet. Then I guess he took the tension up again, and I'm not a ballerina, I can't stand on my tiptoes. All I remember is seeing the camera pan around and then it was like a black iris at the end of a silent film."

In the 1920s-set movie, Fraser's O'Connell is rescued by the intervention of an English Egyptologist, played by Rachel Weisz, who needs the adventurer's help to find the lost city of Hamunaptra. In real life, the actor simply blacked out. "I regained consciousness and one of the EMTs, in a green polo shirt, was saying my name really politely and sort of clapping his hands in front of me," Fraser recalls. "Then the stunt coordinator came over, and he said, 'Hi! Welcome to the club, bro! Last time that happened was Mel Gibson on *Braveheart*! Hahaha!' And I was like, 'What the hell? I want to go home!'"

Sommers' film was a loose remake of 1932's Boris Karloff-starring *The Mummy*. The original movie had been released by Universal the year after the studio found success with director James Whale's *Frankenstein*—the film which had turned Karloff into a star—and Tod Browning's *Dracula*. Universal waited eight years before releasing a second *Mummy* movie, 1940's *The Mummy's Hand*, but then doubled down on this part of the Universal Classic Monsters empire with 1942's *The Mummy's Tomb*, 1944's *The Mummy's Ghost*, and the same year's *The Mummy's Curse*. In 1955, the studio revived the monster for the horror-comedy *Abbott and Costello Meet the Mummy*, which would prove to be the last *Mummy* film produced by Universal for 44 years.

The road that led to Brendan Fraser hanging from a noose began in the 1980s, when aspiring screenwriter Abbie Bernstein learned that Universal was interested in making a new movie about its bandage-wrapped horror icon. "[My agents said] Universal wanted to do a *Mummy* picture, and I should go in and pitch," Bernstein told *Fangoria* in 1999. Bernstein met with Universal executive Josh Donen, who planned on producing a movie in the mold of James Cameron's 1984 science fiction hit *The Terminator.* "Josh said he wanted to do a Mummy that's like the Terminator, a Mummy that got up and started killing people on page one," Bernstein recalled. "The best I could do in my first draft was to have him get up and start killing people on page four. After they read the first draft, they decided that was a little too soon, so in the next draft, he got up and started killing people on page 14." For a spell, George A. Romero circled the project, but he departed before it progressed beyond the script stage. Bernstein herself simply stopped hearing from Donen.

The remake of *The Mummy* was revived by Sean Daniel and Jim Jacks, Universal executives who founded their own production company, Alphaville Films, in 1992. The pair hired Clive Barker to direct the movie and screenwriter Mick Garris to work on the script. The Liverpool-born Barker had made a splash in the mid-'80s with *Books of Blood*, his six volumes of short horror stories, which prompted Stephen King to declare, "I have seen the future of horror and his name is Clive Barker." In 1987, Barker released his directorial debut *Hellraiser.* A bloody, kinky tale, the movie introduced the iconic villain Pinhead and inaugurated a franchise whose third entry, *Hellraiser III: Hell on Earth*, would become Dimension Films' first release.

The Los Angeles-born Garris spent the early 1970s singing with the progressive rock band Horsefeathers. He then secured a low-level job at *Star Wars* director George Lucas' company, which led to him operating R2-D2 at the 1978 Academy Awards. Garris subsequently became story editor on the Steven Spielberg-created anthology TV show *Amazing Stories* and then directed 1988's New Line Cinema-produced *Critters 2: The Main Course.* "Universal decided to do a new version of *The Mummy—Clive Barker's The Mummy*—where his name was in the title, so that tells you it's not your grandfather's *Mummy*," says Garris. "It was set in Beverly Hills. It was sexual, it was depraved, it was scary. The whole time I was writing it, I go, 'The studio's never going to make this.'"

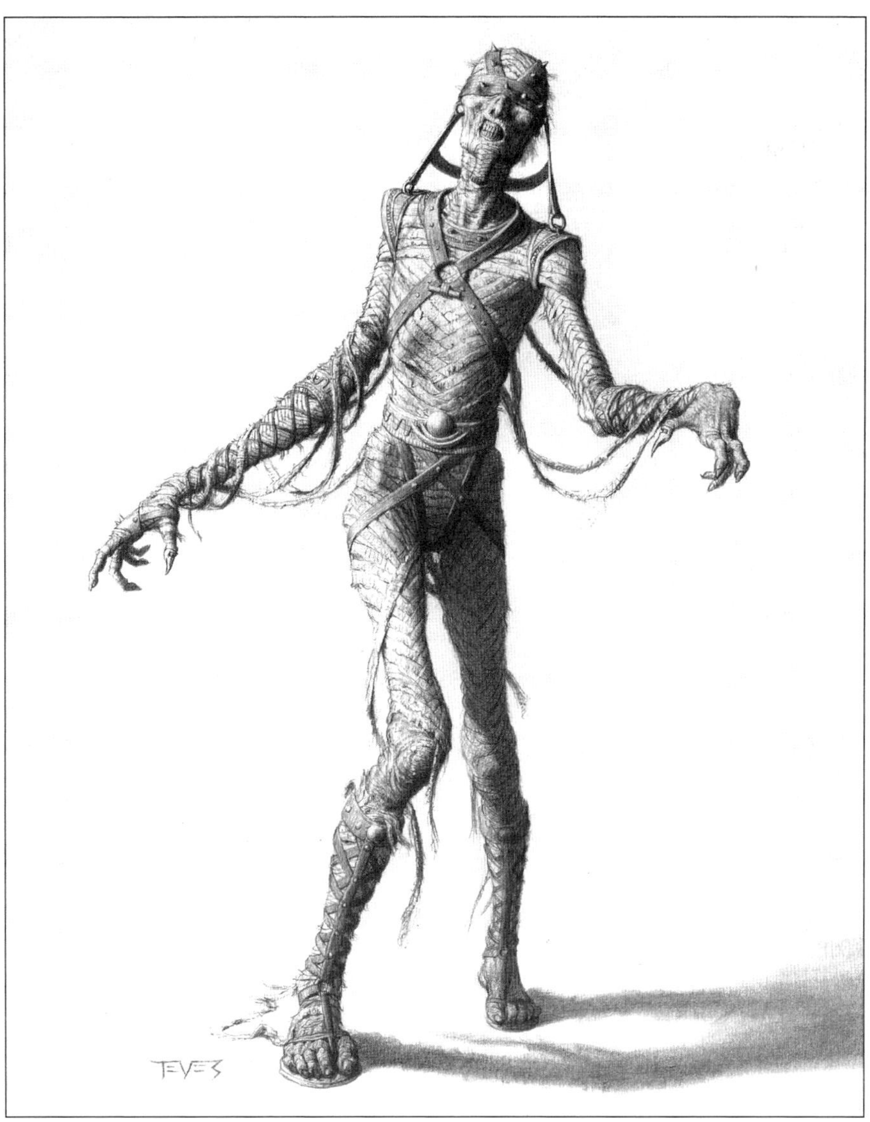

Concept sketch for director Clive Barker's unproduced *The Mummy*.

Barker developed the visuals of the proposed film with makeup effects artist Steve Johnson. "The great thing about this industry is you get to meet your heroes and you really get to hang out with them," says Johnson. "I did so much work with Clive that never saw the light of day. Clive and I used to go to his house, and open a bottle of wine, and just start working on movies that most of the time never happened."

When the screenplay was turned in, Garris' fears were confirmed. "The studio did exactly what I thought, which was to say, 'There's no fucking way we can make this movie,'" he recalls.

Gremlins director Joe Dante also developed a new version of *The Mummy* with a screenplay by renowned independent filmmaker John Sayles, who had written Dante's 1978 horror film *Piranha*. At another point, George Romero looked set to direct a different script by Garris, but that effort, too, came to naught.

The remake's development process had been tracked at a distance by director Sommers, who threw his hat into the ring as he finished up the 1998 horror movie *Deep Rising*. "I told my agent, I said, 'Can you get me a meeting? Because I've always wanted to do a version of *The Mummy*,'" he says. "When I was eight years old, I saw the old Boris Karloff one. It took me to ancient Egypt, and Cairo of the '20s and '30s, and scared the crap out of me."

Sommers grew up in St. Cloud, Minnesota, and studied at USC. The director made his mark in the early '90s directing two live-action movies for Walt Disney Pictures, 1993's Elijah Wood-starring *The Adventures of Huck Finn* and the following year's *The Jungle Book*. Next, he embarked on the production of *Deep Rising*, which was backed, at a cost of around $45 million, by the Disney label Hollywood Pictures. The film tracked the travails of characters played by Treat Williams, Famke Janssen, and Kevin J. O'Connor, among others, as they attempt to avoid a giant monster on an ocean liner. The movie's release was delayed because of the complex computer-generated visual effects involved in creating the creature's lethal tentacles. *Deep Rising* was beaten to cinemas by a slew of other monster movies, including *Anaconda*, *The Relic*, and Guillermo del Toro's *Mimic*. Sommers' film also followed 1997's *Alien Resurrection*, the fourth entry in the *Alien* franchise. *Alien Resurrection* was directed by French filmmaker Jean-Pierre Jeunet, and its so-so box office performance suggested an exhaustion with monster movies. *Deep Rising* was not a hit when it was finally released in January 1998. But by then, Sommers had already gotten the job directing *The Mummy*.

Sommers' pitch for the remake was wildly different from the outré story developed by Barker and Garris. The writer-director planned on making a big-budget, family-friendly period movie. "I love mixed genres," he says. "I wanted it to be romantic and adventurous with scares." Producers Daniel and Jacks brought him in to pitch his vision for *The Mummy* at Universal.

"Usually, a pitch should be maybe 15 minutes, and mine was an hour and 25 minutes," says the director. "I walked out, and Jim was like, 'I don't know what you pitched in there. The studio want to do it for $15 million, and we're trying to get them up to $17 million.' I said, 'I'm going to need that for visual effects alone.' But when I got home, my agent called me and said, 'You got the gig.'" Sommers recalls that his version of *The Mummy* would ultimately cost "around $62 million."

Sommers' editor Bob Ducsay suggested that *School Ties* and *George of the Jungle* actor Brendan Fraser should star in the film. "Bob Ducsay, as soon as he read the script, he said, 'Oh, this is Brendan Fraser,'" recalls Sommers. "It made sense, because we needed somebody who could throw a punch, and take a punch, who could handle some humor."

Sommers had to fight for Rachel Weisz to be cast as the film's female lead, Evelyn Carnahan. After making her film debut in Stephen Norrington's *Death Machine*, the actress had appeared alongside Liv Tyler in Bernardo Bertolucci's 1996 drama *Stealing Beauty* but was much less well known than Fraser and proved a harder sell. "The studio went for Brendan pretty

Rachel Weisz and Brendan Fraser in *The Mummy* (1999).

quickly, but [for the female lead] they started throwing up all these American actresses," says Sommers. "I kept saying, 'Guys, the male is American and the actress should be British. There's a lot of good British actresses!' I bet Rachel auditioned four or five times, because the studio didn't know who she was." Universal eventually consented to the actress' casting opposite Fraser. "They could see it was a great pairing," says the director. Sommers picked South African actor Arnold Vosloo to play the film's lovelorn villain Imhotep, who is mummified in ancient Egypt at the start of the film and slowly regains fleshy form during the movie. The film's supporting cast included *Deep Rising* actor Kevin J. O'Connor and *Four Weddings and a Funeral* star John Hannah.

Fraser had other concerns during the shoot in Morocco than death by strangulation. "The adventure was real," he says. "They sent out a memo on the call sheet describing a type of snake that, I think, had yellow dots on it. They said, if you see this kind of snake, do not go near it. Because, at best, if it bites you, maybe they'll amputate your limb and you'll survive, otherwise you're going to have a neurological disorder for the rest of your life. Anyway, there I was, pissing down a rock, and I look down, and there's the yellow dot snake. I was like, *Fuuuuuuuuuck!* I just ran for it."

Despite the technical issues he had endured on *Deep Rising*, Sommers was determined to keep using computer-generated imagery, a comparatively new—but for the director, exciting—filmmaking tool. The '70s and '80s had been the glory days of practical effects, with makeup artists like Tom Savini, Rick Baker, Rob Bottin, and the KNB team acquiring a reputation as rock stars to the readers of *Fangoria* and others interested in the making of horror or science fiction films. By the late-'90s, visual effects shops like Industrial Light & Magic and Tippett Studio had begun to show what could be achieved onscreen without relying on glue and rubber. ILM, for example, created the liquid alien seen in James Cameron's 1989 science fiction epic *The Abyss*, while Tippett Studio founder Phil Tippett won the Best Visual Effects Oscar for his work bringing to life the dinosaurs in Steven Spielberg's 1993 blockbuster *Jurassic Park*. ILM's John Berton had acted as visual effects supervisor on *Deep Rising* and performed the same role on *The Mummy*. The company was breaking new ground, particularly with the depiction of Vosloo's Imhotep in his desiccated but mobile form. The actor recalls being confused when he was asked to wear an early version of a MOCAP suit. "They put me in one of those motion-capture catsuit things with white ping-pong balls," he says. "They just kept saying, 'It's going to be a skeleton, but it's going to walk like you.' I was like, 'I don't know what the fuck that even means.'"

On January 31, 1999, the Denver Broncos defeated the Atlanta Falcons 34–19 at Super Bowl XXXIII in Miami. Cher sang the national anthem; Stevie Wonder and Gloria Estefan performed during the half-time show; and, as usual, a slew of new movie trailers was screened during the ad breaks. The films being hyped that year included *The Matrix*, *Wild Wild West*, and *The Mummy*, which succeeded in catching the interest of viewers. "At that point, we had mainly the Mummy's face in the sand and the sandstorm chasing the biplane," says Sommers. "It just ignited everything. That 30-second Super Bowl spot was worth its weight in gold."

The Mummy opened on May 7, 1999. The morning of the next day, Sommers received an early call from Universal Studios president Ron Meyer, who told him some stunning news about the film's projected opening weekend box office gross. "We thought, 'Man, after that Super Bowl ad, this film could do $20 million,'" says Sommers. "Ron Meyer [called] at 5:45 am and said, 'Are you sitting down?' I go, 'Hell no, I can't sit down.' He goes, 'The movie's going to open at $45 million.'"

The success of the film could not have come at a better moment for Meyer's company, which had recently released the flops *EDtv* and *Virus*, a big-budget science fiction-horror movie starring Jamie Lee Curtis.. On the same day *The Mummy* was released, *Variety* published an article reporting that Universal Studios' film group had lost $97 million in the previous financial quarter. At the start of the following week, the *New York Post* published an article headlined "How Universal breathed life into 'Mummy'," which noted that Sommers' film had grossed more than the other movies in the top ten combined. *The Mummy* continued to attract audiences through the summer and by the end of that September's Labor Day weekend could claim a domestic gross of $155 million.

Universal swiftly sent Sommers, Fraser, Weisz, Hannah, and Vosloo back to Morocco to shoot a sequel, *The Mummy Returns*. In addition to Vosloo's Imhotep, the sequel's antagonists included the Scorpion King, an ancient warrior who has transformed into a half-human, half-arachnid monstrosity. Sommers cast Dwayne 'The Rock' Johnson as the character. Johnson was a huge star in the wrestling world but had little onscreen experience. "I didn't know anything about the WWE or whatever," says the director. "I saw his stuff and went, 'Oh, he's got such charisma.'"

Sommers recalls that Johnson was sick but game on set. "Dwayne had really bad food poisoning and heatstroke," says the director. "Everybody's in shorts and tank tops, and he would be covered in blankets, just shivering. And he is such a trooper. He goes, 'Just get the camera rolling, and as soon as I hear 'Background,' I'll jump up.' And that's what he did. All the extras start going and I go, 'Action!' and Dwayne, he threw off the blankets and charged forward. That guy gutted it out."

Dwayne Johnson in *The Mummy Returns* (2001).

The Mummy Returns was released in May 2001, and was another huge hit, earning $433 million at the global box office. A Dwayne Johnson spin-off film, *The Scorpion King*, followed the next year. Directed by *A Nightmare on Elm Street 3* filmmaker Chuck Russell, the movie grossed $180 million around the globe and established the wrestler-turned-actor as a box office draw in his own right. Over the next few years, Johnson starred in a string of big-budget films, including 2005's monster movie *Doom*, ascending to superstar status with his role in 2011's *Fast Five*, the fifth entry in the *Fast & Furious* action franchise.

Brendan Fraser reprised the role of Rick O'Connell in 2008's *The Mummy: Tomb of the Dragon Emperor*, for which Sommers ceded the director's chair to Rob Cohen. The threequel earned less than the previous two films but was still a hit, particularly in non-US territories.

Sommers' *The Mummy* would stand the test of time, becoming a cable TV staple and a beloved pop culture artifact. "I don't know what it is," he says. "But people, whenever they find out that I was involved in that movie, that I directed it, it puts a big smile on people's faces."

1999 would come to be regarded as something of a high point for cinema. Two decades later, author Brian Raftery hailed those 12 months as the *Best. Movie. Year. Ever.*, the title of his book that described how cinema audiences were treated to, among other big-screen delights, *Fight Club*, *The Matrix*, *Office Space*, *Three Kings*, *Boys Don't Cry*, *Being John Malkovich*, *Magnolia*, *The Virgin Suicides*, *The Best Man*, and *The Mummy*.

Even if you thought Stephen Sommers' film was too family-friendly to qualify as horror, 1999 was still a banner year for the genre. Following *Scream*, the ears of studio executives had become more open to pitches for horror and horror-adjacent movies, and the results seemed to arrive virtually all at once. At the end of 1999, *Fangoria* editor Tony Timpone wrote in an editorial that horror fans had just enjoyed "what will likely be viewed as one of the genre's best, most profitable and most significant years in a long time."

The first few months of 1999 saw the release of Neil Jordan's horror-thriller *In Dreams*, Katt Shea's sequel *The Rage: Carrie 2*, the Jamie Lee Curtis-starring *Virus*, and Antonia Bird's 19th-century cannibal movie *Ravenous*, whose cast included David Arquette.

The real deluge of genre movies, and the real commercial successes, began with *The Mummy* and the ensuing summer movie season. In July, 20th Century Fox released the giant crocodile film *Lake Placid*, Warner Bros. distributed director Renny Harlin's shark tale *Deep Blue Sea*, and Steven Spielberg's DreamWorks deposited the Shirley Jackson adaptation *The Haunting* into cinemas. Spielberg's company had gained the rights to turn Jackson's *The Haunting of Hill House* into a film after Dimension failed to pursue its own planned version. The movie was directed by *Speed* filmmaker Jan de Bont, who larded the big-budget project with visual effects and a starry cast led by Liam Neeson, Catherine Zeta-Jones, Owen Wilson, and *The Addiction* actress Lili Taylor. The PG-13-rated movie became one of the summer's biggest earners, grossing $91 million at the domestic box office, but the film was maligned by critics and audiences, the latter of whom gave the film a lowly C+ Cinemascore.

The year's release schedule was so packed with new horror movies that September 10, 1999, saw the release of not one but two supernatural thrillers with big name actors: *Stigmata* and *Stir of Echoes*. *Stigmata* starred Patricia Arquette as a Pittsburgh resident who starts to inexplicably bleed from her hands and head. Directed by Rupert Wainwright and produced by Frank Mancuso Jr., a long-time shepherd of the *Friday the 13th* film franchise, the film earned a healthy $50 million at the US box office. The Artisan-distributed *Stir of Echoes* was a showcase for Kevin Bacon as a blue-collar worker in Chicago who discovers he can communicate with the dead. The film was based on a 1958 novel by *I Am Legend* author Richard Matheson and was directed by *Jurassic Park* screenwriter David Koepp. *Stir of Echoes* earned less than half the gross of *Stigmata*, although Bacon would blame the film's lack of success on a different horror movie. That film had arrived in cinemas over a month before *Stir of Echoes* but had still comfortably outgrossed Koepp's movie during its first week of release. "Every step of the way we were compared to them, and it completely fucked the possibility of the movie being seen," Bacon said to *Entertainment Weekly* writer Joey Nolfi in 2017.

The movie about which he was still complaining all those years later came from an obscure filmmaker who had succeeded in terrifying and shocking audiences with his tale of a young boy who sees dead people.

All the time.

M. Night Shyamalan had the hook for his ghost story *The Sixth Sense* at the start of the writing process. The twist, the final act reveal that would turn the movie into both a blockbuster and a pop culture phenomenon, took a little longer.

The Philadelphia-based filmmaker had started writing the film after attending a funeral where he saw a boy talking to himself. Shyamalan began to think about what it would be like for a child if they could see the spirits of people who had passed on. When he returned home, he dreamed up a scene which featured a line of dialog destined to become among the most famous in movie history: "I see dead people."

Shyamalan conceived the film as a serial killer movie similar in tone to *The Silence of the Lambs*, director Jonathan Demme's 1991 movie starring Anthony Hopkins as the psychiatrist cannibal Hannibal Lecter. As Shyamalan developed the screenplay, he abandoned that plan and matched the script's ghost-seeing nine-year-old boy, Cole, with a child psychologist whose marriage is going through difficulties. What the director struggled to figure out was the nature of the problem between the psychologist, Malcolm Crowe, and his wife, Anna. Finally, inspiration struck. In a climactic twist, the film would reveal that Crowe is himself a ghost that can only be seen by Cole. Shyamalan had such confidence in his script that he told his agent he would only sell it for $1 million and on the condition that he be allowed to direct the film. These demands were ambitious. The young filmmaker could claim little reputation in Hollywood, and what track record he had was unimpressive.

Shyamalan got interested in the horror genre after seeing *The Exorcist* at an impressionable age. "We went to my uncle and aunt's who had HBO, and that's where I saw *The Exorcist* for the first time as a kid," says the director. "Slept with my parents for one month, dude. One month, I would not leave their room. I'm still traumatized from that experience a bit. But I so enjoy the genre, and when I was a kid we would just go to the video store and clean out that whole area."

Shyamalan was still studying film at NYU when he made his first film, the 1992 drama *Praying with Anger*, with a small budget made up of money he borrowed from family and friends. The movie starred Shyamalan himself and was barely released, but the filmmaker went on to score a deal with Miramax to write and direct a comedy-drama called *Wide Awake*. After seeing the movie, Harvey Weinstein reduced Shyamalan to tears by telling him that *Wide Awake* could not be saved. The Miramax co-founder ordered reshoots and new edits of the film, which were assembled without the director's input. When the studio released *Wide Awake* in March 1998, the $6 million movie earned a paltry $282,175.

The quality of Shyamalan's *Sixth Sense* script prompted a bidding war between New Line, DreamWorks, Columbia Pictures, and the ultimate victor, Disney's Hollywood Pictures. Walt Disney Pictures' president David Vogel planned for *The Sixth Sense* to be made on a modest budget and star an inexpensive actor, possibly Kevin Spacey. Then Bruce Willis agreed to play Malcolm Crowe, and the budget ballooned to around $40 million.

For the pivotal role of the child Cole, Shyamalan cast Haley Joel Osment, whose credits included *Ally McBeal* and *Forrest Gump*. The director chose Australian actress Toni Collette to play Cole's mother Lynn and New Kids on the Block member Donnie Wahlberg to portray Vincent, a disturbed former patient of Willis' character.

Shyamalan shot *The Sixth Sense* in Philadelphia and filmed in sequence as much as possible to help Osment with his performance. Collette recalls the production as a happy one. "I loved making it, I loved Philadelphia," she says. "I made some very good friends on that film. You know, I think life is energy, and on *The Sixth Sense* there was some definite feeling we all had that it was going to be somehow special. And it did actually come to pass."

Shyamalan's film would be mostly free of both gore and special effects. "Horror films have forgotten that there is a difference between an image that's really disturbing and an image that's spectacle," the director told *Fangoria*. "What I tried to do with *The Sixth Sense* was find as many disturbing and frightening images as I could that would linger with you, because they play on real fears."

In his review for *The New York Times*, Stephen Holden dismissed Shyamalan's film as "gaggingly mawkish supernatural kitsch." Most critics were more positive about the movie, with *Houston Chronicle* writer Jeff Millar ar-

Haley Joel Osment in *The Sixth Sense* (1999).

guing that "there's more fright in any 10 minutes of *The Sixth Sense* than the sensory startle effects *The Haunting* produces in its entire running time."

The Sixth Sense debuted in cinemas on August 6, 1999, Shyamalan's 29th birthday, winning its opening weekend with a gross of $26 million. "I was just shocked," he told *Fangoria* following the film's release. "I thought there was no way we would be number one. We had the least hype of any movie this summer... Our best expectations were for $18 million and third place, and those were pretty high expectations. But we crossed $100 million in 17 days—it's just phenomenal."

The previous month, the grosses of *The Haunting* had dropped 54 percent during the film's second week on release. The box office take of *The Sixth Sense* fell a mere 2 percent over the movie's second weekend in cinemas. The film went to become 1999's second biggest hit in the US (behind *Star Wars: Episode 1 – The Phantom Menace*) and earned $672 million around the world. *The Sixth Sense* was even acknowledged by the Oscars. Shyamalan's film was nominated for Best Picture and Best Director, and Collette and Osment were given nods in the Best Supporting Actress and Best Supporting Actor categories respectively. The movie was also nominated for Best Original Screenplay and Best Editing. While the Academy would ultimately reward other films on Oscar night, the nominations were a rare acknowledgment by the organization of a horror movie's success and qualities.

Remarkably, that August, *The Sixth Sense* had to compete for the public's attention with another big-screen horror sensation. This micro-budgeted film was as rough and ready as Shyamalan's movie was deliberately constructed, yet it would prove just as terrifying and even more influential.

"Attention: Casting Improvisational Feature Film!" ran the ad that appeared in New York's *Backstage* magazine during the late summer of 1997. "Haxan Films is holding an open call for 'The Black Hill Project.' Non-union, with pay, travel, and meals. Shooting October–November in Maryland. Seeking women, men, 18–25, with natural look. EXTREMELY CHALLENGING ROLES: to be shot under very difficult conditions."

Heather Donahue was among the aspiring actors who read the ad and were not dissuaded by its warnings. Donahue had graduated from Philadelphia's University of the Arts with a BFA in theater and had already performed one memorably challenging role in London. "I did this little play called *Fried Blood*," she says. "I was dressed in a black leather dress with thigh-high black boots, and an orange wig, and a red clown nose. I believe it may have crossed the boundaries of experimental theater into the wild, wild world of performance art."

After Donahue arrived for the audition at Musical Theater Works, she was given a sign-in sheet featuring a more detailed description of the nature of the role for which she was trying out. "You are about to read for the most demanding and unpleasant project of your career," the actress was informed. "If you are cast, we are going to drag you into the woods for seven days of hell. 168 hours of real-time improvisational torment. We're not kidding."

The film's directors, Daniel Myrick and Eduardo Sánchez, hoped to use the audition process to test the improvisational skills of potential cast members. When her turn came, Donahue was asked to play someone who was explaining to a parole board why she should be released early from prison after being incarcerated for murder. The actress' response was to say that she did not think she should be let out.

Donahue went on to star in the directors' film about three documentarians who disappear in the Maryland woods while investigating a local legend. Released under the title *The Blair Witch Project*, the movie would prove

Heather Donahue in *The Blair Witch Project* (1999).

to be 1999's most unexpected blockbuster, turning the actress into an instantly famous, though somewhat reluctant, horror icon.

Directors Myrick and Sánchez had become friends while studying film at the University of Central Florida. In 1991, the pair attended a preview screening of *Freddy's Dead: The Final Nightmare* on the UCF campus. Myrick and Sánchez enjoyed the movie, but after the screening started talking about how the horror genre was moving away from the films that had terrified them as kids, like *The Exorcist* and *The Changeling*. The pair had a particular fondness for 1972's *The Legend of Boggy Creek*, a horror film about a Bigfoot-like creature told in the manner of a documentary with interviews and re-enactments. Myrick and Sánchez started developing the idea for a movie about a group of documentarians who vanish while making a film about a witch.

After college, the two aspirant directors teamed up with some friends, including army veteran and fellow UCF graduate Gregg Hale, to form Haxan Films, which initially made commercials and industrial films. One day, over drinks, Myrick mentioned to Hale his and Sánchez's idea for a movie about filmmakers getting lost in the woods. Hale suggested that they could put the actors through a sort of lengthy obstacle course, creating an environment where the cast's natural ability to portray characters who were cold, hungry, and terrified would be enhanced by the fact that they really *were* cold, hungry, and terrified. "We were after complete realism," Sánchez told *Empire* magazine in 1999. "Gregg said, 'Listen, when I was in special forces training, they put us through this P.O.W. camp scenario where we were the prisoners. And after two or three days of being in that camp surrounded by these guys hitting you, and yelling at you in Russian, and not letting you sleep, and hosing you down with water, you start to believe it's really happening.'"

In addition to Donahue, the filmmakers cast two other unknowns, Michael Williams and Joshua Leonard, as the documentary team's soundman and cameraman respectively. The Haxan filmmakers were hoping to raise a budget of around $300,000, but with the start of the movie's shoot approaching, they had managed to secure just $22,000 in funds. Myrick and Sánchez carried on regardless and in October 1997 decamped to Maryland. Once the cast joined them, Donahue was given a Hi8 video camera that Haxan had bought for $500 at a Circuit City store (and would return to the store once the shoot was over), while Leonard received a CP-16 film camera. Donahue would also go into the woods equipped with a knife for protection. As Myrick told *Empire*, "Her mother didn't even want her to do it. So Heather brought a huge hunting knife, which she had on her as a deterrent in case anything went awry."

During the shoot, the cast members, who were asked to use their actual names, were sent to locations marked with flags or milk crates, where they would leave their footage and pick up food and notes with instructions about how to act over the next period of shooting. At night, the filmmakers did their best to freak out the actors, playing the sound of children's cries on a boombox and once leaving a bundle of twigs and real teeth outside their tent for them to find and unwrap.

The Haxan team planned on using the material shot by their cast sparingly in the finished film, which would be presented as a seemingly real documentary about the disappearance of the trio. Following the shoot in Maryland, the real-life filmmakers set about shooting fake interviews and other material that would frame this 'found footage.' Sánchez, who had some experience with web design, set up a site to help spread word about the film. The late '90s was the Stone Age for the internet. Comparatively few people had access to, or interest in, what was still often unironically referred to as 'the world wide web.' In 1997, only 23 percent of Americans were going online. By 1999, that figure had leaped significantly to 41 percent, although many users were still accessing the internet just to check the weather. Still, Blairwitch.com would act as an effective tease for the movie, offering a breakdown of the evidence that had been compiled about the purported disappearance of the filmmakers. Members of the public started posting on the website to discuss whether the trio really were missing.

In November 1998, Haxan found out that *The Blair Witch Project* had been accepted to play at the Sundance Film Festival, which would take place in January of the following year. As Myrick and Sánchez hurriedly finished the movie in time for the event, the pair realized that the power of the found footage material was undeniable and decided to lose the interviews and other framing material.

The Blair Witch Project screened at Sundance in January 1999. The audience included Bill Block, the co-president of indie film studio Artisan Entertainment, as well as the company's head of marketing, John Hegeman. Artisan had recently done well with Darren Aronofsky's directorial debut, the horror-thriller *Pi*, which the company had picked up at the previous year's Sundance. Block and Hegeman were impressed by *The Blair*

Witch Project. The pair's interest in the movie was further piqued after the premiere, when they encountered a clutch of other attendees too frightened to cross the parking lot to their car.

Artisan did not have much competition for the film. Miramax executive Jason Blum was one of those who failed to contract *Blair Witch* fever either before or at the festival. "When I was working for Miramax, before Sundance, a video of *The Blair Witch Project* went to a lot of the buyers," he recalled, many years later, on the *Geek's Guide to the Galaxy* podcast. "I passed; a bunch of people passed. The worst crime was that once it screened at the festival, we still all passed." Artisan eventually paid $1.1 million for the film, a significant figure given its low budget and unusual nature. When word of the deal spread among other executives at Sundance, some joked that the only thing frightening about the film was how much the company had spent on it.

Artisan went all-out to promote the film as a hip movie. The company screened it on 40 college campuses, hiring students to post 'Missing' posters featuring images of the film's cast. The company also relaunched the movie's website, adding documents and video clips to continue the pretense that the events in the film might be real. "*Blair Witch* was one where we started literally from the bottom up," says Jeff Walker, a marketing executive who worked on the movie's campaign. "The fandom loved the idea of this found footage movie that they had discovered. The mainstream audience—they weren't sure if it was real or not." As the marketing and publicity campaigns for the film hyped it up ahead of release, Artisan deliberately kept the movie's cast in the background, fueling the rumors that they really had disappeared in the woods. Donahue's mother even received a sympathy card from someone who believed her daughter was dead.

The Blair Witch Project received its premiere on July 12, 1999, at New York's Beekman Theatre. Artisan put the film in just 27 cinemas the following weekend, with the movie earning $1.5 million. The studio distributed *The Blair Witch Project* wide two weeks later. The film grossed $29 million over three days in 1,101 theaters. The next weekend, which also saw the release of *The Sixth Sense*, Artisan almost doubled the number of cinemas in which the movie was playing, with the film earning another $24 million by the end of the Sunday.

The film's status as a box office phenomenon was confirmed when the magazines *Time* and *Newsweek* simultaneously put *The Blair Witch Project* on their respective covers. The movie's three actors graced the cover of *Newsweek*; Myrick and Sánchez were showcased on the cover of *Time*, with a story written by the outlet's film critic Richard Corliss. "Every now and then, art, whatever form it takes, gets back to its roots," Myrick said in the *Time* article. "When you don't have money and resources, you're forced to get down to the essence of storytelling. Or at least have a good story."

Myrick and Sánchez's micro-budgeted film ultimately grossed $140 million in the US, enough to make it the tenth most successful movie of the year. *The Blair Witch Project* would go on to earn another $108 million around the globe.

The found footage style Myrick and Sánchez had used for *The Blair Witch Project* was regarded as a one-off, unrepeatable trick, even by Artisan. When the Haxan team declined to work on a sequel, the company hired documentary director Joe Berlinger. The filmmaker's tale mostly eschewed the found footage format for a more visually traditional tale, even as the plot took the franchise into a post-modern arena by featuring characters obsessed with the first movie. During post-production on the sequel, which was titled *Book of Shadows: Blair Witch 2*, Artisan took direct control of the project, adding more gore. Starring Kim Director, Erica Leerhsen, and Jeffrey Donovan, *Book of Shadows* opened in October 2000, earning $47 million around the world. That figure likely put the film into profit but represented a dramatic drop-off from the gross of the first movie, and the franchise was placed on a semi-permanent hold.

After the release of *The Blair Witch Project*, Donahue continued to act for several years and scored a role on the Steven Spielberg-produced TV show *Taken*, among other projects. She decided to retire from show business after appearing in the little-seen 2008 horror film *The Morgue*. "They had me siphoning gas, sucking on a tube, to get out of a dire situation, then I choked on what I had sucked out of the tube and died," she says. "When I was lying on wet asphalt with a piece of rubber tubing draped over my cheek having just had a death by mock fellation, I realized that was not the life I wanted. The LA dream happened for me. I got to see what it was like to be on *The Tonight Show*. I got to live that Hollywood dream. Until it became undreamy. And then I had the good sense to move on."

In January 1999, *Variety* announced that *Die Hard* and *Lethal Weapon* producer Joel Silver and *Back to the Future* filmmaker Robert Zemeckis had partnered to form Dark Castle Entertainment. Based at Warner Bros., the company would be dedicated to producing mid-budgeted horror films. The name Dark Castle paid tribute to William Castle, a horror director of the '50s and '60s famous for attracting audiences with theatrical gimmicks. Castle installed vibrating motors on the underside of seats in cinemas showing his 1959 film *The Tingler* that would activate when star Vincent Price exhorted the audience to scream. For 1960's *13 Ghosts*, the filmmaker employed a gimmick called 'Illusion-O,' which involved cinemagoers looking through the red filter of their supplied glasses to better see the movie's apparitions.

Castle himself frequently appeared in the trailers for his films and became a familiar figure to audiences. In the late '60s, the filmmaker achieved both wealth and Hollywood respectability when he secured the movie rights to Ira Levin's novel *Rosemary's Baby* and produced Roman Polanski's adaptation of the book. Ironically, the success of the movie helped make Castle's own directorial efforts seem old-fashioned, and he would directly oversee just one more movie, 1974's Marcel Marceau-starring horror tale *Shanks*, before his death in 1977.

Castle's admirers included John Waters, whose decision to dispense scratch-and-sniff cards to viewers of his 1981 film *Polyester* was a direct tribute to the *Tingler* director's gimmickry, and Joe Dante, whose 1993 film *Matinee* starred John Goodman as a Castle-type impresario. Zemeckis and Silver were two more filmmakers who had grown up watching Castle's movies. Silver had even met with the filmmaker when the future *Lethal Weapon* producer moved to Los Angeles in the 1970s. "He understood what truly scares people is the anticipation of the unthinkable," Silver told the outlet IGN in 2001, "and he developed techniques to exploit audiences' fears and bring a new level of entertainment to the genre and to the movie-going experience."

Prior to forming Dark Castle, Silver and Zemeckis had collaborated as executive producers on the long-running TV show *Tales from the Crypt*. The horror anthology series had premiered on HBO in 1989 and was 'hosted' by a punning, skeletal ghoul named the Cryptkeeper, in real life a puppet-

The Cryptkeeper in HBO's *Tales from the Crypt*.

eered doll. After *Tales from the Crypt* had been screening for several years, the show's producers signed a three-picture deal with Universal. The first fruit of that partnership was 1995's *Tales from the Crypt Presents: Demon Knight*, in which demonic creatures lay siege to a remote hotel-cum-brothel.

Demon Knight was directed by Ernest Dickerson, who had been on the lookout for a horror movie while he was still developing *Blade*. "It's really hard to find good horror scripts, and my agent told me about this *Demon Knight* thing," says the filmmaker. "When I read the script, I thought there was something that could be done with it." Joel Silver wanted Cameron Diaz—about to make a splash with her appearance opposite Jim Carrey in *The Mask*—to play the role of Jeryline, a convict on work release and the movie's heroine. Dickerson was determined to cast a different rising star, the pre-*Scream 2* Jada Pinkett Smith. "I was looking for an African-American, even though that wasn't specified in the script," he says. "Usually, Black folks in those days were the first folks to die in movies. I just felt that Jada is the last person you would think would be the final girl. I arranged a meeting between her and Joel Silver, and I guess she impressed him because he gave me the okay to bring her on."

The movie's makeup effects were the responsibility of Todd Masters, founder of the company MastersFX and a *Tales from the Crypt* veteran. "I could tell Ernest really knew what the fuck he was doing," he notes. "We had no time to prep that movie. We would have lunch together, and doodle shots, and try to figure out what we were going to do next week—and what we were going to do tomorrow!" Released in January 1995, Dickerson's fun, gory film earned $21 million at the US box office, encouraging Universal to continue the deal with the *Tales from the Crypt* producers.

In a brief appearance at the conclusion of the *Demon Knight* end credits, the Cryptkeeper had told audiences to "look out for my next motion picture, *Dead Easy*, coming very soon to a theater near you." The plan was for long-time *Tales from the Crypt* writer-producer Gil Adler to make his directorial debut with the film, a more psychological tale than *Demon Knight*, which he had developed with his writing partner A. L. Katz. Universal had other ideas. In order to strengthen the studio's relationship with Robert Zemeckis, Universal had purchased the script for a vampire film named *Bordello of Blood*, an early, unproduced effort by the director and his *Back to the Future* co-writer Bob Gale. Adler and Katz were now tasked with bringing that screenplay to the screen, to their eternal regret.

To play the film's lead role, a private investigator named Rafe Guttman, producer Silver cast Dennis Miller. The comedian had become well known during his tenure on *Saturday Night Live* and in 1994 had started hosting his own late night talk show on HBO, but he had little acting experience. Silver also handed a role to model Angie Everhart, apparently on the request of her boyfriend Sylvester Stallone, who was starring in the Silver-produced action-thriller *Assassins*.

Adler directed *Bordello of Blood* in Vancouver, an experience he recalls with a shudder. "On Friday nights, Dennis Miller had to do his show, so he wanted to leave at noon, so that was always a problem," he says. "The flies were as big as your fist, and they were all over us. There were issues with the physical production, there were issues with the actors. Everywhere we turned, we had issues."

Released in August 1996, *Tales from the Crypt Presents: Bordello of Blood* earned just $5.7 million at the US box office. The Cryptkeeper did not return after the end credits to announce another film, foreshadowing Universal's decision to pull the plug on a third *Tales from the Crypt* movie.

Following the *Bordello of Blood* debacle, Zemeckis suggested to Silver that, rather than produce original horror films, they should remake old ones, starting with William Castle's 1959 movie *House on Haunted Hill.* This brainwave prompted the formation of Dark Castle, which the pair founded in partnership with *Bordello of Blood* director Gil Adler. "We were initially interested in William Castle and remaking those old movies," says Adler. "I thought that was quite exciting."

The *Variety* article announcing the formation of the company informed readers that Dark Castle "represents the first studio-based challenge to Miramax's Dimension Films, which has dominated the horror genre over the past two years." Adler confirms that the formation of Dark Castle was partly inspired by the success of Bob Weinstein's company. "Success always breeds success, or a desire for more success," says the Dark Castle co-founder. "Seeing Dimension do it successfully, I think Joel and Bob thought the three of us could do it equally successfully or even more successfully."

The Dark Castle founders hired William Malone to direct their new version of *House on Haunted Hill.* The filmmaker had already secured a place in horror history by crafting the Captain Kirk mask worn by Michael Myers in *Halloween* while working at costume manufacturer Don Post Studios. Malone was later recruited by Adler to direct the 1994 *Tales from the Crypt* episode "Only Skin

Deep." "He was a good friend, and this was sort of a 90-minute version of *Tales…*, so he was an obvious choice," says the producer.

The new *House on Haunted Hill* centered around an amusement park magnate named Stephen Price who organizes a party for his wife, Evelyn, at an abandoned (and, as the characters discover, ghost-filled) institute for the criminally insane. To play the larger-than-life Price, the Dark Castle team approached Australian actor Geoffrey Rush, who in 1997 had won the Best Actor Academy Award for his portrayal of pianist David Helfgott in the film *Shine*. Adler recalls that Rush's representative did not believe a genre movie was the next best move for the recent Oscar-winner. "I went to his agent, who basically told me to fuck off, he's never going to do this, he just won an Academy Award," says the producer. "We just wouldn't take no for an answer. We kept going after him, and finally we got the script to Geoffrey, and he said, 'Oh, I'd love to do this.'" The film's producers filled out the cast with *Deep Rising* star Famke Janssen, *Saturday Night Live* cast member Chris Kattan, Taye Diggs, and Ali Larter.

House on Haunted Hill opened on October 29, 1999. Made for a budget of around $19 million, the film earned a healthy $16 million over its first weekend in theaters, commercially trouncing Wes Craven's *Music of the Heart*, which was released the same day.

House on Haunted Hill was not the only 1999 horror film to have a connection with the *Tales from the Crypt* TV show. *Sleepy Hollow* was a big-budget live-action adaptation of Washington Irving's 1820 short story "The Legend of Sleepy Hollow," about a schoolteacher who is pursued through the New York countryside by a ghostly figure known as the Headless Horseman. The movie was directed by *Batman* filmmaker Tim Burton but was initially the brainchild of special effects and makeup artist Kevin Yagher. Early in his career, Yagher had overseen the makeup for Robert Englund's Freddy Krueger on the first three *A Nightmare Elm Street* sequels and had created the original Chucky doll for 1988's *Child's Play*. Yagher also designed the *Tales from the Crypt* host the Cryptkeeper and directed the show's wraparound sequences, as well as a couple of episodes.

Yagher wanted to take his filmmaking career to the next level and agreed to direct 1996's Dimension-backed *Hellraiser: Bloodline*, the fourth entry in the Clive Barker-created franchise. The director would have a difficult time working on the movie with Bob Weinstein, who asked *Halloween: The Curse of Michael Myers* filmmaker Joe Chappelle to oversee extensive reshoots. Yagher ultimately removed his name from the film. "They put the beginning at the end and the end at the beginning and reworked the entire thing," he would later tell *Fangoria.*

Disney had produced an animated version of "The Legend of Sleepy Hollow" in 1949. Yagher believed the material would suit a live-action adaptation and, in the early '90s, began working on the treatment for a film version of Irving's tale, transforming Crane from a teacher to a detective. Yagher accepted his agents' suggestion that he partner with Andrew Kevin Walker, writer of David Fincher's then-unproduced serial killer movie *Seven.* Around the time Yagher was working on *Hellraiser: Bloodline*, the pair began pitching *Sleepy Hollow* and landed a deal with Scott Rudin, producer of 1993's Tom Cruise-starring *The Firm* and both *Addams Family* movies. Rudin, in turn, struck a provisional deal with Paramount to produce the film, with Yagher in the frame to direct. The studio's interest in making the movie cooled after another period film, 1996's adaptation of *The Crucible* starring Daniel Day-Lewis, failed at the box office.

Sleepy Hollow was revived as a possible directing project for a Los Angeles-raised filmmaker named Mike Mendez after his debut movie, the micro-budgeted horror-thriller *Killers*, premiered at the Sundance Film Festival early in 1997. "It was the hottest my career has ever been, sadly," he says. "After *Killers* got into Sundance, I was getting a lot of scripts. I was talking to Dimension quite regularly. They liked to dangle a carrot, like—I think they dangled this carrot to a lot of people—'We don't have a director yet for *Scream 2*, maybe you could be…?' Of course, I was never going to get it, it was always going to be Wes Craven." Scott Rudin was more serious about considering Mendez for *Sleepy Hollow.* As part of his audition for the director's job, Mendez shot a trailer for the film with help from makeup effects artist Tony Gardner, whose credits included *Army of Darkness* and *The Craft.* "They were kind enough to give me $20,000 to make a trailer," says Mendez. "We designed the Headless Horseman with Tony Gardner, and he built a thing that looks very much like the finished one in the film, so it was nice to see that my instincts weren't so off." But as Mendez explains, "Eventually Tim Burton wanted to make the movie, and it made a big difference. When I was doing it, it was going to be an under-$20 million film, and when Tim Burton came on, it became a $90 million film."

HEADS WILL ROLL
A TIM BURTON FILM
Sleepy Hollow
PARAMOUNT PICTURES AND MANDALAY PICTURES PRESENT A SCOTT RUDIN/AMERICAN ZOETROPE PRODUCTION
A TIM BURTON FILM JOHNNY DEPP CHRISTINA RICCI "SLEEPY HOLLOW" MIRANDA RICHARDSON MICHAEL GAMBON
CASPER VAN DIEN JEFFREY JONES MUSIC BY DANNY ELFMAN COSTUME DESIGNER COLLEEN ATWOOD PRODUCTION DESIGNER RICK HEINRICHS EDITED BY CHRIS LEBENZON
DIRECTOR OF PHOTOGRAPHY EMMANUEL LUBEZKI EXECUTIVE PRODUCERS FRANCIS FORD COPPOLA LARRY FRANCO BASED UPON THE STORY BY WASHINGTON IRVING
SCREEN STORY BY KEVIN YAGHER AND ANDREW KEVIN WALKER SCREENPLAY BY ANDREW KEVIN WALKER PRODUCED BY SCOTT RUDIN ADAM SCHROEDER
www.sleepyhollowmovie.com
DIRECTED BY TIM BURTON
THANKSGIVING

Burton was looking for a new project after a clutch of disappointments. His most recent completed film, the alien invasion movie *Mars Attacks!*, had been released in December 1996 and had proved much less successful than *Independence Day*, which had arrived in cinemas five months earlier. Next, Burton spent a year developing *Superman Lives*, which was to star Nicolas Cage as the Man of Steel. In the spring of 1998, Warner Bros. shelved the project, with Burton later blaming differences of opinion (and temperament) between himself and producer Jon Peters.

Burton had become a fan of horror growing up as a lonely child in the Los Angeles suburb of Burbank, where he attended triple bills of vintage genre fare, many of them Hammer releases. The director was familiar with the story of Ichabod Crane and realized that adapting Irving's story would allow him to channel the spooky spirit of the movies he had watched as a kid. In June 1998, *Variety* published an article headlined "Burton eyes *Hollow*," which revealed that the director was in "serious talks to make his next film *Sleepy Hollow*." The article went on to explain that the film was based at Paramount and would be scripted by Andrew Kevin Walker. *Variety* suggested that the film was "being eyed for a fall shoot."

The article did not mention Kevin Yagher, who learned secondhand that the project had been revived as he was working on *Bride of Chucky*. Yagher ultimately shared a 'story by' credit with Walker, as well as overseeing the film's practical effects. "I used to make jokes that I'd step down if Tim Burton came along," Yagher told *Fangoria*. "Tim just happened to be the guy who wanted to do it, so I stepped down."

In the original short story, Irving described Ichabod Crane in less than flattering terms. "His head was small, and flat at the top," the author wrote, "with huge ears, large green glassy eyes, and a long snipe nose, so that it looked like a cock perched upon his spindle neck, to tell which way the wind blew." The *Sleepy Hollow* team planned on reinventing the character to be more pleasing to the eye. In July 1998, *Entertainment Weekly* writer David Hochman reported that Burton and Rudin "have apparently been in hot pursuit of Brad Pitt, Liam Neeson, and Daniel Day-Lewis to play the terrified schoolteacher." Burton always hoped to have his *Edward Scissorhands* actor Johnny Depp star in the film. Depp joined the production after shooting a different horror movie, Roman Polanski's 1999 supernatural thriller *The Ninth Gate*. Burton chose Christina Ricci for the role of Crane's love interest Katrina Van Tassel, and Christopher Walken as the Headless Horseman. The director shot the film in England and packed the supporting cast with veteran British character actors—including Christopher Lee, the star of many Hammer movies.

Sleepy Hollow was a hit, grossing just over $200 million worldwide. Burton's film was nominated for Oscars in the categories of Best Costume Design, Best Cinematography, and Best Art Design, with Rick Heinrichs and Peter Young winning the latter.

Mike Mendez recalls seeing *Sleepy Hollow* on opening night. "I think he did an awesome job," the filmmaker says of Burton. "What are you going to say? It's Tim Burton, they gave him $90 million, and I like the movie. I could be bitter about it, but at the end of the day, I think film fans got the better end of the deal with the Tim Burton one."

Mendez followed up *Killers* with *The Convent*, a berserk tale of demons running amok in the titular abandoned building, whose cast included *Escape from New York* actress Adrienne Barbeau. The film played Sundance in 2000 but was eventually released straight to the home entertainment market. "I made *The Convent* as a reaction to the fact that there was no *Evil Deads* and there was no Peter Jackson-gory films anymore," says Mendez. "The films that were getting greenlit were those kind of bloodless slasher films. I did meet on *I Still Know What You Did Last Summer*, I gave a pitch for that. I should have said, 'I'll do the bloodless bullshit.' Instead, wiseguy that I am, I'm like, 'I'm going to make a no-budget gory movie about zombie nuns.' And Hollywood said, 'You go do that. We're going to go make money.'"

As 1999 drew to a close, fears of mummies, headless horsemen, and other fantastical entities were eclipsed in the minds of the public by worries about the real-world catastrophe that might follow a global meltdown of computers at midnight on December 31. Experts had long been concerned that programmers' use of a two-digit code for denoting years would cause a cataclysmic problem at the end of the century, with computers interpreting the designation '00' as the year 1900 and not 2000. In 1998, President Bill Clinton had signed an executive order that created a Council on Year 2000 Conversion and appointed a Y2K 'czar,' John Koskinen. Around the world, governments and companies spent vast sums of money attempting to fix the issue. There remained a genuine fear that civilization would be destroyed, or at least blasted back to some pre-computer age, as one century turned into another. Those worries were accentuated and exploited by some evangelical Christian leaders, who warned that Y2K could be a harbinger of the apocalypse. Starting in the summer of 1998, Moral Majority leader Reverend Jerry Falwell sold a $28 videotape titled *A Christian's Guide to the Millennium Bug*. The reverend revealed in the video that he planned to stockpile food, gasoline, and ammunition for weapons. "Because if I'm blessed with a little food and my family is inside the house with me, I've got to be sure that I can persuade others not to mess with us," Falwell said ominously.

Arnold Schwarzenegger was not a religious figure, yet the *Terminator* franchise star also hoped to mine dollars out of dread as the countdown to the end of the millennium inexorably continued. On November 24, 1999, Universal released the actor's new film *End of Days*, the last of the year's major movies to utilize tropes from the horror genre. Directed by Peter Hyams, the movie starred Schwarzenegger as a former New York cop who learns that Satan has plans to kick off the apocalypse by impregnating a young woman before the end of the century. The film mixed scares and stunts in a manner designed to take advantage of the public's renewed interest in the horror genre and to show that Schwarzenegger, who had undergone elective heart surgery in 1997, could still cut it as an action star.

End of Days was conceived by USC graduate Andrew W. Marlowe, who also wrote the Harrison Ford-starring 1997 action-thriller *Air Force One*. Marlowe was asked by that film's producer, Armyan Bernstein, if he had any ideas for an Arnold Schwarzenegger movie. "I thought, 'Arnold has fought all these bad guys. Who would be the ultimate bad guy? The Devil,'" Marlowe told *Fangoria*.

In July 1998, *Variety* reported that *End of Days* would be the feature debut of Marcus Nispel. The German-born director had spent the '90s establishing his reputation in the arenas of advertising and music videos, overseeing commercials for Nike and Mercedes and promo clips for Mariah Carey and the Spice Girls. The *Variety* article noted that the film was expected to cost around $100 million.

Nispel subsequently left the project, supposedly because of artistic differences. According to the director, though, the real problem was that he was asked to cut the budget by $10 million shortly before the start of shooting. "I said, 'We would have to lose all the stunts and all the special effects,'" he recalls. "They go, 'We can't do that, it's an Arnold Schwarzenegger movie!' I said, 'Exactly.'" When Nispel suggested that the producers ask Schwarzenegger to cut his substantial wage for the film to fill the gap, they demurred. "They're like, 'No, it's a pay-or-play movie, he's going to walk, and we're going to lose all our money,'" says the director. "I go, 'Well, if we can't have a conversation with Arnold, I'm out.'"

The movie's producers needed to find a replacement quickly if they were to get the movie onto screens before the end of 1999. Schwarzenegger's *Terminator* and *True Lies* director James Cameron suggested Peter Hyams. The filmmaker was a Hollywood veteran whose resumé included 1981's Sean Connery science fiction movie *Outland* and 1997's *The Relic*, about a monster running amok in Chicago's Field Museum of Natural History. *The Relic* was not a big hit but reinforced Hyams' reputation as a safe pair of hands, setting him up to take over from Nispel on *End of Days*.

The movie co-starred Gabriel Byrne, Kevin Pollak, Rod Steiger, Miriam Margolyes, Udo Kier, and up-and-comer Robin Tunney, who played the woman Byrne's Satan wants to impregnate. Tunney had made her film debut in the Brendan Fraser-starring *Encino Man* and appeared in *The Craft* alongside Neve Campbell and Skeet Ulrich. More recently, the actress had been cast in *Supernova*, a space-set science fiction-horror film with a notorious production history. *House on Haunted Hill* director William Malone had pitched the idea for a modestly budgeted movie with the name *Dead Star* in 1990. MGM bought the script (now titled *Supernova*) in 1995. The movie passed through the hands of several directors, from the Australian Geoffrey Wright to Walter Hill—who oversaw the bulk of the shooting—to *A Nightmare on Elm Street 2* filmmaker Jack Sholder to, finally, Francis Ford Coppola. The film's budget ballooned to over $60 million, more than four times what *Supernova* grossed at the domestic box office when it was belatedly released in January 2000.

Despite her experience on the big-budget *Supernova*, Tunney was still taken aback by the demands of co-starring in an Arnold Schwarzenegger vehicle. As the actress recalled to *Entertainment Weekly* writer Josh Wolk prior to the film's release, "One day a fireball was supposed to burst through the front window, and right before they called 'Action,' Arnold turned to me and said, 'Robin, they showed you where the fire extinguisher is in case you catch on fire, right?' I was like, 'Excuse me? No, no, no, I'm holding your hand in this scene, they can't afford to catch you on fire. That's my safety net.' He goes, 'Oh, Robin, I've caught on fire several times.'"

Released in the US over Thanksgiving weekend, *End of Days* had to settle for third place on the box office chart, behind both *Toy Story 2* and the James Bond movie *The World Is Not Enough*. The film's opening weekend take of $20 million was barely more than the amount earned by *Sleepy Hollow*, which had debuted the week before. *End of Days* performed better abroad, but the film's worldwide gross of $211 million represented a mediocre return given its high price tag.

Thanks to the efforts taken around the globe to avert disaster, Y2K proved to be even more of a non-event than Hyams' film. The computers remained on, and the internet stayed connected. Schwarzenegger would star in just a handful more films before being elected Governor of California in 2003. Marcus Nispel, meanwhile, went back to directing ads, at least for the moment. "My first taste of the feature world wasn't good," he says. "I went, fuck that, life is too short, I could make more money doing commercials."

"YOU'RE NOT AFRAID OF THE DARK, ARE YOU?"

Kevin Williamson decided to make his directorial debut with *Killing Mrs. Tingle*, the script he had written before *Scream*, with backing from Bob Weinstein's Dimension. The first-time filmmaker cast Helen Mirren as the tale's titular educator after meeting with an array of actresses, including Sigourney Weaver, Glenn Close, Kathleen Turner, and Sally Field. The movie's students were played by Katie Holmes, Barry Watson, and newcomer Marisa Coughlan. Williamson shot the film in Los Angeles during the early summer of 1998. "That was a fun one," says Julie Plec, who remained close with Williamson and would join his production company Outerbanks in 1999. "Marisa Coughlan was so delightful in the movie, Katie Holmes is just a dreamboat, Helen Mirren was spectacular, and kind, and wonderful, and then Barry Watson is such a good guy. It was one of those very small experiences that was just warm, and friendly, and fun for everybody."

Williamson's plan for *Killing Mrs. Tingle* to be a tonally dark, R-rated film would be upturned by an awful real-life event. On April 20, 1999, two teenagers who attended Colorado's Columbine High School shot and killed 12 of their fellow students and a teacher, before turning their guns on themselves. The incident sent shockwaves through the US, with many blaming violence in movies and video games for the tragedy. On April 28, Republican politician John McCain, the chairman of the Senate's Commerce, Science, and Transportation Committee, held a press conference requesting that President Clinton call an emergency summit to develop a plan for stemming what he called "the flow of media violence to our children."

Sony Pictures released the horror-comedy *Idle Hands* just ten days after the Columbine tragedy. Directed by *Leprechaun 2* filmmaker Rodman Flender, the movie starred Devon Sawa—a teen heartthrob since his appearance in 1995's *Casper*—as a stoner whose hand becomes possessed and goes on a killing spree. *Idle Hands* was placed under a microscope as people sought an explanation for the Colorado killings. At the same press conference where McCain had called for the emergency summit, Democrat senator Joe Lieberman singled out Flender's film for criticism. Lieberman described *Idle Hands* as, "by all reports, another grossly violent film targeted at teens that uses killing as a form of comic relief." The Columbine massacre was referenced in reviews of the movie, even by critics who did not believe Flender's film represented a danger to society. "After the Columbine tragedy, some commentators have wondered if movies like this aren't partly responsible," Roger Ebert wrote in the *Chicago Sun-Times*. "I don't think we have to worry about *Idle Hands*... The only thing this movie is likely to inspire a kid to do is study *Fangoria* magazine to find out how the special effects were achieved." *Idle Hands* was a flop, earning back just $4.2 million of its reported $25 million budget in the US. "The movie got caught up in a political shit storm with certain politicians who hadn't seen the movie but had an agenda to rail against what they thought were the evils of the entertainment industry," director Flender recalled to *SciFiNow* in 2020.

On May 4, 1999, McCain's Senate Commerce, Science, and Transportation Committee held a hearing on the marketing of violence to children. Expert witnesses included William J. Bennett, who had served as Secretary of Education under President Reagan and co-founded the conservative think tank Empower America. As part of his address to the commission, Bennett showed clips from films he argued were irresponsibly violent, including the stabbing of Drew Barrymore's character in *Scream*. "Had enough?" Bennett asked the commission. "That's what a lot of Americans have had, they've had enough. A lot of American parents have had enough."

In June 1999, President Clinton announced that the Federal Trade Commission would conduct a study on whether movie, music, and video game companies were using violent imagery and language to attract young consumers. As part of the announcement, Clinton read aloud from ads for video games, including one that claimed the product was "more fun than shooting your neighbor's cat."

In the wake of Columbine, Dimension was no longer enthusiastic about putting out an R-rated movie with the themes or title of *Killing Mrs. Tingle*. Williamson reworked the film, lightening its tone, so the movie could obtain a PG-13 rating. "It was just darker, and bloodier, and people died," he would recall of his original version on the *Happy Horror Time* podcast in 2023. Dimension released Williamson's film under the name *Teaching Mrs. Tingle* in August 1999. The film grossed an anemic $8 million in the US.

Don Mancini was another screenwriter, and aspirant director, whose plans were derailed by the controversy that erupted about Hollywood's violent output. The prime creative force behind the *Child's Play* franchise wanted to follow *Bride of Chucky* with a fifth movie in the series, one he hoped to direct. Mancini had become friends with Jennifer Tilly during the production of *Bride of Chucky* and planned on having her return for the next film, which he titled *Seed of Chucky*. Mancini pitched Universal on having the actress both voice her *Bride of Chucky* character Tiffany—whose soul has become trapped in the body of a doll—and play 'Jennifer Tilly,' a parodical version of the actress.

After the tragedy in Columbine, Universal put *Seed of Chucky* on hold. "In the wake of Columbine, a lot of fingers were pointed, and some of them were pointed at Hollywood and the entertainment industry in general," Mancini would recall to *Fangoria*. "It sort of put the brakes on the forward motion of this movie, along with a lot of others, particularly at Universal. Chucky was never mentioned in the Columbine case, but pressure was brought to bear on Hollywood in general, and studio heads in particular, to curb their marketing of violent material to teenagers."

The cultural ripples caused by the controversy following the Columbine massacre extended beyond the borders of the US. At the time of the shootings, Toronto-based director John Fawcett and his screenwriting collaborator Karen Walton were prepping to film a werewolf film called *Ginger*

Snaps. The movie hinged around a pair of death-obsessed teenage sisters, Brigitte and Ginger. After Ginger gets her first period, she is bitten by an animal and starts to physically transform.

Fawcett and Walton found their fresh twist on the werewolf genre receiving attention from local media in the wake of Columbine. On June 1, 1999, the *Toronto Star* published an article headlined "Casting directors boycott Toronto teen slasher movie." Written by the newspaper's entertainment columnist Sid Adilman, the story revealed that six prominent local casting directors had refused to work on *Ginger Snaps*. Their decision was driven by the Columbine killings and a subsequent high school shooting in the Canadian town of Taber. According to Fawcett, his ability to cast the film was further hampered by Adilman's article. "We sent Scarlett Johansson a script to see if she was interested in Brigitte," the director told *The Guardian* in 2021, "but her mother had read the [...] article and didn't want her daughter involved."

Fawcett eventually cast Emily Perkins as Brigitte and Katharine Isabelle as Ginger. *Ginger Snaps* played on 80 screens in Canada, but the film failed to secure proper theatrical distribution in the US. After *Ginger Snaps* was released to the home entertainment market, though, it swiftly found an appreciative audience among horror fans. *Fangoria* readers voted to give the movie the magazine's 2002 Chainsaw Award for Best Limited Release Film/Direct-to-Video Film over Guillermo del Toro's *The Devil's Backbone* and Mike Mendez's *The Convent*. Perkins and Isabelle would return for a pair of 2004 franchise continuations, *Ginger Snaps 2: Unleashed* and a 19th-century prequel *Ginger Snaps Back: The Beginning*. "You don't sit down to make a movie thinking, 'I'm going to make a cult classic,'" Walton told the horror website Bloody Disgusting in 2020. "John and I just really wanted to make a movie we would go and see... We weren't trying to make some huge grand feminist theory thing. I was just telling it like it was for me."

Kevin Williamson had written a 35-page treatment for *Scream 3*, which he intended to set at Woodsboro High School. The Columbine tragedy prompted Dimension and Wes Craven to reconsider returning to the original film's setting. "He had a great take on what he thought *Scream 3* should have been," says Julie Plec. "Then Wes, post-Columbine, said, 'I don't want to do kids killing kids right now.' So *Scream 3* had to go in the trash."

Bob Weinstein still planned for Craven to shoot *Scream 3* in the summer of 1999, when the core cast was available. Williamson did not believe he had the time to write a new *Scream* movie from scratch because of his involvement in other projects, including *Teaching Mrs. Tingle*, and dropped out of the film. "Bob Weinstein wanted to make it in Neve and Courteney's hiatus window, and Kevin said, 'I can't do it,' and Bob went and got somebody else," says Plec. "It was inevitable, but that was sad."

Weinstein hired Ehren Kruger, who had written the script for 2000's Dimension-produced action-thriller *Reindeer Games*, to come up with a new screenplay. Kruger would tell *Fangoria* that Dimension had initially wanted to tone down the violence featured in the third *Scream*. "There was one point, when all of this was getting going and Columbine was at its height, when the studio was going to do it bloodless, with no violence at all," said the writer. "Wes kind of came in and said, 'Be serious, guys. Either we make a *Scream* movie or we make a movie and call it something else. But if it's a *Scream* movie, it's going to have certain standards.'"

Kruger's script was set in Los Angeles and took place during the production of film-within-a-film *Stab 3*. The screenplay would subsequently be given an uncredited polish by another writer, Laeta Kalogridis, and Craven also worked on the script. "Ehren's sensibilities weren't the same as Kevin's, and it showed, I think," says Patrick Lussier, who edited the film. "*Scream 3* leans more into the humor and the caper of trying to solve the murder. The joke on the set was that it was very *Scooby-Doo*, to the point where Neve and Courteney gave Wes a *Scooby-Doo* sculpture on one of their last days."

David Arquette and Courteney Cox had become a couple over the course of shooting the first two *Scream* movies, and the pair married in June 1999. "I remember David and Courteney at the read-through [of the first *Scream*], sitting next to each other, and watching that chemistry kind of explode in real time," says Plec. The couple cut their honeymoon short to shoot *Scream 3*.

In addition to Campbell and the Arquettes, the cast for the third film featured Emily Mortimer, Parker Posey, Patrick Dempsey, Scott Foley, Jenny McCarthy, and horror veteran Lance Henriksen. *Scream 3* had a budget of $40 million, more than twice that of the original. After being mostly hands-off on the second film, Bob Weinstein was heavily involved during the production of *Scream 3*. "He would call us every morning before shooting and scream at us for two hours about the script and then Laeta would go off in her trailer and write," producer Marianne Maddalena would recall to Padraic Maroney, author of the 2021 book *It All Began With A Scream*.

Courteney Cox, Parker Posey, and David Arquette in *Scream 3* (2000).

Many critics took a knife to the film, the most recent of a dozen or so movies in the vein of *Scream* that they might have seen in the just over three years since the release of Craven and Williamson's first collaboration. "This *Scream* has been widely marketed as the series' final installment," wrote The A.V. Club critic Keith Phipps. "Better late than never." *Scream 3* was released on February 4, 2000, and earned $89 million in the US, the first film in the series not to cross the $100 million mark at the domestic box office.

Director David Twohy was deep into pre-production on the science fiction-horror film *Pitch Black* and was still searching for an actor to play the movie's third lead character.

Twohy had cast Australian actress Radha Mitchell as a spaceship crew member named Fry and Cole Hauser as a morphine-addicted bounty hunter called Johns. The director was now on the hunt for the right person to inhabit the role of a criminal, Riddick, who would emerge as the antihero of his story about crash survivors attempting to survive on a desert planet full of lethal nocturnal creatures. As the start of shooting approached, the film's backers, Interscope Communications, suggested that the director consider fading but well-known action star Steven Seagal.

Twohy had begun his Hollywood career in horror. He had worked on the screenplay for Mick Garris' directorial debut *Critters 2*, and went on to write *Warlock*, a supernatural horror film directed by future *Halloween H20* filmmaker Steve Miner and distributed in the US by Trimark in 1991. Twohy hit the big time when his screenplay for a film version of the '60s TV show *The Fugitive* became the 1993 blockbuster of the same name, but his directorial debut, the 1996 science fiction film *The Arrival*, failed to set the box office alight. Still, the director refused to consider casting Seagal as Riddick, believing that the *Under Siege* actor was entirely wrong for the role. "I said, 'Not going to do that. Just not going to do that,'" the director recalled in 2021 during an appearance on the podcast *Just the Facts with Alex Zane*. "And they said, 'Well, David, you may have the choice of making the movie with Steven Seagal or not making the movie at all…' And so I said, 'I would rather shut it down.'"

Fortunately for Twohy, Interscope Communications founder Ted Field had another casting suggestion: Vin Diesel. The actor was much less famous

Vin Diesel in *Pitch Black* (2000).

than Seagal but had recently been cast by Steven Spielberg in *Saving Private Ryan*. "Vin and I talked, and then he auditioned, we put him on film with Radha and Cole, and then we cast him off that," Twohy told Alex Zane.

The original script for *Pitch Black*—then titled *Nightfall*—was written by siblings Ken and Jim Wheat, whose screenplay credits included *A Nightmare on Elm Street 4* and *The Fly II*. Interscope executive David Madden had asked the pair to write a film about a planet where ghosts appear after sunset. Interscope liked the brothers' script but decided they didn't want the movie to feature ghosts after all. Once the siblings had rewritten the screenplay, replacing the supernatural antagonists with ravenous aliens, the studio approached Twohy about first doing his own draft and then directing the film.

The shoot for *Pitch Black* took place in Australia, with Twohy filming interiors at Queensland's Village Roadshow Studios and exteriors in the outback town of Coober Pedy around 500 miles north of Adelaide. "Those studios in Queensland are pretty comfortable, but then, on location, we were out in the desert," says Radha Mitchell. "There's this place called Coober Pedy where everybody lives underground. It's an opal mining town; it's the kind of place you go if you want to go off the radar." Mitchell had become well known in her native Australia for starring in the soap opera *Neighbours* and was just starting out on her film career. When she was cast in *Pitch Black*, the actress' most significant big-screen appearance was in director Lisa Cholodenko's 1998 romantic drama *High Art*. "*Pitch Black* had an excitement from the beginning, everybody in it was really bringing their game," says Mitchell. "Everyone was doing push-ups in between takes—and maybe that was Vin Diesel's influence—but there was a real sense of putting everything into it, including sweat."

Mitchell remembers Diesel as being particularly driven in his ambition to make the character of Riddick a memorable one. "He had this action-hero vision even at this point," she says. "In some ways, he was a motivational force for the project, and in other ways, you know, he was kind of difficult. He had opinions and—in the context of not being who he is now—it was a process, at times, getting heard."

The actress recalls the fate of her character being a matter of debate during the production of the film, which would eventually end with Fry perishing. "There was conversation about it, and I was always pro [the character dying]," she says. "Like, 'Yeah, how cool!' In reflection, that was silly; I could have stuck around for the rest of it. But at the time, it was going to be just one film."

Radha Mitchell in *Pitch Black.*

Pitch Black had a trio of young, good-looking stars but a tone and setting far removed from *Scream* and its ilk. Jeff Walker, who worked on the film's marketing campaign, believed that positive word of mouth ahead of the release date would be crucial to the film's success. "That was one that benefited from early targeted screenings as much as any film I ever worked on, because no one was expecting it," he says. "We would do screenings for one or two journalists or a group of fans literally months before it opened. That was one that came out of nowhere as far as the media was concerned—and obviously launched Vin's career." USA Films released *Pitch Black* on February 18, 2000, just a month after the box office failure of the Robin Tunney-starring *Supernova.* Twohy's film grossed $11 million over its opening weekend and went on to become a minor sleeper hit, earning $53 million worldwide.

In May 2000, *Variety* reported that Twohy would follow *Pitch Black* with a film called *Proteus*, the first movie in a three-picture deal he had signed with Dimension and Miramax. *Proteus* was described as "a suspenser about the American crew of a haunted World War II submarine in enemy waters" and was based on a script co-written by *Pi* filmmaker Darren Aronofsky.

Twohy assembled a cast led by Bruce Greenwood and Olivia Williams and shot the film in London, emphasizing atmosphere over jump scares, to the annoyance of the Weinstein brothers. Dimension renamed the film *Below* and released it in fewer than 200 theaters on October 11, 2002. The film earned just $201,000 over its opening weekend.

Twohy would not complete his three-picture deal. Instead, the director reunited with Diesel for a second Riddick adventure. After *Pitch Black*, the actor had starred in 2001's *The Fast and the Furious* and 2002's *XXX*, both hits. Thanks to Diesel's raised profile, he and Twohy were able to secure a budget of around $105 million for a Universal-backed *Pitch Black* sequel, *The Chronicles of Riddick*. The director downplayed the horror elements on the second film, partly because he and Diesel wanted to make a movie more in the fantasy realm than *Pitch Black* and partly to secure the PG-13 rating demanded by Universal. Released in June 2004, *The Chronicles of Riddick* earned $115 million worldwide, over twice the gross of *Pitch Black*, but was still regarded as a box office bomb because of its high budget.

Twohy went on to direct 2009's superior thriller *A Perfect Getaway*, starring Milla Jovovich and *Scream 2* actor Timothy Olyphant. Although Diesel had skipped the second *Fast & Furious* film, 2003's *2 Fast 2 Furious*, he made a cameo appearance at the end of 2006's *The Fast and the Furious: Tokyo Drift*. With the Riddick movies seemingly having run their course, the actor recommitted himself to the *Fast & Furious* franchise. Diesel starred alongside Paul Walker and Michelle Rodriguez in 2009's *Fast & Furious* and then made room for Dwayne Johnson to join the cast for 2011's *Fast Five*. The combination of the *Pitch Black* star and *The Mummy Returns* breakout actor turned the *Fast & Furious* franchise into a global box office juggernaut. *Fast Five* grossed $626 million around the world. The franchise's next two films, 2013's *Fast & Furious 6* and 2015's *Furious 7*, would earn even more.

The failure of *Scream 3* to cross the $100 million domestic box office mark was one of several signs that the public had become less interested in the kind of horror Williamson and Craven pioneered with the original *Scream*. 1998's *I Still Know What You Did Last Summer* and 2000's *Urban Legends: Final Cut* both grossed much less than the original films in their respective series. In 2001, the slasher movie *Valentine*, whose cast was led by

Buffy the Vampire Slayer actor David Boreanaz, proved another box office underperformer; the same year's spooky psychological thriller *Soul Survivors* was a full-on bomb, despite featuring another *Buffy* cast member, Eliza Dushku; the Brittany Murphy-starring tale *Cherry Falls*, about a killer who targets virgins, bypassed cinemas altogether to premiere on the USA Network.

In the spring of 2000, however, New Line proved that audiences could still be enticed to see a slasher film packed with teenagers as long as the villain was Death itself. *Final Destination* starred *Idle Hands* actor Devon Sawa as a New York high school student named Alex who receives a premonition that the Paris-bound plane he has just boarded will catch fire in the air. After Alex, some of his classmates, and a teacher disembark, the plane does indeed explode. During the days that follow, the survivors start passing away and Alex realizes they are being murdered by the Grim Reaper.

The story for *Final Destination* was conceived by a New Line employee named Jeffrey Reddick. "The original idea came from an article I read about a woman who was on vacation and her mother told her to switch flights because she had a bad feeling," he says. "The woman switched planes and the plane she was scheduled to be on crashed. So that idea stuck with me."

Black and queer, Reddick had a difficult childhood growing up in eastern Kentucky during the 1970s. "I was dealing with a lot of racism and homophobia," he says. "I wasn't out yet, but I was just hearing it all around me. There was so much stuff that I could have internalized and [that would have] made me a very rage-filled person. Horror let me let that fear out in a healthy way."

Reddick adored Wes Craven's original *A Nightmare on Elm Street*. "I saw it in a double feature at a drive-in with *Alone in the Dark*," he says. "It just scared the hell out of me." Reddick wrote down his idea for a prequel to Craven's film and sent it to Robert Shaye at the New Line offices in New York. "I'm 14 years old in Kentucky. I have no idea how the film business works," says Reddick. "He sends it back to me and he's like, 'We don't take unsolicited material.' I wrote him back, and I'm like, 'Excuse me, sir, but I've seen three of your movies, so I think you can take five minutes to read my story.' Only the young can be so ballsy. He read my treatment, he got back in touch with me, and I ended up staying pen pals with him and his assistant, Joy Mann, from age 14 to 19."

Like Kevin Williamson, Reddick originally dreamed of becoming an actor. At the age of 19, he moved to New York and studied at The American

Academy of Dramatic Arts. He also secured an internship at New Line, where he would be hired as an executive assistant on a permanent basis. Reddick wrote a spec script for an episode of TV show *The X-Files* inspired by the story he had read about the woman who switched planes. "My friends at New Line read the script and they were like, 'You should develop this as a feature,'" he says. Reddick turned his script into the screenplay for a film he titled *Flight 180*, a supernatural slasher with a final boy instead of a final girl. "I wanted to flip the genre on its head," he says. "I thought it would be interesting to have a male lead going through this."

Reddick sent his treatment to Zide-Perry Productions, a new company founded in 1997 by producers Craig Perry and Warren Zide, who had met working in the New Line mailroom. The trio spent six months working on the concept, sending treatments to New Line and receiving notes from the company. In the initial pitch, the potential victims who got off the plane had no connection with each other and were older than the teenagers who would make up the main cast of characters in the finished film. Reddick was asked to lower their ages because of the success of *Scream* and the other recent teen slashers. "Obviously there were movies that were coming out that seemed to be catering to the demographic," says Craig Perry. When New Line dragged its heels about buying the project, Zide and Perry threatened to sell it to Dimension instead. "They had to shit or get off the pot," says Perry. Facing the prospect of losing the project to their rivals, New Line acquired Reddick's screenplay.

The company initially liked the idea of author and *Hellraiser* filmmaker Clive Barker directing the film. "He was the first person that they [approached]," says Perry. "It just wasn't his. Clive is his own sort of nation state, generating and executing material, so I was not surprised at all [when he passed]."

The company hired director James Wong and his writing partner Glen Morgan, both *X-Files* veterans. The pair pitched that Death would arrange for the killing of the survivors using familiar objects and scenarios in complex or unexpected ways. "They took the idea of 'Let's make Death an invisible force' and [asked] 'Then what would Death do?'" says Perry. "Death would come from a confluence of small things, not necessarily a big thing."

As Zide and Perry were working on *Final Destination*, the pair were also developing the high school sex comedy *American Pie*, which Universal would successfully release in 1999. "Casting *Final Destination* was fascinating, because we were doing *American Pie* at the same time," says Perry. "Every young actor in the world is coming through the casting offices. Tobey Maguire came through, for sure. I remember Topher Grace came through as well."

Devon Sawa was cast as the male lead of *Final Destination*, and *House on Haunted Hill* actress Ali Larter was hired to play Alex's classmate Clear. The supporting cast included Amanda Detmer, *Dawson's Creek* star Kerr Smith, and Seann William Scott, who played the character Stifler in *American Pie*. "Seann couldn't get a job because nobody knew who the fuck he was," says Perry. "He was working in our office building. I'd be going to lunch, and he'd be outside after packing boxes, eating a sandwich. We'd given a VHS of *American Pie* early to New Line and they wanted to find a way for Seann to be in *Final Destination*."

The film would find its connection to Clive Barker with the casting of Tony Todd as a mortician. The actor was best known for playing the killer in 1992's *Candyman*, which was based on Barker's short story "The Forbidden." "We looked at every older Black actor," says Perry, speaking before Todd's death in 2024. "Ernie Hudson. Mykelti Williamson. But there's something about Tony Todd. When he says something to you, outside of the little jet of piss that comes out [of you], you actually listen, because you are realizing: this is important. You can't put a price tag on that."

Director Wong shot the film in New York, San Francisco, Toronto, and Vancouver on a budget of $23 million. The production's most elaborate sequence to shoot was Alex's premonition, in which audiences would see the inside of the plane tear apart. "The plane scene was technically complicated, because you've got the chassis of a plane actually there on top of this 10,000-pound pig iron gimbal that is hydraulically operated by this joystick," says Perry. "You would literally move the joystick like a fighter pilot, and the plane would pitch and yaw. It was just a very technically challenging, and physically challenging, sequence to do, but obviously it worked."

New Line was determined to change the name of the film to something other than *Flight 180*. Perry explains that the company "was worried that it was going to come off like an airplane movie. Would you like to hear some of the alternate titles that were proposed? *On Borrowed Time. Fear the Reaper. The Nth Degree. The Third Eye. In the Know. Coming to Get You.* I don't think it would have helped our cause if it was called any of those things." Perry was happy when the studio settled on the title *Final Destination*. "We got lucky," says the producer.

Devon Sawa in *Final Destination* (2000).

Devon Sawa recalls being "blown away" when he saw the finished film. "James Wong and Glen Morgan were geniuses," says the actor. "There were so many things they were doing that they didn't discuss. They had a vision." New Line released *Final Destination* on March 17, 2000. The film grossed $10 million over its opening weekend and was still in the top ten six weeks later, ultimately earning $53 million in the US.

The film's long run on cinema screens prompted New Line to proceed with a sequel. Jeffrey Reddick suggested that the second film open with a catastrophic highway accident caused by a logging truck whose cargo becomes unchained. Ali Larter and Tony Todd both returned for *Final Destination 2*. Devon Sawa did not come back, despite his character having survived the events of the original film. The actor was struggling with alcoholism and took a hiatus from acting in the mid-2000s. "Getting any movie made is challenging, and a lot of pressure is put on actors," says Perry of Sawa's absence from the film. "For a lot of reasons, it was probably best that he was not engaged in the second one. I'm glad that he is healthy, happy, has a family, and [is] doing the good work that he is doing."

New Line released *Final Destination 2* on January 31, 2003. By the end of the movie's theatrical run, it had earned $6 million less domestically than *Final Destination*. The good news for the movie's producers was that,

by 2003, the film industry was benefiting hugely from a comparatively new and growing revenue source with the DVD format. DVDs debuted in Japan in November 1996 and in the US the next year. This new technology proved wildly popular, and by the end of 2000 the number of movies available to buy on DVD had grown to over 10,000. "DVD offset and allowed for so many more titles to be coming out," says Perry. "It created this whole new revenue stream that allowed more volume to get made."

In March 2005, *The Hollywood Reporter* announced that actors Ryan Merriman and Mary Elizabeth Winstead had been cast in a third *Final Destination* tale. *Final Destination 3* was released on February 10, 2006, and earned $54 million in the US, slightly more than the first film in the franchise. According to producer Perry, "I knew [the DVD] would make so much fucking money for them that the prospect of making a fourth one would be a non-conversation, and it was."

That fourth movie was titled *The Final Destination* and began with a disaster at a racetrack. The film was among the first to be shot utilizing the new 3D technology developed by James Cameron's company Lightstorm Entertainment and showcased in the director's 2009 blockbuster hit *Avatar*. "We always wanted to do 3D," says Perry. "Remember, New Line is very scrappy. They did Odorama with John Waters for *Polyester*. They're totally down with the William Castle school of let's-get-butts-in-seats. So why not do it in 3D?"

The Final Destination was released in the summer of 2009 and earned $66 million in the US, the most money any of the films had grossed thus far.

This box office success was helped by higher ticket prices at 3D screenings and the implication of the movie's title that *The Final Destination* would wind up the franchise. Prior to its release, Perry himself believed the fourth film would be the last. "I figured that we're done," he says. "Then, lo and behold, opening weekend, we're like, 'Uh, okay, here we go.' I don't think the fourth one is good at all, actually it sucks. But it was successful enough to give us a chance to redeem ourselves with *5*."

Final Destination 5 was released in the summer of 2011 and earned a disappointing $42 million in the US. With DVD sales having peaked in 2007 and physical media entering a period of steep decline, New Line decided to press pause on a sixth film. "New Line felt, we're going to sit tight for a little bit," says Perry.

Jeffrey Reddick's creative involvement with the franchise had effectively ended with *Final Destination 2*, but the writer is thrilled to remain associated with the franchise. "As a horror fan, I'm really grateful and humbled by the fact that something I started has had the life and the legs that it has," he says. Reddick is also delighted when fans send him a reminder of one particular sequence from the franchise—which they do with regularity. "Almost every week, somebody sends me a photo of them behind a log truck," he says.

As director William Malone toiled on *House on Haunted Hill* for Dark Castle, Robert Zemeckis was completing his own horror film, albeit not for the company he had co-founded. In 1997, Zemeckis signed a five-year deal with DreamWorks. The filmmaker committed to make *Cast Away*, a co-production with 20th Century Fox, which starred Tom Hanks as a FedEx executive trying to survive on a remote island. The director planned to shoot the movie in two chunks, giving Hanks the opportunity to lose weight for the scenes shot after his character has been marooned for four years. Zemeckis was determined to film both parts with the same crew and was looking for a project to keep them employed during the break. He was also searching for a script in the thriller genre, something that Alfred Hitchcock might have made.

Zemeckis warmed to the screenplay for *What Lies Beneath*, a supernatural riff on Hitchcock's *Rear Window*, about a woman, Claire, who suspects that her neighbor has murdered his wife. To play Claire and her spouse Norman, Zemeckis cast A-list stars Michelle Pfeiffer and Harrison Ford. Pfeiffer had long wanted to appear in a genre film. "When I was little, I used to stay up late at night and watch all of those old horror flicks," she was quoted as saying in the film's production notes. "I used to comb the *TV Guide* for any Frankenstein movie, and my all-time favorite as a child was *The Bad Seed.* Obsessed. Obsessed with *The Bad Seed.*" The hiring of Ford and Pfeiffer was an indicator of the film's lavish budget, which was reported as being in the region of $100 million.

Even critics who wrote positive reviews were rarely ecstatic about *What Lies Beneath*, with Geoff Pevere of the *Toronto Star* describing the film as "a horror movie for people who probably don't generally like horror movies." In *Variety*, Emanuel Levy argued that Zemeckis' film was "not spooky or stylish enough to become a must-see for the goodtimes-hungry summer masses."

Levy was proved wrong after DreamWorks released *What Lies Beneath* on July 21, 2000. The film earned $155 million in the US, making it the eighth most popular movie of the year.

The same year saw Kevin Williamson indirectly aid Bob Weinstein in scoring Dimension's biggest hit to date by helping to inspire 2000's Dimension-produced parody *Scary Movie.* The film was directed by Keenen Ivory Wayans, who, as a producer, had previously taken comedic aim at the wave of early '90s movies by Black auteurs with the 1996 film *Don't Be a Menace to South Central While Drinking Your Juice in the Hood. Scary Movie* not only took Williamson's original title for *Scream* but also parodied that film and *I Know What You Did Last Summer.* Made for $19 million and starring Anna Faris in her first significant onscreen role, Wayans' film grossed $278 million around the globe after the movie was released in July 2000. "It was huge to have an African-American director open an R-rated comedy that was that big," Faris' co-star Regina Hall told *Entertainment Weekly* writer Shirley Li in 2017. "It broke the ceiling for what was possible." Three sequels followed over the next six years, with the franchise comfortably outlasting the craze for teen horror films that had spawned the original movie in the first place.

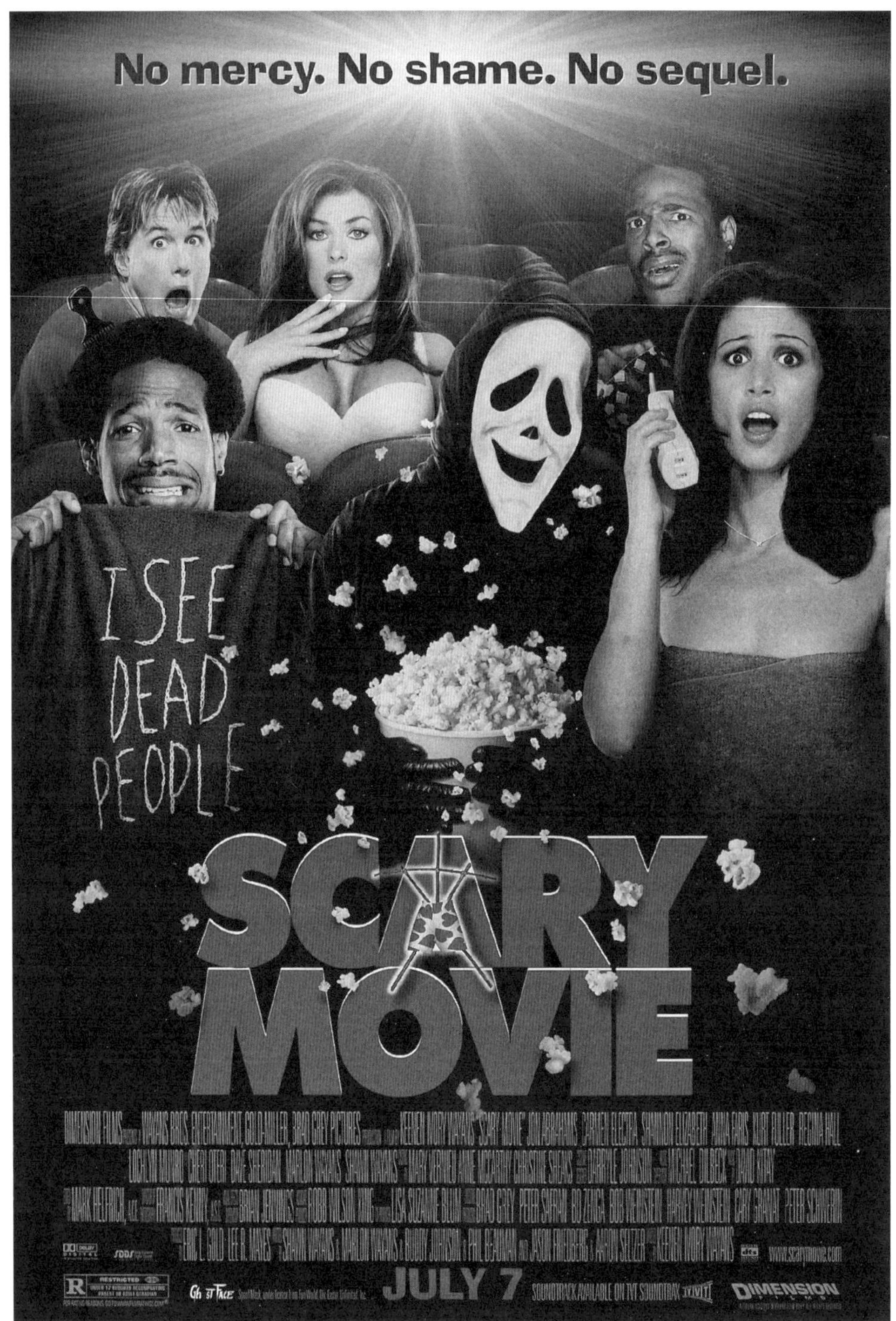
No mercy. No shame. No sequel.
I SEE DEAD PEOPLE
SCARY MOVIE
JULY 7
www.scarymovie.com
DIMENSION

In the spring of 1999, Kevin Bacon was at the Los Angeles visual effects house Amalgamated Dynamics when his wife, fellow actor Kyra Sedgwick, gave him a call. "I'm wearing a black leotard, and there's a guy on his knees and he's rubbing Vaseline on my Johnson," Bacon told his spouse.

Bacon was having grease applied to his genitals as part of the process necessary to create his role in the science fiction-horror film *Hollow Man*. The movie was directed by *RoboCop* and *Starship Troopers* filmmaker Paul Verhoeven and starred Bacon as a brilliant scientist who renders himself invisible but is unable to reverse the process and becomes murderously unhinged. With a cast that also featured Elisabeth Shue and Josh Brolin, *Hollow Man* was the first major movie to tackle the topic of invisibility since John Carpenter's 1992 film *Memoirs of an Invisible Man*. Verhoeven was determined to take advantage of advances in digital effects to make a groundbreaking extravaganza, one that would ultimately cost around $95 million. It was that desire which led to Bacon visiting Amalgamated Dynamics so that technicians could make casts of his head and body.

Unlike many of his famous peers in the acting community, the actor was happy to work on horror projects. "It is a genre I really like," he says. "I like movies that have life or death stakes." Following his appearance in *Friday the 13th*, Bacon had returned to the genre with 1990's much-loved creature feature *Tremors*. "I'm not someone that thinks that all movies are gems, because they're not, but I think *Tremors* is a really well-done movie," he says. "People forget that it was not a box office success, because marketing scary-funny is a tough one to do." 1990 also saw the release of *Flatliners*, about a group of medical students who induce near-death experiences on each other with horrifying results. Directed by Joel Schumacher, the film's starry cast included Bacon, Julia Roberts, and Kiefer Sutherland. "We had a lot of laughs making that movie," says Bacon. "We'd be standing around somebody's body, trying to bring them back to life, and we'd all be laughing."

After *Flatliners*, Bacon enjoyed the most high-profile period of his career, with roles in several acclaimed blockbuster dramas (1991's *JFK*, 1992's *A Few Good Men*, 1995's *Apollo 13*), before he once more returned to horror with 1999's *Stir of Echoes*. Despite the film's trouncing at the box office by both *The Sixth Sense* and *Stigmata*, Bacon remains proud of director David Koepp's movie. "I think that the acting is good, I think the story is scary, I think that the backdrop of working-class Chicago was really well done," he says. "I thought Dave directed the shit out of it."

The *Hollow Man* visual effects were overseen by Scott E. Anderson, who had won an Oscar for his work on 1995's *Babe*. "*Hollow Man* was a nearly impossible script to make," Anderson recalled to the outlet befores & afters in 2020. The shoot would certainly prove a testing one for Bacon. "Honestly, it was really, really challenging," says the actor. "When I got the script, I thought, this is going to be amazing—I mean, most of this is in

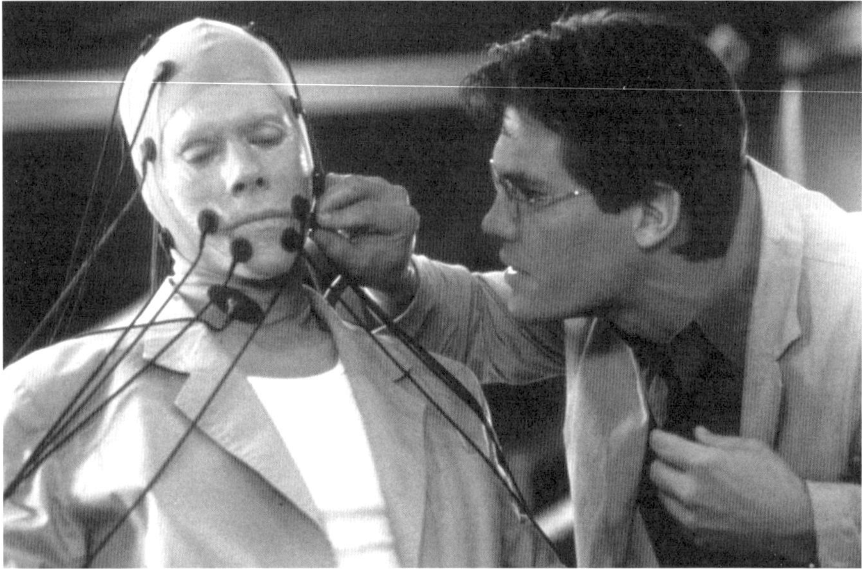

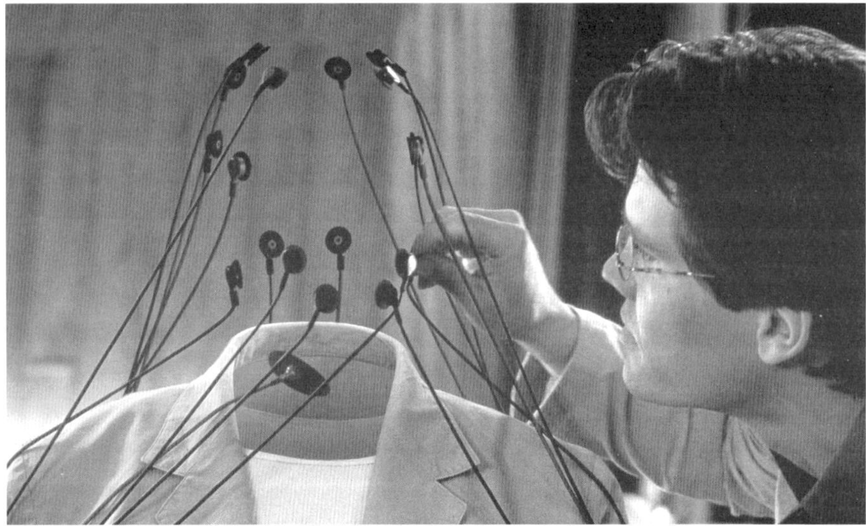

(*From top*) Kevin Bacon and Josh Brolin on the set of *Hollow Man,* and Brolin in the finished film.

voiceover. But Paul Verhoeven felt very strongly that he wanted me to use my body, and the outline of my body, and then have my voice—rightly—interacting with the actors, so they had something to play with. Paul and the effects people were really experimenting with motion control cameras and motion control capture. I [was] often covered in green, with giant green contact lenses that covered my eyes, and [a] green mouth, and green makeup all over, and a green suit."

Sony Pictures opened *Hollow Man* at the start of August 2000. The film was a hit, grossing $73 million domestically and $190 million in all. Bacon had the satisfaction of starring in a film that was not only successful but also pushed at the boundaries of what was possible in the arena of visual effects. "You know, everyone's familiar with the green screen—well, I *was* the green screen," he says.

To Bacon's mild irritation, in the minds of many horror fans, the actor would remain most associated with playing the doomed camp counselor Jack in *Friday the 13th*. "I'm always horrified by the fact that, when it comes to autograph hounds, that's probably the number one picture that I'm asked to sign," he says. "Me, with blood coming out of my mouth and an arrow through my neck. After a while, it just gets to you. You're like, really, do I have to sign another picture of me dead?"

Scream franchise editor Patrick Lussier made his directorial debut with 2000's Dimension-produced straight-to-video *The Prophecy 3: The Ascent,* the third entry in the Christopher Walken-starring horror franchise. "That was amazing," says Lussier. "Chris was great. Because we had him for so few days, he wasn't the main character of the story, but it was great to sort of finish his character's arc."

Dimension next asked Lussier to direct a movie that had a title but precious little else. "They were like, 'We want to make a movie called *Dracula 2000*. We don't know what it is, but we want to do it,'" he says. "The big challenge with *Dracula 2000* is that it had to come out in the year 2000."

Lussier had roughly a year to make the movie from a standing start and teamed with *Prophecy 3* co-writer Joel Soisson to work on the film's story. The pair came up with a modern-day continuation of Bram Stoker's novel in which the body of Dracula is stolen by a gang of criminals who plan to sell the vampire's blood for money. "In the original version that we wrote, the thieves knew what they were stealing, and they were going to sell immortality for a million bucks a shot," says Lussier. With the clock ticking, the filmmaker was aghast at Dimension's decision to hire other writers, including *Scream 3* scribe Ehren Kruger, to rework the screenplay. Equally annoying to the director: in the final draft of the script, the movie's thieves were now unaware that they had stolen Dracula's occupied coffin. "Ehren Kruger came onboard, and did a rewrite, uncredited, and made every single character stupid, which just drove me crazy," says Lussier. "Ehren was just doing the studio notes, so not to badmouth him, but he also got paid a fucking fortune, so he can take the badmouthing." The rewriting process resulted in a delay to the movie's filming. "We didn't start shooting until the end of June," says Lussier, who directed the film in Toronto and New Orleans. "So it was almost six months to the day from the first day of photography to release."

The delay in production did mean that Lussier was able to cast Gerard Butler in the role of Dracula. The then-obscure Scottish actor had impressed the director in his audition but had become seemingly unavailable because of his starring role in the TV miniseries *Attila*. "We had auditions for months," says Lussier. "Gerry was the very first day, but he wasn't available. The best thing those rewrites did is [...] gave us the time for Gerry to be almost finished [with] *Attila*, so he could come be our Dracula."

Gerard Butler in *Dracula 2000* (2000).

Butler's co-stars included Christopher Plummer as an antique-dealing descendant of Stoker's Van Helsing and *Trainspotting* actor Jonny Lee Miller as his assistant. Lussier recalls that, in his and Soisson's original concept for the film, Miller's character "was an apprentice vampire hunter, an apprentice to Van Helsing, so everybody knew what was going on. He had signed on [for] that script. By the time he showed up, we had this complete other version, and his character was dumbed down, and he had no idea what he was doing. Jonny was just like, 'Look, I'll do whatever you want.'" One of the things Lussier asked the actor to do was utter onscreen the (intentionally) hilarious line, "Never, ever fuck with an antiques dealer." "The line 'Never, ever fuck with an antiques dealer'—that was a joke Jonny used to say," the director recalls. "We were like, well, fuck, we have to write *that* in the movie."

The filmmaker wrapped principal photography in early September 2000, but Dimension asked for reshoots, which Lussier started directing at the end of October. Wes Craven acted as executive producer on the film, which would be marketed as *Wes Craven Presents: Dracula 2000*. In an *Entertainment Weekly* article by Rebecca Ascher-Walsh published in November 2000, Craven alluded with obvious weariness to Dimension's handling of the production. "As Patrick says, 'They don't pay you for what you do. They pay you for what they do to you,'" said the *Scream* director. Reporter Ascher-Walsh noted that Lussier would deliver a finished print on December 12, less than two weeks before the film was set to come out. "It shouldn't be normal, but that's the way Dimension makes films," Craven said in the article. "What's the benefit of making movies so fast? There's no benefit whatsoever. It's terribly difficult and completely unnecessary."

Dracula 2000 was released in the US on December 22, 2000. "We came out days before our sell-by date," says Lussier. The film grossed $33 million in the US, much less than the *Scream* movies but much more than Miramax's abortive Oscar play *All the Pretty Horses*, which arrived in cinemas three days after Lussier's film. "Miramax made a lot of prestige films at the time that didn't necessarily make money," says the director. "The Dimension movies, because they could be made for a lot less money and were a lot more popcorn, had a tendency to be more profitable." In many territories, the film was released in 2001. When the movie debuted in the UK during the summer of that year, it was retitled *Dracula 2001*.

Lussier and co-writer Soisson made two *Dracula 2000* sequels for Dimension, 2003's *Dracula II: Ascension* and 2005's *Dracula III: Legacy*, both of which the filmmaker directed in the cheap shooting location of Romania.

"Dimension only wanted one as a direct-to-video thing, which was a big market at that time," says Lussier. "Joel and I had an idea for two, so we said, we'll spend a little bit more going in, and we'll give you two movies. We scheduled them as one movie, shot them at the same time."

The next Dimension project on which Lussier worked—a werewolf movie with the appropriate title of *Cursed*—would prove a much less cost-effective affair.

Legendary Italian producer Dino De Laurentiis had not worked on *The Silence of the Lambs*, but few people were more desperate to see another film about Anthony Hopkins' Dr. Hannibal Lecter. In the early '80s, De Laurentiis had bought the rights to Thomas Harris' first book to feature the cannibal psychiatrist, 1981's *Red Dragon*. To write and direct the film, De Laurentiis had hired Michael Mann, whose credits included directing the 1983 horror movie *The Keep*. Mann's movie starred William Petersen as FBI profiler Will Graham, Tom Noonan as a serial killer known as the Tooth Fairy, and Brian Cox as Lecter. The film was released in 1986 under the title *Manhunter* and was not a box office success.

De Laurentiis had passed on the opportunity to produce the adaptation of Harris' second Lecter novel, *The Silence of the Lambs*. The producer did keep control over the screen rights to the character of Lecter, however, loaning them out to Orion Pictures, which produced the film. "We were afraid to make the movie," the producer's wife and business partner Martha De Laurentiis told *The Guardian* in 2001. "You could be terrible and say no, or you could demand money, which was kind of, 'Why be greedy?' Or you let them use it, and if it's successful, your asset has value."

The value of the Lecter character increased exponentially after *The Silence of the Lambs* became a box office hit and multiple Oscar-winner. When Harris finally finished a third book about the serial killer, titled *Hannibal*, in the late 1990s, Dino De Laurentiis paid $10 million for the film rights. That investment seemed justified after *Hannibal* was published in June 1999 and spent seven weeks at the top of *The New York Times* hardcover fiction chart. De Laurentiis would produce the film in cahoots with Universal and MGM, the latter studio having bought the assets from the struggling Orion Pictures in 1997.

Hopkins was willing to reprise the role of Lecter for a payday of $11 million. Dino and Martha De Laurentiis had less luck securing the services of director Jonathan Demme and Hopkins' *Silence of the Lambs* co-star Jodie Foster, who had played FBI trainee Clarice Starling. The two producers were shooting the submarine thriller *U-571* in Malta when they discovered via Demme's agent Rick Nicita that the director had decided not to make *Hannibal.* To replace him, they approached Ridley Scott, who was also in Malta, working on *Gladiator.* The *Alien* filmmaker initially believed the De Laurentiises wanted him to direct a movie about the famous Carthaginian general Hannibal. "I said, 'Dino, I don't want to do elephants coming over the Alps,'" Scott told *The Guardian.* "'I'm doing a Roman movie now.'"

Once the misunderstanding was cleared up, Scott expressed interest in directing the movie. The filmmaker had concerns about the end of Harris' *Hannibal* novel, in which Starling and Lecter become lovers. Scott, Harris, and screenwriter Steve Zaillian—who had won an Oscar for scripting Steven Spielberg's 1993 film *Schindler's List*—spent four days in a Los Angeles hotel suite coming up with a less romantic conclusion to the film.

After Foster, too, decided not to return for the sequel, the producers and Scott cast Julianne Moore in the role of Starling. The supporting cast included Gary Oldman, who played one of Lecter's former patients, and Ray Liotta, who was cast as a corrupt Justice Department official named Paul Krendler. Working with a reported $85 million budget—four times the cost of *The Silence of the Lambs*—Scott shot the film in the US and Florence, Italy.

With *The Silence of the Lambs*, Demme had tipped his hat towards the horror realm with the housing of Hopkins' Lecter in a subterranean dungeon-like cell, the murders and mutilations committed by Ted Levine's 'Buffalo Bill,' and the casting of George A. Romero in a cameo role. Scott's film boasted a couple of set pieces that planted both feet in the genre. In one, Oldman's disfigured millionaire Mason Verger is attacked by the large pigs with which he had planned to kill Lecter. In another, Hopkins' psychiatrist removes the top of Krendler's cranium and feeds Liotta's character fried sections of his own brain. For the sequence, Liotta requested that he eat chicken on-camera. "Dark meat chicken, it's hard to chew," the actor explained to *GQ* in 2019. "So they had dark meat chicken on the day, and I'm chewing, eating my brain… I was doing a movie in Canada when the movie opened and I heard that people, some just left. Even when I watched it, I said, 'Oh my God, that's just disgusting.' But it was fun to do."

Released by MGM on February 9, 2001, Scott's film was another huge hit. The movie earned $165 million at the domestic box office and another

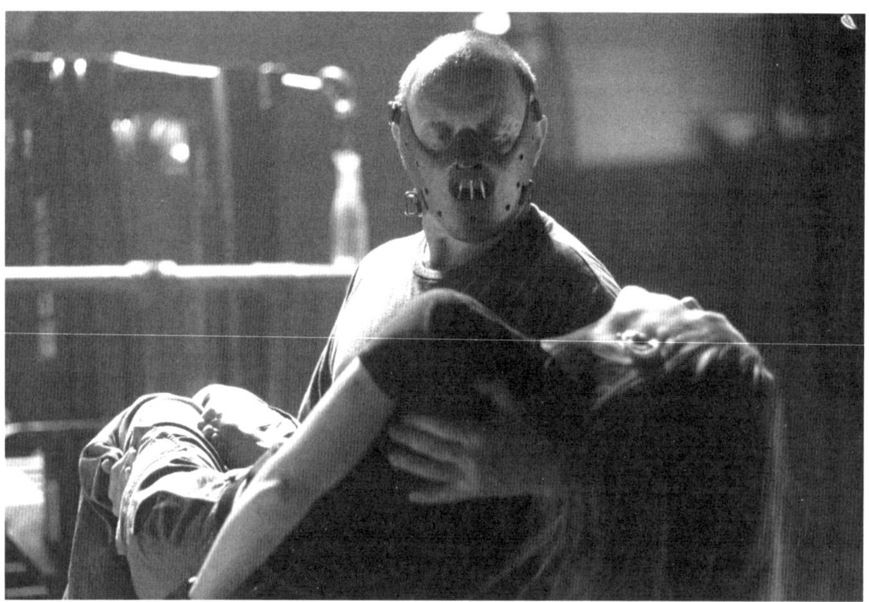

Anthony Hopkins and Julianne Moore in *Hannibal* (2001).

$185 million in foreign territories. Having spent almost a decade waiting to make a *Silence of the Lambs* sequel, Dino De Laurentiis swiftly put in motion another franchise entry. Even before *Hannibal* arrived in cinemas, *Silence of the Lambs* screenwriter Ted Tally had agreed to work on the script for a new version of *Red Dragon*, which would keep the book's original title.

The film was directed by *Rush Hour* filmmaker Brett Ratner and once again starred Hopkins as Lecter, with Edward Norton playing Will Graham and Ralph Fiennes portraying the Tooth Fairy. *Red Dragon* was released in October 2002 and earned $209 million worldwide, much less than Ridley Scott's film. "*Hannibal* came 10 years after *The Silence of the Lambs*, while *Red Dragon* followed *Hannibal* by only a year and a half, so perhaps anticipation for the film wasn't as frenzied this time around," suggested *Entertainment Weekly* writer Dave Karger.

Karger could also have pointed out that much had changed in the real world during the 20 months since the release of *Hannibal*. American soil had come under attack for the first time in 60 years. The country was now engaged in a so-called War on Terror, a conflict with vague parameters and uncertain aims. For many people, what they had seen, and would continue to see, on the news made the mannered mayhem of Hannibal Lecter look like something from a different age.

CHAPTER 5

"SOMETIMES THE WORLD OF THE LIVING GETS MIXED UP WITH THE WORLD OF THE DEAD."

Writer-director Alejandro Amenábar's 2001 film *The Others* had several superficial similarities with Jan de Bont's commercially successful but overstuffed *The Haunting*. The movie was set in a large old house where characters were assaulted by what seemed to be supernatural phenomena, for example. Amenábar's movie also boasted the involvement of major stars. Nicole Kidman played the lead role, and the movie's production entities included Cruise/Wagner, the company co-founded by Kidman's superstar husband Tom Cruise. However, in interviews to support his film, Amenábar emphasized that the movie was very different from de Bont's tale, even going so far as to describe *The Others* as the "anti-*Haunting*." "Nowadays, we have so many pictures with such loud sounds that really hurt your ears, it's like trying to 'Boom!' the audience all the time," the director told Associated Press journalist Anthony Breznican.

In the film, Kidman played Grace Stewart, who lives on the island of Jersey in the English Channel just after the end of World War II. Grace's soldier husband—portrayed by Christopher Eccleston—is missing, presumed dead, and her two young children suffer from a disease which makes them allergic to light. After Grace's servants mysteriously vanish, she employs a new, and somewhat sinister, trio to help maintain her family's mansion-sized house. Meanwhile, her daughter claims that she has started seeing people the audience assumes, at least at first, are ghostly presences.

Atmospherically framed by Spanish cinematographer Javier Aguirresarobe, the film evoked the mood-terrors to be found in Robert Wise's 1963 version of *The Haunting* far more effectively than de Bont's film. In fact, Amenábar's

Alakina Mann and Nicole Kidman in *The Others* (2001).

principal inspirations were two other vintage haunted house movies: 1961's Jack Clayton-directed *The Innocents* and 1980's *The Changeling*, the film which had so disturbed a young Neve Campbell.

Amenábar was born in Chile in 1972. The following year, just a couple of weeks before military leader General Pinochet seized power, his family fled the country and made a new home in Spain. *The Others* director was just 23 and still studying film at Madrid's Complutense University when he directed his first movie, *Thesis*, about a student who discovers that a snuff film was shot at her university. *Thesis* proved a sensation on its release in Spain, winning seven categories at the 1996 Goya Awards. Amenábar followed *Thesis* with *Abre los ojos*, a.k.a. *Open Your Eyes*, in which a man finds himself living different lives in separate realities. *Open Your Eyes* attracted the attention of Tom Cruise, whose company Cruise/Wagner acquired the remake rights. The actor convinced *Jerry Maguire* filmmaker Cameron Crowe to direct an American version, which starred Cruise and would be released as *Vanilla Sky* in December 2001.

Cruise's producing partner Paula Wagner was impressed by Amenábar's script for *The Others* and its climactic revelation that the film's lead character and her two children are not being haunted by ghosts but are themselves dead. Cruise also loved Amenábar's screenplay and gave it to Kidman, who signed on to play Grace. The 12-week shoot for *The Others* took place in Madrid, with exteriors being filmed in the north of Spain.

Cruise/Wagner made the film in collaboration with Harvey and Bob Weinstein, who would be credited as executive producers on the film and distributed the movie in the US. The brothers disagreed about whether *The Others* should be released via Miramax or Dimension. Amenábar's movie had a classy enough patina to possibly attract awards, and Harvey Weinstein believed that Miramax should distribute the film rather than his brother's genre label. *The Others* would eventually be released by Dimension but with Harvey deeply involved in the movie's marketing campaign.

In February 2001, Kidman and Cruise announced that they had split up, but both attended the premiere of *The Others* in Los Angeles on August 7. Cruise's publicist Pat Kingsley ensured that Kidman had disappeared into the cinema before the *Top Gun* star left his limousine to work the red carpet.

Dimension released *The Others* on August 10, 2001, and the film earned a respectable $14 million over its first weekend in cinemas. Strong word of mouth allowed *The Others* to keep its fourth place position on the box office chart the next weekend, when the movie earned almost $11 million. By the end of the second weekend in September, *The Others* had taken in $67 million at the domestic box office.

On the morning of Tuesday, September 11, 2001, America, and the world, watched in horror as the World Trade Center's Twin Towers collapsed in lower Manhattan after al-Qaeda terrorists hijacked two planes and flew them into the pair of buildings. The same day saw another terrorist-piloted plane destroy part of the Pentagon. Passengers on a fourth flight overwhelmed their hijackers, causing the plane to crash in Pennsylvania, killing all onboard.

While a shocked US population grieved the dead, the entertainment industry changed its plans to accommodate the new, terrible reality. *Lethal Weapon* was yanked from TV schedules and images of the Twin Towers were digitally erased from Sam Raimi's upcoming *Spider-Man*. At the start of October, *Variety* published a guest column by MPAA president Jack Valenti in which he laid out his thoughts about how the film business should respond to the crisis. "We have to screw our courage to the sticking place, we have to get on with lives and do our job, to tell visual stories which offer our fellow citizens an interlude so sorely needed at this time," he wrote.

During the period following the attacks, *The Others* continued its successful run in cinemas. The film earned $4.5 million the weekend following the events of 9/11 and $5 million the weekend after that, rising to second place on the chart. When the film finally left US theaters in mid-November, it had grossed $96 million.

In a profile of director Amenábar published by UK newspaper *The Telegraph* at the end of October, journalist Sheila Johnston noted that US film industry observers thought viewers would be turned off by the movie's "languid" pace. Johnston wrote that, with the film still playing in cinemas three months after its release, "Pundits have revised their columns to speculate that audiences, reeling from the events of September 11, crave kinder, gentler movies. *The Others*, with its elegant, old-fashioned quality, restrained but stylish music, and absence of violence, fitted the bill."

Director Brad Anderson established his reputation with a clutch of Sundance-screened comedies, including 2000's Marisa Tomei-starring *Happy Accidents*. But there would be little to laugh about in his next film, 2001's supernatural thriller *Session 9*. The movie tracked a crew of blue-collar workers whose attempt to remove asbestos from an abandoned psychiatric hospital turns hellish (and for many, fatal). At the film's end, the viewer discovers that the men have been murdered by their boss, Gordon, who has previously killed his wife and daughter.

Anderson's movie was a direct reaction to the glossy frights of the *Scream* franchise and its imitators. "*Session 9* evolved out of my need to take a detour into another genre and try something different," he recalled to the outlet Cryptic Rock in 2023. "At that time in the late '90s and early 2000s, the horror genre was still really embedded in movies like *Scream* and *I Know What You Did Last Summer*; mostly cheesy, teenage B-movie-like stories. We wanted to do something that was quite literally horrific, visceral, psychological, and really getting under your skin."

Anderson collaborated on the *Session 9* script with actor Stephen Gevedon, who had appeared in *Happy Accidents*. The pair were inspired to create the character of Gordon—played by Scottish actor Peter Mullan in the film—by the crimes of a financial analyst named Richard Rosenthal. In 1995, Rosenthal had killed his wife, Laura Jane, with a rock and impaled her heart and lungs on a stake after she complained that he had burned their ziti dinner. Another source of inspiration was Massachusetts' sprawling and infamous Danvers State Hospital, the so-called 'birthplace of the prefrontal lobotomy.' Anderson was taken on an unauthorized tour of the building by some 'urban explorers' and later secured permission to shoot the film at the abandoned institution. An extra layer of eeriness would be added to the movie by cinematographer Uta Briesewitz, whose pioneering use of high-definition video gifted a stress-inducing verité feel to the project.

The film's quintet of asbestos-clearers was portrayed by Mullan, Gevedon, Josh Lucas, Brendan Sexton III, and David Caruso. The movie's actors also included *Habit* director Larry Fessenden, who had played a small role in *Happy Accidents*. "This was a defunct asylum, sort of like a panopticon," says Fessenden of the shoot's location. "All of the effects of the people were lying around, tipped-over wheelchairs and files. It's as if they all had to leave very quickly. The crew loved to say it was haunted." Director Anderson killed off Fessenden's workman shortly after he appeared on screen, one of many occasions the *Habit* filmmaker would perish on film. "People love to have me on [to] get killed," says Fessenden. "I have a huge IMDB presence—meaning I have 120 movies that I'm in—but if you analyze the time I'm onscreen, it's probably 13 minutes."

Session 9 was produced and distributed by USA Films, which had been founded by media magnate Barry Diller in 1999. The company had put *Pitch Black* into US cinemas and enjoyed a critical and commercial hit with Stephen Soderbergh's 2000 drug trade thriller *Traffic*. But the commercial chances of *Session 9* were hobbled by USA Films' decision to release the movie on August 10, 2001, the same day as *The Others*. "I got a phone call from a friend who said, 'Hey, have you heard about this movie called *The Others*? 'Cause it sounds a lot like your movie,'" Gevedon recalled to *Fangoria* writer Scott Wampler in 2021. "And I remember calling up somebody at USA Films about this, because there wasn't supposed to be a horror movie coming out that weekend, and the guy I was on the phone with said to me, 'Steve, Steve—you don't have to worry about that. *The Others* is a movie about a haunted house. Yours is a movie about a haunted asylum.'"

In the end, USA Films barely released *Session 9* at all, distributing the movie to a mere 30 cinemas. By the end of its theatrical run, the film had earned just $378,000 at the domestic box office. Brad Anderson would remain in the horror-thriller zone for his next film, though, 2004's *The Machinist*, starring Christian Bale as a troubled and emaciated factory worker.

Session 9 was another movie nominated by *Fangoria* for a 2002 Chainsaw Award in the category of Best Limited Release Film/Direct-to-Video Film, alongside *The Devil's Backbone* and *Ginger Snaps*. Like Fessenden's *Habit*, Anderson's unsettling movie went on to become something of a secret handshake among horror fans. Writing about the movie in 2019, Dread Central contributor Mike Sprague described *Session 9* as "one of the absolute scariest films I have ever seen." "I don't know how it did [at the box office], but it's now a classic," agrees Fessenden. "It really is a scary movie. That's quite rare, if you think about it, a movie that gets under your skin."

Getting under the skin in a different way, *Jeepers Creepers* introduced a new monster to horror audiences when MGM/UA released the film over the Labor Day weekend of 2001, just 11 days before the Twin Towers fell. The film starred Gina Philips and Justin Long as siblings driving home from college who discover what appears to be the corpse-strewn subterranean lair of a serial killer. The murderer turns out to be a winged and seemingly unkillable creature—named The Creeper in the movie's credits—who replenishes his physical form by consuming human body parts. Played by Jonathan Breck, the Creeper was a terrifying invention that helped make the film a surprise sleeper hit that late summer. But some people believed that the movie's real monster was the film's writer and director, convicted child molester Victor Salva.

Salva was raised in the small city of Martinez, 30 miles outside of San Francisco. The director grew up an avid fan of horror movies and spent his teenage years and twenties making short films. Salva was working at a daycare center when a parent recommended that an acquaintance named Rebecca Winters might be able to help him with props for his latest short, *Goblin's Gold*. The director became friendly with Winters and her son Nathan, who was just six years old. Nathan would later recall that Salva began abusing him soon afterwards.

Salva cast Nathan in his 1986 horror short *Something in the Basement*. The film attracted the attention of Francis Ford Coppola, who adopted Salva as a protégé. *The Godfather* director helped finance the younger filmmaker's

1989 feature debut, the horror film *Clownhouse*, whose cast included Nathan Winters and Sam Rockwell. During the production of *Clownhouse*, Rebecca Winters became concerned about Salva's behavior toward her preteen son. The director was arrested, and magazines and videotapes depicting child pornography were seized at his home. Salva pleaded guilty to oral copulation with a person under 14, procuring a child for pornography, and lewd and lascivious conduct. He was sentenced to three years in state prison and was released after 15 months.

Salva returned to filmmaking with the 1995 straight-to-video horror-thriller *The Nature of the Beast*, and the same year's *Powder*, about a young man with albinism who also possesses supernatural powers. The movie starred Sean Patrick Flanery in the lead role and was set to be distributed by the Disney subsidiary Buena Vista Pictures at the end of October 1995. Days before the film's official release, Nathan Winters appeared at a Los Angeles screening of the movie and urged attendees to boycott it. His actions at the event prompted the *Los Angeles Times* to publish an article about Salva with the headline "Disney movie's director a convicted child molester." Despite the controversy, Disney did release *Powder*, which proved successful, earning $30 million in the US. The filmmaker next directed the low-budget 1999 thriller *Rites of Passage*, which starred Dean Stockwell.

Following *Rites of Passage*, Salva moved on to *Jeepers Creepers*, which was produced by Coppola's company American Zoetrope. *Jeepers Creepers* earned $15 million over its opening four days, a record for Labor Day weekend. Salva's gruesome tale even stuck around in the top ten for a couple of weeks after 9/11, going on to gross $37 million in the US. The film's box office was assisted by several enthusiastic reviews. Jae-Ha

Kim was a rare critic who made mention of Salva's crimes, noting in her review for the *Chicago Sun-Times* that the director was a sex offender.

In January 2002, United Artists and American Zoetrope announced that Salva was writing and directing a sequel. Salva's script for *Jeepers Creepers 2* found a busload of high school students and a clutch of adults being picked off by the Creeper as they return from a basketball game. More critics made note of Salva's past, with *Orlando Sentinel* reporter Roger Moore suggesting that the director "must certainly see himself as above this material, but this is all that Hollywood will let convicted child molesters do." Regardless, *Jeepers Creepers 2* topped the box office chart when it was released at the end of August 2003. The film went on to earn $35 million in the US, only slightly less than the first movie.

In contrast to his experience on *Demon Knight*, director Ernest Dickerson did not need to convince anyone that his second horror film, 2001's *Bones*, should star a Black actor. The New Line-produced movie's titular character is a beloved community leader named Jimmy Bones, who is killed in 1979 for refusing to allow the sale of crack cocaine in his neighborhood and years later returns from the dead seeking vengeance. The role was hand-crafted for Snoop Dogg, who had become a hip-hop sensation following the release of his multi-platinum-selling 1993 debut album *Doggystyle* and by the end of the '90s was moving into movies. The rapper wanted to play a Freddy Krueger-esque killer, and the *Bones* script by Adam Simon (director of the Bill Pullman/Bill Paxton 1990 horror movie *Brain Dead*) and Tim Metcalfe was written with the hope of starting a franchise. According to Dickerson, the film was offered to him by New Line as a way of making up for his experience on *Blade*. "When I started really complaining about how they treated me on *Blade*, they asked me to do *Bones*," he says.

Dickerson cast Pam Grier as Jimmy Bones' romantic interest, Pearl. The actress was famous from her roles in 1973's *Coffy*, the same year's *Scream Blacula Scream*, and 1974's *Foxy Brown*, and had enjoyed a career revival with her lead performance in Quentin Tarantino's 1997 film *Jackie Brown*. "I had recently met with Pam Grier for another project that didn't happen," says Dickerson. "Since I had her phone number, I called her up, and I was able to bring her on as the lady lead."

Snoop Dogg in *Bones* (2001).

The movie's lush look was inspired by vintage European releases. "Some of my favorite horror films are Italian horror films," says Dickerson. "I loved the films of Mario Bava, early Argento, Michele Soavi, Pupi Avati. I was in love visually with what the Italians were doing with horror, and I wanted to do that with this."

Dickerson shot the film in Vancouver and enjoyed collaborating with his rap star leading man, who surprised the director with his dedication to the cause. "There was always a problem working with musicians, in that you'd be lucky if they showed up to the set, but Snoop was there every day," says the director. "I actually got him to blush, because he kissed Pam Grier and he had a lifelong crush on Pam Grier. It put me on his good side for life."

The director was unhappy with the way New Line marketed the film at a Black, rather than a more general, audience. "We were shooting in some neighborhoods that were all white," he says. "White kids were coming out of the woodwork to meet Snoop! [But then] they put most of the ads for the movie in African-American neighborhoods. [I] kept telling them,

Snoop's reach is wider than that. You've got to hit white folks, too, you're really ghettoizing the whole movie. As a result, not that many people knew about it."

New Line released the movie on October 26, 2001. *Bones* was only able to place tenth on the box office chart and would go on to gross a disappointing $7 million in the US. "They really blew it, because we got great reviews," says Dickerson. "They just thought it was a Black horror film, that it would only appeal to a Black audience, and because of that it didn't make any money."

Bones had horror competition in the form of *Thirteen Ghosts*, which was released the same day. The film was the second production from Dark Castle and the second to remake one of William Castle's movies. The Dark Castle production once again featured several famous actors, including *Scream* star Matthew Lillard, Oscar-winner F. Murray Abraham, and Tony Shalhoub as a widower who inherits a glass-walled mansion filled with murderous ghouls.

Thirteen Ghosts was the directorial debut of Steve Beck, a visual effects art director whose credits included Steven Spielberg's *Indiana Jones and the Last Crusade* and James Cameron's *The Abyss.* KNB co-founder Howard Berger was in charge of creating the movie's disparate array of ghosts. "Steve wasn't looking at them like, 'Okay, there's Weird Guy #1 and Weird Guy #2,'" Berger would explain in a behind-the-scenes promotional video. "He had a backstory for everybody." The film's ghosts included 'The Jackal,' whose head is encased in a metal cage, and 'The Hammer,' a supernatural fiend with a mallet for a hand and railway spikes embedded in his skull. "I think they came out really well," says producer Gil Adler of Berger's creations. "You don't want to do the same gag over and over."

In his review of *Thirteen Ghosts*, Roger Ebert would claim that "the experience of watching the film is literally painful. It hurts the eyes and ears." Still, the film scored second place on the box office chart over its release weekend in October 2001 and went on to earn $68 million around the globe.

After *Thirteen Ghosts*, Dark Castle moved on from remaking movies (for a few years anyway). But during this period, other companies would revive a host of more recent titles, many of them based on movies far removed, both tonally and geographically, from the output of William Castle.

Behind-the-scenes shots of KNB makeups for *Thirteen Ghosts* (2001).

At the start of director Takashi Shimizu's story "Blonde Kwaidan" in the 2004 anthology horror movie *Dark Tales of Japan*, a visitor to Los Angeles is driven by taxi along Hollywood Boulevard. "This is Hollywood, right?" says the character, played by Tetta Sugimoto, in Japanese. "But it's sure going downhill, huh? It's all reruns lately, right? All reruns and Japanese horror flicks." The visitor's reference to 'Japanese horror flicks' was an in-joke on the part of Japanese filmmaker Shimuzu. Over the previous few years, Hollywood had indeed embraced the notion of remaking of his homeland's so-called 'J-horror' films, including the director's own.

The late 1990s saw a revival of the Japanese horror film, spearheaded by director Hideo Nakata's 1998 movie *Ring*, or *Ringu* as it became known in the US. The source of terror in the movie is a videotape that causes viewers to perish a week after they watch it. The cursed artifact originates from the spirit of a teenage girl named Sadako who was left to die at the bottom of a well. Nakata directed his tale with a stylish austerity that owed much to the tradition of Japanese ghost films like the 1965 anthology movie *Kwaidan* and very little to the blood-drenched mayhem delivered by the likes of Freddy Krueger and Jason Voorhees. "I never really liked the splatter films of the '80s," Nakata told *The Hollywood Reporter* in 2013. "I'm not really into grotesque stuff." *Ringu* was a hit in Japan, grossing more than ten times its $1.2 million budget.

Fangoria editor Tony Timpone devoted most of his magazine's June 2001 issue to "Japan's Scary New Movies." "The Japanese are diving into a pure, unadulterated horror that puts their American brethren to shame," Timpone wrote in his editorial. The cover of the issue featured Sadako staring out at readers from beneath strands of dark hair.

Japan's ghost stories quickly attracted interest from Hollywood executives, with US studios releasing new versions of many supernatural tales from the country and a couple of the movies becoming hits. The first success of this gold rush was director Gore Verbinski's *The Ring*, a big-budget remake of Nakata's movie and one of 2002's most unexpected blockbusters, grossing $249 million around the world.

Although *Ringu* had screened at Canada's Fantasia Film Festival in 1999, the film did not receive a release in the US and seemed destined to become

Nanako Matsushima in *Ringu* (1998).

a title known only to diehard American horror fans. Then, in January 2001, an aspiring producer named Roy Lee and a DreamWorks executive called Mark Sourian watched a tape of *Ringu* at Lee's apartment in Los Angeles. "I'd never seen an Asian movie at the time, other than the Bruce Lee movies or the Godzilla movies," says Lee. "This was a full-blown horror movie that I saw could easily be adapted for the USA."

Sourian, too, was impressed and recommended the film to his bosses at DreamWorks, married producing couple Walter F. Parkes and Laurie MacDonald. The pair saw the potential in an Americanized version of *Ringu* and, according to legend, agreed to pay $1 million for the film's remake rights within three hours of watching the movie. Roy Lee helped set up the deal and would receive an executive producer credit on the finished film.

DreamWorks hired Verbinski, who had made the 1997 hit *Mouse Hunt* for the company, to direct the film and *Scream 3* writer Ehren Kruger to adapt the original movie's screenplay. Gwyneth Paltrow, Kate Beckinsale, and Jennifer Connelly were considered for the lead role of a journalist named Rachel Keller who attempts to save herself and her young son from the supernatural threat represented by the videotape. Verbinski believed they should cast a less well-known actress in the part and got his wish after Naomi Watts signed on to play the role. The British-Australian actress had appeared

Naomi Watts in *The Ring* (2002).

with Nicole Kidman in 1991's Australian drama *Flirting* but had failed to make much of an impact in Hollywood during the years which followed. Although Watts did secure a starring role in 1996's Dimension-backed *Children of the Corn IV: The Gathering*, a straight-to-video horror fourquel was hardly the kind of project likely to propel her onto the A-list. Finally, Watts was cast by David Lynch in the pilot for his proposed TV show *Mulholland Drive*. When the pilot was rejected by ABC, the director turned the material into a feature film. For his work on the nightmarish movie, Lynch shared the Best Director award at the 2001 Cannes Film Festival with *The Man Who Wasn't There* filmmaker Joel Coen. The movie generated enough buzz around Watts' performance to put her in contention for *The Ring*. Verbinski filled out his cast with young actor David Dorfman as Rachel's son Aidan, Martin Henderson as Aidan's father, and *Manhunter* star Brian Cox.

Released on October 18, 2002, *The Ring* earned $15 million over the film's opening weekend, enough to make the movie number one at the box office, but a disappointing figure given its reported $48 million budget. The following Friday, Verbinski's film was knocked out of pole position by *Jackass: The Movie*, yet actually wound up making more than the week before. *The Ring* ultimately grossed $129 million at home and another $120 million in foreign territories. The director came to believe that audiences connected to the film in part because of the 9/11 attacks. "It's interesting because when the genre is elevated, it usually taps into some zeitgeist, right?" he said to Collider in 2016. "*The Ring* deals with the transferable nature of hatred. Its core is a chain letter, and it came right after 9/11. I think there was a sense of 'What did I do to deserve…? What did we do?' That's the terror. The terror doesn't go after the perp. It transfers that horror upon an innocent, somebody else."

In 2001, *The Ring* executive producer Roy Lee had founded Vertigo Entertainment with another producer named Doug Davison. "I was looking for anything I could get made," says Lee. "Horror films appealed to me, because those were the things that I like to see." Lee had dealt with Japanese producer Takashige Ichise to secure the remake rights to *Ringu*. When the American asked Ichise if he had worked on any more films that he felt could be successfully remade in English, the producer sent him a video cassette of 2002's *Ju-On: The Grudge*.

The producer's recommendation was the third film in a franchise created by future *Dark Tales of Japan* co-director Takashi Shimizu. The series had its origins in two short films Shimizu contributed to the 1998 horror anthology TV movie *School Ghost Story G*, which collectively introduced the franchise's supernatural antagonists. One of the segments, "In a Corner," featured the character who would become famous as the long-haired undead Kayako. The other, titled "4444444444," introduced her son, the always alarming Toshio. Producer Takashige Ichise was impressed by Shimizu's work and helped him expand his universe into two straight-to-video films, *Ju-On: The Curse* and *Ju-On: The Curse 2*. These movies established the franchise's non-linear storytelling style and its principal location, a nondescript house where Kayako and her son were murdered by Kayako's jealous husband and where her rage now dooms anyone who enters the abode. After the two films proved successful on video, producer Ichise was convinced that the series should transfer to the big screen, and Shimizu wrote and directed *Ju-On: The Grudge*.

Lee agreed that *Ju-On: The Grudge* had remake potential. The producer recalls that the version of the film he watched "didn't have subtitles, so I would be on the phone with my neighbor and his mother, who's Japanese, going through segments of the movie. We'd add her own subtitles and actually change the story around a bit to make a little more sense when we sent it out to places to see if they wanted to try and adapt it."

Lee partnered with Ghost House Pictures, a new company founded by Sam Raimi and his producer Rob Tapert to make horror movies. Raimi had returned to the genre with 2000's supernatural thriller *The Gift*, which starred Cate Blanchett as a clairvoyant who becomes involved in a murder investigation. The comparatively restrained film was a disappointment at the box office and to horror fans hoping for another slice of horror-comedy mayhem in the same vein as *Evil Dead II* and *Army of Darkness*. The Ghost House founders resolved that the output of their company would more squarely appeal to lovers of the genre.

Raimi and Tapert first saw *Ju-On: The Grudge* at a screening on the Sony Pictures lot in Los Angeles. The pair were impressed by the amount of scares the film delivered, even if Raimi was initially confused by the movie's plot. "That was super-scary," the director said immediately after the screening, according to a profile of Roy Lee published in *The New Yorker*. "Robert and I have a rule that we like to see 15 great scares in a movie, and there were at least that many here, one after the other. Great sound design, green screen craft. Very spooky. I'm not completely sure what happened, though."

Raimi struck a deal with Lee to remake the movie as *The Grudge*. The *Evil Dead* filmmaker asked franchise creator Shimizu to direct the English-language version in Japan with American actors and a budget in the $10-15 million range. Raimi recalls that he told Shimizu, "I loved your movie, and not a lot of people in America will see the movie, they just don't watch a lot of Japanese-language horror films, and I think it would be great to not just remake it in English but to have you remake it." Shooting began in January 2004, with a cast that included Sarah Michelle Gellar, Bill Pullman, and Raimi's brother Ted, as well as franchise veteran Takako Fuji, who reprised the role of Kayako.

Sarah Michelle Gellar in *The Grudge* (2004).

Released in the US on October 22, 2004, *The Grudge* topped the box office chart and earned $40 million over its opening weekend, double some industry estimates. Even executives at Sony, which distributed the film, were surprised by the size of the success. "I wish I could say I had any inclination that we were going to hit the ball so far out of the park," Sony distribution president Rory Bruer told *Variety*. *The Grudge* remained at the top of the box office the next week and by the end of its run at the domestic box office had earned $110 million.

The Grudge was far from the only remake of a foreign language horror film developed by Roy Lee following the success of *The Ring*. "The percentage of development to actual production is fairly low, but since [the original films] were all fairly well thought-out and produced movies that were successful, the conversion rate was much higher," says the producer. The list of English-language remakes of Asian movies on which Lee was credited as either producer or executive producer included 2005's *Dark Water*, 2008's *The Eye*, the same year's *Shutter*, and 2009's *The Uninvited*, as well as sequels to *The Ring* and *The Grudge*. Other producers and executives also mined Asian cinema for horror films that they believed might benefit from the remake treatment (or might benefit them, anyway). In 2001, Dimension acquired the remake rights to Japanese director Kiyosha Kurosawa's Cannes-screened film *Kairo* (a.k.a. *Pulse*) and set Wes Craven to work on an English-language version. The period following the release of *The Ring* would also find US cinemas playing host to remakes of both the South Korean horror film *Into the Mirror* and Japanese director Takashi Miike's *One Missed Call*.

None of these films matched the commercial heights of *The Ring* or *The Grudge*, despite often boasting hefty budgets and heavyweight casts. Brazilian director Walter Salles' remake of Hideo Nakata's *Dark Water*, which starred Jennifer Connelly, John C. Reilly, and Tim Roth, was an early disappointment. Released during the summer of 2005, the filmed earned $25 million at the domestic box office, roughly a fifth of the amount grossed by *The Ring*. "Walter Salles' inclination was to ground what was originally a very scary movie more into reality and take away a lot of the scares," says Roy Lee. "It turned out to be a less effective horror movie and a much better drama."

Hideo Nakata, the director of *Ringu* and the original *Dark Water*, was given his Hollywood shot with *The Ring Two*, the sequel to Verbinski's movie, which was again written by Kruger. Watts and Dorfman reunited for the film, which co-starred Simon Baker and *Carrie* actress Sissy Spacek. *The Ring Two* cost around $20 million more than the first film but earned much less, grossing $75 million in the US after it was released in March 2005. *The Grudge 2* also commercially underperformed when it was released the next year.

Reviewers were often harsh about these sequels, but when Warner Bros. dumped *One Missed Call* into US cinemas at the start of 2008, the critical fraternity combined to completely reject the movie. Directed by French filmmaker Eric Valette, the movie starred Shannyn Sossamon and explored the idea that spirits could communicate with the living via cellphones. "Takashi Miike's original 2003 *One Missed Call* was second-rate technophobic J-horror tripe," critic Nick Schager wrote in his review for Slant, "meaning that Eric Valette's even lousier American remake is something like the next generation of suck." *One Missed Call* would join 1987's *Police Academy 4: Citizens on Patrol* and 1993's *Look Who's Talking Now!* in the exclusive club of films with a zero percent rating on Rotten Tomatoes.

One Missed Call was followed into cinemas by Lionsgate's *The Eye*, about a blind violinist who starts seeing visions after recovering her sight. The film was produced by Cruise/Wagner in collaboration with Roy Lee's Vertigo Entertainment and starred Jessica Alba. The original 2002 film came from Hong Kong directors the Pang brothers; the new version was directed by French filmmakers David Moreau and Xavier Palud, with extensive reshoots overseen by Patrick Lussier. The *Scream* editor and *Dracula 2000* director produced dozens of new script pages with assistance from writer Todd Farmer. "I was a huge fan of the original Pang brothers movie, so I knew that film really well," says Lussier. "[We] wrote 40-some-odd pages of reshoots, a lot of the things that are much more comparable to the original, and shot them in ten days." Released on February 1, 2008, *The Eye* was a bigger hit than *One Missed Call*, although not by much.

American audiences would have the chance to see yet more English-language versions of Asian horror films over the next year. In March 2008, 20th Century Fox released the Joshua Jackson-starring *Shutter*, another Roy Lee production, which found Japanese director Masayuki Ochiai remaking a 2004 Thai film of the same name. The following January, Paramount released *The Uninvited*, an Anglicized version of South Korean director Kim Jee-woon's 2003 film *A Tale of Two Sisters*. The movie was produced by Lee, Walter F. Parkes, and Laurie MacDonald, three of the behind-the-scenes team responsible for *The Ring* remake. *The Uninvited* once again failed to approach the blockbuster success of Verbinski's film, effectively drawing to a close Hollywood's love affair with refashioning Asian horror. "After a while, they sort of felt repetitive and you got some much less successful movies, like *One Missed Call*," says Roy Lee. "There was nothing left that the audience hadn't already seen before, and so it ran its course."

For his part, Patrick Lussier believes that Hollywood studios often ruined English-language remakes of Asian releases by insisting that filmmakers unnecessarily explain the movies' supernatural elements. He accuses executives of employing what he calls 'Coyote logic,' a phrase he learned from his *Mimic* director Guillermo del Toro. "Guillermo used to say this about studio executives," he explains. "'Coyote logic' is a studio executive's version of the Coyote and Road Runner. 'Wouldn't the Coyote be better served if he just used his money that he spends on all these Acme inventions [to] buy himself a good meal?' With the Japanese and Hong Kong movies, there was much more acceptance of the supernatural world. I feel studio executives never fully understood that. Coyote logic is the thing that crushed those films, because there was a need to try to explain it as opposed to just going with it."

For the third Dark Castle release, the company's founders produced an original movie called *Ghost Ship*, based on a spec script called *Chimera*. Written by Mark Hanlon, the *Chimera* screenplay riffed on director John Huston's 1948 adventure classic *The Treasure of the Sierra Madre* and followed a group of marine salvagers who come across a deserted ship with a fortune of gold ingots onboard. The script was refashioned by *U.S. Marshals* co-writer John Pogue, who transformed the movie from a psychological thriller to a supernatural horror film. This switch in genres was dictated by Warner Bros., the studio believing that post-9/11 audiences would find it hard to root for the original screenplay's morally dubious protagonists. Producer Gil Adler recalls that the studio's change of heart about the project "really threw us for what to do. We were sort of rewriting while we were shooting. That's not the best way to make a movie, but we didn't really have a choice."

The original *Chimera* screenplay had attracted a strong cast led by Julianna Margulies and *End of Days* star Gabriel Byrne. When the actors arrived in Queensland, Australia, for the shoot, which began in January 2002, they were surprised to discover how much the script had been overhauled. In a 2014 interview with *The Hollywood Reporter*, Margulies would describe her shock at discovering that she was in "a really awful horror movie." "She said that she signed up for that other movie, not for this movie," recalls Gil Adler. "And I said, 'Yeah, well, that's life in the big city.'"

(*Left to right*) Ron Eldard, Julianna Margulies, and Karl Urban in *Ghost Ship* (2002).

In the film's 1962-set opening, a metal wire slices the ship's passengers and crew horizontally in half. Prepping the film, Adler had balked at the technical difficulties of shooting on water, meaning that the sequence was filmed some distance away from the ocean. "The first scene of that movie, we're on deck and there's a party going on," says the producer. "What I did was, I built that in a field, with kangaroos all around us, and we shot it at night, and it worked very well." The sequence would kick off the film in spectacular fashion and became one of the most memorable horror scenes of the era. "We were hoping for that," says Adler. "We thought, wow, if we can pull this off, that should be cool and what a way to start a movie." Released in October 2002, *Ghost Ship* earned $30 million in the US, much less than *House on Haunted Hill* or *Thirteen Ghosts*.

Following the release of *Ghost Ship*, Gil Adler left Dark Castle to work on a string of big-budget Warner Bros. releases, including 2005's Keanu Reeves-starring superhero-horror movie *Constantine* and 2006's *Superman Returns*. The producer explains that his departure was prompted by a heated call with business partner Joel Silver, which he conducted using his colleague's office phone. "I slammed the phone down so hard, I thought I broke my hand," says Adler. "I broke his phone, which was justice in a way."

The first three Dark Castle movies were not the kind of blockbusters with which Silver was now almost routinely associated. In addition to the first two *Die Hard* movies and four *Lethal Weapon* films, the Hollywood mogul had also produced 1999's *The Matrix*, a huge hit. Silver decided to up the ante on the next Dark Castle production, hiring Halle Berry to play a psychiatrist who wakes up to discover that she is now an inmate at the penitentiary where she works in the supernatural thriller *Gothika.*

Berry's *annus mirabilis* came in 2002 when she became the first Black woman to win the Best Actress Oscar for her performance in the Lionsgate-distributed *Monster's Ball* and was then seen playing the character Jinx in the James Bond movie *Die Another Day*. Berry hoped that her Oscar win would lead to more meaty roles and that Jinx would be given her own film. Neither came to pass. When Silver saw Berry at an event late in 2002, he successfully pitched her on the idea of taking the lead in *Gothika.* The producer assembled a supporting cast that included Penelope Cruz, John Carroll Lynch, and Robert Downey Jr. (the latter on the comeback trail after being brought low, professionally and personally, by substance abuse issues). *Gothika* was directed by French filmmaker Mathieu Kassovitz, who had made his name with the brutal 1995 drama *La Haine.*

Kassovitz shot *Gothika* during the spring of 2003 in Montreal. On May 14, Berry and Downey were shooting a scene when Downey twisted his co-star's arm and badly damaged the limb. "It was sort of a fluke," Berry later said during an appearance on *Late Show with David Letterman*. "It wasn't a day that our stunt coordinator was there because it wasn't a stunt, nobody was in danger, and we were having a really emotional scene, and somehow he just grabbed my arm in just the wrong way with, I guess, enough strength to just *skriiich*."

Warner Bros. opened *Gothika* in the US over Thanksgiving weekend of 2003. The film earned $141 million worldwide, making it Dark Castle's biggest hit to date.

George A. Romero's hopes that the revival of the horror genre would help his own career seemed justified when he was hired to oversee the movie version of the 1996 Japanese video game *Biohazard*—or, as the title was renamed for the European and North American markets, *Resident Evil*. The game was published by the Japanese company Capcom and tasked players with escaping from zombies and other creatures at a research facility owned by the sinister Umbrella Corporation. *Resident Evil* developer Shinji Mikami had been inspired by Romero's *Dawn of the Dead*, which he saw as a teenager. "I was racking my brain trying to come up with something, and then *Dawn of the Dead* came back to me in a flash," Mikami recalled to *PlayStation Magazine* in 1998. *Resident Evil* would sell around 4 million copies worldwide.

Capcom developed a second game, *Resident Evil 2*, and hired Romero to direct a commercial. The director shot the ad at the Lincoln Heights Jail in Los Angeles, with a cast that included Brad Renfro from the upcoming Stephen King adaptation *Apt Pupil*. "I love making the [*Dead*] movies, and it's great that there's a game which is like a flashback to that genre," the director enthused in a behind-the-scenes promotional video. *Resident Evil 2* was released in 1998 and proved even more successful than its predecessor.

In 1997, *Variety* announced that the German production company Constantin had acquired the rights to adapt the game into a movie. Constantin executive Robert Kulzer recruited *Halloween 4* screenwriter Alan B. McElroy to come up with a script. McElroy was already familiar with the game. "I always remember, I was playing *Resident Evil*, by myself, in the basement of our house, I think it was 2:30 in the morning," he says. "The scene where the two zombie Dobermanns come diving through the window, I threw down the controller, turned off the TV. I said, 'I'm done for the night, thank you!'" McElroy wrote two drafts of the film for Constantin before departing the project. "I really tried to stick close to the game in both drafts, and then they decided to go a different way," he says.

Constantin returned to the source, asking Romero to tackle the project. "My guess is, they brought in George Romero because of the name that he brings with it," says McElroy. "He would be very easy to market, to say, 'From the creator of *Night of the Living Dead, Resident Evil*.' I mean, that would have been huge. But something obviously didn't click there, either."

After writing around half a dozen drafts of the screenplay, the *Dawn of the Dead* director was dismissed from the movie version of the video game he had inspired. Romero was aggrieved by Constantin's rejection of the work done by himself and his producer Peter Grunwald. "We busted our balls writing drafts of that screenplay," the director wrote in a 2000 post on his official website. "I'm talkin' marathons, seventy-two hours straight. I really wanted this project… Deep in my heart, I felt that *ResEv* was a rip-off of *Night of the Living Dead.* I had no legal case, but I was pretty resentful. And torn… because I liked the video game. I wanted to do the film partly because I wanted to say, 'LOOK HERE! THIS IS HOW YOU DO THIS SHIT!'"

Romero finally escaped his own personal development hell by writing and directing 2000's low-budget *Bruiser*. The film starred *Deep Rising* actor Jason Flemyng as a man who wakes up to discover that his face has become a featureless mask. In the summer of 2000, Romero visited Chicago for a screening of the film at the Gene Siskel Film Center. He was interviewed by the *Chicago Tribune* and explained that *Bruiser* had been inspired by "frustration with the system and with all this development stuff. It looked like there were just walls all around." In the same interview, the director revealed that producers on a couple of the projects he was developing had asked for script changes to make them more raunchy and outrageous in an attempt to ape the just-released *Scary Movie*. "It's all just what sold last week, and it's very hard to sell somebody an innovative idea," said the director. The article also quoted John Carpenter as saying, "In Hollywood, a director is only as good as the grosses on [his] last film." Unfortunately for Romero, the grosses on *Bruiser* were minuscule.

Romero next decided to revisit the zombie universe of his undead trilogy with a film he titled *Dead Reckoning*. The movie would explore a post-apocalyptic world where the power dynamic between the haves and the have-nots remains firmly in place. The rich live lavishly in a skyscraper called Fiddler's Green and the poor are forced to survive on scraps, all in a city surrounded by the undead. Romero hoped to point up how the well-off could ignore problems like AIDS or homelessness (or zombies) if such issues did not affect their own lives.

Romero's screenplay arrived on the desks of studio executives at the worst possible moment. "I wrote the script and sent it out literally about 48 hours before the World Trade Center disaster, and of course, at that point everybody wanted soft and funny movies," Romero said to Dread Central in 2004. "So I sort of pulled it back and sat on it for about a year and a half."

Resident Evil would finally be brought to the screen by director Paul W. S. Anderson. The British filmmaker had grown up loving horror movies, including those featuring the undead. "The first 18-rated movie that I crept in to see was *Omen III: The Final Conflict* with Sam Neill, which scared the bejesus out of me," Anderson says. "Then—I have no idea why—they projected *Alien* at school and that terrified me as well. When I got a little older, I was a big fan of the Romero zombie movies and the Lucio Fulci movies."

The director made a splash in the UK with his first film, the 1994 Jude Law-starring crime drama *Shopping*, which led to him directing 1995's *Mortal Kombat*. Relatively cheap and light on big-name stars, the video game adaptation earned $120 million around the world and established Anderson as a hot talent. "In the usual Hollywood way of things, when you have a big hit, you're an absolute genius," he says.

Anderson admits that his reputation was damaged over the next few years. His third movie, the Paramount-backed 1997 science fiction-horror film *Event Horizon*, starred Sam Neill and Laurence Fishburne as members of a team exploring an experimental spaceship which has mysteriously reappeared after vanishing seven years previously. Anderson had set out to make the Paramount project a truly terrifying movie, and his early cut was larded with images too extreme for executives. "The first time the studio saw it was the first test screening," says the director. "They saw all this blood and unpleasantness, all the impalings, and people ripping their eyes out, and pulling their intestines out of their mouths. They were just aghast at it. One of the studio executives actually said to me in a horrified way, 'But we're the studio that makes *Star Trek*!' As though somehow I was besmirching *Star Trek* with my horrible movie in space."

Paramount released *Event Horizon* on August 15, 1997. Cursed with competition from the Sylvester Stallone-starring *Cop Land* (released the same day) and the blockbuster *Air Force One*, *Event Horizon* grossed an underwhelming $26 million at the domestic box office. "If I'd been a more experienced filmmaker, I would have pushed back against the studio about the release date," says Anderson. "We should have been released in Halloween, or November. We can't compete against Harrison Ford playing the President of the United States. It wasn't surprising that we got our hat handed to us a little bit at the box office." His next film, 1998's Kurt Russell-starring science fiction-action film *Soldier*, was an even bigger disaster, costing $60 million and earning $14 million in the US. "*Event Horizon*, that was kind of like, 'He's not the genius he was, but he's not an idiot yet,'" says Anderson. "And then I did *Soldier*, and I was a complete idiot."

Anderson believed he had found a way to get his career back on track with *Resident Evil*. "I was in what Hollywood refers to as 'Director's jail,'"

Director Paul W. S. Anderson on the set of *Event Horizon* (1997).

Sam Neill in *Event Horizon.*

he says. "I thought, the phone's not ringing, I'm going to play video games! I played *Resident Evil 1* and *2* back-to-back and became obsessed with it. Clearly the Romero movies had an influence on them. You could also see a lot of John Carpenter in there. You could see this would be an easy flip back into movies." The director wound up spending a month playing *Resident Evil* in his West Hollywood home. "I emerge from my apartment and I literally haven't shaved for four weeks," he says. "I've got a big beard, I've got red eyes, I look crazy. And I say to my producing partner, Jeremy Bolt, 'I've just played this series of video games. We have to get hold of these and turn them into movies.'"

Few zombie films of note had been released since 1985, the year both Romero's *Day of the Dead* and Dan O'Bannon's more comedic *The Return of the Living Dead* had debuted in cinemas. Anderson believed the time was right for a revival of the undead subgenre. "I read a lot about film history, so I was well aware that the movie industry is cyclical," he says. "What was totally unfashionable ten years ago, it's going to come back. I thought, people are ready to see a zombie movie again."

Anderson and producer Bolt discovered that the *Resident Evil* rights were held by Constantin. Fortuitously, the pair had just signed a first-look deal with the German company. "I talked to Constantin and said, 'This is great, you have this property, I really want to make it,'" recalls the director. "They went, 'Well, not so great, we've been kicking it around for a year and a half, we're going to let the rights go.' They said, 'We've spent all this money and we can't afford anymore.' I said, 'It's fine, I'll just write a great spec screenplay.'"

Anderson delivered a script called *Undead*, which he hoped would work as a *Resident Evil* film, but which he could also shoot as an original movie if Constantin did not want to pursue the project. "I thought, there's a zombie movie to be made even if it isn't *Resident Evil*," says the filmmaker. "I presented the screenplay to Constantin and to Samuel Hadida, who ran Davis Film and co-owned the rights. I said, 'If you want to make it as *Resident Evil*, I'll change the title on the front cover, and if not, we'll go make it as an independent zombie movie called *Undead*.' They really liked the screenplay, and we went out and got the movie financed."

The *Resident Evil* team put together the budget by preselling the film in non-US territories. "Romero's movies really resonated outside of America," says Anderson. "Carpenter famously said, 'In France, I'm an auteur. In America, I'm a bum.' Romero was one of those auteurs. *Resident Evil* was financed as an international co-production, even though it was set in America and was shot in English."

Anderson's script did not directly adapt the video games but acted as a prequel to the Capcom franchise. "I was going to make a horror film with a bunch of people dying, and it had to be scary," says the director. "You can do a faithful adaptation, but for people who have played the game, there's no suspense. So that's where my idea came to do the prequel. I thought, [with] a unique bunch of characters, I can kill who I want."

In October 2000, *Variety* announced that Anderson was set to write and direct *Resident Evil*. According to the article, the plot would focus on "a military unit that fights against a powerful super computer that is out of control. In order to save the world, the military unit must combat hundreds of scientists who have mutated into flesh-eating undead due to a laboratory accident." The *Variety* article also noted that the project was "budgeted in the neighborhood of $40 million." Anderson says he actually had much less money with which to make the movie. "How the independent world works is, you go out to the marketplace, and you sell it, like, 'We're making it for $40 million, and your territory is 10 percent of the world, so you give us $4 million,'" he explains. "When it actually comes to making the movie, [they] go, 'Oh, no, no, you don't have $40 million, you've got to make it for $30 million.' To give you the reality, at one point, the budget was 50, and we got it down to 40, and then, to get the green light, we cut it to 30—and that's what we made the first movie for."

Inspired by the *Alien* series and the *Terminator* films, Anderson decided to have the movie's lead character be a woman. The director cast *The Fifth Element* actress Milla Jovovich as his heroine, the amnesia-stricken Alice. Jovovich was already familiar with the *Resident Evil* game and had explored the possibility of producing a film version herself. "It was a happy coincidence," says Anderson. "Cut to another part of Los Angeles, Milla Jovovich is playing the video game with her young brother Marco and really enjoying it. She had started to pursue the rights and discovered that this asshole Paul Anderson had already written a script. That's how she ended up coming onto the project."

Anderson filmed most of the movie in Berlin, whose two halves had been reunited just a decade before. "We shot in Berlin because, [after] the Berlin Wall had come down, it had become the biggest building site in the

Milla Jovovich in *Resident Evil* (2002).

world," says the filmmaker. "There were underground U-Bahn stations that hadn't opened yet, there were building sites with all these pillars and exposed concrete work. It was a wonderful place for us to shoot."

Jovovich's co-stars included James Purefoy, Colin Salmon, and Michelle Rodriguez, who played Rain, a member of the military unit. The actress had portrayed a teenage boxer in director Karyn Kusama's Sundance Film Festival-screened 2000 drama *Girlfight* and was about to be seen in the Vin Diesel-starring *The Fast and the Furious*, which was set for release in the summer of 2001. "We needed another strong element of the casting to push the whole thing over the top," says Anderson. "I met with Michelle in LA, and she felt the role wasn't big enough. I said, 'Don't worry, I'll big up the role for you.'"

Jovovich read Anderson's rewrite on the flight to Berlin and was angered by the changes the director had made to the screenplay. "I almost quit the movie," the actress told the outlet Inverse in 2017. "I was shooting something else, and Paul had hired Michelle Rodriguez to play Rain. And she had just come off *Girlfight* and there was Oscar buzz. She was very hot at that moment, and my hotness had sort of been already four years old by that point. So Paul rewrote the script for her. It pretty much made my character 'the girl,' and Rain was 'the guy.' She got all of my big action scenes, and she became like Alice. And then Alice became this tag-along."

Anderson acknowledges that his rewrite enhanced the character of Rain at the expense of Jovovich's Alice. "To lure Michelle, I'd made her character more important, and when you give more to one character, it seems to make another character less important," he says. "So Milla landed in Berlin, full of piss and vinegar. My poor producing partner Jeremy met her at the airport with a bunch of flowers. I think she just threw the flowers in the bin and said, 'You have a lot of work to do.' I met with Milla, and she laid out her dissatisfaction. I said, 'I totally get it,' and I rebalanced the screenplay to make both her and Michelle happy, and that's what she shot." Anderson and Jovovich would become close off-set, with the pair announcing their engagement in 2003.

The film's practical effects were supervised by Pauline Fowler of the UK-based company Animated Extras. The makeup artist and sculptor's previous credits included 1994's Kenneth Branagh-directed *Mary Shelley's Frankenstein* and 1996's *Mary Reilly*, which had a troubled production. "By the end of that, we were having tee shirts made saying, 'I worked on *Mary*

Reilly and survived,'" she remembers. Fowler first worked with Anderson on *Event Horizon*. "*Event Horizon* was fab, I really enjoyed that," she says. "Because we were both *Resident Evil* nerds, he [then] asked me to work on that."

Fowler was surprised to discover that Anderson's script did not feature the zombified Dobermanns that had so terrified screenwriter Alan B. McElroy.

A zombie in *Resident Evil*.

"The first time Paul sent me the script, the dogs weren't in it," she recalls. "I said, 'You can't have a *Resident Evil* without dogs.' A couple of weeks later, I got the [new] script, and the dogs were in it." Fowler now faced the challenge of creating zombie makeup for real Dobermanns. "My strongest memory is covering this dog with flayed skin, and we walked it down the corridor to Paul to do a screen test," she says. "By the time we got to Paul Anderson, the corridor was covered in gobbets of blood, and this dog had absolutely f-all on it. He went, 'What's that?' We managed to get it down in the end."

Anderson didn't want to just make a zombie film and, following the lead of the video game, the *Resident Evil* characters had much more to fear than the undead. The movie's most memorable killing featured Colin Salmon's team leader being sliced into pieces by a laser grid, and the film climaxed with a battle between Jovovich's heroine and a massive 'Licker' monster. Anderson recalls Constantin chief Bernd Eichinger questioning these choices. According to the filmmaker, "When the pressure was to put a lid on the budget, I remember Bernd Eichinger saying, 'Why do you need laser corridors? Why do you need the Licker? Zombies were enough for Romero, why don't we just do zombies?' I pushed back on that, because I never felt that *Resident Evil* was a zombie movie franchise *per se*. I describe them as science fiction-action thrillers, and they had to have these other components."

Anderson required exterior footage which looked like it had been filmed in the US for a concluding sequence when Jovovich's character walks through the streets of the ruined Raccoon City. The director planned on shooting the scene in Toronto and, on the morning of September 11, 2001, boarded a plane in New York headed to Canada. The filmmaker was still airborne when the al-Qaeda attack on the World Trade Center occurred. "I think my flight was the last to leave American airspace before it was completely closed," he says. "We were all unaware of what was happening; that was before planes had internet. When we landed, it was playing on all the monitors in [the] Toronto airport." The attack delayed the shoot in Toronto and prompted a change in the film's title. "Originally, the screenplay had been called *Resident Evil: Ground Zero*," says Anderson. "After 9/11, obviously, the *Ground Zero* aspect we had to lose."

Sony Pictures signed on to distribute the film in the US through its subsidiary Screen Gems. The label had been set up by Sony at the end of 1998 in a clear response to the success Dimension and New Line had enjoyed with lower budget genre films. As Bloomberg News reported, "Screen Gems' releases might include genre product such as horror and teen-oriented films, as well as independent projects developed by emerging filmmakers." Screen Gems' early releases included *Girlfight* and 1999's Ehren Kruger-written thriller *Arlington Road*. In December 2001, the company's executive vice president of acquisitions and production Clint Culpepper was named president of Screen Gems, a position he would hold until January 2018. "Screen Gems picked up the movie while we were shooting," says Anderson. "It was a piece of business [for them]. They weren't like the European distributors or the Japanese distributor, who were really into it. Clint Culpepper, who was running Screen Gems, said, after the fact, [that] he never understood the screenplay, never understood the movie."

Sony had not guaranteed that *Resident Evil* would receive a theatrical release in the US. The film's future was to be decided by the results of a test screening held by the company in Los Angeles. "If we didn't score over a certain threshold in the first audience test screening, they were totally ready to put the movie to DVD," says Anderson. "And that threshold was fairly high, it was in the 70s, which for a horror movie is hard to achieve. Some of the audience go, 'Am I a bad person if I say that was excellent?' I obviously didn't want the movie to go straight to DVD. It was very stressful."

Anderson flew from Berlin, where *Resident Evil* was being edited, to Los Angeles so the director could attend the screening in Burbank. "This was the night we were going to live or die," he says. "All of the Sony executives were sitting behind me, all of the acquisition people, all of the lawyers."

The film's fate was sealed, positively, by the reaction of the audience to the early death of a supporting character who is killed as they attempt to escape the underground complex. "At the moment when the elevator drops, and that woman gets decapitated, somebody stood up at the front of the audience and went, 'I love this movie!', and the audience literally cheered," says Anderson. "I looked around, and I could see all the Sony executives behind me, they had dollar signs in their eyes. That was the moment we knew we were going to get a theatrical release."

Critics tore apart the film with zombie-like determination. *Detroit Free Press* writer John Monahan claimed, "Even in the dubious genre of movies based on video games, *Resident Evil* is an abomination." "The critical response was muted," says Anderson, with understatement. "I remember [someone] said, 'This is a movie with no audience.' You know, it's been made for nobody. I thought, well, you're wrong. I passionately believed there was an audience. Of course, we were proved right."

Screen Gems released the film on March 15, 2002. By the end of its theatrical run, *Resident Evil* had grossed $40 million in the US and $62 million in foreign territories, much to Anderson's delight. "It's always nice to have a hit," he says. "We did 40 percent in North America and 60 percent in the rest of the world, and as the franchise went on, and got bigger, that divide got wider and wider."

Capcom fast-tracked a second film, *Resident Evil: Apocalypse*, with the backing of the now enthusiastic Screen Gems. "Sony felt they'd missed out, because they saw the business the movie had done all over the world," Anderson says. "They pretty much fully financed all of the films from then on. Although technically still independent movies, they were financed by Sony Pictures."

Resident Evil: Apocalypse was helmed by veteran second unit director Alexander Witt, because Anderson was committed to making 20th Century Fox's *Alien vs. Predator*. "In an ideal world, I would have done *Alien vs. Predator*, then I would have done *Resident Evil 2*," says the director. "But when you're making movies for competing studios, they don't give a damn about, 'Oh, I've got a commitment to make a movie for another studio.'" The plot of the second *Resident Evil* film found Jovovich's Alice trying to escape Raccoon City, which has been overrun by zombies and placed under quarantine by the Umbrella Corporation. The critical community collectively threw up its hands at the movie's arrival, with Roger Ebert describing it as "an utterly meaningless waste of time." Once again, cinemagoers did not care. When Screen Gems released *Resident Evil: Apocalypse* in the US in September 2004, the film won its opening weekend with a take of $23 million and went on to amass a global gross of $129 million.

Constantin and Screen Gems happily greenlit a third movie, 2007's *Resident Evil: Extinction*, which starred Jovovich and *Final Destination* actress Ali Larter. Anderson was busy working on Universal's Jason Statham-starring *Death Race*, and *Highlander* filmmaker Russell Mulcahy stepped in to direct. *Resident Evil: Extinction* proved the most popular franchise entry yet, earning $147 million worldwide.

Anderson remained closely involved with the series, writing and producing both sequels. "On the third one, I actually was on set for the whole thing," he says. "At one point, Russell got sick and was hospitalized, and I literally was on set directing."

The filmmaker considered wrapping up the series after three movies but had a change of heart once *Resident Evil: Extinction* became such a big hit. "A trilogy felt satisfying to me, and I wanted to give it an end point," he says. "The third one is called *Extinction*, because there was an air of finality about it. Equally, I wanted to be able to continue the franchise if I wanted to—and that's pretty much what happened." In December 2008, Anderson confirmed to the outlet IGN that he was writing the script for a fourth *Resident Evil* film.

The director was now far from alone in his enthusiasm for zombies. Six years on from the original *Resident Evil* film, the undead genre had well and truly come back to life.

"THERE WAS SOMETHING IN THE BLOOD."

As Paul W. S. Anderson was shooting *Resident Evil* in 2001, the filmmaker's fellow Brit Danny Boyle was overseeing his own George A. Romero-inspired tale, *28 Days Later*, from a script by novelist Alex Garland. The writer had become famous in his native UK following the 1996 publication of his debut novel *The Beach*. A thriller about backpackers attempting to find their Zen on a remote island paradise, the book was a bestseller, reprinted by publisher Viking 25 times in less than a year. Garland followed *The Beach* with 1998's *The Tesseract*, and struck a deal to write two more books, but began to doubt if the solitary life of a novelist was for him. "I thought: Jesus Christ, I do not want to spend the next 40 years stuck in a room," he recalled to *The Guardian* in 2015. "I had an advance to write two more books and I paid it back because I had an idea for a film about running zombies, which was *28 Days Later*."

Romero's zombie films had made an impression on Garland when he was a child. "I'd seen *Night of the Living Dead* and *Dawn of the Dead* on my neighbor's VCR when I was 13 years old, and I thought, wow!" the writer would recall to entertainment journalist Zaki Hasan. Garland's interest in the zombie genre was reignited by the *Resident Evil* video games. "Probably a year or two before I wrote *28 Days*, *Resident Evil* got released," Garland told Hasan. "Sometimes *28 Days Later* is credited with reviving the zombie genre in some respect, but actually I think it was *Resident Evil* that did it, because I remember playing *Resident Evil*, having not really encountered zombies for quite a while, and thinking: oh my God, I love zombies! I'd forgotten how much I love zombies. These are awesome!"

The writer became friendly with Danny Boyle and his producer Andrew Macdonald while visiting the Thailand set of 2000's big-budget adaptation of *The Beach*, which starred Leonardo DiCaprio. The novelist later pitched Boyle and Macdonald his idea for a movie about a bicycle courier who awakes from a coma to discover that Britain has become overrun by people turned murderously violent by a virus. The infected in Garland's screenplay were not dead, and thus technically not zombies, and sprinted where the undead traditionally shambled. Still, the script clearly owed a debt to Romero's films and borrowed several of the trilogy's plot points.

While Boyle enjoyed some horror movies, like *The Exorcist* and Nicolas Roeg's 1973 film *Don't Look Now*, he was much less familiar with the zombie genre than Garland. So the director had no problem changing up the nature of the threat facing the film's survivors. "No, I don't like zombie movies very much," the director told Amy Raphael, author of 2013's *Danny Boyle: Creating Wonder*. "I find them implausible. Why do zombies just lurch around instead of running after their victims? [...] I immediately said to Alex that if I was going to make the film, the zombies had to run."

Boyle picked new faces as his leads, with Cillian Murphy playing the bicycle courier, Jim, and Naomie Harris and teenage actress Megan Burns portraying fellow survivors, Selena and Hannah. Burns was enthralled by Garland's script, which she was given after her first audition. "I read it on the way home, on the train, and I was thinking, 'I have to do this, it's so good,'" she says. "It was such a visual script [that] as you read it, you could see it playing out. I have to admit that I didn't find it very scary, but I'm into the darkness, and the goth, and the horror. But yeah, instantly I thought, 'If I don't get this part, I'm going to be so sad.'"

Boyle had a small budget of around $6 million but still wanted to depict a post-apocalyptic London. He resolved to shoot on digital video, hiring cinematographer Anthony Dod Mantle, who had worked on Thomas Vinterberg's similarly experimental 1998 drama *Festen*, to help fulfil his vision. In the finished film's most hauntingly memorable scenes, Murphy's Jim wanders through the streets of a deserted London trying to figure out what has happened to England's capital. Boyle filmed the sequence in July 2001, ahead of the main shoot. "We appointed our own marshals in jackets to ask drivers to stop," the director recalled to writer Amy Raphael. "My daughter Grace, who was eighteen at the time, turned up with a few mates. They were all attractive girls. There was a heatwave, they weren't wearing many clothes, and of course the drivers around at that time were mostly men. If I asked them to stop, they'd tell me to fuck off; a beautiful girl leaning into the car did the trick."

Cillian Murphy in *28 Days Later* (2002).

The bulk of the film's shoot began at the start of September. Boyle was still in production when the 9/11 attack occurred in New York. "I think the reason [the film] had the impact that it did is that it was the first one out of the block that touched, not directly but aesthetically and morally, some of the residue of what 9/11 had done to us," he told the outlet Inverse in 2023. "And, in our particular case, it made cities, which feel so immense, suddenly they were utterly vulnerable." At one point, Murphy's Jim pauses in front of a wall on which people have left notes in an attempt to find lost friends and family members. When the film was released, this sight would seem like an eerie reminder of what had happened in New York following 9/11.

The actors who played the infected were recruited from an agency which specialized in finding work for former professional athletes. "We wanted people that could really move," says producer Macdonald. Megan Burns recalls happily hanging out with the cast members playing the movie's lethal virus victims. "People always say to me, 'Wasn't it so scary on set?'"

she explains. "It's like, not really, because you're sat in the makeup chair next to the zombies—the infected—and you're eating dinner with them, so there's not that fear of people who are so lovely. It's a film, isn't it? It's all play-acting."

For the movie's ending, Boyle originally filmed a sequence in which Jim dies after being shot, leaving Selena and Hannah as the last non-infected survivors. After that conclusion tested badly, the director replaced it with a finale where all three lived. Burns remembers preferring the original ending. "I quite liked the idea that it was me and Naomie versus the world," she says. "I thought that was an interesting take on the final girl in horror films. It's like these two girls are left to fend for themselves—still in the bloody ballgowns."

28 Days Later was a hit in the UK, earning $9 million after it opened in November 2002. The movie subsequently proved successful in the US, too, where it debuted in theaters the following June. Following the initial release, distributors Fox Searchlight put out a new version of the movie that included the alternate, and more downbeat, ending. Boyle's film wound up earning $45 million at the domestic box office.

Many reviewers embraced *28 Days Later* and the film's echoes of a reality made more uncertain not just by 9/11 but by a 2003 outbreak of the coronavirus-caused severe acute respiratory syndrome (SARS) that caused more than 700 deaths worldwide. In his assessment for *The Boston Globe*, Ty Burr described the film as "terrifying on the basic heebie-jeebie level, respectful toward its B-movie forebears, and all the more unnerving for coming out in this fretful era of SARS and germ warfare."

The teenage Megan Burns received surprising proof that *28 Days Later* had made a serious impact on the culture when she sat her A-level exams a couple of years after shooting the movie. "I did film studies, and one of the questions was about how the marketing of *28 Days Later* led to its success," she says. "I remember loads of people in the exam room giving me a look like, 'You've aced this, then!' But I still didn't get an 'A' on that paper. I wasn't involved in the marketing of it. I was just a kid, going along, enjoying the shoot."

Critics greeted Uwe Boll's zombie film *House of the Dead* much more negatively than they had welcomed *28 Days Later* and even *Resident Evil* when the German filmmaker's video game adaptation was released in October 2003. "It's hard to write a review worthy of *House of the Dead* and still use correct spelling and grammar," claimed Scott Brown in his review for *Entertainment Weekly*. Jovanka Vuckovic, describing the film for *Rue Morgue*, was similarly damning. "If you want to see what a cinematic piece of dog barf looks like, go see *House of the Dead*," she wrote. Such dim views of the movie were, in large part, shared by its co-writer, Mark A. Altman. "We were like, this is going to be the greatest zombie movie ever made!" he says. "George Romero is going to come and see this and be like, 'Wow!' But obviously that was not to be."

The Japanese company Sega had launched the *House of the Dead* arcade game in 1996. The following year, DreamWorks announced that the company had acquired the film rights for Jesse Dylan, a director of music videos and commercials and son of music icon Bob. That iteration never came to pass, and the project passed into the hands of Mindfire Entertainment. The company had previously produced 1998's *Free Enterprise*, a comedy about *Star Trek* fans. That film was co-written by Altman, who was the president of Mindfire and saw the commercial potential in a *House of the Dead* movie. "I was a huge fan of the arcade game and I love zombie films," he says. "I'm like, this could be really cool. We shopped it around. I had really good meetings. Everybody's like, 'Oh, this seems like a good brand, but it's *zombies*.'" When Mindfire approached Constantin about financing the project, the company demurred because of their prior commitment to produce *Resident Evil*. "They loved it but they're like, we don't want to do two zombie movies," says Altman.

Pressing on, the Mindfire president collaborated on a script for the movie with Dave Parker, who had written and directed 2000's low-budget zombie film *The Dead Hate the Living!* Determined to differentiate their movie from *Resident Evil*, the pair found inspiration in director Jacques Tourneur's 1943 voodoo tale *I Walked with a Zombie*. "We knew *Resident Evil* was happening, they had a much bigger budget than we thought we would have," says Altman. "We developed *House of the Dead* in a different direction. Tonally, it was much more elevated and creepy."

Altman seemingly caught a break when he pitched the project as an investment opportunity to Uwe Boll. The filmmaker had written, directed, and produced the 2000 thriller *Sanctimony*, starring *Starship Troopers* actor Casper Van Dien. Boll had shot *Sanctimony* in Vancouver with finance he had secured by making use of a provision in the German tax code, which allowed investors to write off the money they put into a movie. "My head

David Palffy and Ona Grauer in *House of the Dead* (2003).

of business affairs gets me on the phone with this guy I'd never heard of, Uwe Boll," says Altman. "Uwe was very excited. He was like, 'I want in.' Then the caveat came: 'I'm going to finance it, but I'm also going to direct it.' That's a terrifying thought to any producer. You lose any ability to manage if the director is also the financier. But we had no choice. The license was about to expire."

Altman's worst fears were realized during the Vancouver shoot of the film, whose cast included a group of twentysomething Canadian actors and *Das Boot* star Jürgen Prochnow. "I've worked on a lot of TV shows, a lot of movies, but this was probably my craziest experience," says Altman. "We start shooting, and what I realize is, Uwe had to deliver two movies. At the same time we're shooting *House of the Dead*, he's shooting what was called *House of the Dead: The Funny Version*. We'd do two or three takes of a scene and then he'd go, 'Now, this one is for the funny version. Everyone be funny!' But there was no script for the comedy version. When young actors aren't used to ad-libbing, it's just, 'Fuck this,' 'Fuck-fuck, fuck-fuck,' 'Fuck-fuck-fuck.' Jürgen Prochnow, God bless him, finally snaps and goes, 'Uwe! I signed up to make this script! I don't want to make up lines!'"

Altman's plan for the film to channel the moody atmospherics of *I Walked with a Zombie* was scotched when Boll staged an elaborate action sequence utilizing the 'bullet time' effect previously seen in *The Matrix*. "Uwe's like, 'We're going to do bullet time with zombies,' because he had seen it in *The Matrix*," Altman recalls. *The Matrix* was not the only film to inspire Boll during the shoot. "He would start emulating the things he was seeing," says Altman. "We would all go to see *Fellowship of the Ring* over the weekend, and then on Monday he would throw out the shot list and be like, 'We shoot the scene where he hides in a hole and the zombies come looking [for him]'—exactly the shot from *Fellowship of The Ring.*" According to Altman, Boll's penchant for adding such sequences resulted in important scenes of character development being cut. "They would have to find the money, which generally involved ripping out pages of script," he says. "Uwe always wants the camera to be moving and always something happening. For him, character development is death. It's like ADD filmmaking, which is fine, it's a choice. I mean, it's a Michael Bay approach, right? My feeling is, in horror, you have to feel for the characters. I'm a big fan of Hitchcockian suspense. This was not that."

As Altman watched Boll's first cut of the movie, he was horrified to discover that the filmmaker had punctuated the story with clips from the Sega game. "When Uwe said, 'Can you talk with Sega about getting the video game footage?' I thought it was for marketing stuff," he says. "I didn't know he was going to use it in the movie. I did—and I'm not exaggerating—seventy pages of notes on the cut. And I said, underlined, in all caps, 'IF YOU DON'T LISTEN TO ANY OF THESE NOTES, I BEG YOU TO TAKE THE VIDEO GAME FOOTAGE OUT.' He didn't do any of the notes."

Distributors Artisan released Boll's film in the US on October 10, 2003. Despite the many bad reviews, *House of the Dead* earned a creditable $10 million at the domestic box office and was a hit on DVD. "The theatrical just promoted the DVD," says Altman. "It was the heyday [of] physical media, and it was huge on DVD."

Boll would go on to direct more adaptations of horror video games with 2005's Christian Slater-starring *Alone in the Dark* and the same year's vampire movie *BloodRayne*. These films, too, were poorly received by the critical community, with whom Boll developed a literally pugilistic relationship. In June 2006, the director issued a statement challenging anyone who had given him a negative review to a fight. The next September, Boll boxed and beat a quartet of writers, including Chris Alexander from *Rue Morgue*. "They were badmouthing me, but they showed balls going into the ring," Boll said after the bouts. "Now they are braindead and they will like my movies."

In 2008, Boll followed through on his promise to release a comedic cut of his zombie film. "Many years later, I saw *House of the Dead: The Funny Version* on Amazon on DVD, and I bought it," says Mark Altman. "There's some new footage, and then there's some of the movie, but they did it like *Pop-Up Video*, with pop-ups trying to be funny. I never made it through the whole thing."

Boll and Altman parted ways following *House of the Dead*, but the writer remains surprisingly fond of the German filmmaker. "I liken him to William Castle," he says. "Everything's a stunt. He's larger than life. He's old school Hollywood in that sense. Uwe is one of those people, for all the shit that he gets, and for all his mishegoss, he's a really lovely guy. Would I do a movie with him again? No. Do I wish good things for him? Absolutely."

Halloween 4 screenwriter Alan B. McElroy may have lost out on the chance to help craft the first *Resident Evil* movie, but a couple of years later he would create a different, and similarly prolific, franchise with his script for 2003's *Wrong Turn*. The film centered on a group of twentysomethings who are terrorized by a trio of inbred cannibals in a remote part of West Virginia. McElroy was inspired to write the *Wrong Turn* screenplay by an incident that occurred in the early '90s when he was traveling from his home in Ohio to catch a flight. "My wife and I were driving to New York to take a trip to Jamaica, and it was the middle of the night, and we were in a snowstorm," he says. "We came across a traffic jam, and we were like, well, how long is this going to take?" After looking at a map, the couple decided to circumnavigate the traffic by taking a side road. "As we're doing that, in the dark, in a snowstorm, we're thinking, is this a smart idea?" McElroy continues. "Anything could go wrong!"

Writing his script for *Wrong Turn*, McElroy deliberately steered away from the knowing vibe of Kevin Williamson's screenplay for *Scream*. "I wanted to strip away all of that self-awareness," says the writer. "I felt horror had lost the core of what a horror movie can be, which is to put people in a situation that really is a pressure cooker and force them to face who they are as individuals. I tried to write that kind of movie."

In August 2001, *Variety* announced that the companies Summit Entertainment and Newmarket Group had partnered to produce the film, which was budgeted at $10 million. The article also revealed that legendary special effects artist Stan Winston had joined the project as a producer. The multiple Oscar-winner was well known for his work on the blockbusters *Terminator 2: Judgment Day* and *Jurassic Park*. But Winston loved horror, with his other credits including John Carpenter's *The Thing* and 1988's monster movie *Pumpkinhead*, which he directed. "I read the script, and I thought it was one of the scariest I'd read in ages," Winston would tell the website Moviehole about McElroy's screenplay. Much of the film's budget was provided by Constantin Film, whose Robert Kulzer was a credited producer on the movie. "Stan came onboard as a producer, and Constantin financed it, and we were off to the races," says McElroy.

Wrong Turn was directed by Rob Schmidt, whose feature debut, the Dostoevsky-inspired crime drama *Crime and Punishment in Suburbia*, had been nominated for a Grand Jury Prize at the 2000 Sundance Film Festival. Schmidt wanted to make a horror movie and took a meeting at Dimension about directing a film in the *Hellraiser* franchise. "I called my agent, and I was like, 'They offered me a *Hellraiser*,'" he remembers. "She said she wouldn't represent me anymore if I did the *Hellraiser*. But she took more seriously that I liked the idea of doing horror films."

Schmidt liked the *Wrong Turn* script and started speaking with the numerous producing parties. "I had meetings, I want to say, at three different companies to get approved for it," he says. The large number of production entities would prove an enduring source of stress for the director. "It was like the United Nations to get casting approved," he says. "I don't know what the tiniest country on earth is, but that was me."

Schmidt initially wanted a Black man to play the male lead role of a medical student whose car collides with another vehicle, packed with more potential victims, in the Appalachian woods. "I lobbied for the role to be an African-American actor," says the director. "I was told you can't do that, because we won't be able to sell the movie overseas. I was actually told that they wouldn't be able to sell it in Japan. I'm still to this day shocked by that."

Schmidt cast Desmond Harrington as the film's male lead, Chris, and Eliza Dushku as the movie's final girl, Jessie. To play Dushku's doomed traveling companions, Schmidt chose Kevin Zegers, Lindy Booth, Jeremy Sisto, and Emmanuelle Chriqui.

In McElroy's original script, the film's cannibals—Three Finger, Saw Tooth, and One Eye—were all physically large. Winston suggested that one of the trio be a less imposing character. According to McElroy, "Stan was the one who said, 'What if we create one that is smaller, but more agile and fidgety, and dangerous in that regard?'"

Schmidt shot *Wrong Turn* in Toronto, and he and Winston picked locally based talent to play the film's three cannibals. The pair cast a tall actor named Ted Clark to portray One Eye and an even taller professional wrestler called Garry Robbins to play Saw Tooth. For the role of Three Finger, they picked Julian Richings, whose credits included *Mimic*, *Urban Legend*, and *Cube*. The actor remembers Winston working with him on his character's physicality and distinctive cackle even at his audition. "I was so impressed, he built the character with me," says the actor of the special effects artist, who passed away in 2008. "We figured out the laugh, and we figured out movement, and we figured out a few things, actually."

Richings and his cannibal colleagues had long, physically demanding days during the Toronto shoot, partly because of the makeup and prosthetics that Winston's team applied to them each morning. "It was a very

Emmanuelle Chriqui and prosthetic head in behind-the-scenes shot from *Wrong Turn* (2003).

painstaking process," says Richings. "Mine was four hours to put on and about an hour and a half to take off." Winston's work genuinely alarmed Emmanuelle Chriqui when she caught sight of the cannibal characters. "We saw them out in the woods, literally for the first time, and it was terrifying," says the actress. "One of them made these horrific squealing sounds, and the whole thing was so scary. I was like, wait, wait, wait, this is just a movie."

20th Century Fox released *Wrong Turn* on May 30, 2003, with the film ending the weekend in sixth position on the box office chart. "It was meant to be released closer to Halloween and then it got rushed out at the end of May," says McElroy. "It didn't have the advertising that it should have had." By the end of its domestic cinema run, *Wrong Turn* had grossed $15 million. Fox decreed that the second film in the franchise should be a straight-to-DVD release. According to Rob Schmidt, the studio's decision was made easier by the deals the director and Winston had signed for the first film. "Stan's contract and my contract paid pretty substantially for a sequel if it was a theatrical release," says the director. "So we did not do the sequel, the Stan Winston folks and me." The series would also proceed without input from its screenwriter. "They paid me off," says McElroy.

The franchise's second entry, 2007's *Wrong Turn 2: Dead End*, was the directorial debut of Joe Lynch. Raised on New York's Long Island, Lynch was taken as a small child to see Romero's *Dawn of the Dead* by his mother and spent his teenage years poring over issues of *Fangoria*. The young director successfully pitched his vision for the second *Wrong Turn* film to 20th Century Fox Home Entertainment vice president Tom Siegrist at Los Angeles' Fox Plaza, which famously doubled for the Nakatomi Plaza skyscraper in *Die Hard*. "I came in guns blazing," says Lynch. "I had a 30-page bible, I had the entire opening scene storyboarded. I heard that other directors came in and they were just like, eh, it's a gig, whereas I was like, this is my whole life. When I walked out of Nakatomi Plaza, [I was] dancing around, going, I killed it!"

The script for *Wrong Turn 2*, by Turi Meyer and Al Septien, hinged around a reality TV competition show titled *The Apocalypse: Ultimate Survivalist*, which attracts the attention of the cannibal clan. Lynch cast punk-rock legend Henry Rollins as the show's host and Erica Leerhsen from *Book of Shadows: Blair Witch 2* as the film's final girl Nina.

Lynch filmed *Wrong Turn 2* in Vancouver and was determined to make the best film he could, despite knowing that the movie would not be released on the big screen. "I went into Fox to meet with a certain very big executive right before I shot," says the director. "At one point, he went, 'Look, we can spray diarrhea in a DVD box and put it on the shelf in Blockbuster, and it will sell if the name is *Wrong Turn 2*.' They knew they were cashing in on the name. What we are proud of is the fact that we made it the best diarrhea you could possibly spray into a DVD box ever; it was as if we were eating filet mignon and then spraying diarrhea into it."

The *Wrong Turn 2* DVD was released in October 2007. Bloody Disgusting reviewer Brian Collins wrote that "what could have been a cheap and lazy cash-in turned out to be one of the year's better genre offerings." Such assessments helped drive Lynch's movie to an impressive $9 million in DVD sales.

Fox approached him about making another *Wrong Turn* film before his movie was even released. The director developed a pitch with *House of the Dead* co-writer Dave Parker. "It was almost like an homage to *Assault on Precinct 13*," says Lynch. "In the beginning of the film, Three Finger gets arrested and brought to this police precinct, and then the rest of the family come to get him. They loved the idea, but they said, 'We're going to give you half the money that you had before, and you've got to shoot it in Bulgaria.' I politely passed."

The franchise continued nonetheless. Over the next decade, *Wrong Turn 2* was followed by four more films: 2009's *Wrong Turn 3: Left for Dead*, 2011's *Wrong Turn 4: Bloody Beginnings*, 2012's *Wrong Turn 5: Bloodlines*—whose cast included *Hellraiser* star Doug Bradley—and 2014's *Wrong Turn 6: Last Resort*. The DVD boom was long over by the release of the franchise's sixth entry. The popularity of the format had peaked in 2005, when US sales reached $16 billion. The recession that followed the 2007–2008 financial crisis combined with the rise of streaming services to have a dramatically negative impact on sales. Following the release of *Wrong Turn 6*, Fox put the franchise on ice.

Julian Richings only appeared in the original *Wrong Turn* but continues to be recognized for his portrayal of Three Finger by horror fans. "It makes me laugh, because a lot of people send me posts of my picture with a bow and arrow, and I'll realize that it's from *Wrong Turn 3*, or *4*, or *5*, or something," he says. "I don't like to write back and say, 'Actually, that's not me.'"

Don Coscarelli's *Phantasm* series was among the many horror franchises to reach a commercial low in the early '90s, although the director had started having problems with Hollywood's handling of his saga some years earlier.

The success of 1979's original, independently financed *Phantasm* encouraged Universal to back a sequel, 1988's *Phantasm II*. The studio promised Coscarelli a budget of just under $3 million, roughly ten times the amount he had spent on the first movie. But Universal requested that the director replace *Phantasm* star Michael Baldwin, who had not appeared in a movie since the original film. So the director reluctantly set about auditioning actors for the role of Mike, who had battled Angus Scrimm's dreaded Tall Man in the first film. The list of auditionees included the then-unknown Brad Pitt, who ultimately lost the part to James Le Gros. "I was interviewing every hunky male in Hollywood," says Coscarelli. "Brad Pitt was a good-looking guy, and his reading was really good. He wasn't *the* Brad Pitt back then; this was before he did *Thelma & Louise*. In any case, big mistake on my part obviously, [although] James Le Gros is a terrific actor and he's gone on to a stellar career."

Phantasm II performed poorly at the box office, and 1994's *Phantasm III: Lord of the Dead*—for which Michael Baldwin returned to the cast—suffered the ignominy of being essentially a home entertainment release. "If you were a direct-to-video movie, it's like you were not a movie," says Coscarelli. "So that was tough to endure."

The director had befriended Quentin Tarantino and Roger Avary in the late '80s, when the pair were working at the Video Archives movie rental store in Manhattan Beach. Avary was a *Phantasm* fan and, after winning the Best Original Screenplay Oscar for *Pulp Fiction*, attempted to relaunch the moribund franchise, writing the script for a new movie called *Phantasm 1999*. The planned film would feature franchise veterans Scrimm, Baldwin, and Reggie Bannister, as well as introducing a new character, Colonel Heckleman, the leader of a commando team. To play Heckleman, Coscarelli approached Bruce Campbell, who had impressed the director with his crowd-pleasing antics at a *Fangoria*-hosted event. "I saw him do this stunt, just because he loved his fans," says the director. "He would risk his life, and do this crazy flip on the stage, and they'd give him a standing ovation. I thought, this guy, he's got some magic."

Avary was unable to secure financing for *Phantasm 1999*. As the years went by, the writer would rename his screenplay first *Phantasm 2013 A.D.*

and then *Phantasm's End*, but he never managed to find the $8 million budget for the venture. The screenwriter was even turned down by the Weinsteins, despite Miramax having produced *Pulp Fiction*. According to Coscarelli, the brothers were prepared to back the venture, but only if someone other than the *Phantasm* creator directed the movie. "Roger came back and he goes, 'They passed,'" says Coscarelli. "Roger was given a reason, I later found out, which was, yeah, they'd make it with another director." With *Phantasm 1999* permanently stalled, the filmmaker directed a sequel-prequel titled *Phantasm IV: Oblivion*. Made for less than $1 million, the movie was again released straight to video in 1998.

Coscarelli would collaborate with Bruce Campbell on a very different project, 2003's *Bubba Ho-Tep*. The film was based on a novella by author Joe R. Lansdale, in which an aged resident at an assisted living facility who claims to be Elvis Presley teams up with a Black man who believes he is John F. Kennedy to battle an ancient Mummy. "I was at a bookstore, and I came across a new collection of Joe's short stories," recalls the director. "The logline was, 'Elvis fights a 4,000-year-old Mummy.' I was like, God, there's a movie in that." Many people disagreed about the novella's cinematic potential, as Coscarelli discovered when he attempted to find financing for the film. "It was just a constant series of rejections," he says. "The biggest of all of them was, 'No twentysomething audience is going to want to spend an hour and a half with two old geezers.'"

Coscarelli decided to make the film as a low-budget independent feature, ransacking his own savings to help pay for the movie and receiving financial help from his father. The director cast Campbell as the decrepit 'Elvis,' even though the *Evil Dead* star was only in his early 40s, and veteran actor Ossie Davis as 'JFK.' The *Phantasm* filmmaker shot the movie at an abandoned rehabilitation center in Downey, California, with KNB handling the film's effects.

Phantasm fan J. J. Abrams was one of the people to whom Coscarelli showed an early version of the film. Abrams would soon embark on a major directing career, but was then best known as the co-creator of the TV drama *Felicity*, which had premiered on The WB network in 1998. "I guess he'd seen *Phantasm* when he was 13 or 14 and called me out of the blue," says Coscarelli. "I had this trailer in my driveway that I rented that I made a little editing room in. He stopped in, and watched the movie, and gave me a couple of good suggestions." Coscarelli, in turn, suggested that Abrams meet with *Phantasm* star Angus Scrimm and gave him the actor's phone number. Abrams subsequently cast Scrimm in a recurring role on his new Jennifer Garner spy show *Alias*.

Coscarelli screened *Bubba Ho-Tep* at 2002's Toronto Film Festival, but he was unable to secure a deal with distributors. The director believes that executives did not understand, or care about, Campbell's popularity in the horror community. "Most of the people [in] acquisitions didn't think we had a star in the movie, but we *did* have a star in the movie," he says. "Your traditional marketing people didn't know any of that kind of stuff."

The filmmaker once more dug into his own pockets to self-distribute the film, with assistance from the small Vitagraph Films. Starting in September 2003, Coscarelli toured around the US, joined by Campbell when possible, showing the movie and drumming up publicity for the project. "I thought, oh Christ, I can't just sell this to video, I've got to take a try," he says. "So we started this roadshow thing, Bruce did a little touring, and it was almost a year of my life booking prints and collecting money." *Bubba Ho-Tep* earned positive reviews and proved a hit in the markets where the film played. Coscarelli's movie went on to make more money after MGM released it to the lucrative DVD market, its success primed by the film's limited theatrical run.

In time, both *Bubba Ho-Tep* and the *Phantasm* films would be re-released on DVD and Blu-ray, to be purchased by genre aficionados old and new. "This is why I love horror fans—and I am one myself—we love the tangible objects, right?" says Coscarelli. "We all have our little shelf with [memorabilia from] the time I met that guy and he signed this thing. It just doesn't translate in the streaming world. Back in the good old days of albums, and DVDs, and Blu-rays, the studio could make the thing for a buck and then they'd sell it for twenty. There was a really big profit margin in there. It just doesn't translate in the streaming world. The Best Buys, they don't even have any DVD sections anymore. It's evaporated."

On July 15, 2003, a crowd of journalists and contest-winners gathered at the Bally's Las Vegas casino in Nevada to witness one of the most unusual press conferences in entertainment history. Held to promote what veteran boxing and wrestling announcer Michael Buffer declared to be "an event over 20 years in the making," the affair found Robert Englund arriving in the clothes and makeup of Freddy Krueger and actor-stuntman Ken Kirzinger sporting Jason Voorhees' costume of weathered clothing, hockey mask, and outsized machete. After the two actors were individually weighed, an in-character Englund took a seat to answer questions planted from the crowd as the masked Kirzinger sat silently at the other end of the table.

"Freddy, it seems like this fight is so overdue," asked one female attendee. "Why has it taken so long for you two to get together?"

"Well, first of all, my little piggy, that's Mr. Krueger to you. Beeyatch," replied Englund-as-Krueger. "I'll tell you what took so long. Been waiting for Hockey Puck over here to pass the urine test! Steroid city! Get it?"

The event was promoting the film *Freddy vs. Jason*, which promised an all-out smackdown featuring the two titular slasher villains. The New Line movie was produced by *Friday the 13th* filmmaker Sean S. Cunningham and directed by Ronny Yu. Both Cunningham and Yu were present at the press conference, which, somewhat inevitably, concluded with security guards pretending to restrain the two fictional combatants from coming to blows.

Freddy vs. Jason had certainly been many years in the making. Englund was first introduced to the idea of Freddy battling Jason way back in the mid-'80s, not long after the release of the original *A Nightmare on Elm Street*, when a biker showed the actor his tattoo of the two characters. Englund recalls that the stranger "ripped off his jean jacket with his Hells Angels colors on his back, pulled his pants down, took his shirt off, and said, 'Look, look!' He had a full-torso tattoo of Freddy wrestling with Jason, from his neck to his knees." Englund understood the desire to see the two characters battle. "It had become that adolescent fantasy that teenage boys and fanboys have, much like they did back in the 1930s, sitting on the stoop somewhere, going, hey, who would you think would win between Frankenstein and the Wolf Man?" he says. "Well, they made *Frankenstein Meets the Wolf Man*. They made those movies. So this is nothing new."

Paramount produced the *Friday the 13th* series and was interested in combining the two franchises following the release of 1986's *Friday the 13th*

Robert Englund and Ken Kirzinger in *Freddy vs. Jason* (2003).

Part VI: Jason Lives. The company wanted to license the character of Freddy Krueger from New Line and make the film itself. Robert Shaye similarly hoped to borrow Jason Voorhees from Paramount and have New Line produce the face-off, which led to a stalemate situation between the two corporate entities.

In the early '90s, Sean S. Cunningham teamed up with New Line and secured the rights to the Jason Voorhees character. The studio teased fans with the possibility of a confrontation between the two slasher villains at the conclusion of 1993's *Jason Goes to Hell: The Final Friday*, when Freddy's gloved hand emerged from the earth to drag away Jason's hockey mask. Wes Craven's decision to revisit the universe of Freddy Krueger with 1994's *New Nightmare* put the project on the backburner, but New Line continued to develop the film.

A platoon of scribes would toil on different versions of the *Freddy vs. Jason* screenplay, including *The Crow* screenwriter David J. Schow and future *Battlestar Galactica* reboot creator Ronald D. Moore. "They went through a lot of scripts, they couldn't quite get it right," says Englund. Craven, meanwhile, was not enthused about the idea of his creation Freddy meeting up with Jason. In a 2002 interview with *TV Guide*, the director revealed that he had been approached about working on the project in the mid-'90s, but "couldn't think of a way to do it that wouldn't be laughable."

In March 1997, New Line hosted a lunchtime presentation at ShoWest, the annual event in Las Vegas at which studios attempted to get theater owners excited about upcoming movies. New Line's promotional reel showcased *Austin Powers: International Man of Mystery* and the Wesley Snipes-starring drama *One Night Stand*. According to a *Variety* article, though, attendees were particularly excited about a teaser trailer for *Freddy vs. Jason*. "Perhaps the biggest reaction arose for a promo for *Freddy vs. Jason*, the long-awaited marriage of the *Nightmare on Elm Street* and *Friday the 13th* franchise series," wrote journalist Dan Cox. The *Variety* reporter explained that distributors "applauded and howled at the concept." That concept was still very much at the drawing board stage, however. The promo clip was made up of material culled from previously released movies.

The following August, New Line announced that Rob Bottin, one of Hollywood's best known makeup effects artists, would direct *Freddy vs. Jason*. Bottin did not plan on writing the screenplay but had submitted to the studio a scene-by-scene breakdown of the movie's action and special effects. "Rather than revisit old territory, my intention is to celebrate these characters by way of re-invention—elevating them both to a completely new level of horror, using state-of-the-art techniques," Bottin said in a statement. New Line tapped David Goyer and his writing partner James Robinson to work on the screenplay. When Bottin began to argue with the studio, both he and the writers departed the project.

Future New Line development executive Jeff Katz, who would ultimately help bring *Freddy vs. Jason* to the screen, believes that the influence of Craven's *Scream* helped delay the project going into production. Katz was still attending high school in Detroit during the mid-'90s and followed the development of *Freddy vs. Jason* by reading the array of unproduced screenplays as bootleg copies became available. "Everyone was like, '*Scream* is self-referential, so we have to chase that,'" he says.

With *Freddy vs. Jason* in a state of seemingly endless development, Sean S. Cunningham pitched New Line president of production Michael De Luca on a tenth *Friday the 13th* film. Titled *Jason X*, the movie would send Voorhees 400-odd years into the future and into space. New Line was again keen for the movie to emulate the kind of tongue-in-cheek dialog that had helped make *Scream* such a triumph. "Suddenly all the studio notes were, 'This needs to be more like *Scream*,'" screenwriter Todd Farmer recalled in the 2013 documentary *Crystal Lake Memories: The Complete History of Friday the 13th*. *Jason X* was belatedly released in April 2002 to disappointing box office results and negative reviews. "Jason gets a futuristic makeover and annihilates someone using a giant screwing tool," critic Claudia Puig wrote in *USA Today*. "After sitting through Jason's latest exploits, the audience may find itself identifying with that victim in particular."

Eventually, writers Mark Swift and Damian Shannon satisfied Michael De Luca with their *Freddy vs. Jason* screenplay, which involved Krueger reviving Voorhees to terrorize a fresh batch of victims. "Shannon and Swift were the guys that cracked it," says Jeff Katz. "They understood, you don't have to give the fans exactly what [they want] but give the fans the basic meal or they're going to kill you." In the spring of 2002, *Bride of Chucky* director Ronnie Yu accepted the challenge of bringing the script to the screen.

New Line regarded Englund as an essential part of the package but replaced Kane Hodder, who had played Jason in the previous four *Friday the 13th* movies, with Ken Kirzinger, a stuntman and stunt coordinator. The decision permanently rankled with Hodder, an experienced stuntman himself. "I know things change, people change. But at least give me a reason," Hodder said in 2011. "Even if I don't agree with it, give me a reason why you did that, and it's a lot easier to handle." According to Katz, the company "wanted to turn the page on the Kane-Jason. The idea was to go [with someone] a little taller, a little thinner, and with a big clean mask that Freddy can fuck up. I have a lot of empathy for Kane. It was a design decision, and [it] sucks to be on the other end of that."

Englund and Kirzinger's young co-stars included Katharine Isabelle from *Ginger Snaps*, *Dawson's Creek* actress Monica Keena, and Destiny's Child singer Kelly Rowland. After appearing in George Romero's *Resident Evil* commercial, Brad Renfro was set to return to the horror genre with the movie. But the troubled actor left the film shortly before the start of the shoot and was replaced by Jason Ritter. Renfro would pass away in 2008 from a heroin overdose.

As a teenager, New Line executive Jeff Katz had worked for World Championship Wrestling and suggested the film's promotional press conference in Las Vegas. "I would say, 'This is a fight, you have to lean into this thing,'" he says. "God bless New Line marketing; they got it and went for it."

Released on August 15, 2003, *Freddy vs. Jason* won its opening weekend with a gross of $36 million. By the end of the film's domestic theatrical run, it had earned $82 million, more than any entry in either the *Friday the 13th* or *Nightmare on Elm Street* franchises. "I'm really proud of that film," says Englund. "It really holds up. It's really fun to see on a nice big flat screen with the sound turned up and some cold pizza."

The commercial appeal of older horror franchises was demonstrated again later in 2003 with the release of *The Texas Chainsaw Massacre*. This remake of Tobe Hooper's infamous 1974 cannibal tale was produced by the newly formed Platinum Dunes. The company was founded in 2001 by *Bad Boys* and *Armageddon* director Michael Bay, in partnership with Andrew Form, who was an executive at Simpson-Bruckheimer Films, and Bay's college friend Brad Fuller. "As my attorney reminds me all the time, at that point in my career, I was a dogshit manager with dogshit clients," Fuller recalled during a 2018 appearance on the *Shock Waves* podcast. "And so I said to my wife, 'Michael wants to start a company with me,' and she said, 'That's what you're doing, right?'"

Bay created a cheap but effective teaser trailer for the new *Texas Chainsaw Massacre* in the hope of attracting investors. "When I shot a Mercedes commercial, before the clients arrived, I said, 'I'd like to shoot this chainsaw coming through the door,'" the director told IGN in 2003. "And that's how we sold the movie. We sold it worldwide in three days."

To direct the film, the Platinum Dunes partners approached German filmmaker Marcus Nispel, who was still to make his feature debut following his departure from *End of Days*. Nispel was encouraged to accept the job by his regular director of photography Daniel Pearl, who had been Tobe Hooper's cinematographer on the original 1974 film. "Daniel says, 'You've got to make it, because you're going to hire me, and then I get to shoot the same movie twice,'" says Nispel. "And I go, 'Yeah, let's do it!'"

The notion of remaking horror classics was regarded with suspicion by many fans, despite the beloved status of John Carpenter's *The Thing* and David Cronenberg's *The Fly*. Of course, both Carpenter and Cronenberg were established genre auteurs before embarking on their respective new versions. Nispel had no credentials in the horror movie genre or any other. The director recalls that news of his participation in the new *Texas Chainsaw Massacre* film was received negatively by the online horror community. "It was kind of a prank, you know," Nispel says of signing on for the movie. "Then there was all this venomous internet stuff going down. I go, 'Oh my God, people really take this movie very serious, right?'"

Nispel wanted an actress in the vein of *Carrie* star Sissy Spacek to play the female lead, Erin, who, together with her four friends, is terrorized by the film's chainsaw-wielding Leatherface and his clan. Instead, the Platinum Dunes partners cast the more obviously marketable Jessica Biel, star of the TV show *7th Heaven*. "I feel that the character we are supposed to fear for is waif-like," says Nispel. "What they sent me were, like, cover pages from *Maxim* magazine. I go, 'Well, that's not what I had in my mind at all.'"

Nispel shot the film in Austin, Texas, during the summer of 2002 for a budget of around $9 million. The cast also included *Wrong Turn 2* cast member Erica Leerhsen, *Full Metal Jacket* actor R. Lee Ermey, and Andrew Bryniarski, who portrayed Leatherface. The film's grimy look was dictated

Jessica Biel, Mike Vogel, Erica Leerhsen, Jonathan Tucker, and Eric Balfour in *The Texas Chainsaw Massacre* (2003).

Andrew Bryniarski in *The Texas Chainsaw Massacre.*

by the shooting environment Nispel encountered on the first day of the shoot. "*Texas Chainsaw* was so hot, I almost died," says the director. "We were in that little van, so it was worse than a sauna. All the makeup melted away; the dust of the road would bake in their faces. At the end of the day, we said, well, that's the look."

Nispel was pleased with Biel's commitment to the project. "She was a consummate professional," he says. "My sons showed up, and they were very young, and they were there for lunch break. They noticed there was a woman crying and they go, 'Why is she crying?' I said, 'Oh, that's Jessica in character during lunch.'"

The Texas Chainsaw Massacre was distributed by New Line, which put the film into cinemas on October 17, 2003, just two months after the premiere of *Freddy vs. Jason*. Nispel's film was similarly successful, grossing $29 million over its first weekend in cinemas.

The filmmaker recalls that he and his agent went to see *The Texas Chainsaw Massacre* on opening day at a cinema called The Bridge near LAX airport. "The usher goes, 'The movie's playing like gangbusters," says the director. "He had 15 people reported ill and asking for assistance just in that day already. I go, 'What do you do with them?' He goes, 'We take them out to the parking lot, and they're walking in circles, and then they usually want to go back and continue watching.'" Nispel's film eventually earned $80 million at the domestic box office.

Resident Evil wasn't the only female-led action-horror franchise distributed by Screen Gems in the mid-2000s. While Milla Jovovich enjoyed success portraying an apocalypse survivor who slays zombies, the *Underworld* movies found actress Kate Beckinsale proving her commercial appeal as a vampire who kills werewolves.

2003's franchise-begetting *Underworld* was the feature debut of director Len Wiseman, who grew up in San Francisco making short films in his backyard. After college, Wiseman directed music videos for Megadeth and En Vogue, accumulating an impressive enough reel to score him a meeting at Dimension Films. He thought he would be discussing the possibility of directing a new movie in *The Crow* franchise, which Dimension had continued with the 1996 sequel *The Crow: City of Angels*. But talk soon turned to how Wiseman might tackle a different kind of film. "They were looking to do a werewolf movie and start a werewolf franchise," he says.

To help him work up a pitch, Wiseman teamed with a friend and aspiring screenwriter named Kevin Grevioux. The latter suggested reworking *Romeo and Juliet*, with werewolves and vampires replacing the Montague and Capulet families. "We got really excited about it," says Wiseman. "I started doing drawings for that, went back, pitched it to Dimension, and they said, 'No, we're looking for just a werewolf thing.'" Wiseman's agent encouraged him to keep on developing the pitch with the hope of selling it elsewhere. To further work on the screenplay, Wiseman recruited Danny McBride—not the *Eastbound & Down* actor, but a stuntman-turned-screenwriter of the same name who shared an agent with the director.

Wiseman was determined to direct the project himself. "I'm not dying to make a werewolf movie," he says. "I'm dying to direct a *movie*. It was a real opportunity. Our agent started shopping it to the studios, and we got a lot of attention and a lot of offers to buy the script—if I didn't direct it, because I'd never done a movie before." He came close to striking a deal with Warner Bros. production chief Lorenzo di Bonaventura. "I met with Lorenzo at Warner Bros. and he was like, 'This is a $60 million script!'" says Wiseman. "They almost bought it with me directing it. But at the end of the day, they went, 'You haven't directed a movie yet, this is a *large* movie.'"

Wiseman and McBride had more success pitching the project to Lakeshore Entertainment. The company had produced the 2002 horror-thriller hit *The Mothman Prophecies*, starring Richard Gere and Laura Linney, which was distributed by Screen Gems. Lakeshore was receptive to Wiseman's idea, with president Gary Lucchesi prepared to let him direct the film. "The fact that I did the drawings, I remember that was something that really resonated with Gary Lucchesi," says the director. "He was like, 'If this comes directly from you, and you're not hiring a concept [artist], then I trust you know what you're doing.'" Lakeshore was only prepared to greenlight the movie at a drastically reduced budget level from the $60 million Lorenzo di Bonaventura had estimated the film would cost. "When we started at Lakeshore, the budget was $16 million," says Wiseman. In April 2002, the month after the successful American release of *Resident Evil*, *Variety* announced that Screen Gems had picked up the film's US rights.

Wiseman recalls that the idea of casting Beckinsale came from Lakeshore chairman Tom Rosenberg. "He was the first one to suggest Kate," says the director. "She was more a serious actress in period pieces, and the idea of having somebody that's new to the genre is very interesting. She was looking to do something in a very different genre, and it worked out great."

The daughter of British sitcom star Richard Beckinsale, who had died from a heart attack when she was just five, Beckinsale studied French and Russian literature at Oxford University. The actress played the role of Hero in Kenneth Branagh's 1993 version of *Much Ado About Nothing* and then starred in director John Schlesinger's 1995 movie *Cold Comfort Farm*. 1995 also saw her appearing onstage in a UK production of Chekhov's *The Seagull* alongside Michael Sheen, with whom she became romantically involved. In the late '90s, Beckinsale moved to America and was cast by director Michael Bay as the female lead in his 2001 war epic *Pearl Harbor*.

Beckinsale had a reputation as someone who shone in classy period films. She was not regarded as the kind of actor likely to star in a movie about the centuries-old battle between vampires and werewolves, which was what the screenplay for *Underworld* concerned. Beckinsale, however, was a fan of James Cameron's *Aliens* and Luc Besson's 1990 thriller *La Femme Nikita* and had always been attracted to the idea of starring in an action film. The role of a gun-toting vampire named Selene took her fancy. "As soon as I read it, I wanted to do it," she told IGN ahead of the film's release.

Beckinsale and Sheen had a daughter, Lily, who was born in 1999, but the couple's relationship was strained by Beckinsale's US-based professional life. "I had no work visa to stay in America," Sheen said on the podcast *Changes* in 2020. "I ended up having to get work in Britain because I wasn't really getting any work in America." Beckinsale convinced Wiseman to audition Sheen for the role of Lucian, the leader of the werewolves—or 'Lycans,' as they are called in the film—and the Welshman landed the part. The *Underworld* cast also included Scott Speedman from J. J. Abrams' show *Felicity* and British actor Bill Nighy, as well as Grevioux, who played a werewolf named Raze.

Beckinsale had precious little experience of onscreen combat prior to her involvement in the original 2003 *Underworld*. "I really lived in my head at that point and was very academic, and I was just about managing to walk," the actress would recall to *Entertainment Weekly* writer Josh Rottenberg. She was trained for the film by stuntman and *Underworld* second unit director Brad Martin. During his childhood in Idaho, Martin had become fascinated with stunt work after watching 1978's Burt Reynolds-starring *Hooper* and *The Fall Guy* TV show. The aspiring stuntman moved to Los Angeles, where he started getting work on films like John Carpenter's *Escape From L.A.* and *Alien: Resurrection*. "I did that with Chad Stahelski, the director of *John Wick*," Martin says of the fourth *Alien* film. "He and I were best friends

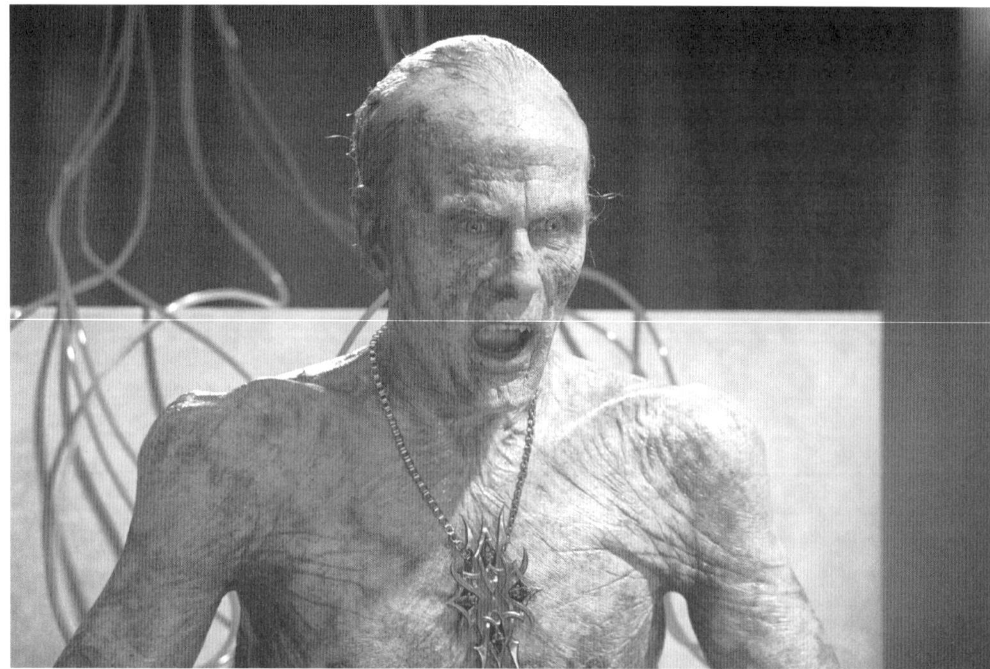

Billy Nighy in *Underworld* (2003).

growing up in the business. I have a picture of Chad and I next to an alien somewhere, it's pretty cool."

Wiseman was set to shoot *Underworld* in Budapest during the second half of 2002. "I didn't own a passport until I went out to go make *Underworld*," he says. "That's how young I was." With Wiseman prepping the movie in Hungary, Martin began the task of turning Beckinsale into an action star. "Kate signed on and we got four weeks with her in LA at a little studio near Sony Pictures," he says. "She didn't know anything, so we started from scratch. I had her on wires, fight choreography, learning to roll, learning to move. Then we went out to Budapest, and we had another couple of weeks there." Martin recalls that he and Beckinsale "had a great relationship. She's got a great sense of humor, but she treats everything super-seriously. There's a few people out there like that. Another one would be Jason Statham, someone who's very anal and very like, 'This has to be perfect.' She's like that, and I love that."

Midway through the shoot, Wiseman edited together a compilation of footage in hopes of enticing Screen Gems boss Clint Culpepper to increase the film's

Kate Beckinsale and Scott Speedman in *Underworld.*

budget and received the best kind of thumbs-up. "Clint Culpepper absolutely loved it," says the director. "They ended up putting in a couple million more."

The relationship between Beckinsale and Wiseman would blossom away from the set. In March 2003, following the end of the shoot, Beckinsale and Sheen announced that they had split, and in June, Beckinsale and Wiseman became engaged. The actress was keen to dispel the rumor that she had left Sheen for Wiseman during the film's production. "The popular notion of how Michael and I broke up—that we were on [the first *Underworld*] and I ran off with the director—is just not true," she told *Entertainment Weekly* writer Josh Rottenberg in 2012.

Screen Gems released *Underworld* in the US on September 19, 2003. The film earned $21 million over its opening weekend, ultimately grossing $51 million in the US and $42 million in international markets. "The release of the film was amazing to me," says Wiseman. "I was so blown away by the advertising campaign. I remember it was up on billboards, and buses, and everything. I was, of course, running around, taking pictures of every billboard, sending them to my family."

Remarkably, the following year, Beckinsale starred in another movie which featured both vampires and werewolves: *Van Helsing*. Written and directed by Stephen Sommers, the film starred *X-Men* franchise actor Hugh Jackman as the vampire-hunter Van Helsing and Beckinsale as a noblewoman called Anna Valerious.

Universal believed this monster-filled movie from the director of *The Mummy* could spawn another highly profitable franchise. The studio gifted Sommers a budget in the region of $160 million, making it among the most expensive films ever made. Universal greenlit a TV expansion of the *Van Helsing* world with a show called *Transylvania*, which was scheduled to debut on NBC in the fall of 2004. The studio also opened an attraction at its Los Angeles theme park devoted to the movie, *Van Helsing: Fortress Dracula*. Released on May 7, 2004, *Van Helsing* grossed a disappointing worldwide total of $300 million, and the film's high cost meant that Universal cooled on the idea of pursuing matters further. Just a couple of weeks after the release of Sommers' movie, *Variety* reported that NBC had shelved *Transylvania*. By the end of 2006, *Van Helsing: Fortress Dracula* had been decommissioned.

Although *Underworld* earned less than half of what *Van Helsing* grossed at the US box office, the much cheaper film kicked off a franchise. Shortly after the release of Wiseman's movie, *Variety* reported that Lakeshore and Screen Gems would co-produce both a sequel and a prequel.

Wiseman directed the sequel, *Underworld: Evolution*, which was shot in Vancouver and found Beckinsale and Speedman's characters on the run from a vampire played by Scottish actor Tony Curran. The film opened in the US on January 20, 2006, and earned over $10 million more than *Underworld* in the US, winding up with a total global take of $111 million.

For the third movie, *Underworld: Rise of the Lycans*, Wiseman ceded the director's chair to the franchise's monster designer Patrick Tatopoulos. Beckinsale only made a cameo appearance in the film, with Rhona Mitra taking the lead role of a vampire named Sonja. Michael Sheen had not appeared in the Wiseman-directed *Underworld: Evolution* but returned for the prequel. *Underworld: Rise of the Lycans* was released in the US on January 23, 2009, the same day that Ron Howard's film version of the play *Frost/Nixon*, also starring Sheen, went wide in cinemas after being nominated for five Academy Awards. Reviewers were less enamored of Tatopoulos' film than they had been of Howard's movie. Under the headline "Underworld 3: Me

No Lycan," *Time* magazine writer Richard Corliss wrote that "the Brit cast attempts to camouflage the silliness by swanning it up, as if the Royal Shakespeare Company had gotten communally drunk and staged an impromptu production of *Dracula Meets the Wolfman.*" The US earnings of the prequel topped out at an unimpressive $45 million.

The November prior to the arrival of *Underworld: Rise of the Lycans* saw the release of director Catherine Hardwicke's *Twilight*, a tale of romance and monsters adapted from Stephenie Meyer's bestselling 2005 young adult novel. Starring Robert Pattinson as a vampire, Taylor Lautner as a werewolf, and Kristen Stewart as the teenage object of their respective affections, the 2008 film was a huge hit, earning $407 million worldwide. Four sequels followed over the next four years, with *Underworld* mainstay Michael Sheen joining the series for its second entry, 2009's *The Twilight Saga: New Moon*, as the leader of an Italian vampire coven. The blockbuster success of the films eclipsed those of Wiseman's *Underworld* series and led some people to incorrectly believe that he had ripped off the *Twilight* movies. "Here's what's funny," says the director. "Because *Twilight* was such a massive, massive success, people—like, at Comic-Con—would ask if *Underworld* was inspired by *Twilight.* I get that a lot, as years go on. It's like, 'You did a dark, gritty version of *Twilight.*' I go, 'No, they did a glossier, romantic version of [*Underworld*].'"

The box office triumph of *Freddy vs. Jason* led Universal and its subsidiary Focus Features to take *Seed of Chucky* off the shelf, a possibility that Don Mancini had long anticipated. "I always knew that looming on the horizon was *Freddy vs. Jason*," he told *Fangoria.* "If it did well, come hell or high water, someone was going to want to make another Chucky movie. Sure enough, *Freddy vs. Jason*—coincidentally directed by Ronny Yu, who did *Bride of Chucky*—grossed $30 million-plus its opening weekend. Sure enough, the Monday following that, we got the call that they wanted to make *Seed.*"

The 'seed' of the title was the Billy Boyd-voiced Glen/Glenda, the nonbinary offspring of Chucky and Tiffany, who is uninterested in pursuing his father's murderous ways. Gory at points, *Seed of Chucky* as a whole seemed more interested in delivering jokes than scares, with Jennifer Tilly obviously having a ball playing a version of herself and director John Waters similarly camp as a doomed photographer.

Chucky and Jennifer Tilly in *Seed of Chucky* (2004).

Focus Features' newly established genre division Rogue Pictures released *Seed of Chucky* on November 12, 2004. The film earned just short of $3 million over its opening weekend, much less than *Bride of Chucky*. Mancini would come to believe he had too enthusiastically foregrounded queer themes for audiences of the time. "With *Seed of Chucky*, I think I felt emboldened by the success of *Bride* to go even further and push the queer aspects of the story even further," he says. "And as we know, that didn't go so well, because it was so queer, that movie, that I think it didn't go down so well with a lot of the young, straight, male horror audience."

Horror fans had also moved on, at least for the moment, from the arch and comedic tone that had become the hallmark of the Chucky films. Cinemagoers were instead hungry for tougher, bleaker, and more visceral material. A new group of filmmakers would establish their reputations serving up exactly that.

CHAPTER 7

"I WANT TO PLAY A GAME."

James Wan and Leigh Whannell spent the world premiere of their film *Saw* nervously walking around the lobby of the Egyptian Theatre in Park City, Utah. Directed by Wan and written by Whannell—who also played one of the film's lead roles—the horror-thriller was screening as part of the 2004 Sundance Film Festival. Lionsgate had announced days before the start of Sundance that it had purchased the film. But the movie's reception at the event would influence the scale of its theatrical distribution and even whether *Saw* would be released in cinemas at all. The pair of Australian filmmakers remained apprehensive about how their down-and-dirty collaboration, made for less than $1 million, would be received by attendees. "James and I spent the entire screening out in the lobby of the theater, pacing around," Whannell would recall to The A.V. Club in 2010. "We did get somebody come out and say that they just couldn't handle it. I distinctly remember that. Two young women walked out, and I accosted them. 'What's going on? Why are you leaving?' They said they couldn't handle it anymore."

Saw starred Whannell and Cary Elwes as a pair of seeming strangers who awake in a filthy windowless bathroom with their ankles chained to pipes and a dead body lying between them. Elwes' character, a surgeon called Dr. Lawrence Gordon, correctly guesses that they have fallen foul of the Jigsaw Killer, a notorious criminal whose habit of placing his victims in often fatal traps is detailed in a series of flashbacks. It was likely one of these 'games' that prompted the early departures from the screening. Certainly, *Saw* was the first Sundance film to feature a junkie (played in Wan's film by Shawnee Smith) digging a key from the stomach of her drug dealer to free herself from a metal 'reverse bear trap' attached to her head.

Despite the gruesome nature of the film, which climaxes with Elwes' surgeon removing one of his feet with a hacksaw, *Saw* caused little stir at the festival. The review from *Variety* critic Dennis Harvey described the film as "a crude concoction sewn together from the severed parts of prior horror/serial killer pics" but admitted that Lionsgate might "draw B.O. blood." *Saw* did much more than that. The film's record-breaking success would be a game-changer for Lionsgate and for the wider horror genre, helping to unleash a geyser of profits and a tidal wave of onscreen gore.

James Wan was born in the Malaysian city of Kuching and moved with his family to Perth, Australia, when he was seven. The director's first exposure to the horror genre came via his mother and father. "My parents were not afraid to let me see horror movies," he says. "I saw them and was terrified by them, and from then onwards I was bitten by the bug." Wan was particularly frightened by *Jaws* and *Poltergeist*. "*Jaws* made me terrified of the ocean and going to the beach," he explains. "*Poltergeist* made me afraid of toys that could potentially be haunted and also the idea that the nice, loving suburban house that you live in could actually be plagued by supernatural malevolent forces."

Whannell was born and raised in Perth. Like Wan, he was deeply affected by *Jaws*, which he saw at the age of five and which scared him so much that he became terrified of taking a bath. The writer explored the horror and science fiction genres as he got older. "I grew up in the VHS era," he says. "The '80s was the height of practical effects. I just loved that era, films like *The Terminator*, *RoboCop*, *The Thing*, *The Fly*."

Wan and Whannell met in 1995, taking the Media Arts course offered by Melbourne's Royal Institute of Technology. The pair bonded over their love for the kind of commercial cinema that was regarded with suspicion by many of their fellow students. After leaving film school, they attempted to come up with an idea for a movie that they could shoot cheaply. The pair were inspired by the early, micro-budget offerings of Kevin Smith and Robert Rodriguez and the example of *The Blair Witch Project*. One day, Wan called Whannell with a pitch about two men in a room and a dead body lying between them. After speaking with his friend, Whannell opened his diary, where he had previously sketched a word in a heavy-metal font, with blood dripping down from the letters. Whannell called Wan back and said, "If we can call it *Saw*, then fine."

The pair's plan was for Wan to direct *Saw* and for Whannell to star in the movie, using $5,000 that the latter had saved working as a film critic on a TV show called *Recovery*. Once Whannell had written the script, their manager Stacey Testro convinced them to try to secure more backing for the project. Los Angeles-based literary agent Ken Greenblatt thought he might be able to sell the script and asked Wan and Whannell to fly to the US for meetings with potential buyers. As a calling card, Wan shot the script's reverse bear trap sequence, with Whannell playing the part later portrayed by Shawnee Smith. They filmed the scene over two days, pulling in favors to assemble equipment and a crew, and transferred the edited result to DVD.

James Wan and Leigh Whannell in 2010.

They received a positive response from Evolution Entertainment, a Los Angeles-based management and production company founded in 1998 by Mark Burg and Oren Koules. The pair had recently produced *John Q.*, a New Line-distributed thriller starring Denzel Washington, which had opened at number one when it was released in February 2002. "We made the movie for $28 million, it grossed $100 million, it took us seven years to get the movie made," says Burg. "You get your first producer's statement, and I think they said they had lost, like, $40 or $44 million on the movie. We were like, screw this, if we ever make another movie, let's do it ourselves."

Wan and Whannell's DVD had been brought to the attention of Evolution's head of production Gregg Hoffman by an agent friend. "About two or three minutes into it, my jaw hit the floor," Hoffman was quoted as saying in the finished film's production notes. "I ran back to my office with the DVD and the script and showed it to my partners." Koules remembers thinking the DVD was "incredible" and swiftly devoured Whannell's screenplay. "I'm like, if this could keep up with the short, these guys really have it," says the producer. "We got the script and every page I was like, please don't suck, please don't suck, aw, this is *good*."

When Wan and Whannell arrived in Los Angeles, they received a warm welcome from the producers. "James and Leigh landed, they took a cab to our office," says Burg. "We looked at them and were like, 'Okay, we'll let you guys make the movie.' They were like, 'We love America! We've been here an hour, and we already have a greenlit movie!' Their agents then set them up with a bunch of other meetings, and they went and did the town, and nobody else was greenlighting the movie. I think they got an offer of 250[k] for the script, 300[k] for the script. People wanted the script but weren't committing to make [the movie]. We were like, 'This movie's greenlit.' We figured we had friends, we could get actors to do the movie, we're making it for a million."

In search of outside financing, the producers approached Lionsgate. The company had been founded in 1997 by Canadian businessman Frank Giustra with the plan of focusing on films with mid-range budgets. "I felt Canada needed an entertainment company modeled much like a US studio, creating commercial blockbuster-potential products that have global appeal," Giustra said to *Variety* about the company, which had offices in both Vancouver and Los Angeles. Under the leadership of CEO Jon Feltheimer, Lionsgate began to acquire other companies, buying Trimark in 2000 and Artisan three years later.

Trimark executive Peter Block transitioned over to Lionsgate following his company's purchase, becoming president of acquisitions and co-productions. The position allowed him to buy or finance films principally for the home entertainment market, but which might also have theatrical potential. Over the next few years, Block would work on a variety of non-horror Lionsgate films, including 2003's *Girl with a Pearl Earring* and 2005's multiple Oscar-winning *Crash*. Together with his fellow Lionsgate executive Jason Constantine, Block also set about expanding the company's genre output. Many of those films featured much more violent and gory material than was to be found in the sleek slasher movies that had followed the release of *Scream*. "What was happening [in] the early aughts is people kind of pulled back, everything was going in a safer way," says Block. "As other companies were cutting their movies down to PG-13, I was trying to think of a way we could get a foothold and a niche."

When the Evolution Entertainment founders arrived at Lionsgate with Wan and Whannell's demo DVD, they were swiftly directed to Block. "*Saw* was brought in by Mark Burg and Oren Koules," says the executive. "They showed [the DVD] to the vice chairman and chairman. They got a minute into the thing, and they were like, 'We don't even want to watch the rest. Take it down the hall and show it to Block.'"

Lionsgate had rapidly established a reputation for releasing films that other studios had deemed too hot to handle. The company became the US distributor of Kevin Smith's 1999 religious comedy *Dogma* after Miramax got cold feet about the movie and acquired the rights to Alejandro Iñárritu's 2000 drama *Amores perros*, which featured sequences of dogfighting. In August 2001, the company released *O*, a high school reworking of *Othello*. Dimension had acquired the film in 1999 but then stepped back from the movie following the Columbine massacre. In an article published shortly before the release of the movie, *Los Angeles Times* journalist Patrick Goldstein described Lionsgate as "one of the few remaining film companies that hasn't lost its nerve when it comes to backing movies that offend, titillate, and outrage."

Prior to *Saw*, the company had released a clutch of horror and horror-adjacent movies, including an adaptation of the 1991 book *American Psycho*. Author Bret Easton Ellis' novel centered around investment banker and serial killer Patrick Bateman, a horrifying figure as obsessed with designer clothes and pop music as he is with killing people. Ellis' publisher Simon & Schuster balked at the explicit violence featured in the novel, giving the book back to the author. *American Psycho* was snapped up by Sonny Mehta, editor-in-chief of Knopf, who published the novel through the paperback line Vintage Books.

Producer Edward R. Pressman developed a big-screen adaptation, first with *Re-Animator* filmmaker Stuart Gordon and then with David Cronenberg. Following these false starts, the producer approached Mary Harron, director of the 1996 independent drama *I Shot Andy Warhol*, starring Lili Taylor as the radical feminist Valerie Solanas. Harron collaborated on the *American Psycho* screenplay with actress Guinevere Turner, who had starred in and co-written the 1994 comedy-drama *Go Fish*. "We wanted to lean toward satire," says Turner. "We certainly didn't want to do the level of gruesomeness in the book." The screenwriters did go the route of straight horror for a sequence in which Bateman pursues a sex worker with a chainsaw. "We were like, we need one set-piece that brings all the classic horror tropes, and horror fans will not walk away unsatisfied," she continues. The screenwriter recalls receiving notes from Lionsgate asking that she and Harron make Bateman more likeable. "Various executives were like, 'He's not very sympathetic,'" she says. "We were like, 'He's a serial killer!'"

For the role of the tanned, fitness-obsessed Bateman, Harron wanted to cast the relatively unknown British actor Christian Bale. "He flew to New York to audition for Mary in person," says Turner. "He was pale, and thin, and had the David Bowie-esque teeth. He didn't really look the part, but he just really *got it.* This is before we all knew that give Christian Bale six months and he could turn into a hippopotamus."

Lionsgate executives opted to go a different casting route. On May 17, 1998, *Variety* reported that the studio had agreed to pay *Titanic* actor and freshly minted movie superstar Leonardo DiCaprio $21 million to portray Bateman. Harron told Lionsgate that she would refuse to direct the film without Bale playing the killer. "Mary did not want to do the Leonardo DiCaprio version," says Turner. "I'm like, wow, that's so much integrity that I don't think I would have!"

The studio moved on, recruiting Oliver Stone to develop the film with DiCaprio. But the *Titanic* star subsequently dropped out of the project, choosing instead to star in Danny Boyle's *The Beach.* Around four months after the DiCaprio announcement, Lionsgate reached out to Harron. The director assumed that the company was getting in touch to reach a financial settlement with her. Instead, Lionsgate told Harron that she could make the film after all and eventually agreed to Harron's demand that Bale play the lead role. The film's supporting cast would include Chloë Sevigny, Reese Witherspoon, Willem Dafoe, and Jared Leto. The latter's character in the movie is slaughtered by an axe-wielding Bateman after Bale delivers a speech about the merits of Huey Lewis and the News' song "Hip to Be Square."

American Psycho received its world premiere at the Sundance Film Festival in 2000. "We premiered to much hoopla, and then, by the end of the movie, to polite clapping," says Turner, who also appeared in the film as another of Bateman's victims. "You could feel that the audience was not loving it. People were like, 'I'm not sure what the f[uck] that was.'"

Lionsgate opened *American Psycho* in mid-April 2020 on 1,200 screens. As *LA Weekly* writer Manohla Dargis noted, that was "an optimistic number for an art-house satire about a wealthy sociopath who stores female body parts in his gleaming Ultra Line refrigerator." *American Psycho* earned a relatively humble $34 million worldwide. But the film had a longer tail in

Christian Bale in *American Psycho* (2000).

pop culture than many more commercially successful movies, thanks in part to Bale's subsequent casting as Bruce Wayne in Christopher Nolan's trio of Batman films. Images and footage from the movie would also proliferate on the internet, helping to gift Bale's crazed investment banker an unexpected second life. Many years after the release of the film, Turner became an assistant professor of film at New York's Syracuse University and was surprised to discover that her students knew all about her and Harron's collaboration. "I said, 'Can you explain to me why you are so interested in this movie that came out before you were born?'" she recalls. "This one girl goes, 'Um, the memes!' I'm like a rock star because of it."

Two years after the arrival of *American Psycho* in cinemas, Lionsgate released the horror film *Frailty*, the directorial debut of Bill Paxton. The actor also starred in the film as a mechanic, 'Dad' Meiks, who tells his two sons that God wants them to kill demons who have disguised themselves as humans. One of his children believes in his father's holy crusade, while the other reluctantly concludes that his father has gone insane.

Paxton's blockbuster credits included 1995's *Apollo 13*, 1996's *Twister*, and his friend James Cameron's *Titanic*, but the actor had a fondness for genre films. Early in his Hollywood career, the Texan had worked as a set decorator on 1981's Roger Corman-produced science fiction-horror movie *Galaxy of Terror* and memorably played a vampire in Kathryn Bigelow's *Near Dark*. "I've always thought that sci-fi, fantasy, and horror have been relegated to the back of the bus," Paxton told *Fangoria* writer Anthony C. Ferrante, "and it's funny, because those films are what built this business, going all the way back."

Frailty was developed by *Child's Play* franchise producer David Kirschner, who had fallen in love with the screenplay by newcomer Brent Hanley. Kirschner initially approached Paxton to act in the film only. "I wanted Tom Hanks to be Dad, somebody that you trust implicitly, [but] I knew I would never get him," says the producer. "CAA represented me, and they came back with Bill Paxton. I thought, 'Oh, wow, that's really interesting.'" When Kirschner met with Paxton, the actor surprised him by saying that he wanted to direct the film as well as star in it. "I invited him over to the house for lunch, and this is the first time I saw him," remembers Kirschner. "He was kind of sheepish, and smiled that great charming smile of his, and said, 'I was thinking that I'd like to direct it.' I remember smiling, but inside thinking, 'Oh shit, [I] did not see this coming.' I very politely said, 'Bill, I'm concerned, because you've never directed anything before, I don't know if you can do this.' He proceeded to pull out storyboards he had drawn. They were phenomenal, not just the art—he was a very good artist—but the angles, the ideas behind it. I was blown away."

Kirschner agreed to let Paxton direct the film and secured a commitment from Matthew McConaughey to co-star in the movie, but was unable to sell the project. "I could not get a studio to buy this film, for obvious reasons, right?" says the producer. "It's children, murder in the name of God, there's so many things stacked against us." Kirschner used his own money to keep the project on track. "I went to my wife and said, 'I can't sell this at any studio, but I want to make this film,'" he recalls. "I said, 'I know I said we would never do this, but I would like to put up $100,000 [to] hold studio space, because I'm going to lose Matthew McConaughey, I only have him for a short window.' She said, 'Okay.' Well, that turned into $4 million. That was our nest egg, that was the future. I must confess, it was pretty tense in this house because of that. Finally, I was so fortunate to have Lionsgate come in and be my white knight."

Jeremy Sumpter, Matt O'Leary, and Bill Paxton in *Frailty* (2001).

Kirschner was impressed by Paxton's commitment during the shoot. "He was the first one there in the morning, the last one to leave, the first guy to move furniture—which you're not allowed to do, but he did it—anything to move the day along," he says. According to the producer, he and Paxton were left alone by Lionsgate as they worked on the movie. "Ten days had gone by, and I called Mike Paseornek, he was the head of physical production," Kirschner remembers. "I said, 'How come you're not coming by the set, are you guys unhappy with what you're seeing?' He said, 'David, my philosophy is, if it's working, there's no reason for us to be there. Bill's doing a great job.'"

Paxton invited James Cameron to look at an early cut of the movie. "We were editing, and Bill says to me, 'Would you be okay if Jim comes by?'" says Kirschner. "I said, 'Jim who?' He said, 'James Cameron.' I said, 'Just as a fanboy, I would be thrilled.' Anyway, he came in, he watched the film, he had one note, to change something from the beginning to the end, and it changed the entire film [for the better]. I mean, that's why he's James Cameron."

The producer had a much less happy experience ahead of the film's release when he was targeted by religious extremists. "There was a steady stream of hate mail that came in," he says. "What they said was, they'd put a bullet in my head. It was very frightening."

Frailty was among the first films executive Peter Block championed after Lionsgate bought Trimark. "When we merged the companies, Tom Ortenberg, who was running theatrical for Lionsgate, let me see a cut and I was like, we can do gangbusters off video, and got behind it in a big way," he says. "I was a big Bill Paxton fan, but that movie was just really accomplished."

Lionsgate's promotional campaign for the film foregrounded positive quotes from Cameron, Stephen King, and Sam Raimi, who had directed Paxton in his 1998 thriller *A Simple Plan*. The movie's poster featured a close-up of McConaughey's face. "It doesn't really look like him, but it's a great image," says Kirschner. "There wasn't very much money. Lionsgate were kind of new to this. I was just thrilled to get the film made and say to my wife, 'Here's our nest egg back.'" The film received positive reviews, including a rave from Roger Ebert, who described Paxton's film as "an extraordinary work, concealing in its depths not only unexpected story turns but also implications, hidden at first, that make it even deeper and more sad."

Frailty performed modestly after Lionsgate released the film in US cinemas on April 12, 2002, but would have a healthy second life on DVD. "To me, it's the perfect example of [when] people say they don't like horror movies, show them *Frailty*, show them *The Others*," says Block. "It's like, 'Yeah, you do!'"

Paxton only directed one more film, 2005's golf movie *The Greatest Game Ever Played*, before passing away in 2017 following heart surgery. The reputation of his directorial debut continued to grow, and in 2022 *Entertainment Weekly* writer Katie Rife included *Frailty* on a list of the best horror movies of the 2000s. "I think Bill's looking down from heaven being very proud," says Kirschner. "Not that I even believe in heaven, but I think he would be so proud."

Lionsgate began to earn its reputation as a horror-friendly company in earnest by acquiring the first film from rock star Rob Zombie. The genre aficionado and former Parsons School of Design student had directed several of his band White Zombie's videos during the mid-'90s. In August 1997,

Variety reported that Zombie was set to make a third movie in *The Crow* franchise, titled *The Crow: 2037*, from his own script, but the project fell apart before shooting could begin.

Next, Zombie wrote an original screenplay, *House of 1000 Corpses*, about a murderous criminal clan living above the lair of a psychopathic surgeon named Dr. Satan. The film was greenlit by Universal Pictures after the success of *Scream*, but Zombie's movie would be far more grisly and disturbing than Wes Craven's film and the wave of glossy attractions that followed. "I was never a fan of those movies," says the director. "I come from two different places. One is classic '30s horror, where the monster is the star, the sympathetic monster. The other one is the '70s, where all bets are off. Whether it's *Last House on the Left* or *Texas Chain Saw Massacre*, you're Fucked City if you're watching those movies. When it became more like teens from shows like *Dawson's Creek* or whatever, it became a whole different vibe."

The director shot the movie on the Universal lot in the summer of 2000. "That part was really exciting," he says. "They would set up the tables in front of the *Psycho* house, and we'd eat lunch up there." Zombie's film starred Bill Moseley, Karen Black, Sid Haig, and the director's future wife Sheri Moon as the movie's psychotic Firefly family. Rainn Wilson played one of their victims who perishes in the process of being turned into a monstrous 'Fish Boy' by Moseley's character. "That was the first big movie role that I ever did," says Wilson. "I was hacked in half, my torso is attached to a fish's tail and revealed to my screaming girlfriend. The shoot was a blast, it was fun to be part of."

Zombie was making his film at a time when Hollywood's output was still being scrutinized following the Columbine massacre. In September 2000, the Federal Trade Commission published its study about the way the entertainment industry marketed products to teenagers and children. The *Los Angeles Times* described the result as a "scathing" overview of how "movie studios, record companies, and video-game manufacturers used everything from comic books to television cartoons to systematically market violent adult fare to young consumers under age 17." On September 27, 2000, the Senate's Committee on Commerce, Science, and Transportation held a hearing to consider the Federal Trade Commission report. The session was chaired by Senator John McCain, with the assembled panel of witnesses comprising more than half a dozen senior studio executives, including Universal

Pictures' chairman Stacey Snider. In her prepared statement, Snider defended Universal's marketing of R-rated films to teenagers. "There are many films we released in the recent past which were R-rated, but that would be more than appropriate for certain young filmgoers to see with their parents," she said. "I am referring to thought-provoking stories like *In the Name of the Father*, *The Hurricane*, or *Schindler's List*, which derived their power from their intensity and still would be suitable viewing for certain mature children." Snider did not mention the upcoming *House of 1000 Corpses*.

After attending a test screening of Zombie's film, the executive resolved that Universal would not be releasing the movie. "I went down to the lobby, and I was like, 'Hey, it went great, right?'" says Zombie. "And all [Stacey Snider] said to me was, 'Come to my office tomorrow, we've got to talk.' I was like, well, that doesn't sound particularly good. I went the next day, and she basically said, 'This movie is unreleasable.'"

MGM expressed an interest in distributing *House of 1000 Corpses* and, according to Zombie, began to pay the production's bills as he continued to edit the film. That relationship also ended after Zombie appeared on a segment of the MTV show *Movie House*, speaking with Ben Affleck on the set of the actor's 2003 superhero film *Daredevil*. Zombie told Affleck that Universal had dropped *House of 1000 Corpses* because the studio found the film morally objectionable. "MGM is going to put it out," Zombie said. "Appar-

Sid Haig in *House of 1000 Corpses* (2003).

ently, they have no morals over there. They're happy for some blood." The story that MGM wanted to distribute the movie was subsequently reported by *Variety* in a story which ran on June 5, 2002. The outlet included Zombie's tongue-in-cheek assertion about MGM having "no morals" in their report. The director would claim that his joke resulted in the studio deciding not to release the film after all.

Zombie's travails had been tracked by Lionsgate executive Peter Block, who believed that the controversy surrounding the film could be a marketing plus. Block suggested to Lionsgate CEO Jon Feltheimer and vice president Michael Burns that they should acquire the film. "I remember running with glee down the hall to Jon Feltheimer and Michael Burns going, 'We need to buy this project,'" he says. "And they're like, 'Why?' I'm like, 'You can't get free publicity better than this, this is what we strive for.' They're like, 'But it's supposed to be depraved and appalling.' I'm like, 'Won-derful!' And it was every depraved, appalling thing I'd hoped for."

In August 2002, Lionsgate announced that the company had secured the rights to the movie and would be releasing it theatrically the next year. The deal was negotiated for Lionsgate by Block, Jason Constantine, and Tom Ortenberg. Zombie was delighted that his film had found a home. "Lionsgate was kind of small and personable," he says. "Peter Block was a really good dude and really into doing genre stuff. They were cool."

Lionsgate's VP of theatrical marketing Tim Palen oversaw the film's release campaign. The Colorado-raised photographer and executive had previously worked at Sony, which he describes as "a nightmare and killed my soul every day." In 2000, Palen was looking for a job when he went to see the Lionsgate-distributed *Amores perros*. "I had never heard of Lionsgate," he says. "The next day, I sent a cold letter to a tangential friend who worked [there] and said I want to work for a company that makes movies like that." Palen recalls that Tom Ortenberg "had an opening and I started right away." The marketing executive describes his early years at the company as "dangerously exciting. We were on life support many times. The first movie I worked on there was *Monster's Ball*. I was told afterwards they were down to their last million dollars, and if that film didn't work, they were going to shut their doors."

Since the release of *Scream*, horror movies had routinely been marketed with posters that showcased the famous visages of their young, easy-on-the eyes stars in a gallery of so-called 'floating heads.' Palen took a different

tack with the horror films released by Lionsgate. "I remember being really enamored by the *Scream* phenomenon and that veneer of poppiness," he says. "When it came to most of my stuff, I just didn't have that luxury to make it look like penny candy, because I didn't have enough money." Palen was determined to reflect the infamy accrued by *House of 1000 Corpses* with the film's publicity materials. In stark contrast to the floating heads featured on the posters for *Scream*, *I Know What You Did Last Summer*, *Urban Legend*, and *Final Destination*, the primary image for the *House of 1000 Corpses* campaign was a single, madly staring ghoul. The film's teaser trailer, meanwhile, declared that "The movie some didn't want you to see isn't being released—it's being unleashed." "That movie was branded as horrific and too much," says Palen. "It was a marketing dream to be able to jump in the saddle on something like that."

Before *House of 1000 Corpses* debuted in theaters, Palen would become equally enthusiastic about, and inspired by, Lionsgate's next horror purchase.

A few weeks after Lionsgate announced their acquisition of Zombie's movie, another gruesome debut premiered at the Toronto Film Festival. Directed and co-written by Eli Roth, *Cabin Fever* tracked a group of vacationing friends as their relationships, and bodies, are torn apart by a flesh-eating virus.

The Massachusetts-raised Roth had been inspired to write the movie by a skin disease he contracted working on a horse farm in Iceland with his brother during the summer of 1991. "My dad had been to Iceland, met someone whose niece had a horse farm, and she'd just had a baby and needed help," says Roth. "He was like, 'I'm sure my boys would love to come out.' I was 19, my brother was 21. They had an old barn, and we had to clean it out. It was filled with 20-year-old hay, and it was dusty, and I got this skin infection. I remember scratching and scratching. I can still feel it. I went to shave—it was so itchy that shaving and ripping the skin off felt good." Roth's alarmed hosts insisted that he seek treatment at a hospital. "This doctor, thank God, said it was some kind of ringworm infection, gave me this cream, and it healed," he says. "But that was what sparked the idea."

Roth had set his sights on becoming a horror filmmaker at the age of eight, after his father took him to see *Alien* and the preteen was intrigued by the credit 'directed by Ridley Scott.' "It's crazy that I had this idea from eight years old—I'm going to make horror movies—and to actually pull it off," he says. The *Cabin Fever* director grew up reading *Fangoria* and watching horror films from the '70s and early '80s, a period he would come to regard as a golden age for visceral genre cinema.

Roth studied film at NYU's Tisch School of the Arts in the early '90s, where he conducted research work for director David Lynch. "I spent years researching a Nikola Tesla project for him," Roth confirms. "We called him 'Mr. X,' because you couldn't say 'David Lynch' around NYU film school without everyone having a heart attack."

After leaving NYU, Roth began working on the screenplay for *Cabin Fever* with his college friend Randy Pearlstein. Roth knew from the start of the writing process that the screenplay's most important scene—at least in terms of its horrifying potential—was a sequence in which one of the female characters unwittingly removes chunks of flesh as she shaves her legs. "Usually, I start with an image, and I'll build a movie around it," he says. "Girl shaves her legs off? I started there." Roth planned on having Pearlstein star in the movie. "We wrote *Cabin Fever* for our friends," says the director. "We wanted Jay Mohr, Mary McCormack, Steve Zahn. Like, all the young actors that we knew—and Randy. We wrote it in three weeks. Then no one wanted it. People were like, 'You can't have a disease as a killer.'"

Roth sought low-level film crew positions as he continued to seek finance and honed the *Cabin Fever* screenplay. "I worked on *Private Parts*, the Howard Stern movie, and I would sit and tweak the script," he says. "I spent six years actively meeting with people, getting rejected." Roth enjoyed *Scream*, but the success of Wes Craven's film did not help his search for finance. "Everyone was doing *I Know What You Did Last Summer* kind of stuff," he says.

Roth relocated to Los Angeles, where he was hired by David Lynch to help launch the director's website. "He's like, 'We're going on the net!'" says Roth. "He made these shorts that I was producing. We would just film these random things. If you look up 'Pierre and Sonny Jim' on YouTube, that's me and David doing these puppets. I was there when he got *Mulholland Drive* back together. I was working with him for a long time. David was like an older brother to me, and he taught me so much about directing."

In addition to working for the *Blue Velvet* auteur, Roth created an animated TV series called *Chowdaheads*, which he produced with another college friend, Evan Astrowsky. "Evan was like, 'Whatever happened to *Cabin Fever*?'" says Roth. "I'm like, 'I can't finance it.' He's like, 'Well, let's take another run at it.'" Astrowsky partnered with producer Lauren Moews, who in turn brought in Sam Froelich, president of the North Carolina-based production company Down Home Entertainment. "Sam had financed *George Washington* by David Gordon Green," says Roth. "Sam was willing to put up $250,000. We started there."

Roth shot the movie in North Carolina during the second half of 2001 with a cast that included Rider Strong from the TV show *Boy Meets World*, Jordan Ladd, and Cerina Vincent, whose character Marcy would be the focus of the leg-shaving sequence. Shortly before the start of shooting, Roth saw some of his promised finance disappear and had to alternate between directing scenes and trying to make up the shortfall with producer Moews. "These dentists who were going to put in half a million dollars pulled out a week before shooting," says the director. "So then it was, like, my Aunt Gladys giving us $10,000 so we could buy film, and my dad took money out of his retirement. We all developed health problems from the stress of making that movie."

The film's grotesque practical effects were created by KNB thanks to Lynch. "We did *Mulholland Drive*, we've done a couple of things with David Lynch," says KNB's Greg Nicotero, speaking before Lynch's passing in 2025. "When *Cabin Fever* came up, David said, 'I've got this young guy who's interested in doing a movie, and we don't have a lot of money.' We did it as a favor to David, and that's how we were introduced to Eli."

When Roth came to shoot the leg-shaving scene with Cerina Vincent, he learned that he would be unable to use the prosthetic appliances created by KNB. "We built these prosthetics that would peel off the leg like a banana," says the director. "The day we went to shoot it, we opened the box,

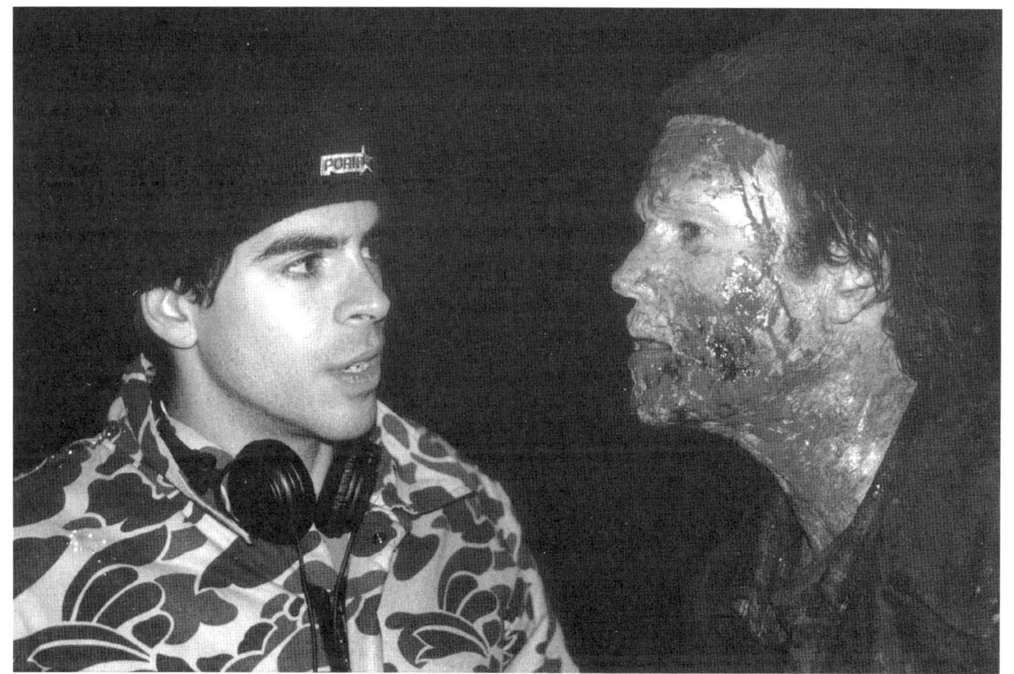

Director Eli Roth and Arie Verveen on the set of *Cabin Fever* (2002).

and the prosthetics had frozen in transit, and they were ruined." KNB's on-set makeup artist Garrett Immel suggested applying a bloody makeup to Vincent's leg, covering the fake gore with shaving foam, and then having the actress seemingly scrape off her upper layer of skin with a bladeless razor. "When we shot it, Cerina played the scene beautifully, [but] I was so depressed," says Roth.

Prior to the screening of *Cabin Fever* at the Toronto Film Festival, Roth's film had been hyped up by Harry Knowles, founder of the popular Ain't It Cool News movie website. "Ain't It Cool News was the site that everyone looked to for movie buzz back then," says Roth. "I spoke to Harry for an hour on the phone. He wrote this piece saying, 'I haven't seen this movie, but I just have a feeling this is going to be the one.'"

When Roth arrived at a crucial early Toronto screening for journalists and distributors, he discovered a line of people waiting to see the film. "That buyers' screening, it was in a mall at the multiplex at ten in the morning," he says. "I remember getting off the escalator and being like, 'What's everyone waiting in line for?'" Roth was delighted to discover at the film's public premiere that the audience was horrified by the leg-shaving sequence. "People were screaming in the scene!" he says.

Lionsgate executive Peter Block saw *Cabin Fever* in Toronto and was impressed by Roth's work. "I knew I wanted it right away," he says. "It's scary, and it's gross, and it's fun, and all of those things work together." Block's fellow Lionsgate executive Jason Constantine had a similarly positive reaction. "The lights go out and within seconds, within minutes, people are not just, like, laughing, they're laughing hysterically," Constantine would recall on a commentary track for the *Cabin Fever* DVD. "You're kind of looking around going, these are jaded industry execs laughing hysterically… So it's like suddenly you realize, okay, lightning in a bottle. There's magic here."

Block and Constantine were interested in acquiring the film for Lionsgate, but had competition from several of the company's rivals. "We had eight studios bidding," says Roth. "It was up to, like, $8 to $9 million." Block believed that Roth's film had theatrical potential, and Lionsgate won the day by promising the *Cabin Fever* team that the company would spend $12 million on prints and advertising, or P&A. According to Roth, "Lionsgate's like, look, we can give you $3.5 million—we made it for $1.5 million, so everyone makes their money back—but we can guarantee it will be the biggest release we've ever done."

When Lionsgate tested the film, though, the results were not encouraging. "The theatrical department wanted to test it, mostly because nobody [at Lionsgate] really wanted the movie," says Block. "*Cabin Fever* was literally one of the worst testing films we ever had, which has nothing to do with the quality of the film, it's just people didn't know [what to expect]. When you looked at the tests, people who rated it 'Poor' said, 'Too funny,' or some people said it was 'Too scary.' I'm like, 'These are positives!'"

Roth recalls Lionsgate CEO Jon Feltheimer expressing concern about the film's content. "They paid $3.5 million, and committed $12 million in P&A, and then they were panicked about it," says the director. "Jon Feltheimer was really concerned about the language. I'm like, 'Jon, 'fuck' is not a swear word anymore.' It was a year of fighting, and recutting, and arguing, which was good preparation for what the rest of my life was going to be."

Lionsgate marketing executive Tim Palen soon realized that one of the film's prime publicity assets was its voluble director. "Tim was the one who was like, 'Eli's the star,'" says Roth. "I was like the *GQ* version of the horror director, but I loved all these crazy sick movies." Palen credits Roth for

TERROR...IN THE FLESH.
CABIN FEVER
CATCH IT!
www.cabinfevermovie.com

inspiring his approach to the campaign for *Cabin Fever*—whose poster featured an image of trees and a cabin forming the shape of a skull—and subsequent horror releases. "He's such an aficionado," says Palen of the director. "He imprinted this thing on me of it being fine art. That was the approach that we took with a lot of those projects, and that was where we found the most salvation."

Pulp Fiction director Quentin Tarantino was tipped off about Roth and his movie by KNB during the lengthy shoot for his two *Kill Bill* films. "KNB were like, 'There's this kid who wants to bring back old-school '80s cabin splatter, like *Evil Dead*,'" Roth remembers. "'He's a super nerd for horror and he wants to go out and make the most crazy, shocking movies.'" In June 2003, *Cabin Fever* screened as part of the Los Angeles Film Festival at West Hollywood's Sunset 5 cinema, and Roth was surprised to learn that Tarantino was standing outside. "Everybody was like, Quentin Tarantino is waiting on line," says the director. "I went outside, and I'd covered myself in blood, and I was like, 'Quentin, do you want to come and hang in the VIP section?' He was like, 'No, no, no, I'm cool.' He stayed and watched the movie. He had questions after, he was going crazy."

The next day, Tarantino called Roth and invited him to his home for a screening of the 1966 kaiju movie *The War of the Gargantuas*. "I went over to his house, we watch *War of the Gargantuas* on 35[mm]," says Roth. "I'm in his theater next to him and it's, like, Howard Berger, Greg Nicotero, and a bunch of actor friends of Quentin's." Roth and Tarantino swiftly bonded over their deep knowledge of horror movies. "It was like two aliens who had found each other," says Roth. "We were nerding out about the font on ads for made-for-TV horror movies, and taglines, and the law that the bigger the video box, the worse the movie was. Like, *Evil Dead* was a case that was barely the size of the videotape, but *Three on a Meathook* was basically a Captain Crunch box."

A month later, Roth received an important endorsement from Peter Jackson, whose first two *Lord of the Rings* films—2001's *The Fellowship of the Ring* and 2002's *The Two Towers*—had proved to be blockbuster hits. In the summer of 2003, Roth screened *Cabin Fever* at the Wellington Film Festival in New Zealand. During his visit to the country, the director met Jackson and his *Lord of the Rings* trilogy co-writers Fran Walsh and Philippa Boyens. "I was at the Wellington Film Festival and I got the print to Peter Jackson," he says. "Peter Jackson loved it, he stopped production on *Return of the King* to screen it for the crew, and then I had lunch with him, and Fran

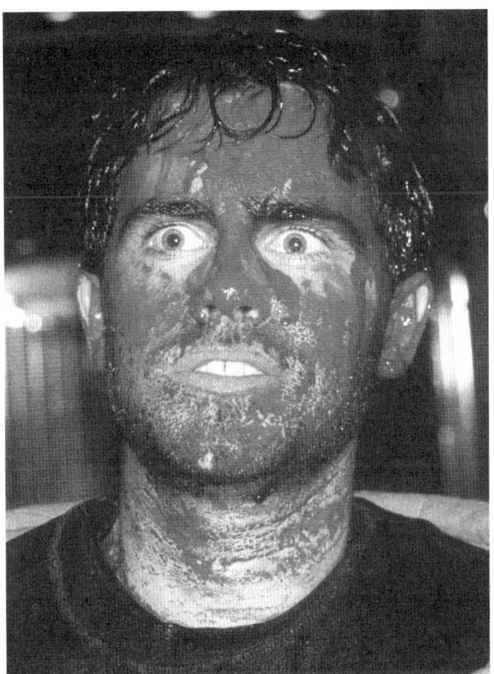
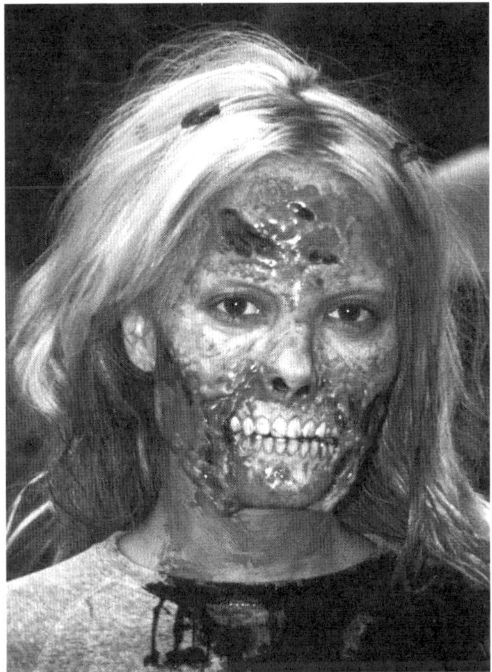

(*Left*) Rider Strong and (*right*) Jordan Ladd on the set of *Cabin Fever*.

Walsh, and Philippa Boyens. The biggest deal to me in film school was *Bad Taste*, *Meet the Feebles*, and *Braindead*, so it was just a wild time. Peter was like, 'We can't believe you made a 'cabin' picture, we haven't seen that since *Evil Dead*! This is the most fun I've had!' Fran said, 'Peter, you should give him a quote, remember Stephen King did it for *Evil Dead*, which is the reason we all saw *Evil Dead*.'"

Jackson agreed to provide positive quotes about the film, including the director's description of the movie as "Bloody, and I do mean bloody, fantastic." "Peter's the hottest director in the world, and he so generously gave me these quotes, and it completely changed everything," says Roth. "It doesn't matter what the critics think. The fans were like, 'Oh, Peter Jackson loves it. *Now* I'm excited.'"

Lionsgate released *House of 1000 Corpses* on April 11, 2003. Zombie's film earned $4.6 million during its first week on screens, a respectable amount given that the movie was available to watch in just 595 theaters. *House of*

1000 Corpses later became a success on DVD. "Lionsgate will even admit, 'We have made so much fucking money off this movie, it's ridiculous,'" says Zombie.

Cabin Fever opened on September 12, 2003, and earned $8.4 million over its first weekend. Roth's film went on to gross a total of $21 million domestically and another $9 million around the world. "I remember seeing it in England, and girls were running out of the theater crying at the leg-shaving," says Roth. "I was so happy." *Cabin Fever* also proved popular when the film was released on DVD. Block describes Roth's movie as "a huge success for the company. Between *Corpses* and *Cabin Fever*, we really had come out and cemented ourselves."

Roth regards 2003 as a watershed year for his preferred strain of hard-edged horror. "2003 was the year that it all came back," he says. "It started in April with *House of 1000 Corpses*, August was *Freddy vs. Jason*, September was *Cabin Fever*, October was Marcus Nispel's *Texas Chainsaw Massacre.* Suddenly, it was back!"

Tarantino helped spread the word about Roth to the moviegoing public in the spring of 2004 as he promoted *Kill Bill: Volume 2*. Asked by *Premiere* magazine to name a young director who gave him great hope for the future, Tarantino replied, "Well, the young director whose work I saw that I was, like, really, really excited by is Eli Roth, who did *Cabin Fever.* I think he's exactly what the horror genre has needed."

Roth was thrilled by Tarantino's comment. "That's like the cool kid in high school going, 'Hey, man, get in my car,'" he says. "Everyone's like, 'Whoa, he's riding shotgun in the cool kid's car?'"

Peter Block was impressed by the *Saw* demo DVD brought into Lionsgate by producers Mark Burg and Oren Koules. The sight of Leigh Whannell stuck in the reverse bear trap appealed to him less as a horror fan than as a reader of crime novelist Agatha Christie. "I'm a huge locked room mystery fan," he says. "Maybe more than a horror fan, I am a guy who loves puzzles. So I saw it as a puzzle. How does a person get out of this, right? I don't think Mark and Oren knew exactly what they had. People weren't really making low-budget movies at that time, there was a certain threshold you didn't cross going down. They were like, 'We're looking for a partner.' I said, 'Is there a script?'"

Block quickly discovered that the *Saw* screenplay featured puzzles and twists aplenty. The executive enthusiastically talked up the project to Jason Constantine and another acquisitions executive named Eda Kowan. "I was like, 'This is awesome, we could definitely get this out straight to video, I know exactly how to sell it,'" he says. "'We should make this movie.'" Lionsgate made Burg and Koules an offer they seemingly couldn't refuse. "My enthusiasm got the better of me," says Block. "I came in and I'm like, 'Yeah, we'll definitely put up half.' As soon as I said that, instead of being the pursued, I became the pursuer. I never had to work so hard to close a deal."

Encouraged by Block's enthusiasm, Burg and Koules decided to finance the film themselves and took out a second mortgage on their Highland Avenue headquarters to pay for the venture. They also founded a subsidiary, Twisted Pictures, to produce thriller and horror films, beginning with *Saw*.

The *Saw* team cast Tobin Bell as John Kramer, a.k.a. the villainous Jigsaw, who, in the film's surprise denouement, reveals that he has been playing dead as the corpse lying between the characters portrayed by Elwes and Whannell. Bell was born in Queens, New York, and studied at the Actors Studio. The future *Saw* star was in his mid-40s when he finally got his break, playing an FBI agent in Alan Parker's 1988 drama *Mississippi Burning*. Over the next 15 years, Bell racked up an impressive list of film credits, even if his parts were often small, appearing in Martin Scorsese's 1990 gangster epic *Goodfellas* and Sam Raimi's 1995 western *The Quick and the Dead*. "We had no money, so we were limited to working with really good actors, and not stars," says Burg. "Somebody brought up Tobin's name, and it was a done deal." The film's cast also included Michael Emerson, Monica Potter, Ken Leung, and Danny Glover, who played an obsessed cop pursuing Jigsaw.

James Wan directed *Saw* in Los Angeles, the film's small budget requiring him to complete the shoot in a tight 18 days. Burg recalls that Bell insisted on playing Kramer for the many scenes in which his character is lying on the floor pretending to be dead. "He did not want us to make a dummy for him, which we probably couldn't have afforded anyways," says the producer. "We couldn't afford anything on that movie. The movie was 900 grand."

In the film, Jigsaw communicates with Shawnee Smith's Amanda on video via a puppet avatar, nicknamed 'Billy' by the movie's creators. Wan had already made a prop for the short, and the film's producers suggested that the same doll be used for the feature version. "I made the puppet in my bedroom in my small little apartment back in Melbourne," says Wan.

Shawnee Smith in *Saw* (2004).

"It's made out of clay, wrapped-up newspaper, ping pong balls for eyes, and it's very, very crudely constructed, but it was effective enough for the first movie."

Block was still keen for Lionsgate to acquire the film. The executive visited Wan's set during the shoot and found himself lending a hand to proceedings. "When Danny Glover speeds along and arrives outside Jigsaw's lair, that's just a couple of people, including [me], pushing on the back of that car," he says. "The car didn't move at all."

Saw was edited by Kevin Greutert, who was stepping up after working as an assistant editor for several years. Greutert recalls the experience as being a baptism of fire. "I was in the 'editing room,' which was James and Leigh's apartment in downtown Hollywood, where I lived for four months solid," he says. "I never left it. We truly lived and breathed *Saw* all day for four months."

Lionsgate executives Block and Constantine were impressed by Wan's work. "James, obviously, [is] such a talented filmmaker and was able to use good old-fashioned filmmaking techniques, even on a low budget, for great effect," Constantine would recall in the 2015 documentary *Game Changer: The Legacy of Saw*. "For instance, how many people think they see Cary Elwes' character take the saw and saw all the way through his leg? It's never on-screen. Everyone thinks they saw it." Constantine was particularly taken with the film's conclusion. "The original *Saw* is one of the greatest twist endings of all time," the executive said. "You can make a shortlist of the movies that have the greatest twist endings, and it's the original *Planet of the Apes*, it's *Sixth Sense*, it's *Usual Suspects*, it's *Saw*."

Twisted Pictures signed a distribution deal with Lionsgate after every other company turned the project down. "Miramax, Warners, Screen Gems, everyone passed," says Koules. "People were scared of the film." As had been the case with *Cabin Fever*, some of Block's colleagues at Lionsgate were doubtful about the film's chances at the box office. "When that movie was done, it worked great," he says. "But the company didn't know. We work in a business of follow-the-leader. There was nothing before *Saw* that really suggested success. You didn't have anything to go on, and I think people were very conservative and scared."

In the second week of January 2004, Lionsgate publicly announced that it had acquired the worldwide rights to *Saw* in a deal negotiated for the distributor by Block and Constantine. The announcement release revealed that Lionsgate would premiere the film in the Midnight section at the upcoming Sundance Film Festival. "We snuck it into Sundance, pretty much against the company's wishes," says Block. "People reluctantly went to the screening and were very upset with what they saw—except the fans weren't, the fans loved it."

Block was determined to get *Saw* a theatrical release and asked Tim Palen to see the film at a screening in Burbank, hoping to recruit the marketing executive to his cause. "*Saw* was not supposed to be released theatrically," says Palen. "It wasn't on my radar. I went to Burbank, didn't even know it was horror, and literally my head just blew off my shoulders. When the reveal happens at the end, the whole audience stood up and clapped. Immediately after the screening, I went up to Tom Ortenberg in the lobby and said, 'That is a giant movie. Like, seriously, what are we doing?'"

Lionsgate eventually pulled the trigger on a theatrical release for *Saw* after two more positive test screenings. "[*Saw*] was still a direct-to-video title," says producer Mark Burg. "Lionsgate was still not convinced that it was a theatrical movie. And it was their head of marketing, Tim Palen, that insisted on doing a research screening, and the research screening was so incredibly successful that they didn't believe the results. They called up Oren and were like, 'How many of your friends did you bring to the research screening?' We were like, 'We didn't bring anybody, this movie works.' Then they did a second research screening in Vegas, and they didn't tell us until lunchtime where the screening was, and the screening in Vegas tested higher than the [previous] one. Then they agreed to do a theatrical release."

A few months prior to the planned Halloween season release of *Saw*, in the summer of 2004, Lionsgate scored one of its most profitable horror hits to date. The micro-budgeted *Open Water* starred Blanchard Ryan and Daniel Travis as scuba divers left behind by their boat. The movie had screened at the 2004 Sundance Film Festival and was bought by Lionsgate for $2.2 million. Written and directed by Chris Kentis, the movie's shoot saw its two lead actors interacting with real sharks, a production story that proved chum to entertainment journalists. Released on August 6, *Open Water* earned $30 million at the domestic box office and would be followed by 2006's straight-to-DVD *Open Water 2: Adrift*.

Meanwhile, Tim Palen was going all-out to pique the interest of potential *Saw* audience members by teasing the extreme nature of the film. Among the publicity initiatives was a website that included clips from the movie and asked viewers, "How fucked up is that?" "It was this perfect storm of being at a company like Lionsgate, where there were no guardrails or some board that was super conservative," he says. "We just sat around as a marketing group, and we decided [that] the real magic of this movie is [that] the concept is so fucked up. Like, your head's going to be ripped apart if you don't dig the key out of the body in front of you? That is so fucked up. It was just really leaning into what was magical about the movie."

Palen arranged for film posters to be given out to potential audience members, which featured images of severed body parts. "The bloated limbs that we passed out at Comic-Con—the severed foot and the severed hand—we had to call them 'international posters,' because the MPAA would have revoked our rating," he says. "Honestly, seeing fanboys rolling it up for their backpacks like it was the most precious fine art piece they'd ever seen was validation. It was like, we're on to something here." Lionsgate also promoted *Saw* via a campaign encouraging people to donate blood to the American Red Cross in exchange for a ticket to see the film. "The street teams said, 'This is a really good idea, we can actually plug into the blood drives regionally,'" says Palen. 4,200 pints of blood were donated as a result of the blood drive. "It sort of was a joke that we would never really do," the marketing executive says. "Then it worked, and then it became a burden that we had to do every time."

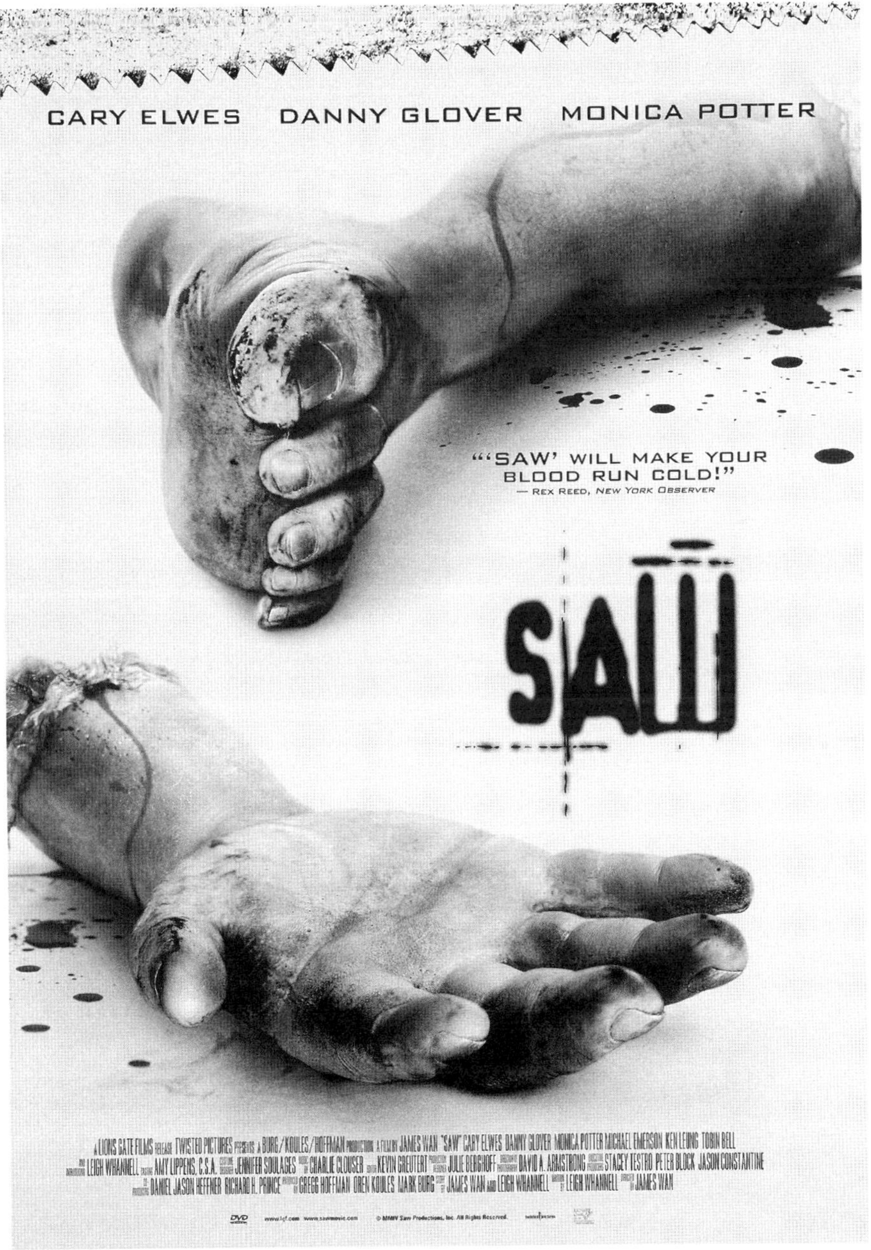

Lionsgate released *Saw* on October 29, 2004. Roger Ebert described the movie as "a fictional machine to pair sadistic horrors with merciless choices, and so the question becomes: do we care enough about the characters to share what they have to endure? I didn't." But many people did care—or at least were intrigued enough to check out this low-budget entry into the Halloween market. *Saw* earned $18 million over its initial weekend in theaters, enough to place third behind *The Grudge* and *Ray*. The film went on to earn $55 million at the domestic box office, making it the second most successful Lionsgate release after Michael Moore's recent documentary *Fahrenheit 9/11*. In all, Wan and Whannell's $900,000 film would gross a jaw-dropping $103 million worldwide.

CHAPTER 8

"DEMONS EXIST, WHETHER YOU BELIEVE IN THEM OR NOT."

After *Resident Evil*, *House of the Dead*, and *28 Days Later*, the public's renewed enthusiasm for zombies was further demonstrated in the spring of 2004 when Universal Pictures released *Dawn of the Dead*. A remake of George A. Romero's 1979 movie, the new version was directed by first-time filmmaker Zack Snyder and written by James Gunn.

Growing up in St. Louis, Missouri, Gunn had fallen in love with horror movies and, in particular, with Romero's shopping mall terror tale. "I was a huge fan of *Dawn of the Dead*," he recalled to *St. Louis Magazine* in 2011. "In fact, I had the poster for the original movie on my wall throughout high school."

In the early '90s, Gunn moved to New York to study creative writing at Columbia University. Needing a summer job, he approached Lloyd Kaufman at the New York-based, independent production company Troma Entertainment. Founded in 1974 by Kaufman and fellow Yale alumni Michael Herz, Troma specialized in low-budget horror like 1984's *The Toxic Avenger* and 1986's *Class of Nuke 'Em High*. Kaufman was looking for someone to write the script for his latest project, a comedic reworking of *Romeo and Juliet* called *Tromeo & Juliet*. Gunn took on the task for a payment of $150.

After *Tromeo & Juliet*, Gunn wrote a screenplay called *The Specials*, a comedy about superheroes. He gave a copy of the screenplay to his actor brother Sean, and Sean handed it to an acquaintance, Jamie Kennedy. The *Scream* star in turn recommended the script to a talent manager named Peter Safran, who helped get the project off the ground. *The Specials* was produced by *House of the Dead* co-writer Mark A. Altman. "It was tough, because the budget wasn't a lot of money," says Altman of the film's production. "James came out of Troma, and so the budget never scared him. Rather than saying, 'Why can't we do something?' [he said,] 'What can we do with the resources we have?"' Directed by future *The Last of Us* TV show co-creator Craig Mazin and released in September 2000, the film was not a success. Still, *The Specials* put Gunn on the Hollywood map, and Warner Bros. president of production Lorenzo di Bonaventura hired him to write the script for a live-action version of the children's cartoon *Scooby-Doo*. The 2002 film starred Sarah Michelle Gellar, Matthew Lillard, Linda Cardellini, and Freddie Prinze Jr. and grossed $275 million worldwide.

The idea to remake *Dawn of the Dead* came from a producer named Eric Newman, whose company Strike Entertainment had a first-look deal with Universal. Newman secured the rights to make a new version of Romero's film from the director's former producing partner Richard P. Rubenstein and asked Gunn if he was interested in writing the script. "I was being offered *Jabberjaw*, and *Magilla Gorilla*, and *Hong Kong Phooey*, and *The Wonder Twins*," Gunn told IGN in 2006. "Those things really didn't fucking interest me, so I was happy that Eric was willing to take a risk and let me do a horror movie."

By the early 2000s, the original *Dawn of the Dead* was widely acknowledged to be a horror masterpiece. Any attempt to remake the film would likely have raised the hackles of horror fans, but the hiring of the man who had written *Scooby-Doo* to work on the screenplay provoked a furore on the internet. The online agita was fueled by an article Harry Knowles wrote for Ain't It Cool News headlined, "When there is no more room in hell, James Gunn will write a remake of *Dawn of the Dead*!!!" Gunn later recalled that he received death threats after Knowles posted the article in August 2001.

The announcement that the film was to be directed by Zack Snyder would hardly have reassured Romero purists. The director had spent the '90s making commercials for the likes of Audi and Nike alongside ZZ Top and Rod Stewart music videos. In the wake of 9/11, Budweiser entrusted him to direct their 2002 Super Bowl TV spot "Respect," in which the brand's famous Clydesdale horses bowed down in front of the New York skyline.

Snyder and Gunn kept Romero's mall setting and, as a result, his critique of rampant commercialism. But the collaborators agreed to add an element to their *Dawn of the Dead* that would increase the project's onscreen energy and the threat to the film's living characters. Taking a leaf out of the *28 Days Later* playbook, the pair decided that their zombies would have the ability to run.

Snyder assembled a cast which included Sarah Polley, Ving Rhames, Ty Burrell, and *Wendigo* actor Jake Weber. "Our goal was always to have good

Jake Weber, Sarah Polley, Mekhi Phifer, and Inna Korobkina in *Dawn of the Dead* (2004).

actors. We didn't want Carmen Electra in this," producer Eric Newman told *Fangoria*, referring to the *Baywatch* actress' appearance in Dimension's *Scary Movie.* Snyder tipped his hat to the original movie by gifting cameo roles to Ken Foree, Scott Reiniger, and Tom Savini, all of whom had appeared in Romero's version. The director shot much of the film at Toronto's Thornhill Square shopping mall, part of which was set for demolition, during the summer of 2003.

The look of the film's zombies was the responsibility of David LeRoy Anderson, who ran the Los Angeles-based makeup effects company AFX Studio with his wife, *A Nightmare on Elm Street* star Heather Langenkamp. The undead ghouls in Romero's *Dawn of the Dead* had been physically set apart from the living by their blue-green skin. For the new version, Snyder requested that Anderson come up with a more visceral makeup design. "Zack's prompt was: make it real," recalls the makeup artist, who won Oscars for his work on 1996's *The Nutty Professor* and 1997's *Men in Black.* Anderson studied images of diseased and decomposing flesh in the hope of arriving at makeups that would satisfy the director. "I had to look at forensic information and comprehend the process of dying and decaying as a palette and a texture," he says. "I wasn't surrounding myself with historic zombie concepts, I was surrounding myself with these horrible images."

The stunt people and extras playing the zombies were often running on camera, which, combined with the hot Toronto weather, meant that the performers looked increasingly grotesque. This development both surprised and delighted Anderson. "It was ninety degrees with a hundred percent humidity," he remembers. "We utilized a technique that involved gelatin, and gelatin has a very low melting point. As soon as the performers started running, the gelatin started melting, and they became even better."

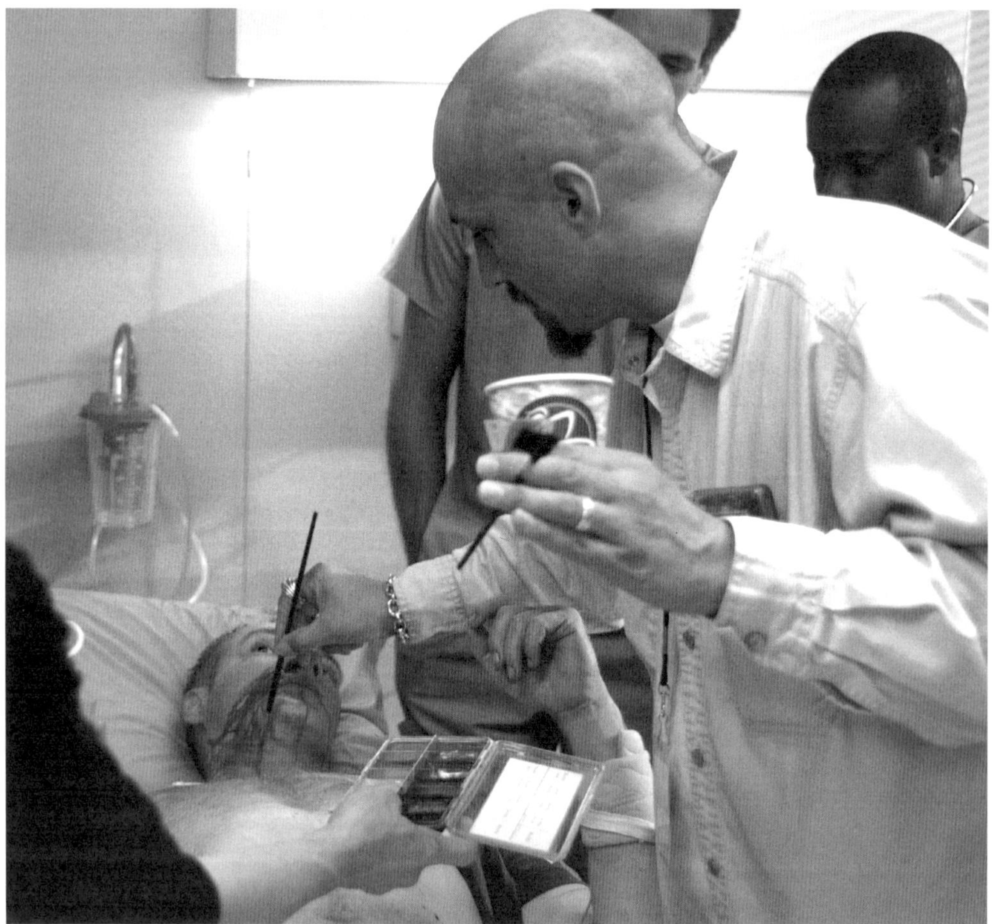

David LeRoy Anderson applying makeup on the set of *Dawn of the Dead.*

Universal released *Dawn of the Dead* on March 19, 2004. The film faced strong competition from another violent tale of resurrection: *The Passion of the Christ.* Director Mel Gibson's religious epic had come out in February and proved an unexpected commercial juggernaut, claiming the top spot at the box office for three weeks in a row. Ahead of his film's release, Gunn noted that *Dawn of the Dead* at least had numbers on its side. "Well, you could see a movie with one guy rising from the dead, or you can see one with thousands," the screenwriter told IGN. *Dawn of the Dead* earned $26 million at the domestic box office over its opening weekend, $7 million more than *The Passion of the Christ.* The movie ultimately grossed an impressive $59 million in the US and another $43 million around the world.

Fans of the film included Stephen King, who believed that the movie tapped into fears provoked by the 9/11 attacks and broader geopolitical issues. Snyder's film began with Polley's character going to bed on a normal day but waking up to see her husband being turned into a ravenous, violent zombie by a preteen neighbor. This prologue was capped off by a startling opening credits sequence that showed the collapse of civilization, soundtracked by Johnny Cash's doom-laden "The Man Comes Around," and began with a shot of Muslims at prayer. Ruminating positively about the film several years later in *Fangoria,* King had little doubt that the image was designed to echo real-life concerns. "It's here that Snyder demonstrates exactly what this inspired remake is about, and how well he knew what was driving our fear-engines at that particular point in time," the *Carrie* author wrote. "What we see in that brief black-and-white shot is what looks like a thousand devout Muslim worshippers, bowing to Mecca in unison—an image of mass belief that most Americans found troubling. By 2004, only three years downriver from 9/11, rampant consumerism was the last thing on our minds. What haunted our nightmares was the idea of suicide bombers driven by an unforgiving (and unthinking, most of us believed) ideology and religious fervor. You could beat 'em or burn 'em, but they'd just keep coming, the news reports assured us."

Remarkably, *Dawn of the Dead* was not the sole Universal-distributed zombie film of 2004. In September, the studio's Focus Features/Rogue Pictures subsidiary released the British horror-comedy *Shaun of the Dead,* starring Simon Pegg. The movie was directed by Edgar Wright, who shot *Shaun of the Dead* in London at the same time *Dawn of the Dead* was filming in Toronto. According to Wright, "I heard later that at Universal it would be a joke for people, saying, 'We're making films called *Dawn of the Dead* and *Shaun of the Dead*? What the hell is this?'"

Wright and Pegg had first worked together on the 1996 sitcom *Asylum*, bonding over their love for Romero's *Dawn of the Dead*. The pair collaborated again on the Channel 4 show *Spaced*, which starred Pegg and Jessica Hynes and premiered in the UK in 1999. On the third episode of the show, Pegg's character Tim plays *Resident Evil 2* all night and then hallucinates that he is shooting zombies. "I wrote a scene where Tim is playing the game under the influence of amphetamines and starts to live it out," says Pegg. "Which was just an excuse, really, to shoot a sequence where I was jumping around killing zombies."

After making two seasons of *Spaced*, Wright and Pegg started writing *Shaun of the Dead*. The screenplay revolved around a twentysomething slacker who tries to survive the undead apocalypse by holing up in a London pub with his girlfriend, his mother, his best friend, and a couple of other acquaintances. The horror-comedy was partly inspired by Pegg's discussions with his real-life pal Nick Frost at their local hostelry in north London about how to carry on living in a world overrun by reanimated corpses. According to Wright, "Simon and Nick were living together, watching a lot of Romero, playing a lot of *Resident Evil*, and they would have these survivalist fantasies of what they would do if a zombie outbreak happened." Wright and Pegg's script stuck closely to the zombie rules established by Romero's trilogy of undead films. In their screenplay, the characters were threatened by shambling corpses rather than sprinting ghouls or *Resident Evil*-style monsters.

The pair were still writing *Shaun of the Dead* when they learned about *28 Days Later*. The two friends were horrified to discover that Danny Boyle was also making an undead tale that took place in the UK capital. Wright and Pegg had decided to write *Shaun of the Dead* in part because the zombie movie had lain fallow since the mid-'80s and, like Paul W. S. Anderson, the two friends believed that the time was ripe for a revival of the subgenre. The news that the renowned Boyle was working on a similar-sounding movie which would beat their own project to screens was particularly devastating to the relatively unknown Wright. "While we were doing our first draft of the script, I vividly remember Simon calling me and saying, 'Hey, uh, you know Danny Boyle's doing a zombie film?'" he says. "I was like, 'What?!' He said, 'Yeah, it's this Alex Garland thing, *28 Days Later*.' I'd heard about that title, but I didn't know it was a zombie film. I was like, 'Argh, no! Oh, we're fucked!'"

The pair persevered with their own screenplay and had almost completed the first draft by the second week of September 2001. With Pegg busy shooting a TV sketch show called *Big Train*, Wright volunteered to finish the screenplay himself at their central London office. "I said, 'I'm going to go in, and I'll write the final pages up to the end, and then you take a pass at it,'" says the director. "And the day that I went in on my own was September 11, 2001." At first, Wright believed that the attack on the World Trade Center meant that no one would be interested in seeing their apocalyptic horror-comedy. "There was this moment of, like, we can't make this film," he says. "There's nothing funny about death after 9/11. Then that started to change, and suddenly the film felt more urgent in a way because of that. In the same way that zombies over the years have been a metaphor for other problems in society, they started to feel like they slotted right into this 21st-century angst."

Wright's producer Nira Park struggled to find the $6 million the director required to shoot the movie. "We'd come from TV, and some said, 'Hmm, but is it really a film? It just feels like an episode of TV,'" she says. "Most people said that, to be honest. The majority of them wrote back and said, 'Thanks, but no thanks.' I got rejection after rejection." Park eventually struck a deal with Working Title Films, the producers of *Four Weddings and a Funeral* and *Notting Hill*, whose movies were distributed in the US by Universal. Wright shot *Shaun of the Dead* in London during 2003, with a cast led by Pegg, Frost, Kate Ashfield, Penelope Wilton, and *Underworld* actor Bill Nighy.

George Romero was among the first people to see Wright and Pegg's self-described 'rom-zom-com.' The director was in Florida, and *Shaun of the Dead* executive producer Jim Wilson set up a screening for him in the beach town of Sanibel during March 2004. Romero was joined at the screening by a security guard employed by Universal for fear that the filmmaker might attempt to pirate the movie. "I remember thinking, 'Well, George Romero's not going to pirate it,'" says Wright. "Even if he did, he's the one person who'd be entitled to some share of the profits!" Romero described his reaction to *Shaun of the Dead* in a 2008 interview with the website Cinemablend. "I flipped for it," he said. "It came with their phone numbers, and I called them up immediately. They just said, 'Oh, we just wanted to

Dylan Moran, Kate Ashfield, Simon Pegg, Nick Frost, Lucy Davis, and Penelope Wilton in a promotional photo for *Shaun of the Dead* (2004).

know that you weren't going to slap us down.' And I said, 'How could anybody slap you down for this?' It was just so loving."

The director was happy to give a positive quote about the film, and his assessment of it as "An absolute blast!" would appear on the movie's publicity materials. The *Shaun of the Dead* team approached other horror notables, including Sam Raimi, Peter Jackson, John Carpenter, and Stephen King, in the hope that they would also blurb the film. "We had a good hit rate," says Wright. "That was pretty amazing. The only person who never got in touch was John Carpenter. I think he doesn't really watch much new stuff. Stephen King gave it a rave [review], which was just mind-blowing to me, having been a teenage Stephen King fan."

Eli Roth first met Wright in February 2004, at London's Empire Awards. "I just really loved him," says Roth. "We got each other right away. We were kind of the same graduating class. At the same time, I was about a year ahead of him in terms of when our films came out." After the *Cabin Fever* director saw *Shaun of the Dead*, he talked up the film to Quentin Tarantino. "Quentin's like, 'I've got to see this movie, let's do a screening at my house,'" he remembers. "I talked to Nira Park and Universal and I said, 'Let's get a print.' It was this awesome screening. It was me, Kevin Smith, all of Quentin's friends, so many actors."

In July 2004, Wright and Pegg appeared on a panel to promote *Shaun of the Dead* at San Diego Comic-Con. Roth agreed to portray an aggrieved horror fan in the audience who accused the pair of making "a total rip-off" of Romero's *Dawn of the Dead*. "Edgar's like, can you come to Comic-Con and we'll do a bit?" he says. "I pretended I was an outraged fanboy that just didn't get the joke."

When the ArcLight Hollywood cinema hosted a *Shaun of the Dead* screening, the event was attended by Wright, Roth, Tarantino, and Greg Nicotero. The KNB founder had already seen and loved the film, and made up audience members, including Roth, as zombies. "You just couldn't believe it," says producer Park. "Edgar's heroes were reaching out, and were so generous about it, and so nice about it. It was incredible."

Director Edgar Wright and Mark Donovan on the set of *Shuan of the Dead.*

Shaun of the Dead was released in the US on September 24, 2004. The film placed eighth at the box office, no mean feat for a small British movie. *Variety* deemed the appearance of Wright's film in the top ten as "a big surprise," and the movie continued to perform well over the next month. It ultimately grossed $13.5 million at the domestic box office and $30 million worldwide.

Bob Weinstein had continued to pursue his ambition of making a werewolf movie after Dimension rejected Len Wiseman's *Underworld* pitch. His dream finally became reality when Dimension released 2005's *Cursed*, a movie which had long been a nightmare for many of the principals involved.

"Oh, *Cursed* was a mess," said Wes Craven, who directed the movie from a screenplay by Kevin Williamson. "It was just a film where there was no script. The script was constantly being worked on, constantly changed. We shot for 11 weeks and threw almost everything away because Bob Weinstein wanted to change everything. We laid off for five months, and Kevin virtually wrote a new script. There could be a book written about that thing."

The film began life as a very different project. In August 2000, *The Hollywood Reporter* revealed that Williamson was set to write and produce an original thriller called *Cursed* for Dimension. The article described the film as concerning a serial killer in New York and "being in the vein of *The Silence of the Lambs*." Bob Weinstein tasked Williamson with rewriting the script so it more closely resembled *Scream* than Jonathan Demme's Oscar-winning film.

Back in October 1998, Craven and his producing partner Marianne Maddalena had signed what *Variety* described as "an exclusive, multimillion-dollar film deal with Dimension Films and its parent company Miramax Films." Under the terms of that deal, Craven would direct *Scream 3* and two other films. The director developed an adaptation of Christina Schwarz's bestselling mystery novel *Drowning Ruth*, but the project never got off the ground. Instead, Bob Weinstein hired Craven to direct the English-language version of *Pulse*, the 2001 Japanese chiller from writer-director Kiyoshi Kurosawa. The filmmaker was just weeks away from shooting the movie when Weinstein asked him to leave the project and direct *Cursed*.

Scream editor Patrick Lussier recalls that the director did not like Williamson's now much-altered script. "It wasn't a movie Wes wanted to make," he says. "He had wanted to make *Pulse*, and he had his whole crew hired for *Pulse*, and then they pulled the plug on that. In order to keep his crew employed, he took *Cursed*, which they were trying to twist his arm into doing. He said, 'This movie's not going to work, it's not scary enough, it's not funny enough.' And [Dimension] knew better, or said they did, and backed up the money truck."

Weinstein hoped that the reteaming of Craven and Williamson would result in another *Scream*-sized hit. "Bob just wanted Wes and Kevin to partner again," says Craven's former assistant Julie Plec, who was a co-producer on *Cursed*. "He was going to market the entire movie as the return of the dream team, and he basically just made it happen. When Bob got those things in his head, it was difficult to say no. So Wes signed on, and Kevin signed on, and the process began. It was a wild ride."

Craven cast Jesse Eisenberg, Christina Ricci, and *Scream* actor Skeet Ulrich as strangers who are attacked by a werewolf on a remote stretch of Los Angeles' Mulholland Drive. Other roles would be played by Milo Ventimiglia, Shannon Elizabeth, Mandy Moore, Omar Epps, Robert Forster, John C. McGinley, James Brolin, Heather Langenkamp, and Scott Baio, who was cast to portray a version of himself. To oversee the film's werewolf effects,

Jesse Eisenberg and Christina Ricci in *Cursed* (2005).

Weinstein recruited Rick Baker, winner of the first-ever Best Makeup Oscar for his work on 1981's horror classic *An American Werewolf in London*.

Plec recalls being surprised by how much Williamson's script had changed. "Kevin's original take was a woman in New York City who got bitten and had to deal with the dark side of herself, and all that that meant," she says. "And then, somehow, it became a movie in which Scott Baio, as himself, is the bad werewolf, and the final act of the movie takes place in the Hollywood Wax Museum. I remember reading that version of the script and being like, '*Huh*.'"

Craven began shooting what he assumed would be the R-rated venture in Los Angeles during March 2003. In July, with four weeks of filming left, Dimension put the production on an extended hiatus. *The Hollywood Reporter* ran an article on the stoppage the following month. Journalists Ian Mohr and Chris Gardner passed along the official Dimension line that the hiatus was planned, but reported that, according to their sources, "top executives at the Miramax Films genre arm weren't happy with the film's ending or how the special effects were progressing, specifically the look of the film's lead lupine."

Lussier joined the production just prior to the hiatus. "They stopped shooting before they shot the ending," he says. "Dimension Films very much got cold feet about what they were seeing in dailies, cold feet about the werewolf." Dimension had two options: keep the bulk of the footage and rework the planned ending, or essentially start the shoot again. "One version is, you spend $5 million to finish it and retweak whatever you can," says Lussier. "The other version is, you spend $20 million to basically shoot a new film, which is what they did. Which was an *insane* decision."

Very little of the footage from the initial shoot would make it into the finished movie. "You had these three stories: Skeet's story, Jesse Eisenberg's story, and Christina Ricci's story," Lussier explains. "In the original movie, they're all strangers, they all meet on the side of the road. There was probably 85 [or] 90 minutes of material. I recut a lot of that material. Of that, there are only 12 minutes in the final film, so tons of it was thrown out. It was just bizarre."

In December 2003, *Variety* published an article revealing that Portia de Rossi, Michael Rosenbaum, and Joshua Jackson had joined the cast of "the troubled Dimension Films project" and that Craven had resumed shooting the month previously. The list of actors who would not make the final cut included Mandy Moore, Omar Epps, Robert Forster, John C. McGinley, Heather Langenkamp, and Skeet Ulrich. Eisenberg participated in the reshoots, but his character of a bullied high school student was now not a stranger to Ricci's TV producer, but her brother. In an interview posted by Movieweb in December 2003, Ricci revealed that they were "essentially reshooting" the whole movie.

Rick Baker did not rejoin the production for the reshoot, with KNB taking over the makeup effects. "That movie went through a lot of changes, and there was a lot of people sticking their fingers into it," says the company's Greg Nicotero. "At one point, I think, when you have the Weinsteins commenting on werewolf stuff, Rick just kind of went, 'Guys, I'm out. This isn't what I signed up for.' And I respected him for that."

The first *Cursed* reshoot would be followed by two more. "It just didn't stop," says Lussier. "I was supposed to be on it for six weeks, I was on it for 19 months. It paid off my mortgage, that film." Plec also recalls being well remunerated for working—and, as she admits, for *not* working—on the film. "They put me on a weekly [wage] and two years later I was still getting paid every single week," she says. "Even when the movie shut down, I would stay, getting paid, because we were waiting on script pages. We shot that movie four times. By the end of it, we made tee shirts that said, 'Cursed 4: Back for More.'" According to Lussier, *Cursed* would ultimately cost "in

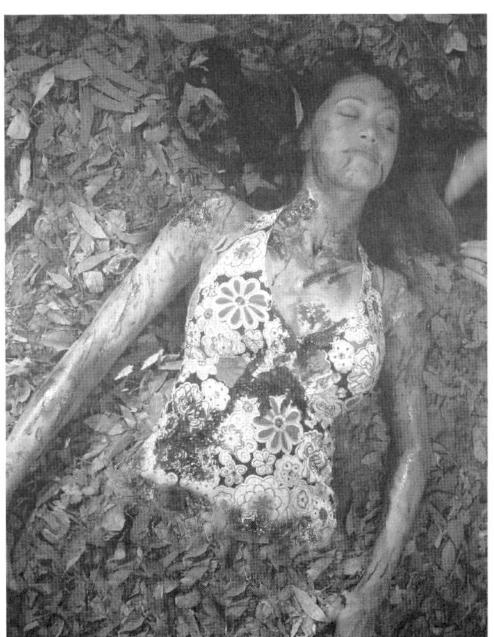

Behind-the-scenes shots from *Cursed* of (*left*) Shannon Elizabeth and (*right*) werewolf makeup.

the vicinity of $100 million, regardless of what you read. Bob Weinstein used to say, years later, 'This company lost a lot of money on werewolves.'"

Fangoria devoted the cover of its March 2005 issue to the film, promising, "Wes Craven tells all." The interview with the director began with him saying that he was unsure whether the movie was finished or not. "I hope it's over," the filmmaker told writer Marc Shapiro. "I talked to Bob Weinstein recently, and he's talking about making it a PG-13 movie. I can't win at this point, so I'm just going to walk away. I'm way past what my contractual obligations are to this film. If Bob wants to spend the rest of his life making this movie, that's fine. But I'm going to go on and do other things."

Weinstein did indeed cut out much of the film's gore to secure a PG-13 rating. Dimension finally released *Cursed* on February 25, 2005, with the film earning $9 million over its first weekend in theaters. In all, *Cursed* would gross just $19 million at the US box office.

After wrapping the werewolf film, Craven directed DreamWorks' *Red Eye*, a thriller starring Rachel McAdams as an airplane passenger attempting to outwit Cillian Murphy's terrorist. The film was released just six months after *Cursed* and finally gave Craven a hit away from the horror genre. Costing a reported $26 million, the thriller grossed $57 million in the US and $96 million worldwide.

Dimension's version of *Pulse* would eventually be directed by first-time filmmaker Jim Sonzero and star Kristen Bell. Released in August 2006, the film barely managed to earn back its reported $20 million budget at the US box office. Even so, Bob Weinstein released a pair of straight-to-DVD sequels via his new Dimension Extreme label, 2008's *Pulse 2: Afterlife* and the same year's *Pulse 3*.

Craven continued to regret his participation in *Cursed*. Following *Red Eye*, the filmmaker did not direct another feature until 2010's poorly received supernatural slasher film *My Soul to Take* and blamed his public travails on *Cursed* for the long gap. "The *Cursed* experience was so screwed up," he told Ain't It Cool News writer Steve Prokopy in 2009. "I mean, that went on for two and a half years of my life, for a film that wasn't anything close to what it should have been… I did learn from the *Cursed* experience not to do something for money… In general, I think it's not worth it, and part of the reason my phone hasn't rung is that that story is pretty well known."

Shortly before *Cursed* debuted in cinemas, Bob Weinstein's Dimension followed Lionsgate's lead into darker and more violent cinematic territory by acquiring Australian movie *Wolf Creek*. Writer-director Greg McLean's film about three backpackers being stalked and tortured by a killer was inspired by real-life murder cases. "I was developing another script about a bad guy in the outback, and it never really cracked for me," he says. "I was doing a lot of research about true cases that happened in Australia and, when I looked into these true cases, it just came to life, because what really happened was so much more terrifying than anything I could come up with."

After the film was bought by Dimension, *Wolf Creek* screened at the 2005 Sundance Film Festival and was reviewed by *Variety* critic Dennis Harvey, who warned potential viewers about the bleak nature of McLean's tale. "Harrowing and unpleasant, Aussie horror pic *Wolf Creek* invites comparisons to *The Texas Chain Saw Massacre* not just for content, but because both are based—albeit faintly—on real-life serial murder cases. Dimension Films caused a stir by buying US rights, supposedly sight-unseen, for $3.5 million weeks before the pic's Sundance bow. They should have little trouble scaring up a profit on that investment, particularly if the pic is sold as a more conventional genre item than it really is." *Wolf Creek* was a success when Dimension released the less-than-festive film on Christmas Day, 2005, earning $16 million in the US.

After *Wolf Creek*, McLean directed the Dimension-backed *Rogue*, about a man-eating crocodile, which starred Michael Vartan and Radha Mitchell. In the years since Mitchell had starred in *Pitch Black*, the Australian actress had established a reputation outside the horror genre, with roles in Tony Scott's 2004 thriller *Man on Fire* and the following year's Woody Allen-directed comedy-drama *Melinda and Melinda*. She recalls receiving pushback from her representation about the possibility of appearing in McLean's creature feature. "The agent's like, 'Don't do it, I don't want you to do it,'" Mitchell says. "I ended up wanting to do it." Dimension gave the film a straight-to-DVD release in the US after McLean's movie was beaten to cinemas by a rival killer crocodile movie from Hollywood Pictures called *Primeval*. "They shelved this film in the US, which was kind of a tragedy," says Mitchell. "At that time, it wasn't seen. But somehow people are always asking me about *Rogue*. People that are into horror really appreciate the movie."

Stephen King's *Creepshow* collaborator George Romero had appreciated Zack Snyder's *Dawn of the Dead* and its sprinting zombies far less than the author. In a 2005 issue of *Time Out*, *Shaun of the Dead* star Simon Pegg interviewed Romero, who described the remake as "more of a video game. I'm not terrified of things running at me; it's like *Space Invaders*. There was nothing going on underneath."

Romero was speaking with Pegg to promote his revived *Dead Reckoning* project, which was finally being released under the title *Land of the Dead*. After 9/11, the director had both retitled and somewhat reworked the *Dead Reckoning* script, inspired by the Republican administration's response to the attack on the World Trade Center.

On September 20, 2001, nine days after the Twin Towers fell, President George W. Bush spoke at a joint session of Congress to announce that US foreign policy would focus on tackling terrorists via a War on Terror. The majority of the al-Qaeda members responsible for the 9/11 attacks were citizens of Saudi Arabia, an oil-rich country friendly to the US, and the Bush administration decided to wage its war in other parts of the globe. In October 2001, US military forces began operations in Afghanistan, capturing the capital of Kabul the following month. In March 2003, American and British forces invaded Iraq, securing Baghdad three weeks later. At the start of May that year, Bush made a televised victory speech on the aircraft carrier USS *Abraham Lincoln*, standing in front of a huge banner that declared 'Mission Accomplished.' The message proved premature, and American troops would remain in Afghanistan and Iraq for years to come.

Romero believed that Bush's War on Terror gave his screenplay added resonance. "I pulled it back out and said, 'This is stronger now,'" the director told *Fangoria*. "There were scenes in it that were there before, like an armored vehicle going down the street in a little village, mowing people down, wondering why they were pissed off at us, and suddenly that resonated so much after you'd seen it on CNN, with tanks mowing people down. A lot of it I really didn't have to change."

In September 2004, *Variety* announced that Universal had acquired distribution rights to *Land of the Dead* and that Romero would direct the film with a budget of $15 million. The filmmaker understood that the studio's decision to back the project was partly based on the box office returns of *28 Days Later* and the *Dawn of the Dead* remake. "Because of the success of those films, Universal was willing to pony up a little more dough," he told the outlet JoBlo.

Director George Romero on the set of *Land of the Dead* (2005).

Romero shot *Land of the Dead* in Toronto. The film's stars included John Leguizamo, Simon Baker, Dennis Hopper, and Asia Argento, the daughter of Italian horror director Dario Argento, who had helped finance the original *Dawn of the Dead.* Hopper played the film's villain Kaufman, the ruler of Fiddler's Green and a character reminiscent of both Vice President Dick Cheney and Secretary of State Donald Rumsfeld. A clutch of notable horror film folk made cameos as zombies in the movie. Tom Savini portrayed his (now undead) biker character from Romero's *Dawn of the Dead*, while Simon Pegg and Edgar Wright also made brief appearances. "George fell in love with *Shaun of the Dead*," says KNB's Greg Nicotero, who directed second unit on the film. "I don't remember if it was George's idea or my idea, but we were collectively like, 'You guys have to be zombies in it.'"

Pegg and Wright were planning to make their next film a cop comedy called *Hot Fuzz*, which would be released in 2007. The pair's choice to not follow *Shaun of the Dead* with another horror film was reinforced by a conversation they had with Romero. "Before we went back to London, we had a quick coffee with him, and he asked us, 'What are [you] doing next?'" says Wright. "We said, 'We're writing this cop action-comedy.' And George Romero said, 'Oh, so not a horror? So you're getting out?' That really stuck with me, because I feel like probably George Romero felt that he had been pigeonholed in the horror genre somewhat."

Eugene Clark in *Land of the Dead.*

Land of the Dead grossed around a third of the amount earned by Snyder's *Dawn of the Dead* after the film was released on June 24, 2005. Speaking with *Fangoria*, Romero would blame Universal for the film's disappointing commercial performance. "The US marketing campaign was a dud, no posters went up in the theaters, the TV spots were barely there," he said. "Universal really misunderstood the value of the picture and didn't know what to do with it."

Romero had good reason to grouse about the release date Universal had chosen for *Land of the Dead.* The studio put his film into cinemas during the busy summer movie season and less than a week before the arrival of Steven Spielberg's *War of the Worlds.* Starring Tom Cruise and made for many times the budget of Romero's film, this new adaptation of author H. G. Wells' alien invasion tale earned $64 million over its opening weekend. During the same period, *Land of the Dead* grossed just $2.7 million and fell to tenth place on the box office chart. "It came out in the summer, a week after *Batman Begins* and five days before *War of the Worlds*, and that's a tough position to be in," Romero later pointed out to *Fangoria.*

Few people regarded Steven Spielberg as a horror filmmaker. Yet the director of *Duel*, *Jaws*, and *Jurassic Park* had been directly responsible for some of cinema's most memorably terrifying moments. Spielberg had also produced a slew of horror movies, including 1982's *Poltergeist*, the 1983 anthology film *Twilight Zone: The Movie* (for which he also directed a segment), and 1999's *The Haunting*.

Spielberg had spent much of the '90s depicting real-life historical horrors with the films *Schindler's List*, *Amistad*, and *Saving Private Ryan*. The world's most famous director headed back to the terror tale genre with the encouragement of Tom Cruise. The *Top Gun* star had enjoyed working with Spielberg on 2002's Philip K. Dick adaptation *Minority Report*. When the actor visited the set of Spielberg's next film, *Catch Me If You Can*, the pair talked about reuniting. "He mentioned three movies; *War of the Worlds* was the third," Cruise was quoted as saying in the film's production notes. "We looked at each other, and the lights went on."

The *War of the Worlds* script was initially written by Josh Friedman, who would go on to create the TV series *Terminator: The Sarah Connor Chronicles*, and was then reworked by *Stir of Echoes* filmmaker David Koepp. The protagonist of the finished screenplay was a Brooklyn crane operator and very

Tom Cruise in *War of the Worlds* (2005).

imperfect father named Ray Ferrier, who attempts to transport his two children from New York to Boston in the wake of an alien attack. Cruise had intended his next production to be the third *Mission: Impossible* movie, with *Narc* filmmaker Joe Carnahan set to direct a script by Frank Darabont. Then Carnahan departed the project in June 2004 and was replaced by J. J. Abrams. With the *Felicity* and *Alias* creator needing time to co-write and prep his directorial debut, Cruise and Spielberg fast-tracked *War of the Worlds*. In August 2004, *Variety* reported that the film had been put on "a crash pre-production schedule" and that shooting was due to begin in November.

Spielberg filled out the main cast with Dakota Fanning and Justin Chatwin, who played the children of Cruise's character, and Tim Robbins as an unhinged fellow survivor. Working with a $128 million budget, Spielberg shot in a variety of locales, including New Jersey, Connecticut, and Los Angeles. The PG-13 film featured several horrifying sights, such as a burning passenger train hurtling along railway tracks and a river full of corpses. The fake bodies were provided by *Blade II* makeup effects artist Steve Johnson, who had hoped to create much more work for the movie. "The original script was quite different, it showed the alien species toward the end," he says. "We were creating an entire mechanical animatronic alien." The special effects artist recalls that the script also featured "these huge pods, and aliens came out of them. We made a full-size pod that was one of the most amazing things I've ever done, [but] they cut the pods out of the film. The producers felt badly. They said, 'Well, we have this scene where there's a hundred dead bodies floating down this river, and you can do that.'" Johnson explains that making sure the faux corpses were in the frame of Spielberg's cameras was "actually kind of difficult. They float around the bend, how do you catch them and restage it, a hundred dead bodies, for take two? It ended up being a big job."

The *War of the Worlds* visuals echoed the attacks on the Twin Towers in scenes which found buildings blasted into rubble and American citizens turned into dust. Spielberg's inclusion of 9/11-inspired imagery was picked up by media outlets. At the end of June 2005, the *Los Angeles Times* ran an article on the film that described *War of the Worlds* as "the first major-scale Hollywood production bringing Sept. 11 imagery to the multiplex."

The story that really dominated the *War of the Worlds* publicity campaign was Tom Cruise, his new relationship with *Dawson's Creek* actress Katie Holmes, and his leading position in the Church of Scientology. During his

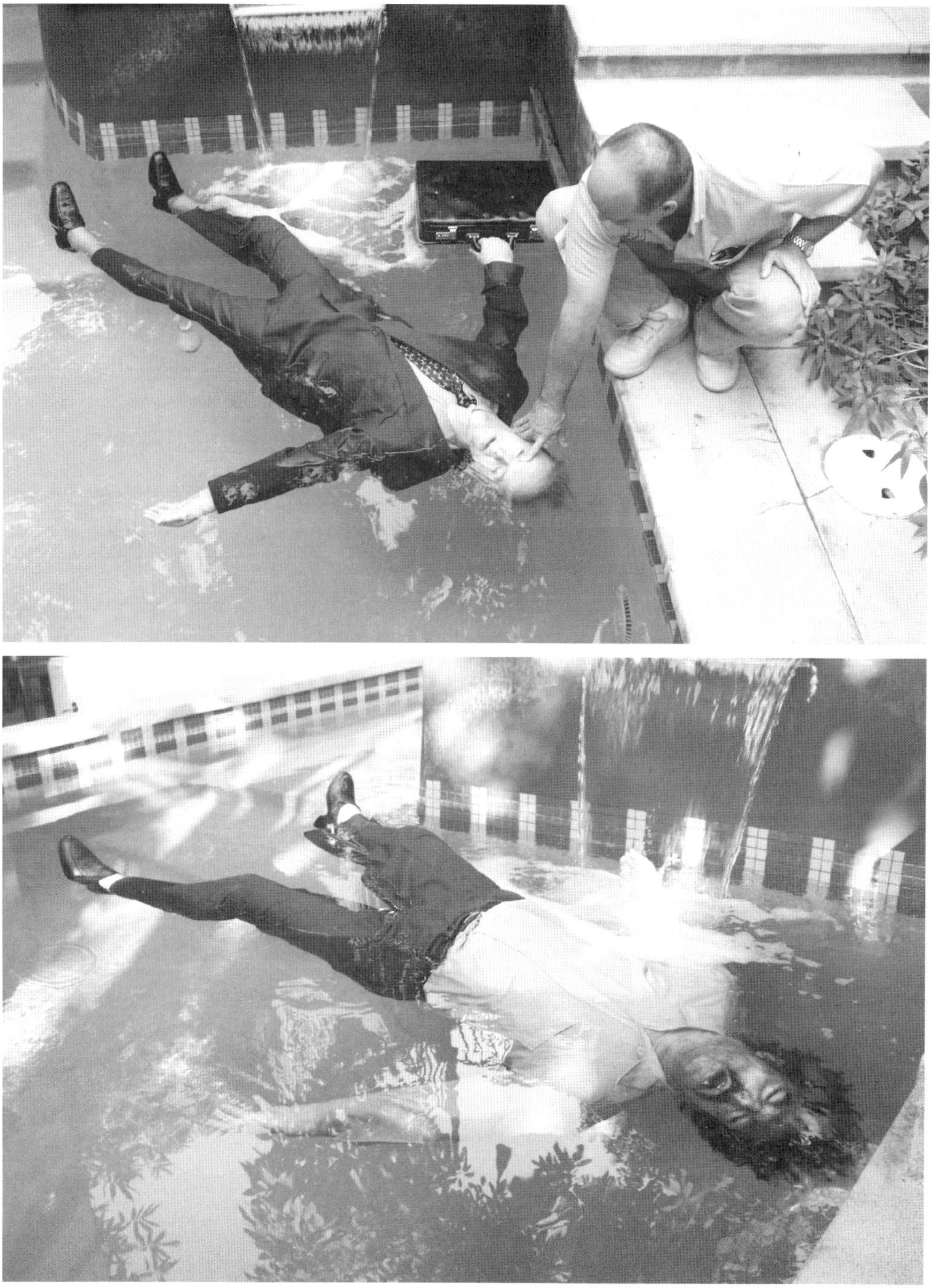

Fake corpses being tested for *War of the Worlds*.

instantly infamous appearance on *The Oprah Winfrey Show*, ostensibly to promote *War of the Worlds*, an excited Cruise repeatedly punched the floor and jumped on the host's couch, before going backstage and returning with Holmes. On June 23, NBC's *Today Show* broadcast an interview with Cruise conducted by host Matt Lauer. In the course of the increasingly heated exchange, Lauer said that cynics were suggesting Cruise's relationship with Holmes was a publicity stunt and asked the actor about his statement that actress Brooke Shields' use of antidepressants to help with postpartum depression was irresponsible. As Cruise argued his case, an onscreen crawl read 'War of the words.'

Spielberg was reportedly irritated with the way Cruise handled himself on the film's promotional tour. But the media's focus on the star's personal life and opinions did not stop *War of the Worlds* grossing a satisfactory $603 million at the worldwide box office, becoming the director's most successful film since 1997's *The Lost World: Jurassic Park*.

As a director, Spielberg moved away from genre terrors after *War of the Worlds*, turning his attention to 2005's *Munich* and 2008's *Indiana Jones and the Kingdom of the Crystal Skull*. The *Jaws* auteur would continue to help horror stories make it to the screen, however. The director's company DreamWorks was among the producers of 2008's *The Ruins*. Adapted from Scott B. Smith's 2006 novel, the film was a gory, R-rated tale of young American tourists menaced by carnivorous vines at an ancient Mayan temple. *The Ruins* was the directorial debut of fashion photographer Carter Smith. "I've loved the horror genre since I was a kid," he says. "As a queer kid who spent a lot of time alone, it was definitely a place of solace. Horror movies and the pages of *Fangoria*, it wasn't where I would see people like me, but I felt like I was part of something."

The director's short film *Bugcrush* won a jury prize at 2006's Sundance Film Festival and attracted the attention of Spielberg. "I never imagined that *The Ruins* would be my first film," says Smith. "*Bugcrush* got me in the room for *The Ruins*. It was Steven Spielberg seeing that short, and kind of being obsessed with it, that got me the job."

Smith shot *The Ruins* in Australia, with a cast including Jena Malone, Shawn Ashmore, and Joe Anderson. DreamWorks and the company's distribution partner Paramount released the film in the US on April 4, 2008. *The Ruins* grossed a disappointing $22 million at the worldwide box office but found a fan in Stephen King. "The Scott Smith-scripted adaptation of his novel isn't quite as creepy as the book, but the sense of dismay and disquiet grows as the viewer begins to sense that no one's getting away," King wrote in *Fangoria*. "With its cast of mostly unknowns, this would play well on a double Halloween bill with Snyder's *Dawn* remake."

With the release of *Resident Evil* and *Underworld*, the Sony label Screen Gems had helped breathe new life into cinematic zombies, vampires, and werewolves. Next, the company would perform the same service for the exorcism film.

William Friedkin's Oscar-winning 1973 blockbuster *The Exorcist* had failed to inspire similarly successful sequels. Director John Boorman's 1977 film *Exorcist II: The Heretic* was an infamous disaster that Friedkin would describe as "the worst piece of shit I've ever seen" during a 2019 appearance on *The Movies That Made Me* podcast. In the late '80s, William Peter Blatty, author of the original novel *The Exorcist*, teamed with the newly founded Morgan Creek Entertainment and directed *The Exorcist III*. Released in August 1990, Blatty's movie performed modestly at the box office.

In 1997, Morgan Creek began developing a prequel to Friedkin's film, which would feature a younger version of Max von Sydow's character Father Merrin. The company hired Paul Schrader, the writer of *Taxi Driver* and director of the 1982 horror film *Cat People*, to oversee the movie. Schrader cast Stellan Skarsgård as Merrin and began shooting the $38 million-budgeted film in November 2002.

When Morgan Creek president James G. Robinson was dissatisfied with the result, the company employed *Deep Blue Sea* filmmaker Renny Harlin to take over the prequel. Harlin retained Skarsgård in the lead role but shot an almost completely new film, doubling the budget of the whole project to more than $75 million. The director's film, *Exorcist: The Beginning*, was released in the US in August 2004, and grossed $48 million at the domestic box office, a slight return given the cost of the enterprise. Schrader's original version, *Dominion: Prequel to the Exorcist*, would be completed and put out the following year, to improved reviews but very little financial return.

The exorcism subgenre was revitalized by 2005's Screen Gems-distributed *The Exorcism of Emily Rose*. The film was directed and co-written by Scott Derrickson, who grew up in a blue-collar neighborhood of Denver, Colorado. Derrickson started making Super 8 films with the camera of his car dealer father and at Halloween constructed haunted houses in the basement of his home. "I used to bring the neighborhood kids around and charge them to go through my basement of scary things," he says.

At the age of 17, Derrickson moved to California, attending the Christian college Biola and then USC film school, where he first saw Italian director Dario Argento's 1977 horror classic *Suspiria*. "I grew up on slasher movies and then I saw *Suspiria*," he says. "I didn't know horror could be so operatic and such high art. From that point on, I devoured everything."

Derrickson and another USC graduate Paul Harris Boardman successfully pitched to write the screenplay for 2000's *Urban Legends: Final Cut*. The pair were also among the clutch of screenwriters who worked on the script for Dimension's Patrick Lussier-directed *Dracula 2000*. In a 2017 message on social media, Derrickson recalled that Bob Weinstein told him that the movie "needs a rewrite. Shoots in two weeks. It's called *Dracula 2000*. It's terrible. But I'm making it anyway." According to Derrickson, when he asked the Dimension chief why he was making the film if the script was terrible, Weinstein replied, "Because it's called *Dracula 2000*."

In August 1999, *Variety* reported that Dimension had signed Derrickson and Boardman to a three-picture deal. The principal fruit of that pact was 2000's straight-to-video *Hellraiser: Inferno*, the fifth entry in the Clive Barker-created franchise. Written by Derrickson and Boardman and directed by Derrickson, the film starred Craig Sheffer as a corrupt cop whose investigation of a murder leads him to the hellish realm of Doug Bradley's Pinhead. "My reach [exceeded] my grasp," says Derrickson of the film, which he made for just $2 million. "The budget that I had for that movie didn't fit the script, that's for sure. But I also had a lot to learn about how to make something scary."

Over the next half-decade, Derrickson and Boardman worked on a slew of scripts, nearly all of which would remain unproduced. Among the screenplays the pair wrote during this period was the first draft of what would become 2014's Derrickson-directed *Deliver Us from Evil*, starring Eric Bana and Joel McHale. Their script was based on the 2001 non-fiction book *Beware the Night*, which detailed the career of NYPD officer and paranormal investigator Ralph Sarchie. When Derrickson visited New York to meet with Sarchie, the cop recommended that he read another book called *The Exorcism of Anneliese Michel*. "He said, 'It's the most well-documented case of demonic possession I've ever read,'" the director remembers.

Written by anthropologist Felicitas D. Goodman, *The Exorcism of Anneliese Michel* documented the case of a young German woman who underwent 67 exorcisms in the year prior to her death from malnutrition in 1976. After Michel's passing, her parents and two priests were put on trial and convicted of negligent homicide. Derrickson was electrified by the story. The director believed that an adaptation of Goodman's book could satisfy his desire to make movies with spiritual themes and refresh the exorcism movie by marrying the subgenre with that of the courtroom drama. "I contacted the author, and I optioned it for $100, and then I wrote the script on spec, and that became *The Exorcism of Emily Rose*," says Derrickson.

The filmmaker was inspired not just by Goodman's book but by audio recordings of Anneliese Michel which the author sent him. "She became friends with the two priests, who gave her all the recordings of these exorcisms," he says. "There were something like thirty audio cassettes. She gave them to me, and I listened through all of them. Absolutely horrifying. They are truly the stuff of nightmares." Derrickson and Boardman's screenplay relocated the events to America and related the story of Emily Rose in flashback from the perspective of different characters, a structure inspired by the work of Derrickson's cinematic hero, *Rashomon* filmmaker Akira Kurosawa.

The script proved a tough sell, thanks to the poor box office track record of *The Exorcist* franchise in the decades since Friedkin's film. "I took it around town, and everybody passed on it," says Derrickson. The director did not approach Screen Gems, believing the studio would be unlikely to take on the project. "Sony's Screen Gems was a new company," he says. "They had made the first *Underworld*, [but] they hadn't made much."

Screen Gems president Clint Culpepper got his hands on a copy of the screenplay and reacted with extreme positivity. "I get a call on Monday morning that says, 'Screen Gems is going to make your movie,'" recalls Derrickson "I'm like, 'What?! I haven't even met with them. What are you talking about?' I'm always going to be grateful to Clint for having the vision to see what that movie could be."

Derrickson cast Tom Wilkinson as a priest who is put on trial for his involvement in the death of Emily Rose and Laura Linney as the lawyer of Wilkinson's character. Linney had acted alongside a relatively unknown actress named Jennifer Carpenter in a 2002 Broadway production of *The Crucible* and suggested that the director look at her for the part of Emily Rose. In her audition, Carpenter genuinely unnerved Derrickson with her

Jennifer Carpenter in *The Exorcism of Emily Rose* (2005).

performance of a possessed person. "Jennifer came into the room and, just in front of us, did the kind of things that she does in the movie," the director says. "I remember watching her in this psychotic state that she seemed to be in, and the way she moved her body, and the sounds she was making. I got frightened, it felt so alien and unhinged." Carpenter's audition prompted Derrickson to reassess his approach to the film. "I thought to myself, okay, not only am I going to cast her, but I'm going to cut almost all the visual effects," he says. "*This* is what's scary, this person's performance right here. I realized, this is how you get around *The Exorcist.* You can't go over *The Exorcist*, you'll never conquer that movie, but you can go *under* it! That, to me, was the idea, making the terror the result of this naturalistic performance, and that's how the movie worked."

Released in the US on September 9, 2005, *The Exorcism of Emily Rose* comfortably won its opening weekend with a gross of $30 million. The film would go on to amass worldwide earnings of $145 million. *The Exorcism of Emily Rose* proved to be the rare original horror blockbuster that did not beget a sequel, with Derrickson moving on to direct 2008's Keanu Reeves-starring remake of the science fiction classic *The Day the Earth Stood*

Still. But the success of the film helped usher in an onslaught of similar tales, including 2006's *An American Haunting*, 2009's *The Haunting in Connecticut*, 2010's Eli Roth-produced *The Last Exorcism*, and 2011's Anthony Hopkins-starring *The Rite*. "No one had really made a successful exorcism movie since *The Exorcist*, and [our] movie relaunched the possession and exorcism genre," says Derrickson. "I'm very proud of that fact."

On the Monday following the US release of 2004's *Saw*, Lionsgate and Twisted Pictures released a statement announcing that a sequel would come out one year later. That film would not be directed by James Wan. Ahead of the *Saw* screening at Sundance, the director and Leigh Whannell had been encouraged by their representatives to strike a deal for another movie, in case the film turned out to be a failure. Whannell suggested to Wan that their next project concern a possessed ventriloquist dummy, and the pair successfully pitched the idea to Universal.

Billy the Puppet in *Saw II* (2005).

Wan's unavailability to direct *Saw II* did not dissuade Lionsgate from its plan to release the sequel just 12 months after the first movie. With the clock ticking, Twisted Pictures executives Mark Burg, Oren Koules, and Gregg Hoffman recruited aspiring filmmaker Darren Lynn Bousman to turn his screenplay for a film called *The Desperate* into *Saw II* with help from Whannell. "*The Desperate* was clearly a *Saw*-esque film," says Lionsgate's Peter Block. "We had to move so quickly, and Mark and Oren had gotten the script and sent it over. The real question was, can we rejigger it to work?"

Bousman was raised in Kansas City and had bonded with his father via their ritual of watching movies at the end of the week. "Every Friday night after school, we would go to Blockbuster and pick a movie based only on the box," he says. "The horror section, the fantasy, the sci-fi, had the coolest box art. Horror became a bonding experience with my dad."

After studying film at Florida's Full Sail University, Bousman moved to Los Angeles, where he got an assistant job at a talent agency and started writing the script for *The Desperate*. "The original pitch of it was, a group of people who are desperate in their lives [for] something—a cancer treatment, custody of the kid—play in a game called 'The Desperate'," he says. "They go into a house, and the doors are locked, and they play this murder game with a ticking clock."

Bousman asked friends of his working as assistants at other agencies to write assessments (known as 'coverage') of his unfinished screenplay. "I had a bunch of friends write fake coverage," he says. "Twisted Pictures said, 'We've heard about this script, we think we're the perfect people to make it.' That was my kick in the ass to get the script finished."

He signed a deal to direct *The Desperate* with Twisted Pictures. When the company's executives realized that *Saw* was set to become a box office hit, they suggested turning his screenplay into *Saw II*. Bousman was unhappy about the notion. "I'm fresh out of film school, think my farts don't smell," he says. "I'm like, 'I'm an *artiste*, I'm not a sequel guy!' Then I had this awakening. I was like, 'I'm fucking stupid. I have an opportunity at 24 years old that most people never get.' And I dove in, and it was the best decision of my life."

Bousman had directed the video for a track by Los Angeles-based industrial metal band Static-X but could claim no real experience as a narrative filmmaker. Twisted Pictures was forced to seriously consider him as a candidate for the *Saw II* directing gig because of the deal he had signed for *The Desperate*. "When it got turned [into] *Saw II*, I was immediately kicked off," says Bousman. "I think they talked about going to Renny Harlin. I've had the same lawyer for 20 things [because of] this one thing that she did. In the contract for *The Desperate*, it says that I am 'attached to direct *The Desperate* or any variation thereof.' I remember that my lawyer goes, 'Why don't look you look at subparagraph 3, subsection 16?'"

Bousman still had to convince Lionsgate that he should be allowed to take over the company's new cash cow. "Mark and Oren said, 'We're going to back you on this, but you've got to go into Lionsgate and sell yourself hard,'" he recalls. "[I'm] fresh out of Kansas. I don't know shit about anything. I go into Lionsgate, and I'm sitting in a room full of just execs, and every word I'm saying is a fucking lie. They're like, 'Why should you direct it?' I said, 'Because I've been directing horror shorts since I've been a kid, and I've won festivals on my horror shorts.' I remember Pete Block leans forward and goes, 'Great, we need to see the horror shorts that won at festivals.'"

For his part, Block confirms that he had doubts about Bousman's claims. "It's funny, because Jason Constantine, who I worked with for many years, is the most believing soul you've ever met," says the executive. "I'm like, 'Jason, just assume everybody's lying, just assume it's all puffery!' He's like, 'Well, Darren said he made some shorts.' I'm like, 'Yeah, let's just *see* these things.'"

The problem for Bousman was that he *didn't* have anything to show the executives. "I remember leaving Lionsgate, and calling my mom, and saying, 'Mom, I need money right now,'" he recalls. "I got together with some friends, and we shot a short film on 16mm. I didn't know what the fuck I was doing. That was the short that ended up getting me *Saw II*."

Bousman worked with Whannell to write the *Saw II* script, based on his screenplay for *The Desperate*. "I had a few weeks to adapt *The Desperate* into *Saw II*, so I did my best Jigsaw impressions," he remembers. "Leigh gets the script after that and goes, 'No, no, no.' There was a two- or three-week period when Leigh and I would sit in Twisted Pictures every day. It was this crash course in filmmaking with Leigh Whannell." Bousman had a more distant relationship with Wan, an executive producer on the sequel. "James was this phantom figure that I was terrified of," he says. "AOL Instant Messenger was a big thing, and that was really the only way that I talked with James. I had this constant fear that I was going to get the message that he wanted to return."

Tobin Bell and Shawnee Smith came back for the second film and *Sixth Sense* actor Donnie Wahlberg joined the *Saw* family, playing a cop whose son is kidnapped by Bell's John Kramer. *Saw II* had a budget of around $4 million and Bousman admits to suffering from a king-sized case of imposter syndrome during the shoot. "I had bullshitted my way from sleeping on

Director Darren Bousman and Shawnee Smith on the set of *Saw II*.

a friend's couch to being on set," he says. "I felt like at any moment they were going to realize I didn't know what the fuck I was doing." Block recalls that Bousman could be an idiosyncratic presence on set. "He came in with all his insecurities, and his pills, and his playing with his hair, and everything, but he had a passion," says the executive. "One thing about Darren? He was committed. He was a crazy person, but I loved him, and I still do."

In June 2005, Lionsgate released the twisty and graphic French serial killer film *High Tension*. The movie starred actresses Cécile de France and Maïwenn as friends attempting to survive the murderous attentions of Philippe Nahon's truck-driving psychopath. *High Tension*, originally released as *Haute Tension* in France in 2003, was directed by Alexandre Aja from a script by the French filmmaker and his writing partner Grégory Levasseur. Lionsgate released a dubbed version of Aja's movie in over 1,300 cinemas. But *High Tension* failed to find a substantial audience, grossing less than $2 million over its opening weekend.

Tim Palen believes that the company made a mistake giving the movie such a wide release. "Candidly, we were working on the campaign, and it all went south," he says. "Cécile de France came to Joshua Tree, where I have a studio, and we did photographs. I mocked up a poster, and I blew it up really big, and put it on my wall in my office. The Lionsgate producer came in[to] my office and was like, 'That's a big movie!' That started the ball rolling of, 'We're going to dub this movie,' instead of celebrating what it was, which was a French-language, homoerotic horror movie. The English-ification of it was where it went off the rails." Palen admits that the movie "was considered a failure at Lionsgate, and it shouldn't have been, because it's such a great movie."

Cécile de France in a promotional shot for *High Tension* (2003).

While not a big box office player, *High Tension* would come to be regarded as an important early entry in the so-called 'New French Extremity.' This grouping of brutal and transgressive films also included Claire Denis' 2001 cannibal movie *Trouble Every Day*, Gaspar Noé's unrated 2003 film *Irréversible* (another Lionsgate release), 2008's *Inside*, and 2009's *Martyrs*, overlapping and intersecting with the corresponding wave of extremity developing in the US.

The month after *High Tension* debuted in cinemas, Lionsgate released Rob Zombie's *The Devil's Rejects*, a sequel to *House of 1000 Corpses*, which once again starred Bill Moseley, Sid Haig, and Sheri Moon Zombie. To gin up interest in the movie, Lionsgate decorated billboards with a poster that showed the movie's characters posed in a manner that aped a specific Leonardo da Vinci painting. "We did a collage *à la* 'The Last Supper,'" says Tim Palen. "I know that the Catholic Anti-Defamation League were up in arms about it." *The Devil's Rejects* outgrossed its predecessor, earning $17 million at the US box office.

Palen courted more controversy with his original poster for *Saw II*, which featured a pair of severed human digits. "The first iteration of the posters were the dismembered fingers, and the MPAA lost their minds," he says. "We weren't a signatory, so I always thought, 'Well, fuck you, then.' But their recourse is to say, 'If you don't listen to us, then we can forbid you from using the rating, which means you can't book certain theaters,' and you're fucked. We had to reissue the poster, cropping the base of the fingers so they were no longer dismembered. Such bullshit. There were people at [other] studios that were ratting us out, too. I know people for sure at Paramount were calling the MPAA, saying, 'He's doing it again!'"

Saw II took pole position on the box office chart over Halloween 2005 with a haul of $31 million during its first three days of release. The film went on to earn $147 million at the global box office, $44 million more than Wan's original. Its success confirmed that the grimier, gorier brand of horror pioneered by Rob Zombie, Eli Roth, and the creators of the original *Saw* had been embraced by a mainstream audience. "When *Saw II* opened at $30 million, suddenly this was a major business," says Roth. "And everyone was paying attention."

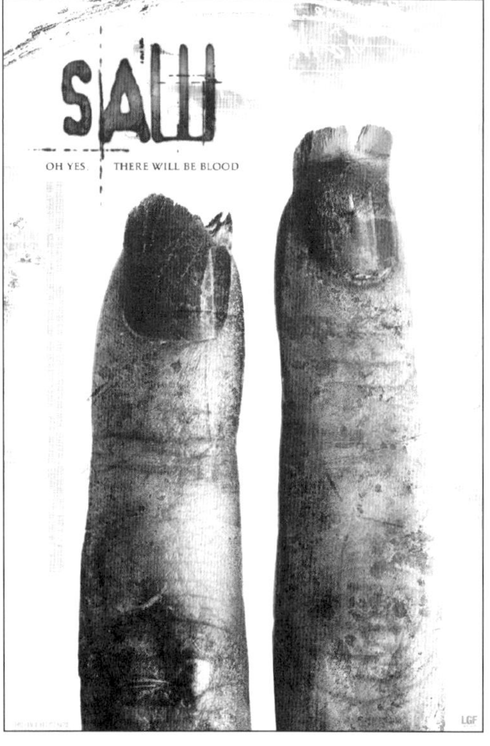

(*Left*) Original poster for *Saw II* and (*right*) widely released version.

"WELL, NOW THAT IS SOME FUCKED-UP SHIT."

In January 2006, just two months after the release of *Saw II*, Eli Roth's second film hit US cinema screens. Titled *Hostel*, the movie tracked a group of American tourists who are tortured and, in a couple of cases, killed by wealthy members of a secret club in Slovakia.

The idea for a film with the name *Hostel* had originated with a producer named Chris Briggs, who was interested in making a movie about backpackers. Roth developed the concept, combining the title and the milieu with an organization he had been told about by Ain't It Cool News founder Harry Knowles, which supposedly allowed customers to kill people in South-East Asia for a fee.

Roth considered several other options before deciding to make *Hostel* his second film. Thanks to the success of *Cabin Fever*, the director was regarded as a hot talent in Hollywood, and the most obvious career move for him was to tackle a project with a much larger budget than his debut. The director struck a deal to write a teen comedy called *Scavenger Hunt* for Universal and developed an adaptation of the Richard Matheson short story "Button, Button" with *Donnie Darko* director Richard Kelly (Kelly would later bring the story to the big screen as 2009's *The Box*). For a spell, Roth contemplated signing on to direct a movie version of TV show *The Dukes of Hazzard*, a project subsequently taken over by filmmaker Jay Chandrasekhar. "I got offered $350,000 to direct *Dukes of Hazzard*," Roth says. "I thought, 'I don't want to do this, but I'm running out of money here, and what am I supposed to do? Like, what's the move?'"

The filmmaker was increasingly drawn to the idea of making another low-budget horror film. Roth was inspired by some of the movies he had seen coming out of Asia, including Takashi Miike's notorious *Audition*. The

Japanese director's 2000 film starred Ryo Ishibashi as a widower who takes part in a fake casting audition, hoping to find a new partner. Ishibashi's character connects with one of the auditionees, portrayed by Eihi Shiina, leading to a phantasmagoria of dismemberment and torture. "No movie has made me cringe worse than *Audition*," says Roth. The director was similarly impressed by South Korean filmmaker Park Chan-wook's *Sympathy for Mr. Vengeance*, which he saw in October 2002 at the Sitges Film Festival. "I was like, 'Oh, this is the best film I've seen in years,'" he says.

The director was further pushed in the direction of making a second lean and mean movie by his appreciation for, and competitive attitude toward, Wan and Whannell's *Saw*. "I liked *Saw*, I thought the twist was fantastic," says Roth. "I love James, I took him around Hollywood and helped promote *Saw*. But there's always that competitive nature of like, 'I don't want this movie stealing my thunder.'"

Roth was given the final shove in the direction of making *Hostel* by Quentin Tarantino shortly after turning down the *Dukes of Hazzard* gig. "I had the idea for *Hostel*, and I went to Quentin's house—I remember it photographically, like it happened this morning," he says. "I'm like, 'I just turned down a movie for a TV show I know and like, but I didn't love the script, I don't know how to make that a movie.' He goes, 'Forget about that, what ideas do you have?' I go, 'Well, I have this one idea, but I think it's too sick, I don't know if anyone will ever even see it.' I tell him the idea for *Hostel* and he goes, 'I've got fucking chills right now. This is the best idea for a horror movie I've heard in ten years.' I was like, 'I need to go home and write.' I wrote it in ten days."

In March 2005, *Variety* announced that Roth would direct *Hostel* for Sony's Screen Gems label, with Jay Hernandez from the 2001 romantic drama *Crazy/Beautiful* set to star. "Screen Gems knew that *Cabin Fever* had sold so many DVDs it was crazy," says Roth. "Basically, Sony were like, anything under $5 million, do whatever you want, because we know, with your name, the DVD will sell."

The director shot *Hostel* on a budget of around $4 million in the Czech Republic, with a cast that also included future *Suits* star Rick Hoffman, Slovakian actress Barbara Nedeljáková, and, in a cameo, *Audition* filmmaker Takashi Miike. Journalist Bill Schulz covered the *Hostel* production for the men's magazine *Stuff* and was cast as a victim who would be seen in the film having his testicles removed by a client of the movie's secret organization.

A torturer in *Hostel* (2005).

"Every person who was behind the camera in *Hostel* was in front of the camera getting killed," says Schulz. "Eli said, 'Do you want to get your balls cut off in a scene?' And I said, 'I sure as fuck do.'"

When the footage shot by Roth proved too disturbing for Sony, Screen Gems president Clint Culpepper approached Lionsgate about taking on the film's US distribution. "Somebody at Sony watched the dailies and said, 'If Sony releases this, it's going to be damaging for the company,'" says Roth. "So, Clint Culpepper called Lionsgate and said, 'You guys just worked with Eli, do you want another one?'" Some Lionsgate executives were also uneasy about the material the director had shot. "People at Lionsgate started going, 'Hey, man, your dailies are crazy,'" he says. "I was like, 'I thought I was done with Lionsgate. You keep pulling me back in!'"

Concerned about the possibility that *Hostel* might not get a theatrical release, Roth asked Tarantino to be credited as 'presenting' the film in publicity and marketing materials as a way of reinforcing the movie's cine-

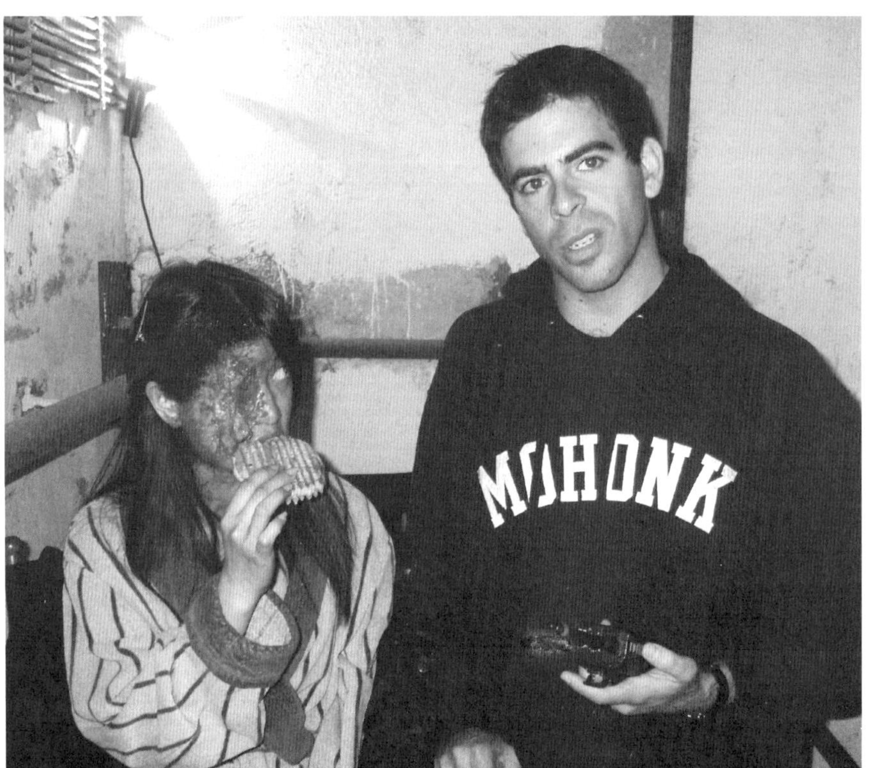

Jennifer Lim and Eli Roth on the set of *Hostel.*

matic credentials. "*Hostel*, again, [was a] low-testing movie," says Roth. "I said to Quentin, 'If you want to put your name on it, now's the time, because they might not go theatrical with this.' And so, Quentin did it as 'Quentin Tarantino presents.'"

The *Hostel* marketing campaign began with the release of a teaser poster featuring the stark image of a surgical clamp, a daguerreotype by photographer Mark Kessell. "We were struggling [with] how to kick off this campaign," says Tim Palen. "I was on this track of, like, I need some fine art element that fast-forwards us out of the world of snuff. That was a tough road, that piece, even with Eli. He embraced it and said, 'This is fantastic,' and then he sent this, like, 20-page email of, 'I know I said 'Yes,' and now I think this is the most horrible idea, I plead with you, do not put this out.' I was like, 'It's going out today.' I knew there were going to be other beats coming after it. You can't reverse engineer. You can't plant your flag and say, 'This is the snuffiest movie in history,' and [then] go, 'But it's really artful!' But you *can* go the other way."

Hostel was released in the US on January 6, 2006. Roth's movie won its opening weekend with a gross of $19 million. "When that thing opened at $20 million, people were shocked, because it was so violent," says the director. *Hostel* would go on to gross $81 million around the globe. Roth recalls the swift production and successful release of the film as an exhilarating experience. "Nothing was as fast as *Hostel*," he says. "I was possessed. And then it worked. So you're like, oh, this is easy! Cut to: *never happens again*."

The new wave of violent horror cinema was noted, and given a name, by film critic David Edelstein. In January 2006, following the release of *Hostel*, *New York* magazine published an article by the writer titled "Now Playing at Your Local Multiplex: Torture Porn." "Explicit scenes of torture and mutilation were once confined to the old 42nd Street, the Deuce, in gutbucket Italian cannibal pictures like *Make Them Die Slowly*, whereas now they have terrific production values and a place of honor in your local multiplex," wrote Edelstein. "As a horror maven who long ago made peace, for better and worse, with the genre's inherent sadism, I'm baffled by how far this new stuff goes—and by why America seems so nuts these days about torture."

The writer spent the rest of the article mulling over possible causes for the rise in onscreen violence, from the quest by filmmakers to have a visceral impact on audiences to the aftermath of the attacks on the Twin Towers. "Fear supplants empathy and makes us all potential torturers, doesn't it?" he wrote. "Post-9/11, we've engaged in a national debate about the morality of torture, fueled by horrifying pictures of manifestly decent men and women (some of them, anyway) enacting brutal scenarios of domination at Abu Ghraib. And a large segment of the population evidently has no problem with this." The phrase 'torture porn' proved enduring and, over the next few years, would be routinely applied to the horror genre's more extreme output.

The success of boundary-pushing horror filmmakers like Rob Zombie and Eli Roth was also acknowledged by UK film journalist Alan Jones. In the April 2006 issue of the magazine *Total Film*, Jones wrote a six-page article about the directors headlined "The New Blood." A sidebar accompanying the feature identified Zombie, Roth, Neil Marshall, Alexandre Aja, and Greg McLean as members of a distinct group which the writer named 'The Splat Pack.' "We were all seeing [that] horror was getting more violent," says Jones. "I threw everybody in that I knew at the time and called it The Splat Pack."

In the article, Jones explained how Roth and his peers were clawing ground back for bloodier material after years of what the writer described as "watered down horror" such as "all those toothless remakes of Asian hits starring Jennifer Connelly, Naomi Watts, and Sarah Michelle Gellar." Roth told the journalist that interest in extreme horror had been fueled in America by 9/11 and its aftermath. "Right now, Americans feel unsafe in their own country," the director said. "They are scared of an unseen enemy they can't do anything about. They are so wound up, they want to scream. And where can you do that? At the cinema, that's where."

Directors Eli Roth and Rob Zombie in 2011.

Jones also spoke with *Dawn of the Dead* screenwriter James Gunn, who prophetically warned that audience tastes would likely change again before long. "*Saw*, *The Devil's Rejects*, and *Hostel* are all terrific movies and much better than what came before," said Gunn. "But pretty soon, the audience will have had enough of them, too, and be looking for something different."

For the moment, the profitability of the *Saw* films and *Hostel* was unarguably helping Lionsgate's bottom line. In August 2006, *Fortune* magazine published an article about the company headlined "Last of the indies." Reporter Barney Gimbel informed readers that CEO Jon Feltheimer and vice chairman Michael Burns, "have built nine-year-old Lions Gate into the Southwest Airlines of the movie industry: a disciplined, no-frills, profitable independent studio. Last year the 18 films the company released grossed $344 million at the nation's box office, and 15 of them made a profit, a phenomenal success rate in Hollywood." Gimbel mentioned the rewarding releases of *Crash* and the Tyler Perry-starring 2005 hit *Diary of a Mad Black*

Woman. The writer also devoted space to *Hostel* and the *Saw* movies, pointing out that the second film in the latter series had earned $87 million in theaters and another $90 million in DVD sales. "There is no one else in Hollywood who could have made and marketed these films better," *Saw* franchise producer Mark Burg was quoted as saying in the article. "There are even *Saw* conventions now."

Lionsgate executives continued to look for low-budget movies with theatrical potential from raw (in every sense) filmmakers. In April 2006, the company gave a limited release to British director David Slade's Sundance-screened *Hard Candy*, starring Elliot Page as a teenager who kidnaps and psychologically tortures a sexual predator, played by Patrick Wilson. "One of my favorite experiences was when I bought *Hard Candy*," says Peter Block. "I remember walking in [to the screening] and I heard somebody behind me, who didn't know what I looked like, saying, 'Oh, if ever there was a Peter Block movie, this is it.' Good to know!" In contrast to their approach with *High Tension*, *Hard Candy* was promoted as more of an arthouse film and was given a limited release, to good effect.

That summer, Lionsgate released *The Descent*, about an all-female group of spelunkers who battle subterranean monsters, and each other, in a cave system beneath the Appalachian Mountains. The movie was written and directed by British filmmaker Neil Marshall, whose feature debut, 2002's werewolf movie *Dog Soldiers*, had been a box office success in the UK. "*Dog Soldiers* was a very testosterone-y, blokey kind of movie, and I wanted to do something different," says the filmmaker. Marshall was also responding to the challenge laid down by one of the writers who reviewed *Dog Soldiers*. "Some critic said, 'Well, *Dog Soldiers* is okay, but it's not very scary. When is a British filmmaker going to make another truly scary film?'" he recalls. "I thought that was a gauntlet to respond to. *Dog Soldiers* had been given a 15 certificate in the UK, and I was determined that *The Descent* should get an 18. I always felt horror films should be for adults. I wasn't interested in doing PG-13 horror movies."

The director assembled a cast which featured relative newcomers Natalie Mendoza, Alex Reid, and Shauna Macdonald. He shot most of the movie at London's Pinewood Studios, where production design Simon Bowles built the subterranean locales seen in the film. "There isn't a real cave in the whole movie," says the director.

Marshall had a couple of inspirations he combined for the look of what he calls the film's 'crawlers,' the cave-dwelling creatures that pick off the spelunkers as the film progresses. "I had this notion of something like Nosferatu-meets-Iggy-Pop," he says. Marshall hired theater actors he knew who had appropriately Iggy-esque frames to play the creatures. "There was very little prosthetics on them beyond the face and a little on the back," says the director. "The rest was their own physique but with lots of body paint and tons of lubricant all over them to make them look slimy and disgusting. I worked very closely with the actors to figure out how the crawlers would move. I was trying to capture the essence of how spiders behave, how they'll sit for ages and suddenly just move and scuttle."

Marshall got hints that he had succeeded in making a truly terrifying film while he and his editor were piecing the movie together during post-production. "Jon Harris, who cut it, would test out some of the jump scares on the accounting department, because they were working down the corridor," he remembers. "He would bring them in, and sit them down, and say, 'Do you think this works?' If they were screaming or shouting, I'd think, 'We're doing something right.'"

The Descent was released in the UK by distributors Pathé. Worried about the impending release of Screen Gems' similarly plotted but much pricier film *The Cave*, the company rushed Marshall's movie into theaters on July 8, 2005. "We beat them by a month or two," Marshall notes. His film also beat *The Cave* at the UK box office, earning $4.8 million to the latter's $2.9 million.

Lionsgate had secured the US distribution rights to the film prior to the movie's UK release. "They were getting a reputation as *the* horror distributor in the US at that time," says Marshall. Near the end of movie's UK version, Shauna Macdonald's character Sarah seemingly escapes from the film's ravenous monsters. In the closing moments, viewers discover that this happy ending is a fantasy and Sarah is still stuck in the cave system with the crawlers amassing around her. Lionsgate screen-tested the original film and a new edit that removed the final twist. The company told Marshall that he could choose which version the company released, but that the truncated film would receive a wider theatrical release. "Myself and the producer thought, 'At this point, the version that we want to be seen has been out right across the world,'" says the director. "'What the hell, let's let them do it.'"

Released in the US on August 4, 2006, Marshall's low-budget movie earned $26 million at the box office. Peter Block has no doubt that the

Shauna Macdonald in *The Descent* (2005).

movie's successful theatrical run was helped by the removal of the original version's final scene. "Do I think it's a better movie? No," he says. "I just think it was a better *performing* movie to get us what we needed for the theatrical."

Even in its edited form, *The Descent* would be swiftly recognized by fans as among the horror genre's scariest white-knuckle rides. "Every one of these movies had a PR hook, right?" says Block. "So, *Saw* had the you-will-not-believe-the-twist, don't tell anybody. Rob Zombie had your-parents-don't-want-you-to-see-this-movie. *Open Water* had real sharks. *The Descent* didn't have any of those things. It was just maybe the best of the bunch."

Lionsgate also decided to sequelize *House of the Dead* with 2005's *House of the Dead 2*. The film was directed by Michael Hurst, whose credits included the 1999 thriller *New Blood*, and once again written and produced by Mark A. Altman. Starring *Saw II* actress Emmanuelle Vaugier and Sid Haig from *House of 1000 Corpses*, *House of the Dead 2* detailed a zombie outbreak at a university. "In my opinion, it's way better than *House of the Dead*," says Altman. "We made that for $2 million, very little money, but I think it's more ambitious and more interesting. But Lionsgate ended up selling it to the Syfy channel because they got a really good deal."

Although *House of the Dead 2* did not receive theatrical distribution in the US, Altman speaks warmly of Lionsgate's Peter Block and Jason Constantine, both of whom were executive producers on the film. "In this business, you encounter a lot of real assholes," he says. "Jason and Peter are wonderful. Peter was the king of horror at that time. Jason Constantine is one of the great people in this industry. They were super supportive. I wish we could have done more stuff together."

New Line had moved swiftly to put another Freddy vs. Jason film on track after the release of the original movie. Executive Jeff Katz suggested adding Bruce Campbell's character from the *Evil Dead* films to the mix with a film titled *Freddy vs. Jason vs. Ash*. In October 2003, Katz and his fellow executive Stokely Chaffin sent a memorandum to New Line president of production Toby Emmerich with the subject line "Round Two: *Freddy vs. Jason*—Why Ash Works."

Katz spent over a year negotiating with Sam Raimi and producer Rob Tapert—whose first *Evil Dead* had been distributed by New Line—trying to strike a deal for *Freddy vs. Jason vs. Ash*. "We wanted Ash to kill Freddy and Jason," he says. "I know there's some revisionist history that [the *Evil Dead* team] walked away because we wanted Freddy and Jason to win. That's complete bullshit. At the end of the treatment, Ash drove off with Freddy's glove dangling like dice from his rear-view mirror. You cannot win much bigger than that. We tried to make the deal with Raimi and Rob. I think they wanted to get a pound of flesh out of Bob [Shaye] from stuff on the original *Evil Dead* and that contributed to them being more aggressive. We ultimately couldn't get it done."

Katz struck out again when he tried to help get a *Bubba Ho-Tep* sequel off the ground. The end of Don Coscarelli's original film had featured the on-screen promise that Elvis would return in a movie titled *Bubba Nosferatu: Curse of the She-Vampires*. The tease was initially meant as a joke by Coscarelli, but when *Bubba Ho-Tep* proved popular on DVD, he began to think about actually making the movie. The director wrote the treatment for a sequel-prequel in which Elvis battles vampires who are in league with the singer's manager, Colonel Tom Parker. "Elvis fans hate Colonel Parker's guts because they blame him for his descent into drugs, for his crappy movies, and [for] the fact that he never toured outside of America," says Coscarelli. "How else would he have this control if it wasn't for some level of vampirism?"

Coscarelli intended to cast Campbell as Elvis and Paul Giamatti as Parker. The *Sideways* actor was an admirer of Coscarelli's work and had been put in touch with the filmmaker by Eli Roth. "Eli was shooting *Hostel* in Prague, and I was shooting this movie *The Illusionist*," says Giamatti. "We talked about me actually killing somebody in that movie, but it never panned out. I told him how much I liked Don. *Bubba Ho-Tep*, to me, is like some kind of weird perfect movie. And Eli knew Don."

Jeff Katz was another fan of *Bubba Ho-Tep* and was interested in helping Coscarelli make the sequel. The New Line executive also believed that Coscarelli's *Phantasm* franchise was ripe to be relaunched. At the same time as pitching *Freddy vs. Jason vs. Ash*, Katz was negotiating a deal with Coscarelli to remake the 1979 film. "I was like, *Phantasm*, that's an undervalued one to go and get," he says. "You can make a definitive version of that for modern audiences. The spheres—if you can't market that, you're an idiot—and I like Don personally very much."

In March 2005, *The Hollywood Reporter* revealed that New Line was in "final negotiations" with Coscarelli to bring *Phantasm* back to the big screen. The outlet went on to note that the new *Phantasm* was "being developed as a relaunch and as a possible trilogy." Coscarelli planned to have the now 79-year-old Angus Scrimm reprise his signature role as the Tall Man. The director also wanted the characters played by Scrimm's fellow *Phantasm* veterans Michael Baldwin and Reggie Bannister to return in the movie's third act. New Line, though, was keen to start over with a whole new cast. "I wanted Giamatti to be Reggie," says Katz. Coscarelli was uncomfortable with the idea of recasting the roles and decided not to proceed with the project. "I was especially very close to Angus Scrimm, and it just felt weird to replace him in a bigger budget movie," says the director. "So it went away."

Katz had no more luck with *Bubba Nosferatu*. Although Giamatti agreed to play Colonel Tom Parker and Dwayne Johnson expressed an interest in participating, Campbell got cold feet about the project. "We had Giamatti and The Rock," says Katz. "We were ready to make that movie, and Bruce walked off." Coscarelli explains that Campbell had problems with both the screenplay and fitting the shoot into his schedule. "He said he had issues with the script," recalls the director. "He had also gotten cast in *Burn Notice*, which had taken up a lot of his time, and he was directing his own movies."

Giamatti would eventually get to work with Coscarelli when the director cast him as a journalist in the horror-comedy *John Dies at the End.* Adapted from the novel by 'David Wong' (a.k.a. author Jason Pargin), the film starred Chase Williamson and Rob Mayes as 'spiritual exorcists.' It was an unusual project even by Coscarelli's standards, with the finished film's KNB-created practical effects including a door handle shaped like a penis and a monster made from cuts of frozen meat. Coscarelli partnered with Giamatti and his company Touchy Feely Films on what proved to be a lengthy search for financing. The result was eventually distributed by Magnet Releasing—the genre arm of Mark Cuban's Magnolia Pictures—at the start of 2013. "I've made some weird movies through the years," says Coscarelli. "There's a fanbase that really worships them, and then there's studio types that don't get them. Thank God Paul turned up."

The box office successes of *Freddy vs. Jason*, Marcus Nispel's *Texas Chainsaw Massacre*, and Zack Snyder's *Dawn of the Dead* encouraged studio executives to dust off other well-known horror IP. The ensuing decade saw an unprecedented wave of genre remakes as distributors tempted cinemagoers with new versions of *Black Christmas*, *The Omen*, *When a Stranger Calls*, *Prom Night*, *Fright Night*, *The Stepfather*, *The Hills Have Eyes*, *House of Wax*, and more.

Several of the remakes mined the filmography of John Carpenter. The once prolific *Halloween* auteur had seemingly abandoned directing after 2001's *Ghosts of Mars.* A future-set action-horror film, the movie starred Natasha Henstridge, Ice Cube, Jason Statham, and Pam Grier as characters battling an army of possessed miners on the surface of the Red Planet. KNB oversaw the movie's makeup effects, and Greg Nicotero recalls the shoot being a tough one for Carpenter. "We had some great people in that cast and some not so strong people in that cast," he says. "Overall, I think John had some frustrations with some of his actors." *Ghosts of Mars* earned just $8 million at the domestic box office when Sony released it in the summer of 2001.

As Carpenter entered a period of semi-retirement, several of his movies were reimagined by younger filmmakers. 2005 alone saw new versions of *The Fog* and *Assault on Precinct 13* arrive in cinemas, the latter with a starry cast headed by Ethan Hawke and Laurence Fishburne. Dimension, meanwhile, still held the rights to the *Halloween* franchise and hired Rob Zombie to direct a 2007 remake of Carpenter's original film, which starred Scout

This holiday season, the slay ride begins.
BLACK X-MAS

WHEN A STRANGER CALLS
COMING SOON
www.SonyPictures.net

PROM NIGHT
A NIGHT TO DIE FOR
IN THEATERS APRIL 11

ELISHA CUTHBERT
CHAD MICHAEL MURRAY
BRIAN VAN HOLT
PARIS HILTON
JARED PADALECKI
PREY.
SLAY.
DISPLAY.
HOUSE OF WAX
MAY 6

Taylor-Compton as Laurie Strode, Tyler Mane as Michael Myers, and Malcolm McDowell as Dr. Loomis. Speaking with *Fangoria* to promote the film, Zombie mused on the rush to remake well-known horror films. "Nothing is safe," he said. "Everything will be remade. I guarantee you that in 20 years, they'll be remaking *House of 1000 Corpses* because someone will like the title." Zombie's *Halloween* was a box office hit, and the filmmaker would go on to direct 2009's *Halloween II*, which featured Mane's Myers killing a nurse played by future Oscar-winner Octavia Spencer. "She is such a sweetheart," Mane says of *The Help* actress. "The scene was, I'm stabbing her behind the nurse's booth. Of course, I'm not stabbing *her*, I ended up stabbing a sandbag, and Rob was like, 'Go for it!' I think I stabbed that thing about 30 times as hard as I could, and he's going, 'Give me one more!' It was one of the viciousest-looking kills and one of my favorites."

2011's Universal-produced *The Thing* was not a remake of John Carpenter's movie but a prequel that depicted the titular creature's bloody infiltration of the Norwegian research station seen in the 1982 movie. The film was a commercial failure and earned the ire of horror fans when they discovered that the practical effects overseen by makeup artists Alec Gillis and Tom Woodruff Jr. had been replaced by computer-generated monsters.

Tyler Mane and Scout Taylor-Compton in Rob Zombie's *Halloween* (2007).

For his part, Carpenter seemed happy to cash the checks that came his way because of these remakes without offering creative input. The director told IGN that his involvement with the remake of *The Fog* consisted of coming in, saying hello to everybody, and going home. "I'm just a fucking bum, okay?" he said.

Wes Craven was more hands-on than Carpenter with several remakes of his films, producing a new 2006 version of *The Hills Have Eyes* and then a 2007 sequel. The 2006 movie was the first American film overseen by *High Tension* director Alexandre Aja. The French Aja and his creative partner Grégory Levasseur suggested to Craven that the new film's desert-dwelling antagonists be mutants, the victims of nuclear testing. "We pitched the idea to Wes, and I think he really connected to it—this idea of an American family having to face an enemy that, indirectly, they [as Americans] had created through that testing," Aja would recall to Joseph Maddrey, author of the 2024 biography *The Soul of Wes Craven*. "To us, it was a direct line to the September 11th attacks, where Americans faced terrorists that the CIA had trained years before, when the terrorists were still on their side. That was the subtext that really got us excited."

Subtext became text in 2007's *The Hills Have Eyes 2*, which was directed by German filmmaker Martin Weisz and written by Craven and his son Jonathan. The movie pitted National Guardsmen against the mutants, deliberately echoing the situation in Iraq and Afghanistan, where American soldiers remained on the ground. "I certainly feel strongly about the horrible situation that young troops have been put in by going there without really an adequate plan and without the imagination of the leadership to say [that] we're in a totally different kind of war," Craven explained ahead of the film's release. "Every day you have people willing to blow themselves up. How do you fight that? How do you even get your head wrapped around that? So [there's] that sense of getting involved with something where you don't understand the enemy at all. Because they must be animals—but no, goddamn it, they're people and they're smart. That's really scary. So yeah, that was very much floating around the room when we were writing."

Variety reviewer John Anderson recognized the film as a critique of the administration's foreign policy. "Horror sequels and remakes? What they usually signify is one more trip to the well, with a bucket of blood," he wrote. "But while *The Hills Have Eyes 2*—a sequel to a remake—may inhabit familiar geography, screenwriters Wes Craven and son Jonathan have shifted the dramatic landscape [...] the entire scenario adds up to an unmistakable critique of the war in Iraq." For the most part, the film was harshly reviewed by critics, who seemed exhausted by watching so much onscreen gruesomeness in the years since the release of *House of 1000 Corpses*. Terry Lawson of the *Detroit Free Press* described the movie as "another by-the-numbers, don't-mess-with-the-formula screen filler aimed at the gore-hound fan boys who sustain all these franchises while bemoaning their sameness." Where Aja's *The Hills Have Eyes* earned $41 million at the domestic box office, Weisz's sequel grossed just $20 million in the US.

Craven also produced a remake of *The Last House on the Left*, which was released in 2009. This new version of Craven's infamous revenge film cost around $15 million and starred Tony Goldwyn. Made by Greek director Dennis Iliadis, the movie earned $32 million domestically and found a firm fan in Stephen King. Writing in his regular column for *Entertainment Weekly*, the author gave the movie the number two slot on his list of 2009's best films, behind Kathryn Bigelow's *The Hurt Locker*. "Easily the most brilliant

remake of the decade, and not just because the 1972 original was such a crap-fest," wrote King. "This beautifully photographed—but hard to watch—movie is the standard by which all horror/suspense films should be judged."

Aja followed *The Hills Have Eyes* with 2008's Kiefer Sutherland horror film *Mirrors*, a loose reworking of the South Korean movie *Into the Mirror*. The Frenchman next directed 2010's Dimension-backed *Piranha 3D*, which was based on Joe Dante's 1978 film *Piranha*. The new version featured considerably more nudity and gore than the original tale. KNB's Greg Nicotero helped turn the final act of the film into a literal bloodbath as killer fish terrified vacationers and a wet tee shirt contest host played by Eli Roth at a lake resort. "The idea was that this was *Saving Private Ryan* meets *Girls Gone Wild* with a little bit of *Jaws* thrown in," says Nicotero. "There's one sequence where they're trying to get all the kids out of the water and some of them are getting chewed up. We came up with a whole bunch of really fun gags, and Alex said, 'Yeah, let's just do them all.'"

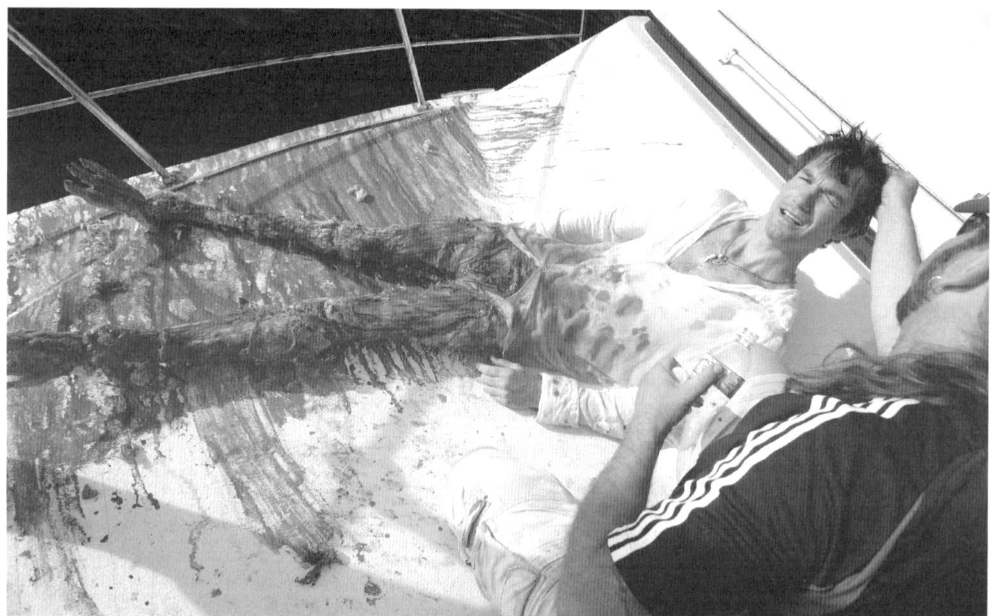

Jerry O'Connell on the set of *Piranha 3D* (2010).

Many of the era's cinematic retellings were made by Platinum Dunes. In October 2003, with the *Texas Chainsaw Massacre* remake still in cinemas,

Variety announced that MGM had partnered with the company to produce a remake of the 1979 horror hit *The Amityville Horror*. The new film starred Ryan Reynolds, Melissa George, and Chloë Grace Moretz and earned $65 million in the US. Platinum Dunes returned to Leatherface's cannibal clan for 2006's Jonathan Liebesman-directed prequel *The Texas Chainsaw Massacre: The Beginning* and then retooled 1986's *The Hitcher* for a 2007 remake, with Sean Bean replacing Rutger Hauer as the villain.

The company also set about reviving the *Friday the 13th* franchise, hiring *Freddy vs. Jason* veterans Damian Shannon and Mark Swift to write the screenplay and Marcus Nispel to direct the production. Platinum Dunes' movie shared a title with Sean S. Cunningham's original 1980 film, in which Jason Voorhees only appeared at the end as a child. The new movie would showcase the adult, hockey mask-wearing version of the slasher icon, played by Derek Mears. Nispel's film co-starred *Supernatural* actor Jared Padalecki, Danielle Panabaker, and Willa Ford.

The original Camp Crystal Lake slasher tale took place and was shot in New Jersey. To Nispel's dismay, Platinum Dunes decided that the new version would be filmed in Austin, where the director had endured the blisteringly hot *Texas Chainsaw Massacre* production. He describes the shoot as "horrible and completely ridiculous. It's called Camp Crystal Lake, and there were no camps and there were no lakes anywhere. We went to Houston to shoot a camp, and we had to drive to get to a lake, and then we had a house that had a little bit of a man-made pond that we played as the edge of the lake—so that was that." Nispel's film was released on February 13, 2009, and by the end of the day had grossed a remarkable $19 million in the US, adding a further $24 million over the weekend.

Having successfully revived Jason Voorhees, Platinum Dunes moved on to Freddy Krueger. In January 2008, *Variety* reported that the trio of founders had been tasked by New Line to create a new franchise based on *A Nightmare on Elm Street*. The first film would be a remake of Craven's original movie directed by music video and commercial veteran Samuel Bayer, whose credits included the video for Nirvana's "Smells Like Teen Spirit." Jackie Earle Haley was cast as Freddy, and Rooney Mara signed on to play Nancy.

The new version of *A Nightmare on Elm Street* was made without the involvement of the original movie's writer and director. In an interview published by IGN on June 6, 2009, Craven seemed genuinely upset at the idea of the remake. "Yes, it does hurt, it does, because it's such an important film for me," he said. "Unfortunately, when I signed the original contract, I gave up all rights to it and so there's nothing I can do about it."

New Line released Bayer's film on April 10, 2010. The movie earned $63 million at the US box office but was excoriated by critics and widely disliked by horror fans. The big winner at the 2011 Fangoria Chainsaw Awards was *Black Swan*, with Darren Aronofsky's tale of a mentally unravelling ballet dancer being named Best Wide-Release Film and Natalie Portman adding the Best Actress Chainsaw Award to the Oscar she had already won for her performance. Platinum Dunes' *A Nightmare on Elm Street* was voted Worst Film. *Fangoria* managing editor Michael Gingold noted that fans found the movie "several cuts below the Wes Craven original."

The Platinum Dunes executives came to understand that their company's reputation was tarnished by association with the film. "Two years, we did not make another movie," Brad Fuller would recall during a 2018 appearance on the *Shock Waves* podcast. "Because, at that point, we were as cold as ice."

Jeff Katz had departed from New Line by the time the remake was greenlit. The executive says he "never would have done the movie. It's a bad idea. Replacing Jason is one thing, multiple guys have played him, he does not talk. Replacing Freddy? He's a character, and it's a beloved actor. You're not replacing Jason, you're replacing James Bond, you'd better get it right. With love to Brad and Andrew [Form]—who I like—they're not horror fans, they're businessmen. They would tell you, this was a business thing with *Texas Chainsaw* that worked, and they kept going, God bless them. I don't fault them. But this was one that anybody could have told you, don't do that."

New Line decided not to proceed further with the hoped-for *Nightmare on Elm Street* franchise, declining to take up Katz's suggestion that the company make *Freddy vs. Freddy*, starring both Jackie Earle Haley and Robert Englund. "I called an executive at New Line I knew at the time [and said], 'The only way to do it is to merge Robert and Jackie, because the fans, they're rejecting Jackie,'" he says.

Englund would revive his version of Freddy Krueger for a 2018 episode of sitcom *The Goldbergs* called "Mister Knifey-Hands" but later claimed that he had aged out of making another *Elm Street* movie. "I won't don the fedora or strap on the claws again," he said in 2023. "I'm just a little too old."

While James Gunn had helped kick off the horror remake craze with his screenplay for Zack Snyder's *Dawn of the Dead*, the writer nightmared up an original tale for his next genre project. At the start of 2005, *Variety* announced that Gunn was making his directorial debut with the film *Slither*, which would be shot in Vancouver and distributed domestically by Universal. The article described the movie as "taking placein a South Carolina town where an inhabitant becomes infected by an alien parasite. It spreads to other townsfolk while its original host turns into a loathsome-looking baddie. Pic will rely heavily on prosthetic effects."

Gunn planned *Slither* as a throwback to the special effects extravaganzas he had enjoyed growing up. "My inspirations were the in-your-face, fun, over-the-top, gory horror films of the 1980s," he recalled for Film Threat ahead of the movie's release. "*Re-Animator*, *The Fly*, *The Thing*, *Return of the Living Dead*, *Basket Case*, *Evil Dead II*. With the exception of a couple of terrific filmmakers like Eli Roth and Rob Zombie, horror has become so boring and by-the-numbers as of late. We needed some fucked-up color in the marketplace: thus, *Slither*."

The film's prosthetics were the responsibility of Ernest Dickerson's *Demon Knight* collaborator Todd Masters. The makeup artist was happy to learn that Gunn wanted the movie's effects to be practical whenever possible. "We were really fortunate to have a supporter like James for practical effects," he says. "Even if it's well-made CG, it can just become a big graphics show. You can tell there's no soul behind it. We were hoping on *Slither* that people wouldn't forget how cool this shit is."

Gunn cast Nathan Fillion as the town's police chief, Elizabeth Banks as a teacher, and Michael Rooker as her husband, Grant Grant, who horribly mutates after coming across the alien creature. The horror-comedy's real star would prove to be its array of deliriously grotesque effects. In the finished movie, Grant Grant grows tentacles and impregnates an old flame named Brenda (played by actress Brenda James) with alien spawn, causing her to swell until she is a massive sphere. The 'Brenda' prosthetic was built at Masters' Los Angeles workshop and then transported via truck to the shoot in Vancouver. "It was quite crazy," he says. "One of my people in my office got highway information on the height of the overpasses all the way up Interstate 5, and we got the lowest truck we could find, and that's what determined how big Brenda was. It is, like, 12 feet wide and 13 feet tall. I actually think it is the world's largest prosthetic."

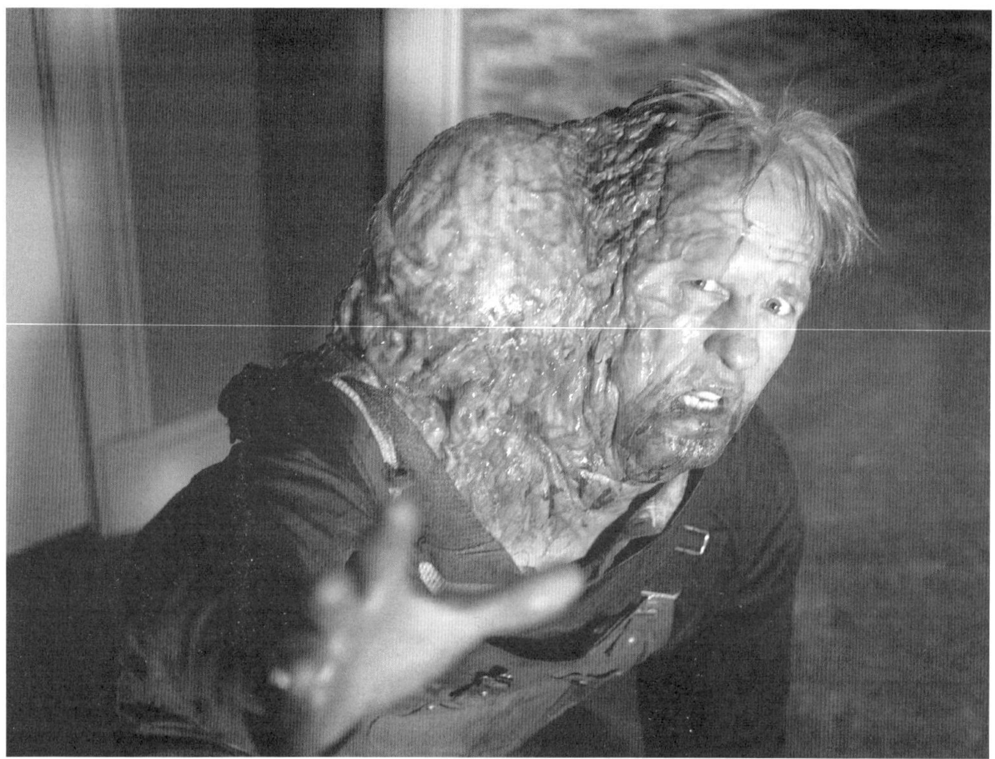

Gregg Henry in *Slither* (2006).

Masters and his team used a petroleum-based material employed in the manufacture of sex toys to make the large number of prosthetics that Gunn required. "This was the material that they were [using to] make fleshlights," says Masters. "This material was just amazingly flexible, and still held detail, and felt really good—not that I ever tried it like *that*."

Masters' heavy use of the material was appropriate. Several of the prosthetics seen in the film resembled human erogenous zones, from the breast-like Brenda-monster to the orifice belonging to the first alien creature seen in the movie. "The funny thing about James is, even when things get tense, it's fucking hilarious," says Masters. "We're shooting this yellow organism, and James screams across, 'Why does everything you fucking do look like a sexual part?!' He's calling me out on the yellow organism, which literally has a vagina sculpted on top of it. And I go, 'Okay, here's your script, it actually says in the script, 'The yellow organism has a yellow vagina on it.' This isn't a coincidence!'"

Universal released *Slither* on March 31, 2006. The film placed a lowly eighth on the box office chart over its first weekend in theaters, earning less than $4 million and slipping out of the top ten the following week. Gunn's movie went on to gross $7.8 million at the domestic box, a disappointment given its reported $15 million budget. The director would come to believe that he had overestimated the appeal of films mixing horror and humor. "Yeah, if somebody had shown me a breakdown of what horror-comedies had done in the past before I made *Slither*, I probably would have thought twice about it," he says. "Horror-comedies as a rule have not made big money."

Gunn had teased a sequel to *Slither* in the movie's post-credits sequence. But the film's box office performance made that second film a non-starter. "I brought up *Slither 2* to one of the producers not too long after," says Masters. "He basically threw me out of his office." Still, the makeup artist has kept the outsized Brenda prosthetic safe, just in case anyone does decide to make *Slither 2*. "At the end of [shooting] *Slither*, the production manager goes, 'What do you want to do with this thing?'" he recalls. "I'm like, 'I can't really throw her away, I mean, she's kind of a historical piece.' Yeah, Brenda is in a warehouse below a shopping center in Tacoma, just waiting for the sequel."

Brenda James, Nathan Fillion, Don Thompson, and Jennifer Copping in *Slither*.

To James Gunn's delight, *Fangoria* helped publicize *Slither* by featuring an image of Michael Rooker in full monster makeup on the cover of its April 2006 issue. "I don't really collect articles or covers," says Gunn. "But I do have my *Fangoria* cover up in my office. *Fangoria* was a huge magazine to me growing up." In August, *Fangoria* announced that *Slither* had been nominated for three of its Chainsaw Awards, whose winners would be announced at a ceremony in October. The event was the first Chainsaw Awards to be televised, a sign of the horror genre's popularity.

The initial Fangoria Chainsaw Awards ceremony had taken place in May 1992, at the Hilton Los Angeles Airport. The event was hosted by Bruce Campbell, and presenters included Sam Raimi and *Halloween* franchise actress Danielle Harris. Campbell returned to MC the 1993 event, at which Quentin Tarantino presented the Best Independent/Low-Budget Film trophy to director Dan O'Bannon's H. P. Lovecraft adaptation *The Resurrected.* The 1994 event was hosted by Linnea Quigley, star of O'Bannon's 1985 zombie film *The Return of the Living Dead.* The big winner was the Campbell-starring *Army of Darkness*, which took home Best Wide-Release Film and Best Actor, among other trophies.

Fangoria stopped holding the Chainsaw Awards as an in-person event after 1996. The new, televised iteration of the ceremony was the result of a partnership between the magazine and the cable network Fuse. An August 2006 press release about the event revealed that the traditional list of awards had been junked in favor of categories with more attention-grabbing names. *Hostel* would claim the most nominations, competing for Killer Movie, Most Thrilling Killing, Dude You Don't Wanna Mess With, Relationship From Hell, and Best Butcher. Other movies with multiple nods included *The Devil's Rejects*, *Underworld: Evolution*, *Final Destination 3*, *The Descent*, Peter Jackson's remake of *King Kong*, and the Samuel L. Jackson-starring *Snakes on a Plane.*

The rebranded Fuse Fangoria Chainsaw Awards was a much more lavishly staged show than the modest functions of the '90s. The event took place at the Orpheum Theatre in downtown Los Angeles and featured musical performances by bands Avenge Sevenfold and 30 Seconds to Mars. The ceremony rarely seemed to take the horror genre too seriously. Presenters dug around in the rib cage of a prosthetic corpse for the cards that revealed category-winners. Host Jamie Kennedy appeared in comedy sketches that found him stalked by a mysterious figure, ultimately revealed to be *Scary Movie* star Regina Hall.

One attendee who struck a more serious note was Mick Garris. The writer-director was present in his capacity as executive producer of the Showtime series *Masters of Horror*, which won the Killer Television Award. "I'm proud to be a horror guy," Garris said after taking the stage. "I love this genre, and I believe in it, and it will always live, and it will always be popular, and with *Masters of Horror* we wanted to show that horror was more than just remakes and sequels. So thank you so much for letting us be truly nasty."

Garris had good reason to be proud. For his anthology show, the filmmaker had succeeded in corralling and showcasing a lineup of true horror legends who were keen to show that they still had the gory goods.

Masters of Horror had its origins in 2002, when Garris organized a dinner for a group of director friends famous for their contributions to the genre. The meal took place at Café Bizou, a French restaurant in the Los Angeles neighborhood of Sherman Oaks. The list of attendees included

First Masters of Horror dinner in 2002 with *(from left, in front)* Larry Cohen, *(behind)* Stuart Gordon, John Carpenter, Don Coscarelli, film historian and archivist Bob Burns, Guillermo del Toro, John Landis, William Malone, Tobe Hooper, and Mick Garris.

Garris, John Carpenter, Stuart Gordon, Tobe Hooper, Joe Dante, William Malone, Guillermo del Toro, *An American Werewolf in London* director John Landis, *It's Alive* filmmaker Larry Cohen, and Don Coscarelli. "I was a little nervous going to it, because I didn't know how many people I really knew," says Coscarelli. "I walked in the door and there's Mick and John Landis at the bar. They go, 'Don! Come over and have a drink!' From that moment on, it was just so easy and natural."

The group took the name 'Masters of Horror' from a Bruce Campbell-hosted documentary of that title, which screened on Showtime in 2002. The film was produced by *The Convent* auteur Mike Mendez and his fellow horror filmmaker Dave Parker. *Masters of Horror* had begun life as a bonus feature for a planned DVD release of movie clips called *Masters of the Macabre* from a short-lived Universal Pictures division called FlixMix. "I had access to Universal letterhead and fax paper," says Mendez. "I realized I could write to Wes Craven and John Carpenter and say, 'I'm working for Universal Pictures' and it's not a lie." Mendez and Parker attracted an impressive array of interviewees, including Craven, Carpenter, George A. Romero, and del Toro. "He was a young 'un at that time," says Mendez of the Mexican filmmaker. "I had to fight for [him]. 'I think this Guillermo kid is going somewhere!'"

The interviewee footage was orphaned after the first couple of DVDs released by FlixMix failed to shift sufficient units. "Universal realizes nobody gives a shit about compilation discs," says Mendez. "I pitched to my boss, 'What if we made a documentary?' We cut a sizzle reel, gave it to a sales guy, and he sold it to Showtime."

At the dinner in Sherman Oaks, del Toro started using the name 'Masters of Horror' to describe the gathered diners. "There was a party at a table next to ours celebrating a birthday," says Garris. "They sang, 'Happy birthday,' we all joined in, and, at the end of it, Guillermo del Toro stood up and said, 'The Masters of Horror wish you a happy birthday!' That was a joking name, but we kind of adopted for the dinners."

The Masters of Horror meals became regular events, often taking place at Hamburger Hamlet on Sunset Boulevard. The list of attendees grew to include, among others, Eli Roth, Quentin Tarantino, *Pet Sematary* director Mary Lambert, Darren Bousman, and Ernest Dickerson. "Oh, they were great," says Dickerson of the dinners. "Somebody I became really tight with was Tobe Hooper. He became my bourbon-drinking buddy."

Bousman recalls one memorable dinner attended by British filmmaker Ken Russell, the idiosyncratic director of 1980's *Altered States* and 1988's *The*

Lair of the White Worm. "I have weird people that I geek out over," he says. "I get sat next to Ken Russell [and] I was like, 'Holy shit! I am literally sitting here with an idol! And he's having a cheeseburger right next to me.'" Russell proved a cantankerous presence at the event, to Bousman's delight. "He is the most angry curmudgeon that I've ever met," says the director. "He was so unimpressed. It was like, he is my spirit animal!"

In 2007, Roth contributed an article about the Masters of Horror dinners to MTV.com. "There's a real bond between horror directors, because we know what it's like to put these ultra-violent movies out there, and have the fans love them, and have press attack us," he wrote. Bad reviews were not the only complaint of the attendees. The Masters of Horror had plenty of war stories to share about the battles they had fought trying to get their cinematic visions into theaters. "People like John Carpenter and Tobe Hooper were really cynical about what had happened to their careers," says Garris. Hooper, like Carpenter, had suffered recent professional setbacks with neither 2000's *Crocodile* nor 2004's *Toolbox Murders*, getting a theatrical release in the US. "At all those dinners, the conversation would turn to, 'Wouldn't it be great if we could be the masters of our own fate [with] our own movies?'" says Garris.

The director realized that the small screen might offer a route by which his friends and peers could work without interference. Garris suggested that they combine to create a series of films, titled *Masters of Horror* and released on DVD, with each director tackling a self-contained tale. He struck a deal with the company Anchor Bay, best known to horror fans for releasing the *Evil Dead* films to the home entertainment market. Anchor Bay brought on board the cable channel Showtime to help finance the project. This deal gave the directors almost complete *carte blanche*. "There were five rules," says Garris. "I don't remember all of them, but no adults killing children and [no] frontal male nudity. Everybody was excited about it. Even though it wasn't a lot of money, it was a lot of freedom."

In March 2005, *Variety* announced that Showtime had "nabbed rights" to *Masters of Horror*. The show was described as "a series of 13 hourlong films to be helmed and/or written by the genre's top names," with the list of filmmakers including Garris, Carpenter, Landis, Hooper, Coscarelli, Dante, Gordon, Cohen, and Dario Argento. The final roster of talent would also boast *Audition* filmmaker Takashi Miike and Lucky McKee, director of the 2003 film *May*.

The directors who oversaw the episodes were all male, despite Garris having approached a clutch of women filmmakers to participate. "One of them, I didn't know it at the time, had health issues," he says. "A couple of other directors who had done horror stuff did not want to be included in a show that brands you as a horror director."

Most of the *Masters of Horror* episodes were filmed in Vancouver, with each director allotted ten days to shoot their respective stories. Don Coscarelli's episode, the Joe R. Lansdale adaptation "Incident On and Off a Mountain Road," starred Bree Turner as a character facing off against a serial killer. Coscarelli realized after arriving in Vancouver that he truly would be given the freedom to make his episode as horrific as he liked. "Mine was the third one to film," says the director. "I showed up, and Dario Argento was filming, and people were coming back [from the] set going, 'This the most brutal, bloody thing I've ever seen.' I'm going, 'My episode is so tame, I've got to amp it up.' It was a challenging moment."

John Carpenter's contribution was called "Cigarette Burns" and starred Norman Reedus as a dealer of rare films who is hired by a character played by Udo Kier to find the last surviving print of a lost, and infamous, movie. Garris admits that the *Halloween* director had been in no rush to join the project. "Carpenter, he wasn't a difficult sell, but it took him a little while," says the executive producer. "Then he had so much fun making it, and it became the most beloved episode of season 1."

The show's many makeup effects were provided by KNB, whose founders Howard Berger and Greg Nicotero were familiar with several of the *Masters of Horror* directors, including its executive producer. "Howard and Greg are really good friends of mine," says Garris. "We had Howard Berger on set every day. There's no greater way to start a day than with Howard Berger starting the monster makeup."

Critics were generally positive about *Masters of Horror*, which premiered on October 28, 2005, with Coscarelli's episode. *Variety* reviewer Brian Lowry wrote that, while "Incident On and Off a Mountain Road" may not have been subtle, "for aficionados of the horror genre it's the kind of stylish gorefest that should keep them up at nights." Coscarelli remembers that his tale "even got a rave review in *The National Enquirer*. Go figure!"

The director who arguably used his freedom on the show to the most memorable effect was Joe Dante. In the years since the 9/11 attacks, the *Gremlins* director had become enraged by the actions of the Bush admin-

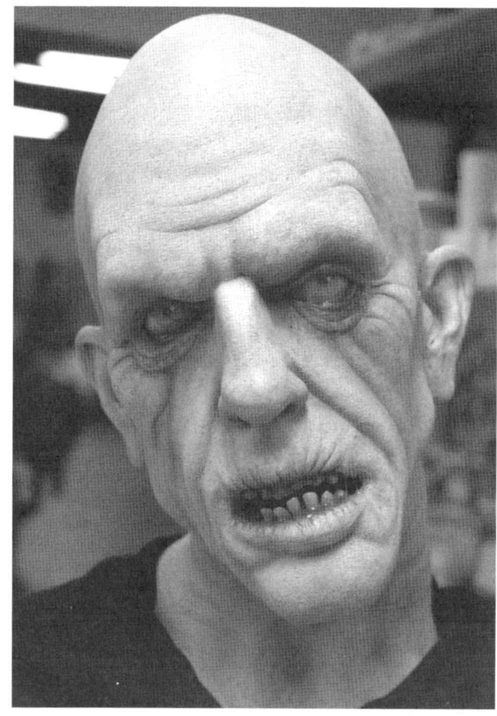

Behind-the-scenes shots of KNB makeups for *Masters of Horror*.

istration and what he regarded as the media's support of the President's War on Terror. Dante channeled that anger for his episode "Homecoming," which was written by Sam Hamm, based on a 2002 short story by Dale Bailey. In the tale, a political consultant played by Jon Tenney responds on a live TV news show to the grieving mother of a dead soldier who demands to know the point of her loss. "If I had one wish," says Tenney's character, "I would wish for your son to come back, because I know he would tell us all how important this struggle is." Soon afterwards, the deceased veteran and other fallen soldiers start returning from the dead as zombies—not to eat people, but to vote Bush out of office. "Nobody was coming out against the Bush administration, nobody was satirizing it, and it took our little movie [to do that]," says Garris. "The ability to inject social consciousness into a story is one of the great things about horror, they're great metaphors."

Dante's episode was praised by Slate contributor Grady Hendrix. "While Dante's film will no doubt raise hackles, my guess is that most members of the military would get a kick out of this flick that praises the troops in Iraq

A zombie in Joe Dante's *Masters of Horror* episode "Homecoming" (2005).

while offering up the politicians and pundits who sent them there as finger food for the undead," he wrote. "Some big brains have tried to make a statement about the war in Iraq, and every single one of them should be standing in line, heads hung low, waiting to get their artistic licenses revoked. Who would've thought that where Michael Moore (*Fahrenheit 9/11*), Sam Mendes (*Jarhead*), and Steven Bochco (*Over There*) got it so wrong, the director of *Looney Tunes: Back in Action* would have gotten it so right?"

Hendrix's prediction that the episode would raise hackles was proven correct. "I got death threats and stuff, but I mean that's to be expected," says Dante. "There were a lot of people who hated it and there were a lot of horror movie fans who resented the intrusion of politics into their favorite genre, which I think is pretty ridiculous."

Showtime may have been happy to screen Coscarelli's extreme violence and Dante's political satire, but the network drew the line at what Takashi Miike depicted in his episode, "Imprint." The period tale starred Billy Drago as a journalist who visits a remote brothel looking for the love of his life. While the show was stylish, and even beautiful, the episode also featured torture, nudity, and close-up shots of aborted fetuses. Garris had traveled to Japan for the shoot and was aware that the *Audition* director's tale featured extreme material. "I knew it would be controversial, but I didn't think it would be controversial to the point where the network would not even air it," he says.

On January 19, 2006, *The New York Times* reported that Showtime had canceled the broadcast of the episode. "We thought, well, great, we're going to advertise the DVD as the episode that Showtime was too chickenshit to air," says Garris. "But when Walmart found out about it—they, at the time, sold 40 percent of America's DVDs—they wouldn't carry it. The way we got around it was, when we did the first box set, they didn't realize what was going on, and it was included."

Garris was determined that his acceptance speech at the 2006 Chainsaw Awards should cut through the levity of the proceedings. "People make fun of horror, people don't respect it, and there had been enough of that," he says, recalling the event. "I didn't choose to only make horror movies, but I'm happy to live in that world. I didn't want to joke around about it, and I wanted to give some weight to the awards."

The second season of *Masters of Horror* premiered in October 2006 with a Tobe Hooper-directed Ambrose Bierce adaptation called "The Damned Thing" and wound up the following February with "Dream Cruise," by Japanese director Norio Tsuruta. This time, it was John Carpenter who tackled a hot button topic with his episode "Pro-Life," about a teenager trying to get an abortion after being raped by a demon. Written by Drew McWeeney and Rebecca Swan, the tale starred Caitlin Wachs and Guillermo del Toro regular Ron Perlman. "When the second season got greenlit, I said, 'John, would you do one in season 2?'" says Garris. "And he said, 'You know what? I think I'd like to do that.' Because he had a good time."

In 2006, Anchor Bay had been bought by Liberty Media, owner of the Starz cable network, which in turn sold *Masters of Horror* to Lionsgate. When Lionsgate asked for more money from Showtime, the cable network passed on backing a third season. The company subsequently struck a deal for the show to continue on NBC. In September 2007, the network's co-chairman Ben Silverman announced that he had commissioned a 13-episode season of *Fear Itself*, essentially a retitled *Masters of Horror*, with plans for NBC to screen the show the following summer. Garris would come to rue the decision to transplant his creation to NBC. "Lionsgate took it to

Showtime and said, 'We want twice as much money,'" says Garris. "Showtime said, 'No thanks.' And then they turned to NBC and cut its balls off."

Garris set to work recruiting directors and sifting through scripts but changed his mind about remaining with the project following the start of a writers' strike in November 2007. "We developed all 13 of the scripts before the strike, and then the other producers said, 'We'll bring in these non-union writers and they can do that,'" recalls Garris. I said, 'I can't do that, I'm on strike, I'm a writer.'"

Fear Itself continued into production with a lineup of filmmakers that included Stuart Gordon, Mary Harron, Larry Fessenden, and Ernest Dickerson. The latter directed a werewolf story called "Something with Bite," starring *The Wire* actor Wendell Pierce. "NBC changed *Masters of Horror* to something called *Fear Itself*, but they took all of the gonads off of it and ruined it," says the director. Working on the series did give Dickerson the opportunity to reconnect with his *Day of the Dead* collaborator Greg Nicotero. "What happened was, I wanted a werewolf," he says. "The producers told me, 'What do you mean, you want a werewolf? We don't have money for a werewolf.' I said, 'There's a werewolf in the script!' I asked Greg if he had something, and he said, 'Yeah, come down to the shop.' He had a beautiful werewolf costume, so Greg gave it to me."

NBC screened the first episode of *Fear Itself*, "The Sacrifice," on June 5, 2008. Directed by Breck Eisner, the story attracted 5.26 million viewers and placed third for its time slot. The audience for the following week's episode, the Brad Anderson-directed "Spooked," collapsed to just 2.93 million, prompting *Variety* to declare that the show was "clearly not working." NBC agreed. After airing eight episodes, the network paused the show for the 2008 Olympics. The hiatus proved permanent.

The mild-mannered Garris would remain aggrieved by the way he and his creation had been treated. "It was the biggest heartbreak of my career," he says. "I basically talk about it being that they kidnapped and raped my baby."

CHAPTER 10

"MY MOTHER TOLD ME TO BE WARY OF FAUNS."

Silent Hill was another horror film that received multiple nominations at the 2006 Chainsaw Awards, competing in the categories of Chick You Don't Wanna Mess With, Creepiest Kid, Sickest FX, and Looks That Kill. The video game adaptation starred Radha Mitchell, Laurie Holden, and Alice Krige, whose chilling portrayal of a cult leader named Christabella would affect the actress as much as it did cinemagoers. "I had no idea that, for me, Christabella would be a journey into the heart of darkness," she says.

Alice Krige in *Silent Hill* (2006).

The South Africa-born actress's first experience of working in the genre came with 1981's Peter Straub adaptation *Ghost Story*, an anonymously titled but eerie film that co-starred Hollywood legends Fred Astaire and Douglas Fairbanks Jr. After *Ghost Story*, Krige spent two seasons acting with Britain's Royal Shakespeare Company and then scored a notable supporting role in 1987's Mickey Rourke drama *Barfly*. The actress returned to horror with the 1992 film *Sleepwalkers*, about incestuous shapeshifters, which was written by Stephen King and directed by Mick Garris. Krige committed to her role of the energy vampire Mary Brady with the same diligence as she had her Shakespearean parts, even basing her portrayal of Brady on the character of Volumnia in the Roman tragedy *Coriolanus*. "The more I worked on it, the more I thought, 'Well, she's actually a tragic heroine,'" she says. Krige achieved a higher level of fame, particularly among science fiction fans, playing the Borg Queen in 1996's *Star Trek: First Contact*.

Silent Hill was directed by Christophe Gans, a French filmmaker whose period horror movie *Brotherhood of the Wolf* became a sleeper hit when Universal Pictures released it at the start of 2002. Gans first played *Silent Hill* shortly after the Japanese company Konami released the game in 1999. The director became obsessed with this horror-survival adventure set in a mysterious town populated by cultists and supernatural creatures. Gans was friendly with *Pulp Fiction* co-writer Roger Avary and reached out to the American for help with the screenplay. A hardcore gamer, Avary was familiar with *Silent Hill* and agreed to assist with the script.

In addition to Krige, Gans cast Radha Mitchell in the lead role of Rose and Laurie Holden as a cop named Cybil. Young actress Jodelle Ferland portrayed both Rose's daughter Sharon and Alessa, the supernatural force who has created the horrors that dwell in the town of Silent Hill. Mitchell was unfamiliar with the game but agreed to appear in the film after meeting with Gans. The actress recalls that, as had been the case with *Rogue*, her agent argued against her taking the role in Gans' horror movie. "[My] agent was like, 'Please don't do this movie, I will pay you not to do this movie,' just hated it," she says.

Gans shot *Silent Hill* in Ontario, where his crew built more than 100 sets. The director would follow the trend, in the horror genre and beyond, of employing both CG and practical effects. But for the film's terrifying creatures, the director went the practical route whenever possible so that Mitchell and other cast members would have physical performers to react against. "The sets were amazing, and the creatures were amazing," says Mitchell.

Radha Mitchell in *Silent Hill.*

"The crazy scene with the nurses, they dressed everybody up. We were acting with them. The result was these incredible visuals."

Krige once again prepared for her role with care. The actress played *Silent Hill* (even though the games did not feature her character) and read up on what she regarded as relevant subjects, like the Spanish Inquisition and American cults. Krige found the shoot itself a disturbing experience. She approached breaking point shooting the climactic scenes inside Silent Hill's church, during which her character oversees the immolation of Holden's cop and threatens the life of the young Sharon, before Christabella herself is torn apart by a writhing mass of barb wire. "It was very difficult," she says. "Mary Brady in *Sleepwalkers*, she's clearly in the realm of fantasy, but Christabella could be cutting off heads somewhere. The last two weeks of *Silent Hill*, we were just in that church burning people."

Sony's TriStar Pictures released *Silent Hill* on April 21, 2006. The film faced tough competition from Dimension's *Scary Movie 4*, which had opened the previous Friday and earned $50 million over the next seven days. Gans' tale was able to knock the spoof movie into second place, raking in $20 million that first weekend of release and going on to gross $100 million worldwide.

Following the film's successful release, Avary developed a sequel to *Silent Hill.* The project was put on hold after the screenwriter was involved in a 2008 car crash in Ojai, California, which caused the death of his passenger. The following year, he pleaded guilty to vehicular manslaughter and drunken driving.

British filmmaker M. J. Bassett took over the project, and *Silent Hill: Revelation* was released in October 2012, earning $17 million in the US. The cast of the second *Silent Hill* movie featured several actors from the first film, including Radha Mitchell. "I was there for a couple of days," she says. "The director was lovely, and it was fun to pop back in. But I was a bit like, 'Hmm, this is my movie! What are they doing to it?'"

Alice Krige did not appear in the sequel and was happy to put the role of Christabella behind her. "This is the effect that it had on me: I had a little dog called Skipper, little girl, she didn't have a tail because they'd cut it off before we rescued her," she says. "[After shooting *Silent Hill*,] I was dropped at the gate and Skipper was there, wagging her whole body. I got out of the car, and I walked up to the gate, and Skipper stopped wagging, and looked at me, and she backed off. She would have nothing to do with me. Three weeks later, I went away to do another film and when I came back, Skipper was at that gate, and I got out of the car, and it was like, 'Oh, you've come back without Christabella this time.'"

Although Guillermo del Toro had attended the original Masters of Horror dinner and helped christen the group of auteurs, he never directed an episode of the show. "Guillermo is the James Brown of movies, hardest working man in show business," says Mick Garris. "Guillermo wanted to [direct an episode] but we knew from the beginning that was never going to work."

Del Toro had become one of Hollywood's most in-demand filmmakers thanks to *Blade II* and his Ron Perlman-starring comic-book adaptation *Hellboy*, which came out in 2004. Following the release of those two movies, the Mexican was offered several big-budget superhero tales to direct. He opted instead to make a comparatively small, Spanish-language film called *Pan's Labyrinth*, a fairytale, but one featuring some of the most horrific moments yet to be found in his filmography.

Del Toro conceived *Pan's Labyrinth* as a sister film to 2001's *The Devil's Backbone*, a movie that he believed had been rendered out of date by the events of 9/11. "When I finished that movie, I showed it in Toronto," the director told *The Guardian* in 2006. "It was September 9, 2001. We got rave reviews, lots of applause, people telling me 'Great movie,' blah-blah-blah. Then I take a plane cloaked in my *petit bourgeois* happiness at how well my film was received, landed in Los Angeles, and then September 11 happened. That was when I realized that (a) I don't know shit and (b) whatever I had to say about brutality and innocence had just changed."

Set in Spain during World War II, del Toro's script for *Pan's Labyrinth* centered on a 10-year-old girl named Ofelia, whose pregnant mother has married a military captain tasked with hunting down anti-Fascist rebels. The film's young heroine meets a faun, who gives her a series of tasks, promising her immortality if she successfully completes them. Del Toro had difficulty finding finance for the movie. Peter Block, who had worked with the director on Trimark's home entertainment release of *Cronos*, was among those to turn down the project. "Guillermo is like, 'I really want to show you this other picture, and I want to give it to you first,'" says Block. "He gave me *Pan's Labyrinth*, which he was going to make as a Spanish-language, adult fairytale fable, with a lot of special effects. I was like, 'This is spectacular, but I don't know how we make this or release this,' and I passed. I was, I think, the first person to pass on *Pan's Labyrinth*, which haunts me to this day."

Del Toro eventually secured a budget of around $18 million, a modest amount given the fantastical sights he planned on showing audiences. The director cast Ivana Baquero as Ofelia and Sergi López as her stepfather Captain Vidal. After meeting Doug Jones during the reshoots for *Mimic*, the director had picked him to play the half-man, half-fish character Abe Sapien in *Hellboy*. Del Toro now approached the actor about portraying the crucial role of the Faun. Jones was delighted about the idea of appearing in a very different kind of terror tale. "In my monster heyday, I got offered a lot of horror films that were very formulaic," he says. "I'd just read one of those, and then Guillermo del Toro emails me this script for *Pan's Labyrinth*. After turning the last page closed, I'm wiping tears away, going, 'Oh my gosh! I have to be in this movie.'"

Del Toro wanted the actor to also portray a second creature, the Pale Man, a grotesque and emaciated creation who eats children and sees through eyeballs he places in stigmatic palm slits. "I thought he was being a cheap ass that wanted two characters for the price of one—which he got, by the way!"

(*From top*) Doug Jones as the Pale Man in *Pan's Labyrinth* (2006) and attending the 2007 Academy Awards.

says Jones. "But I also understood that the Pale Man was the creation of the fauns, therefore having the same actor play both scenes made kind of sense."

During the shoot, Jones was preoccupied with learning the Faun's Spanish dialog. The actor put the Pale Man to the back of his mind, not really considering the truly terrifying nature of the encounter between Ofelia and his second character. "The week that we took to film the Pale Man scene came, and I'm like, 'Oh, here's *that* character, right,'" says Jones. "When I saw the murals around the ceiling of the Pale Man's history of eating children and the pile of kids' shoes, I realized, 'Oh, *this* is a moment. The Pale Man is waking up for the first time in a while, so he's hungry, and here's a child who woke him up by breaking the rules, eating something off my table.' That was a totally horrific scene."

The fantasy world of *Pan's Labyrinth* was far removed from the zombie universe of George A. Romero. Yet the Pittsburgh director's undead tales helped inspire one particular aspect of Jones' Pale Man performance. "Guillermo told me he wanted the Pale Man to be very disjointed and gallopy as he chased Ofelia," says the actor. "When we rehearsed the scene down the hallway, I did it like I was told. Guillermo said, 'No, Dougie! No! I want you to think George Romero zombie!' So I came at her much slower, much stiffer. That made it much scarier."

Pan's Labyrinth would elevate del Toro to the upper echelons of Hollywood's most-admired filmmakers. After premiering at the 2006 Cannes Film Festival, the movie earned $83 million around the world. *Pan's Labyrinth* was nominated for six Academy Awards, including Best Original Screenplay and Best Foreign Language Film. At the Oscars ceremony, the movie won in the categories of Cinematography, Art Direction, and Makeup. Doug Jones was unsurprised by the film's success. "When I read the script, I was like, 'Oh, this is an award-winning movie,'" he says. "When you have a monster [in] the film and you're getting that kind of critical acclaim, that's a Guillermo del Toro specialty."

Lionsgate planned on releasing a third *Saw* movie during the 2006 Halloween season, but Darren Bousman was unsure about returning to the franchise. Then, in December 2005, *Saw* series producer Gregg Hoffman unexpectedly passed away at the age of 42. Bousman had become friends with Hoffman during the production of *Saw II* and was shocked by the loss. "Gregg Hoffman was my mentor," says the director. "He was the umbrella that protected me from the hailstorm, and the rain, and all that shit."

In the wake of Hoffman's passing, Bousman agreed to direct another *Saw* film from a script by Leigh Whannell. "I didn't make a lot of money on [*Saw II*]," he says. "They made me a much more substantial offer to come back." The third *Saw* film would once again be prepped at a fast clip and then shot in Toronto. "Once it started working, [Lionsgate] wanted one every year," says Peter Block. "But they didn't get greenlit until November, which meant it was a mad dash to get them out by October every year."

Wan and Whannell had regarded the original *Saw* as a Hitchcockian thriller. The series' producers came to believe that the franchise's traps were its main selling point, and increasing emphasis was placed on Jigsaw's diabolical tests. *Saw III* would prove to be the most gruesome entry to date, with one of John Kramer's victims twisted apart on a mechanized rack, another frozen to death onscreen, and a third almost drowned by rotten pig carcasses. "Fans reacted to traps and gore," says Block. "So that's where the franchise went."

Bousman admits that there was competition between him and his filmmaking peers about who could put the most extreme material onscreen. "One of the things that was cool is that I was on a text chain with Eli Roth and Rob Zombie," he says. "I was doing *Saw III*, and I sent a photo of a character ripping a chain out of his jaw. Eli wrote back, 'You fucking asshole.' I was like, 'Gotcha!'" Roth has similarly fond memories of the period and of the sense of camaraderie he felt with his fellow horror auteurs. "It was an amazing time," he says. "After *Hostel*, it really went haywire. It was me, and James Wan, and Leigh Whannell, and Darren Bousman, and Alex Aja. We were all friends, and we were all trying to outdo each other. We sort of hijacked pop culture for a while."

Bousman was determined that Tobin Bell's Jigsaw should perish at the end of *Saw III*. "I said, 'We've got to do something completely unexpected,'" he recalls. "'So what are we going to do? Kill him, that's what we've got to do.' I remember it was a huge issue."

Producer Mark Burg was unsure that killing off Bell's character was a good idea. "I remember being in Oren's dining room with Darren Bousman, and Darren insisting that Jigsaw dies in *Saw III*, and I'm going, 'I don't know,'" he says. "We got talked into it." Block recalls that Bousman was allowed to kill the franchise's villain partly because of Lionsgate's belief that the third *Saw* film would be the last. "When we got to number three, we were like, this can't go on forever," says the executive.

A promotional shot of Tobin Bell for *Saw III* (2006).

Jigsaw was not the only major *Saw* franchise character on Bousman's kill list. The conclusion of *Saw III* would also see the death of Shawnee Smith's Jigsaw-victim-turned-accomplice, Amanda. "I killed them all," says Bousman. "Of all of my *Saw* films, *Saw III* is my favorite, because it felt like that 'Fuck you!' ending that I wanted it to have."

The budget of *Saw III* was around $10 million, more than ten times that of James Wan's original movie. For the production, Bousman asked for three versions of the 'Billy' puppet to be constructed: a detailed 'hero' prop, a stunt doll, and a third Billy in case one of the others was damaged. The director recalls Wan visiting the shoot in Toronto and raising his eyebrows at its comparatively lavish nature. "James sees multiple Billy dolls sitting there, he sees all the shit that I have," says Bousman. "I'm grinning like an idiot, and he says, 'Bousman, move over, you're standing on my coattails.' I was like, oh my God, that might have been the best insult that I've ever gotten from anyone. He was joking, because he had none of this. He goes, 'On *Saw*, we had a smelly warehouse, and you've got cranes, and you've got three Billy dolls.' It was pretty funny."

Saw III grossed $164 million around the globe, a new record for the franchise. Bousman believes that the film's success was aided by the death of Jigsaw, who, in the film, is fatally wounded with a buzzsaw by one of his victims. "That moment caused such anger, and rage, and cheers in the audience," says the director. "'What?! He's dead? Oh my God!' I love when you can do shit like that in movies."

While Bousman swiftly directed two sequels to James Wan's *Saw*, the Australian director had struggled to make the ventriloquist dummy movie he and Whannell had pitched to Universal Pictures. Titled *Dead Silence*, the film starred Ryan Kwanten as a man who discovers that the murder of his wife is in some way connected to a long-dead ventriloquist named Mary Shaw and her puppet. The film's dummy was once again named Billy, this time onscreen as well behind the camera.

Whannell detailed the difficulties of making *Dead Silence* in a 2011 blog post he titled "Dud Silence: The Hellish Experience of Making A Bad Horror Movie." In the post, the writer described how his delight at selling the pitch to Universal turned sour when he began to write the screenplay. "With terror, I realized that what I had pitched was not a story—it was an image. A vague concept. A visual motif," he wrote. "When I tried to wrap a story around it, it was like trying to make a tarantula wear a leather jacket." After sending his draft to Universal, Whannell was asked to rewrite the script in a manner that more clearly established the supernatural rules of his tale. The Australian spent a year sweating over his screenplay before the studio brought in another writer to further work on it.

Wan shot *Dead Silence* in Toronto. The director was inspired by the vintage gothic horror releases of Hammer Films and hoped the movie would demonstrate that he was no one-trick pony. "I wanted to try something different," the director recalled in an interview with *Fangoria* to promote the film. "Leigh and I just felt like we wanted to go off and try a ghost story." In the same interview, Wan bridled at the media tagging him as a member of the director group responsible for the so-called torture porn subgenre. "If anyone knows Leigh and myself, they'd know that we are the happiest guys in town," he said. "To be branded as part of a group of guys who created this torture genre is really strange to me."

Dawn of the Dead makeup artist David LeRoy Anderson oversaw the practical effects on the movie, which had a much bigger budget than *Saw*. To build the Billy doll, the AFX Studios founder enlisted the help of his father, Lance Anderson, a makeup effects designer in his own right, whose credits included John Carpenter's *The Thing*. "I knew it was right up his alley because there were mechanics involved," says the younger Anderson. "It was old school, Dad's old school, and he loved it. I made the eyes, but he sculpted the face. We did it authentically, as somebody who makes dolls would do. We made a hero and a backup. We sent them off to Canada, and I never saw them again. I'm sure James has got them. I'm hoping Billy's safe in his house somewhere."

The best efforts of Wan and his collaborators could not turn *Dead Silence* into a hit. When Universal released the movie in March 2007, it earned just $16 million at the US box office, $64 million less than *Saw III*. Wan moved away from the horror genre with his next film, the Kevin Bacon thriller *Death Sentence*. Released six months after *Dead Silence*, the film earned $9.5 million domestically, an even less impressive amount than his previous film had grossed. Wan's fans—those that remained—would have to wait four years to see his next movie.

From Dusk Till Dawn director Robert Rodriguez was visiting Quentin Tarantino in the early 2000s when he saw a one-sheet on the living room floor of his friend's house. The poster was for a 1957 double feature of B-movies *Dragstrip Girl* and *Rock All Night*. Rodriguez had the same one-sheet and suggested to Tarantino that they make their own double bill of movies. "I said, 'Hey, why don't you direct one and I'll do the other?'" Rodriguez would recall to *Entertainment Weekly* writer Chris Nashawaty. "Right away he said, 'And we've got to call it *Grindhouse*!' It happened that quickly."

Rodriguez and Tarantino struck a deal to make the films for the Weinsteins, who were on the verge of departing from Disney to form The Weinstein Company. In May 2005, the siblings announced the initial slate of movies to be released by their new production entity. The list included *Grindhouse*, which at the time was titled *Grind House* and was scheduled for release in spring 2006. An article in *Variety* revealed that Tarantino "hopes the pic will spawn a series of *Grind House* films."

Rodriguez's half of the double bill, *Planet Terror,* was set in a small town whose citizens become victims of a bioweapon called DC2, turning them into grotesque zombie-like creatures. The director had been initially prompted to think about making an undead movie by KNB's Greg Nicotero around the time they were both working on *The Faculty*. "I got *Resident Evil 2*," says Nicotero. "I remember showing it to Robert and going, 'We should make a zombie movie.' That was part of the impetus for *Planet Terror*. He used to come to LA, and we would have all-night movie marathons at my house, and he gave me the first, like, 20 pages of *Planet Terror*. That was his homage to zombie movies. It's as if you took John Carpenter and George Romero and put them together, that's what *Planet Terror* is."

Rose McGowan in *Planet Terror* (2007).

The director updated his script to reveal that a group of soldiers had become affected by DC2 after killing Osama bin Laden on the Afghan border. "These kind of exploitation movies always seized on something that was happening during the day, even before Hollywood wanted to talk about them," Rodriguez would explain, promoting *Grindhouse* on the *Charlie Rose* talk show. "I thought, 'Well, if I'm going to do a zombie movie, let's make it an infection that comes back from the Iraqi War.'"

The director assembled a cast that included Freddy Rodriguez, Bruce Willis, Michael Biehn, Jeff Fahey, Josh Brolin, Marley Shelton, and Rose McGowan. The *Scream* actress portrayed a go-go dancer, Cherry Darling, who spends much of the film with a machine-gun leg after her original limb is torn off by a group of infected 'sickos.'

Nicotero worked on both *Grindhouse* films. The KNB co-founder recalls the *Planet Terror* production as having "that cheeky no-rules vibe. Everything was big: the blood was big, the squibs were massive. Every time somebody

Director Quentin Tarantino and Kurt Russell on the set of *Death Proof* (2007).

melted, every time something happened, it was really over the top. That gave us a good opportunity to do some really outrageous effects."

Tarantino also decided to make a horror film, *Death Proof*. Inspired by a recent immersion in slasher movies, he came up with the idea of a character called Stuntman Mike, who uses his own car as a murder weapon. The director had planned on casting Mickey Rourke but was unable to make a deal with the actor's representatives. He eventually cast John Carpenter's favorite leading man, Kurt Russell. The *Death Proof* actors also included McGowan, Rosario Dawson, Eli Roth, *Cabin Fever* actress Jordan Ladd, and stuntwoman Zoë Bell.

Nicotero's most difficult task on *Death Proof* was depicting the moment when four young friends (played by Ladd, Monica Staggs, Vanessa Ferlito, and Sydney Tamiia Poitier) are killed by Stuntman Mike when Kurt Russell's character drives into their car. "We lifecast all the actresses [with] the

Behind-the-scenes *Death Proof* image of the dummies doubling for Sydney Tamiia Poitier and Monica Staggs.

expressions and in the exact positions they were going to be in before the crash," he explains. "Then, between me and Jeff Dashnaw, the stunt coordinator, and John McLeod, the effects guy, we came up with all these different rigs, and we shot all of that onstage. They built the interior of the car so you could simulate the impact over and over again, and then we put the dummies in and shot it." Nicotero realized his efforts had been worthwhile when he heard about the reaction of Tarantino's editor Sally Menke to the footage. According to the KNB co-founder, Menke called the director and said, "These are some of the greatest dummies I've ever seen in my life, because I can't tell the difference between the dummies and the real girls."

To make the double bill more of an authentic experience for viewers, Tarantino decided that *Grindhouse* should feature trailers for non-existent exploitation movies. Rodriguez volunteered to make a trailer for the imaginary action film *Machete*, with Danny Trejo playing the titular role of a mercenary. Rob Zombie, Edgar Wright, and Eli Roth also agreed to direct faux clips.

Roth recalls that Zombie stunned his fellow filmmakers with the promo clip for a movie called *Werewolf Women of the SS*. In part a parody of 1975's notorious Canadian exploitation film *Ilsa, She Wolf of the SS*, the elaborate trailer featured appearances by veteran Zombie collaborators Bill Moseley, Tom Towles, and Sheri Moon Zombie, as well as Udo Kier and Nicolas Cage. "We're like, 'Jesus, we've got to really step it up,'" says Roth. "So I made the *Thanksgiving* trailer."

The filmmaker had first dreamed up the idea for a slasher film called *Thanksgiving* as a child with his friend Jeff Rendell. "We grew up in Massachusetts, where the Pilgrims landed," says Roth. "Thanksgiving, as you can imagine, is a massive deal there. We also came of age in that era of holiday slasher films, starting with *Black Christmas* and *Halloween*. Our dream was to make a slasher film around Thanksgiving." The fake trailer's horrifying sights included a beheading at a parade and a human corpse presented for consumption in the manner of a roast turkey. "We put together this parade in Kladno in the Czech Republic, and we had the Kladno majorettes, and Mike McCarty and Kevin Wasner from KNB made a human turkey body," says Roth. The fake trailer footage also featured the sight a near-naked female trampolinist about to land on a sharp knife. "Everyone was like, 'This is going to ruin your career,'" says the director. "I'm like, 'I don't care, this is what it's all about, coming up with the craziest shocking moment, and seeing if you can sneak it into 3,000 cinemas.'"

On the set of Eli Roth's *Thanksgiving* trailer for *Grindhouse* (2007).

Wright, meanwhile, directed the trailer for a film called *Don't*, whose cast included Nick Frost, Simon Pegg, Lucy Punch, *Event Horizon* actor Jason Isaacs, and future *Succession* star Matthew Macfadyen. "I did mine in two days for, like, a hundred grand," says Roth. "Edgar did his in a day or two. We just had a blast doing it."

The Weinsteins had agreed to back the project believing that Tarantino and Rodriguez would make a pair of 60-minute movies for a combined budget of $40 million. As the length, cost, and ambition of *Grindhouse* expanded, the brothers suggested that the two films be released separately, but the directors refused. The Weinsteins were forced to push the release of the film, first from the spring of 2006 to December of that year, and then to April 2007.

In his review for *The New York Times*, critic A. O. Scott described *Grindhouse* as an "exuberant, uneven tribute to the spirit of trash cinema." To Roth's delight, Scott encouraged readers "not to miss the trailer for *Thanksgiving*." "It was like I had won the 'Who had the most shocking moment of the whole thing' contest," says the *Hostel* director. "You know, it's always a competition with directors. Quentin's like, 'I'm going to do the craziest car chase ever,' and Edgar's like, 'I'll do Nick Frost in a diaper,' and Rob's like, 'I'll have the werewolf women, and Nazis, and Nicolas Cage.' And [*The New York Times*] are like, 'No—girl on the trampoline.'"

Grindhouse placed fourth on the box office chart over its first weekend in cinemas, behind the comedies *Blades of Glory*, *Meet the Robinsons*, and *Are We Done Yet?* During its first three days on release, the movie earned a catastrophically low $11 million. The film's gross was just $1 million more than the amount earned by the much less hyped *The Reaping*, a Hilary Swank-starring horror film from Dark Castle that opened on the same day.

While *Grindhouse* was a bomb, Tarantino remained proud of the project. "I'm in London doing press on the film before opening weekend," Tarantino recalled to *Empire* magazine. "And I go to Edgar Wright, 'Hey, let's you, and me, and your friends go see it on Friday night in Piccadilly... And we walk in the theatre and there's about 13 people in there. On the opening 8:30 show, all right? That was a rather humbling experience. But we sat down, and watched it, and had a good time. Edgar was like, 'That was very impressive. I think I would have turned around and walked out of there. The fact you said, 'Fuck it,' and sat down, I admired that.'"

Grindhouse would have a remarkably fertile after-life with the project's fake trailers inspiring a clutch of real movies. Rodriguez co-directed 2010's *Machete*, starring Danny Trejo and Michelle Rodriguez, and then directed 2013's *Machete Kills*, which featured a cameo from Elon Musk. In Canada, prints of *Grindhouse* had included the trailer for a fake action-comedy called *Hobo with a Shotgun*. The trailer's director Jason Eisener later used the clip as the basis for a feature film, which starred Rutger Hauer and played at the Sundance Film Festival in 2011.

In 2010, Roth was interviewed by Cinemablend in his role as producer of the upcoming *The Last Exorcism*. The *Hostel* filmmaker confirmed that he and Jeff Rendell were developing the screenplay for a feature version of the *Thanksgiving* trailer. In fact, fans would have to wait more than a decade to see a *Thanksgiving* film as Roth and Rendell struggled to find a feature-length framing for their kills. "After we made the trailer, we thought, well, now we never have to make the movie, we did the best parts, they turned out great," says Roth. "And then, for years, the fans would re-post [the trailer] every year going, 'Why haven't they made this?' And we really didn't know what it was about."

---

28 Weeks Later was yet another film inspired by President Bush's War on Terror and, in particular, the occupation of Iraq. With Danny Boyle and Alex Garland occupied making their science fiction film *Sunshine*, the *28 Days Later* sequel was directed by Spanish filmmaker Juan Carlos Fresnadillo, who also co-wrote the script. The film starred Robert Carlyle, Idris Elba, Jeremy Renner, Rose Byrne, and a teenage Imogen Poots, and was set in a London (now free of the rage virus) being repopulated under the control of American troops. "There were lots of ideas," says producer Andrew Macdonald. "We knew the time thing was very important. Could it be *28 Minutes*? Could it be *19 Days*? One of the ideas was about a crack military team that came in to find Tony Blair and they'd be in these underground bunkers." Macdonald and his collaborators eventually pursued a different route. "What we thought was really interesting, because of Iraq, is what would happen when you tried to reboot a whole country," says the producer. "The disease comes back, and it gets out of control, and the Americans just say, 'Kill everybody.'" Released in 2007, *28 Weeks Later* was positively reviewed and performed decently at the box office, though less well than its cheaper predecessor.

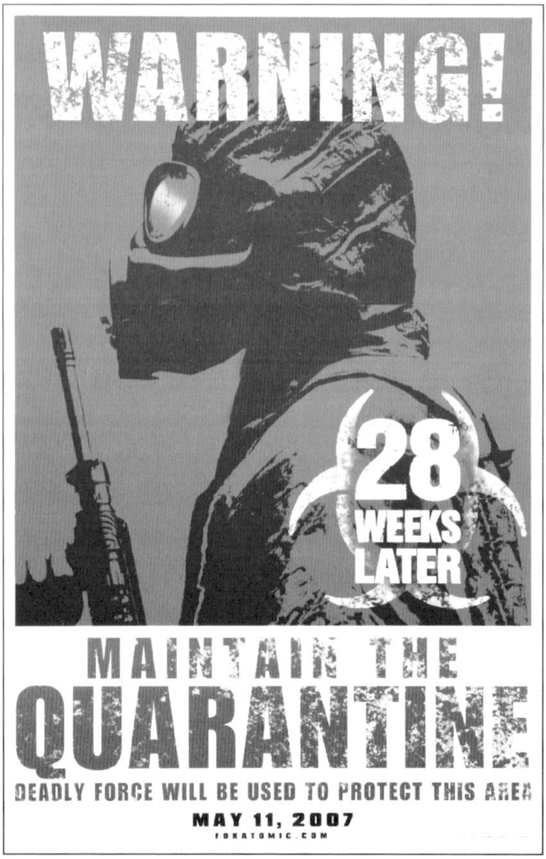

Macdonald had tried, and failed, to get Cillian Murphy to make a cameo in the film. The actor was much in-demand following his performance in *28 Days Later*, with roles in Boyle's *Sunshine* and Ken Loach's 2006 historical drama *The Wind That Shakes the Barley*, as well as the Wes Craven-directed *Red Eye*. *Batman Begins* director Christopher Nolan even asked him to audition for the role of Bruce Wayne after seeing a still of Murphy in Boyle's original zombie movie. Nolan eventually cast Christian Bale in the role but chose the Irish actor to portray villain The Scarecrow. The pair would continue their collaboration on subsequent films, including 2017's *Dunkirk* and 2023's *Oppenheimer*, for which Murphy won a Best Actor Oscar. "There was one moment when I tried to persuade Cillian to become an infected in [*28 Weeks Later*]," producer Macdonald confirms. "He said he wanted to go on holiday, and I said, 'I'll buy you a trip to Barbados if you appear in the film for ten minutes.' But it never happened."

When Adam Green was eight years old, his parents sent him to a summer camp in Pembroke, Massachusetts. "It was called Camp Avoda," he says. "The camp was a miserable place for me. They had us cleaning toilets and scrubbing floors. I never understood why that's what we did at camp." Green received an answer many years later as he promoted his first proper film, 2007's franchise-inaugurating slasher movie *Hatchet*. "When I was touring *Hatchet*, somebody explained to me from the audience that '*avoda*' in Hebrew means 'work,'" says the writer-director. "So my parents actually sent me to Camp Work."

Green's camp experience directly inspired him to create the mass murderer who would haunt the *Hatchet* franchise, a disfigured and seemingly unkillable supernatural maniac named Victor Crowley. "The counselors told us to stay away from this one cabin, otherwise 'Hatchetface' would get us—it was basically the cabin where they drank and partied," he says. "That was all they had for their story." Green's older brother had already showed him some slasher movies, starting with 1981's *Friday the 13th Part 2*, and the pre-teen Green used his knowledge of the genre to craft a tale about Hatchetface. "That night, when we were going to sleep in my cabin, I launched into this whole story about a deformed man who was hiding in the house, and the door got lit on fire, and his dad tried to save him and hit him in the face with a hatchet, and now he haunts the area," he recalls. "22 years after that story, I finally made the movie."

Green moved to Los Angeles in 2000, hoping to pursue a career as a writer-director. He wound up working as a production assistant on movie sets and paying his rent by DJing at the Rainbow Bar & Grill on the Sunset Strip. In 2004, Green visited New Orleans to attend the bachelor party of a high school friend. The trip prompted him to write a script hinging on the character he had developed at Camp Avoda. "There's nowhere else like New Orleans," says Green. "There's voodoo shops, and cemetery tours, and there's the swamps, which are just an awesome setting—at least I thought so."

The *Hatchet* script featured an abundance of gruesome murders, like the slasher films from the '80s that Green loved, but also channeled the humor of *An American Werewolf in London* and *Scream.* When Green's agent attempted to sell the screenplay, there were no takers. "People didn't know what to make of *Hatchet,*" he says. "They were like, 'Is it funny or is it graphically violent, because you've got to pick a lane.' And I'm like, 'Well, no, that's the point.'"

Hatchet was rescued from the rejection pile by Green's friend Sarah Elbert, who helped produce the annual Halloween shorts that the director made with his company ArieScope Pictures. Elbert had just worked on the bonus features for a box set of the *Friday the 13th* movies and arranged for Green to meet with filmmaker John Carl Buechler. A legendary figure in Hollywood's horror community, Buechler had directed 1988's *Friday the 13th Part VII: The New Blood* and provided special makeup effects for a slew of other movies, including *Re-Animator* and *A Nightmare on Elm Street 4: The Dream Master.* Buechler agreed to help Green with his project and offered to speak with *Friday the 13th* franchise veteran Kane Hodder about playing the role of Victor Crowley. "He was like, 'I'm driving out to the set of *The Devil's Rejects*, because Kane is coordinating [the stunts], I could give him the script,'" says Green. Around a week later, Green found himself on the phone with the one-time Jason Voorhees, talking about him playing Victor Crowley. "I think it was timing, because he had recently been unceremoniously replaced as Jason for *Freddy vs. Jason,*" the director says, explaining Hodder's interest in *Hatchet.* "All of a sudden, there's this new character that he would get to play, and be the first one to play it, because by the time he played Jason, six other people had portrayed the character."

Green cast Hodder as both Victor Crowley and Crowley's father, who accidentally kills his son trying to save him from their burning house. The actor-stuntman would be joined in the film by Robert Englund, who played the movie's first victim, and *Candyman* star Tony Todd, who made a cameo as New Orleans businessman Reverend Zombie. The director cast newcomer Tamara Feldman as the film's heroine Marybeth and future *Avatar* actor Joel David Moore as male lead Ben.

The *Hatchet* team eventually put together a budget of $1.5 million from private investors, helped by the recent success of low-budget horror films like *Saw* and *Cabin Fever.* "It was mainly one person, which was incredibly fortunate for us," says Green. "Lionsgate were acquiring movies made at that budget level and then putting them out in a major way. *Cabin Fever. The*

Director Adam Green on the set of *Hatchet* (2007).

Descent. *Saw*, of course. There were so many successes happening that I think that made them feel like it was worth the risk."

Green and producer Elbert shot *Hatchet* at the Sable Ranch in Santa Clarita during the summer of 2005. The pair's core collaborators included Green's ArieScope co-founders, cinematographer Will Barratt and producer Cory Neal, as well as cameraman BJ McDonnell. The cast and crew were surprised to discover that Sable Ranch was playing host to another slasher film, of sorts: a porn movie called *Camp Cuddly Pines Powertool Massacre*. The film starred Stormy Daniels, later to prove a thorn in the side of President Donald Trump during his political career. "We were mainly shooting at night," Green recalls. "So we would show up around five in the afternoon, and there was a food truck, and we noticed they were shooting some kind of porn right where we were eating. It wasn't until recently that we realized Stormy Daniels was in the movie."

Hatchet received its world premiere at the Tribeca Film Festival in April 2006. "I'm watching all these executives walking in—New Line and Lionsgate—and you're thinking, 'Here's the moment,'" says Green. The director recalls the event as "such a magical night, the response from the audience was way beyond what we could have hoped: cheering, laughing, screaming." Green was brought down to earth when his sales representative expressed doubts about the film being picked up for theatrical distribution. "Back then, a theatrical release was so important, because that made your movie legitimate," the director says. "I went back to my hotel room, and I fell on the floor, and I cried the hardest I've ever cried in my life."

Lionsgate's Peter Block was among the studio executives who declined the opportunity to acquire Green's film. "What Adam remembers is that I walked out of the Tribeca screening," he says. "I don't remember that. I remember being really tired and saying, 'I don't know what this is.' Lionsgate didn't need it at the time."

Green felt aggrieved that he was unable to get distribution for his original slasher tale when studios were greenlighting so many sequels and remakes. "[Hollywood] is always chasing a trend," he notes. "Something opens strong, and then everything has to be like that. The example I always give is the *Prom Night* remake. It was huge. It [grossed], like, $50 million. No one will ever talk about that movie again. I'm not slamming the film, I don't know if I ever saw it. But there's other stuff where, ten years later, 20 years later, they just keeping getting bigger."

To drum up interest in the film, Green hit the international genre festival circuit, screening *Hatchet* at FrightFest in the UK and the Sitges Film Festival in Spain. The director publicized the movie with a poster whose tongue-in-cheek tagline repurposed the criticism offered by one of the executives who had turned the film down: 'It's not a remake. It's not a sequel. And it's not based on a Japanese one.'

Finally, Anchor Bay signed on to distribute the film, but Green struggled to secure an R rating for his film from the MPAA. "They gave *Hatchet* an NC-17," says Green. "I'm like, there's no sex, there's very little swearing, no one even smokes a cigarette. None of the killing is realistic in any way." Green was forced to trim his movie's gore and violence. "I had to cut so much out," says the director.

Anchor Bay released *Hatchet* on September 7, 2007, in 93 cinemas including Hollywood's ArcLight Theater. The film placed 39th on the box office chart, earning just $100,000 over its opening weekend. But the movie proved a hit when it was released on DVD. "It did really well the first week and then word of mouth started," says Green.

In November 2009, Bloody Disgusting broke the news that Green would write and direct a second *Hatchet* movie. After he was unable to strike a deal with Tamara Feldman for her to reprise the role of final girl Marybeth, the director cast *Halloween* franchise actress Danielle Harris in the role. Green's enthusiasm for blood and gore would once again find him in conflict with the MPAA. "Even after us cutting two minutes out of the movie, [the MPAA] told us that we just couldn't kill people like this," he said to *Entertainment Weekly* at the time. *Hatchet II* would ultimately be released in an unrated version via the AMC theater chain on October 1, 2010, but cinemas pulled the film from screens after just a couple of days. "I assume it probably had something to do with the controversy online about an unrated movie playing in theaters," said the director shortly after the film's release.

The cast of *Hatchet II* included an uncredited Joe Lynch, who played an alligator hunter. Green had met the *Wrong Turn 2* director at a movie screening in Los Angeles hosted by visual effects artist 'Spooky' Dan Walker. "Spooky Dan is like the mayor of the horror community out here, he would have these backyard screenings," says Green. "I'm standing in one corner of the yard, holding court, and I notice there was someone else doing the same thing in the other corner. The competitive side of me was like, 'Who's that?' He was thinking the same thing. When the movie started, we sat down next to each other to size each other up, and that was history from then forward." The pair would go on to be fast friends and collaborators on an array of ventures, including the 2011 horror anthology film *Chillerama*, for which Green directed a segment titled "The Diary of Anne Frankenstein," and the long-running podcast *The Movie Crypt*.

Green wrote the script for a third *Hatchet* movie and nominated cameraman BJ McDonnell to direct the movie. McDonnell shot much of the film in New Orleans, with a cast that included Kane Hodder, Danielle Harris, Derek Mears, Sid Haig, *The Texas Chainsaw Massacre 2* star Caroline Williams, and *Gremlins* actor Zach Galligan. Green was on hand in Louisiana to witness, and help out with, what proved to be a difficult shoot. "We shot half of that movie in a real swamp," he says. "Every night, someone went to urgent care. The bugs were so bad. It was miserable. If I could go back, I would set *Hatchet* in Hawaii, because it's miserable shooting in a fucking swamp."

Distributors Dark Sky Films gave *Hatchet III* a limited release in 2013, with the film once again proving popular on DVD. The director firmly

Kane Hodder in *Hatchet III* (2013).

believed that the third *Hatchet* movie would definitely be the last. "Yes, it was *over*," says Green. "Little did I know!"

In January 2006, *Variety* reported that Eli Roth was in talks with Screen Gems and Lionsgate to make a second *Hostel* film. Again written and directed by Roth, the sequel would feature a trio of female tourists—played by Bijou Phillips, Heather Matarazzo, and *Texas Chainsaw Massacre* remake actress Lauren German—checking into the titular establishment with terrifying and gory consequences.

Journalist Bill Schulz returned to Prague to cover the sequel's shoot for *Maxim* magazine. The writer would once more appear onscreen, doubling for Jay Hernandez in a dream sequence during which the chest and stomach of the actor's character is sliced open. "Not to brag, I was the lead," says Schulz. "Jay didn't have to be in the scene. I'm playing his torso—and no one would ever think that, looking at my torso—while they pull intestines

Heather Matarazzo in *Hostel: Part II* (2007).

out." Schulz was surprised when Roth told him that the main victims in the sequel would be women. "He's like, 'All right, so here's the deal with the second one—it's going to be like the first, but this time I'm torturing women,'" says the writer. "He's like, 'I'm going to get so much shit for this.' I've got my stupid little tape recorder and I'm like, 'Yeah, dude, this isn't going to be good!' I didn't mean 'good' quality-wise. I'm like, 'The reaction is going to be terrible.'"

The *Hostel: Part II* teaser poster featured an eyeball-grabbing image of boar flesh, a photograph taken by Tim Palen. The marketing executive recalls that he "actually saved the receipt, because when we submitted it to the MPAA, they said, 'It's not approved because it's too graphic,' and we had to prove to them that it was not human."

On June 8, 2007, the day *Hostel: Part II* was released, CNN posted an article headlined "'Torture Porn' helps Lionsgate roar." Written by financial journalist Paul R. La Monica, the write-up noted that Lionsgate shares "have surged 24 percent in the past 12 months." La Monica reported that

HARMONY FARMS
2824 FOOTHILL BLVD
LA CRESCENTA CA 91214
818-248-3068
Sale
ID: 0002
Merchant: 8010013467
12/01/06 15:35:04
NOVUS
XXXXXXXXXXXX2208
Appr Code: 001431 Invoice#: 8
Total: $ 68.49
Customer Copy
THANK YOU

Teaser poster for *Hostel: Part II*, with receipt for purchase of boar flesh.

analysts were seeing even bigger gains ahead thanks to *Hostel: Part II*, which some box office experts were predicting could make $20 million over its opening weekend.

To the disappointment of Lionsgate shareholders, *Hostel: Part II* was a commercial letdown. The film cost $10 million, more than twice as much as the first movie, but earned $8 million over its first weekend of release, $11 million less than the original *Hostel* had grossed. In a message on his Myspace page posted later in the month, Roth blamed the pirating of the movie for the film's comparatively poor performance. "A stolen workprint (with unfinished music, no sound effects, and no VFX) leaked out online before the release, and is really hurting us, especially internationally," he wrote. The director encouraged readers to see *Hostel: Part II* in theaters or risk studios not financing more R-rated horror movies. Nikki Finke, founder and editor-in-chief of the entertainment news outlet Deadline, wrote a post about

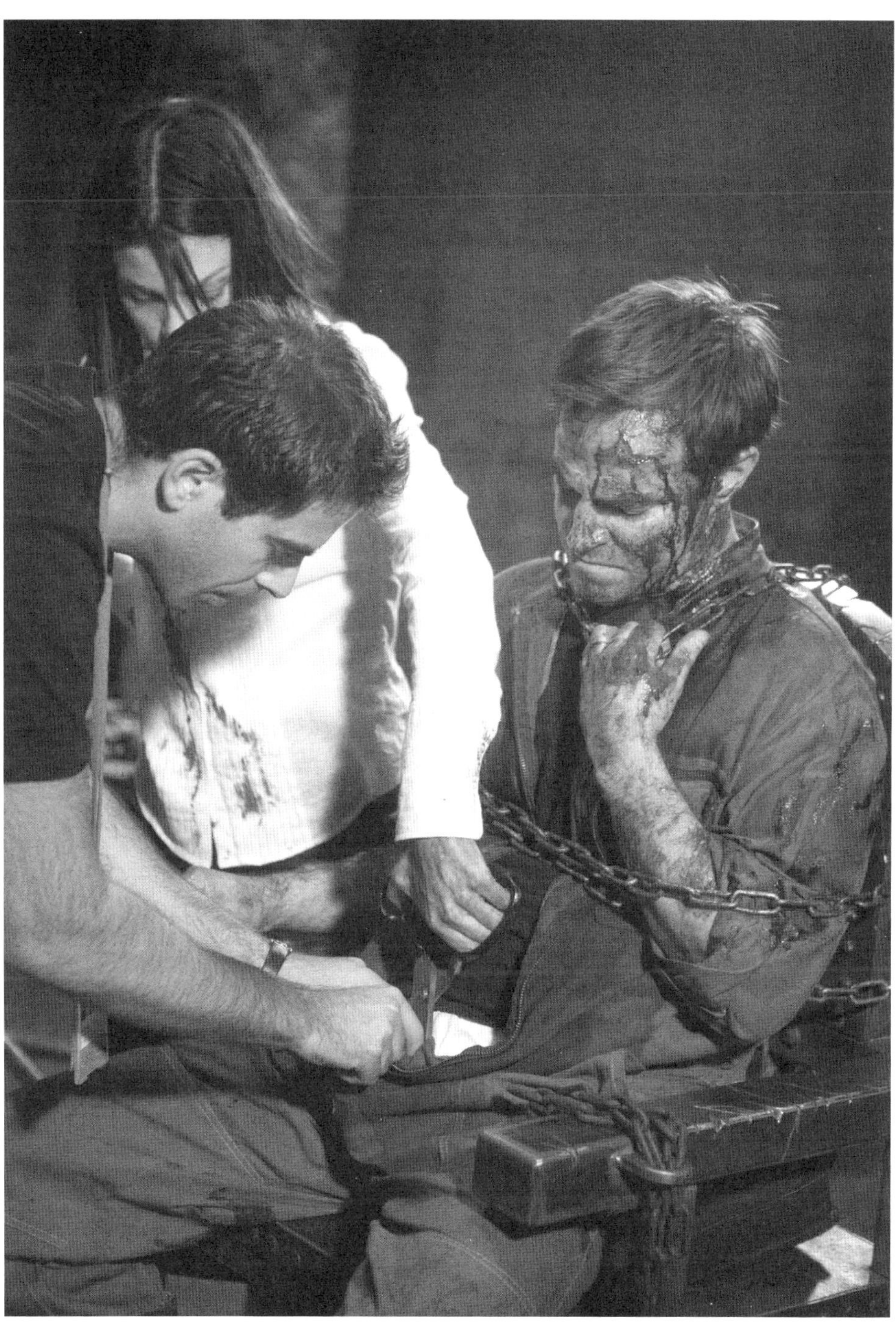

Eli Roth, Lauren German, and Roger Bart on the set of *Hostel: Part II*.

the director's statement with the headline "Eli Roth Reacts Badly To *Hostel II* Failure; Says R-Rated Horror In Serious Jeopardy." In her article, the famously caustic Finke described Roth's writing as "more like whining."

Palen, meanwhile, believes that Roth's decision to change the sex of the victims in *Hostel: Part II* contributed to the movie making less than its predecessor. "Everybody wants to see douchey frat boys who do horrible things get punished," he says. "When innocent schoolgirls are being tortured, then it really is torture porn."

Oversaturation of the market, too, likely contributed to the *Hostel* franchise's declining returns. Roth's film was not just following the many Lionsgate movies featuring extreme material (including, of course, the original *Hostel*). It also came after Dimension's *Wolf Creek* and *Turistas*, a jungle-set tale about human organ theft from 20th Century Fox's new genre label Fox Atomic, released in December 2006.

Lionsgate contributed further to that oversaturation in July 2007, when the company put out *Captivity*, starring Elisha Cuthbert as a model who is drugged, kidnapped, and psychologically tortured. *Captivity* opened in over 1,000 theaters but earned just $2.6 million in all at the US box office. It was followed into cinemas just two weeks later by TriStar Pictures' *I Know Who Killed Me*. The film starred Lindsay Lohan as a high school student who disappears and then returns mutilated and claiming to be someone else. The movie's director Chris Sivertson insisted that he was inspired stylistically by Alfred Hitchcock, David Lynch, and Brian De Palma. Reviewers mostly assessed the movie as another *Saw*-inspired cash grab. *New York Post* critic Lou Lumenick described the movie as "a sleazy, inept, and worthless piece of torture porn." *I Know Who Killed Me* was another box office disappointment, earning $7 million in the US.

In his statement on Myspace, Roth announced that he was taking a "long overdue" break and that audiences would not see "a film directed by me in cinemas until at least next fall." In fact, Roth's next movie as director would be *The Green Inferno*, which was not widely released until 2015. A third *Hostel* film, the Las Vegas-set *Hostel: Part III*, was made without his input and sent straight to video in 2011. "The knives were out on *Hostel II*," says the filmmaker. "Nikki Finke wanted my head on a platter. Everyone was like, 'This movie's a failure.' I bought a *house* from that 'failure.' I'd *love* to fail like that every time. After that, I was like, 'You don't get another movie from me.' I felt like I needed to regain the love of doing this again. And I stopped for five years."

The box office returns of *Saw III* banished all thoughts among the franchise's producers of ending the series as a trilogy. Shortly after the film's release, Lionsgate and Twisted Pictures announced that a fourth entry was in the works. Production designer David Hackl, who had worked on the two previous entries, was set to direct *Saw IV*. When Hackl's wife fell ill, Bousman agreed to return and direct his third *Saw* film. The script for *Saw IV* was by Marcus Dunstan and Patrick Melton. The writing duo had been thrust into the Hollywood spotlight when their script for a monster movie called *Feast* was chosen to be turned into a film on season 3 of the Miramax-produced reality show *Project Greenlight*. While Dimension would give *Feast* just a small release in 2006, the exposure put them on the radar of Hollywood genre producers.

The death of Jigsaw at the end of *Saw III* presented the franchise's overlords with a problem going forward, given that the series had become synonymous with Tobin Bell's character and his traps. The producers of the *Friday the 13th* series had faced a similar problem after killing off Jason Voorhees and solved the issue by reviving the slasher icon as a supernatural character in 1986's *Friday the 13th Part VI: Jason Lives*. The *Saw* team took a different route, making clear to audiences that Jigsaw was able to continue his campaign of terror by having set up traps, and acquired accomplices, before his death. "We found a way of bringing him back in flashbacks," says producer Mark Burg.

Saw IV was released on October 26, 2007. The movie's first weekend domestic earnings of $31 million were less than both *Saw II* and *Saw III*, but the film comfortably claimed the number one slot. Worldwide, *Saw IV* earned $139 million.

According to Bousman, he continues to receive complaints from his behind-the-scenes collaborators about killing off Jigsaw in *Saw III*. "I still get shit from Lionsgate and Mark when they're trying to find clever ways to bring him back twenty years later," he laughs.

"THERE'S SOMETHING IN THE MIST."

George A. Romero's *Night of the Living Dead* was a loose and unauthorized adaptation of Richard Matheson's 1954 book *I Am Legend*, the same novel that informed Ernest Dickerson's pitch for *Blade*. Matheson later encountered Romero, who explained that he had not gotten rich from his directorial debut. "I came up with an idea for him and I met him for lunch," recalled the novelist. "And the first thing he said to me, putting his arms up as if I was about to strike him, he says, 'Didn't make any money from making *Night of the Living Dead*!'"

Matheson came up with the core idea for his post-apocalyptic, Los Angeles-set vampire tale as a teenager after seeing 1931's *Dracula*. "I thought if the world was full of vampires, it would be more frightening than just one," the writer told *The New York Times* in 2007. The novel had been officially adapted as 1964's *The Last Man on Earth*, with Vincent Price playing the movie's protagonist. Warner Bros. acquired the rights to *I Am Legend* in 1970, and the following year released another adaptation, *The Omega Man*, starring Charlton Heston.

Matheson took a dim view of the two official *I Am Legend* adaptations. The author had agreed to write the screenplay for *The Last Man on Earth*, but the script was reworked by other hands and Matheson asked for the pseudonymous credit of 'Logan Swanson.' *The Omega Man* swapped out the author's vampires for mutant victims of biological warfare. In an interview for the Archive of American Television, Matheson said that the film "was so far removed from my novel, it didn't even bother me."

In the mid-'90s, Warner Bros. production executive Lorenzo di Bonaventura hired screenwriter Mark Protosevich to work on the script for a new film version of Matheson's novel. Protosevich had attracted the attention of di Bonaventura with his screenplay for *The Cell*, a science fiction serial

killer thriller that New Line would release in 2000 with Jennifer Lopez playing the lead role. The writer was thrilled about getting the opportunity to adapt *I Am Legend*, later telling *Fangoria*, "I'm a tremendous Richard Matheson fan and I have always felt that that story had never been done justice, and so it was really amazing being offered something that's a personal favorite as an assignment. I took it as a crusade to do it well."

Ridley Scott developed the project to star Arnold Schwarzenegger. Special effects artist Steve Johnson designed and built a practical monster in the hope of making many more for Scott's film. "That movie went on for years, and years, and years," says Johnson. "It was a huge-budgeted film, and we wanted to create something that was worthy of such a great story. We did it with translucent materials, [with] veins painted from the inside, so you'd get a translucent skin tone for a vampire who has been living out of the sun for years. At this point, translucent silicone makeups were not the norm, so we were kind of putting our dicks on the chopping block with that. Then it just never happened." In December 1997, *Variety* reported that Warner Bros. executives were "choking on the budget [...] which is hovering at around $108 million." The studio subsequently shelved the film.

In the early 2000s, the adaptation was revived by Will Smith. Protosevich wrote a new draft of the screenplay, with the actor set to star in the film and his *Bad Boys* collaborator Michael Bay interested in directing. The project was scuppered by the release of *28 Days Later*, which the principals believed was too close to the film they planned to make. Smith would tell *The New York Times* that Danny Boyle's film seemed to "snatch the concept."

I Am Legend was resurrected again by screenwriter Akiva Goldsman, whose credits included 2004's Smith-starring *I, Robot* and who had a production deal at Warners. Goldsman completed a new draft of the script, which relocated the movie from Los Angeles to New York City (although the finished film would ultimately feature material by both Goldsman and Protosevich). Smith agreed to play the lead role of scientist Dr. Robert Neville, and the $150 million-plus project was fast-tracked by Warner Bros. after the start date for the actor's superhero movie *Hancock* was pushed back. The studio hired *Constantine* filmmaker Francis Lawrence to direct the movie, and the *I Am Legend* shoot finally began in September 2006.

Steve Johnson did not work on the film. The special effects artist had left the US for Costa Rica in the spring of 2006 after failing to secure the contracts for both Sam Raimi's *Spider-Man 3* and Spike Jonze's *Where the Wild Things Are*. "Basically, I lost $20 million on the same day," he says. "I just snapped. I probably went temporarily insane. I had outstanding loans of two or three million dollars. I said, 'Fuck it, I'm closing my company, I'm going down to the jungle, and I'm going to heal.'"

To portray the film's creatures, director Lawrence started by using prosthetics-wearing actors but, a week into the shoot, decided the monsters would need to be enhanced with computer-generated effects. Johnson continued to monitor the progress of the movie, and the production's decision

Will Smith in *I Am Legend* (2007).

to heavily employ CGI, from afar. "I heard they went to every effects studio in town and said, 'Hey, can you make these crazy vampires?'" he says. "They ended up doing it digitally because they worked down the amount of prep time. They fucked themselves in the long run."

The production's most expensive sequences included a nighttime flashback scene shot by the Brooklyn Bridge in which Smith's Neville attempts to have his wife and child escape Manhattan via helicopter. Shooting the scene cost north of $5 million and involved 14 government agencies, a crew of 250 people, and 1,000 extras. As *The Hollywood Reporter* journalist Joseph Steuer wrote, "Creating such a tableau would be difficult in any large city, but accomplishing it in post-Sept. 11 New York seems nothing short of Sisyphean."

Reviews of the completed film tended to be positive, although some reviewers took issue with the look of the monsters. "A big part of the reason for this movie's nose dive around the one-hour mark is that, seen up close, the infected just aren't that scary," wrote Slate critic Dana Stevens. "As rendered by a combination of CGI and motion capture, these beings—speeded-up zombies on the *28 Weeks Later* model, wearing only torn trousers *à la* Incredible Hulk—are too familiar to elicit more than a mild 'eww'; and the movie trots them out so often that they start to become almost cute."

Released in the US at the end of 2007, *I Am Legend* grossed $77 million over its first weekend in cinemas, the biggest December opening of all time. The film went on to earn $245 million at the domestic box office and $585 million in all.

The blockbuster status of *I Am Legend* did not overly impress Richard Matheson, who later gave his verdict on the film to *Fangoria.* Asked what he thought about the movie in a 2011 cover story on the novelist, Matheson replied, "I thought it was extremely well-produced… and yet another example of them failing to adapt my book."

After 2005's *Land of the Dead*, George Romero directed two more zombie movies. In 2007's found footage release *Diary of the Dead*, a film student documents the undead apocalypse, uploading his footage to the internet. Romero originally wrote the script as the pilot for a TV show. Later, the director received funding to turn his screenplay into a feature, one influenced by the public's enthusiasm for the recently launched YouTube

George Romero on the set of *Diary of the Dead* (2007).

platform. 2009's *Survival of the Dead* was a neo-western—inspired by William Wyler's 1958 film *The Big Country*—about two feuding families on an island who continue to fight each other even after the dead come back to life. The film's cast included Alan Van Sprang and *Wrong Turn* actor Julian Richings.

Both movies were much cheaper ventures than *Land of the Dead* and were independently produced. Romero seemed content, at least in public, with his return to low-budget filmmaking. "I was happy to get back to my roots," he said in an interview that appeared in the February 2014 issue of *Sight & Sound*. "I had problems with *Land*. I loved Dennis Hopper, but I was very uncomfortable to see that one of the biggest line items on the budget was his expensive cigars."

The rush to remake horror films, combined with renewed interest in the zombie genre, led to the director's *Day of the Dead* being revived twice via straight-to-DVD releases. In 2005, Anchor Bay distributed the sort-of sequel *Day of the Dead 2: Contagium*, and a loose remake of Romero's film written by *Final Destination* creator Jeffrey Reddick followed three years later. The new *Day of the Dead* was directed by *Halloween H20* filmmaker Steve Miner and starred Mena Suvari, Nick Cannon, and Ving Rhames, playing a different role from the one he had portrayed in Zack Snyder's *Dawn of the Dead.* Horror fans greeted the film unenthusiastically, in part because it veered so wildly from Romero's original. "Through the development process, they kept stripping away everything that was related to *Day of the Dead,*" says Reddick. "If you look at me talking early on in the process, it's like, 'I think fans are going to be happy!' Later on, I was like, 'It's a movie!'"

In February 2010, US distributors Participant Media released a remake of Romero's low-budget 1973 film *The Crazies,* about a biological weapon that drives people to violence and insanity. Directed by Breck Eisner on a budget of around $25 million, the new version co-starred Timothy Olyphant and Radha Mitchell and earned $54 million worldwide. "I think the film was uplifted by having a budget that the first movie didn't have," says Mitchell. "My character was the pregnant doctor, so she didn't get to engage in too much action. The fun part, from an acting perspective, was that sequence in the car wash drive-through, where I got to have it out with a zombie."

The undead subgenre continued to be explored and tweaked outside the US. Norwegian filmmaker Tommy Wirkola co-wrote and directed 2009's grotesque, hilarious *Dead Snow,* in which a group of vacationing friends face off against Nazi zombies. "Nazis have always been the ultimate villains in movies," Wirkola told the website Eat My Brains. "Combine that with zombies, and you really get something no one would sympathize with."

Another twist on the zombie subgenre was delivered by Spanish filmmakers Jaume Balagueró and Paco Plaza with their 2007 movie *Rec.* The film starred Manuela Velasco as a TV reporter named Ángela, whose ride-along with a team of Barcelona firemen descends into violence and death when the residents of an apartment block become infected with a mysterious disease. The two directors and their co-writer Luiso Berdejo added a supernatural element to the basic zombie template and, as Romero did on *Diary of the Dead,* made use of the found footage format employed by the *Blair Witch Project* filmmakers.

In August 2007, Screen Gems announced that the studio had struck a deal to remake *Rec.* The new film would be produced by Vertigo Entertainment's Roy Lee and Doug Davison. "I actually started development before the Spanish-language movie was done," says Lee. "I had gotten a copy of the script, and I was like, 'This is amazing.' We got to see the original movie while we were prepping the remake. Minute things were adjusted because we saw what

things really worked in the actual movie and tried to make sure we had those in the remake."

Screen Gems commissioned filmmaker John Erick Dowdle and his sibling co-writer Drew to make the English-language version of *Rec*. Titled *Quarantine*, it dropped the original movie's supernatural plot line but kept the found footage format. The film starred Jennifer Carpenter from *The Exorcism of Emily Rose* as the new version's TV reporter and *Pan's Labyrinth* star Doug Jones as a doomsday cult member who infects himself with a mutated form of rabies. "Yes, I was 'Thin Infected Man' in *Quarantine*," says Jones. "The filming crew get up to my apartment and there I was, this saggy, old, infected, vile-looking man in nothing but tighty-whitey underwear." The actor recalls that Carpenter declined to meet him before the shooting of their scene together began. "When she's coming face-to-face with me in that dark apartment, that was the first time ever seeing me in makeup," he says. "She was genuinely terrified of me. Between takes, she ran away, bless her heart!" The Dowdles' remake was released in October 2008, earning a respectable $31 million at the domestic box office.

The zombie genre proved popular away from the big screen. In 2003, former *Saturday Night Live* writer Max Brooks published *The Zombie Survival Guide*, a comically straight-faced manual about what to do during an undead apocalypse. Brooks (son of *Young Frankenstein* filmmaker Mel Brooks) next wrote 2006's bestseller *World War Z: An Oral History of the Zombie War*, the film rights for which were acquired by Brad Pitt's production company Plan B.

Image Comics, meanwhile, struck gold with writer Robert Kirkman's *The Walking Dead*. The saga debuted in 2003 and related the adventures of a police deputy named Rick Grimes who wakes from a coma to discover that the world has been overrun by zombies. Kirkman had been writing the comic for a couple of years when *The Shawshank Redemption* director Frank Darabont expressed interest in transferring the story to the small screen. Darabont was a huge fan of the zombie genre, having first seen *Night of the Living Dead* at the age of 14. "It was 1974 and it came to one of the revival houses in LA," he says. "It was already kind of a legendary film. My friends and I all went and were very affected by it."

Darabont had long thought about playing in the Romero-created undead sandbox but was aware that the zombie genre seemed to have limited commercial appeal prior to the 2000s. "To be a fan of zombie literature, or films, was a really sub-cult thing for many decades," he says. The filmmaker realized he might have found a suitable vehicle for his zombie ambitions when he picked up the first collection of *The Walking Dead* comics at his local Burbank comic store. Darabont developed *The Walking Dead* as a TV show and approached NBC about backing the series. "The moment they got a look at the script, they passed," he recalls.

Darabont reluctantly put the idea of adapting *The Walking Dead* on the back burner but assured Kirkman that he hadn't given up on bringing his undead tale to the screen. "He told me early on, 'Don't worry, man. I'm going to get this thing made,'" the comics writer recalled in a 2010 interview with the Pads & Panels website. "I'm kind of like, 'Yeah, all right, buddy. That's real nice of you to say, but I know how things work. You're probably just blowing smoke up my ass.'"

Frank Darabont still had a horror itch. The writer-director would scratch it in unforgettable fashion with *The Mist*, his 2007 adaptation of Stephen King's 1980 novella. In King's tale, a group of supermarket employees and customers are terrorized by otherworldly creatures that emerge from a mysterious fog. The characters' predicament is made worse by a religious fanatic named Mrs. Carmody, who decides that their situation is a punishment from God. King had been inspired to write the story in the course of visiting a supermarket with his young son Joe after a storm. "I was halfway down the middle aisle, looking for hot-dog buns, when I imagined a big prehistoric bird flapping its way toward the meat counter at the back, knocking over cans of pineapple chunks and bottles of tomato sauce," King would write in his 1985 anthology *Skeleton Crew*, which included *The Mist*. "By the time my son Joe and I were in the checkout line, I was amusing myself with a story about all these people trapped in a supermarket surrounded by prehistoric animals."

Darabont believed that adapting *The Mist* would allow him to create a film that unnerved viewers but also said something important about America's increasingly polarized society. Speaking to SlashFilm writer Eric Vespe in 2022, the director would explain: "If you look at the year I made that movie, look at the world that we were in, the political situation here in the US, the cultural situation, the divide that has now become a chasm, was very much in evidence."

Darabont's parents were Hungarian refugees who had brought their son to America when he was still a baby. Barely out of the crib, the future director fell in love with horror, watching the classic Universal horror movies on TV. Darabont began his film career working as a PA on the Linda Blair-starring 1981 horror movie *Hell Night* after being hired by the movie's line producer Chuck Russell, another aspiring filmmaker. Around the same time, Darabont secured permission from Stephen King to make a short film out of his story "The Woman in the Room." He spent three years working on the project, with King giving his thumbs up to the result. After Russell was hired to direct 1987's *A Nightmare on Elm Street 3: Dream Warriors*, he asked Darabont to help him rework the script. Darabont went on to co-write Russell's 1988 remake of *The Blob* and 1989's Chris Walas-directed *The Fly II*.

Darabont considered making *The Mist* as his directorial debut but decided instead to adapt King's prison-set novella *Rita Hayworth and Shawshank Redemption*. *The Shawshank Redemption* underwhelmed at the box office when it was released in September 1994 but was nominated for seven Academy Awards and rapidly became beloved. Darabont followed that movie with another King adaptation, 1999's Tom Hanks-starring *The Green Mile*. The supernatural drama was a hit with cinema audiences and with the Academy, which nominated the film in four categories. Darabont's third movie,

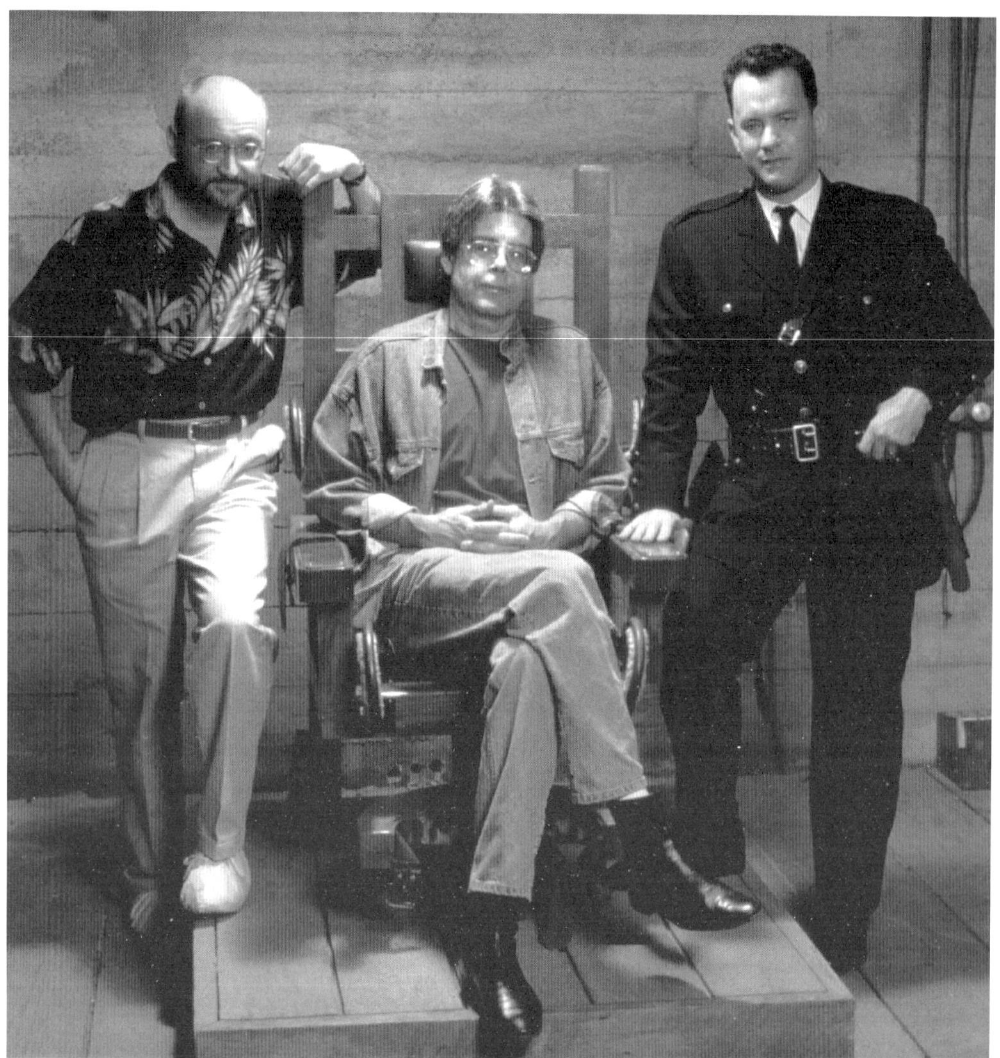

Frank Darabont, Stephen King, and Tom Hanks on the set of *The Green Mile* (1999).

2001's Jim Carrey drama *The Majestic*, was a bomb, but the director had proved himself to be a major filmmaker, particularly when the film he was making adapted a story by Stephen King.

Darabont was now ready to direct *The Mist*, although his version would have one big difference from King's original. The novella ended with the story's artist protagonist David Drayton and his son Billy driving into the mist and to an uncertain future. Darabont planned a far more definitive conclusion. In his ending, the Draytons would leave the supermarket with a couple of other survivors to discover that Lovecraftian monsters have seemingly taken over the world. David kills his own son, desperate to save Billy from a worse fate. Soon after, military vehicles arrive, the implication being that the danger has passed. "I sent [the script] to Steve King," Darabont recalled to Eric Vespe. "And he wrote back, and he said, 'I read it. I love your ending. I'm sorry I didn't think of it, because I would've written that instead.'"

Stephen King remained a prolific writer and was a totemic figure to younger horror-loving filmmakers like Darabont. But the post-*Scream* period had been a lean period for big-screen adaptations of the author's more terrifying tales. King's reputation as his generation's pre-eminent writer of adaptable horror fiction had been cemented with Brian De Palma's 1976 adaptation of King's debut *Carrie* and Stanley Kubrick's 1980 version of *The Shining*. Over the next decade, a slew of major horror releases mined the novelist's rapidly growing bibliography, from director David Cronenberg's *The Dead Zone* to John Carpenter's *Christine* to Mary Lambert's *Pet Sematary*. King himself both wrote and directed 1986's *Maximum Overdrive*, based on his short story "Trucks," which was a box office flop.

The month after *Maximum Overdrive* premiered in cinemas, Columbia Pictures released *Stand by Me*, a much more successful King adaptation despite not being a horror film. *Stand by Me* was directed by Rob Reiner, who in 1987 co-founded Castle Rock Entertainment, a production company named after the fictional Maine town that appears in many of King's tales. Reiner scored another success with *Misery*, an adaptation of King's 1987 book about a romance novelist named Paul Sheldon who finds himself at the mercy of his 'number one fan,' the deranged nurse Annie Wilkes. With a screenplay by William Goldman and stellar performances from James Caan and Kathy Bates, the 1990 film was a hit, and Bates won the Best Actress Award at the 1991 Oscars. Reiner's company followed *Misery* with 1993's *Needful Things*, adapted from King's recent horror novel. But moving forward, Castle Rock would lean into King's less genre-based material, producing Darabont's *The Shawshank Redemption* and *The Green Mile*.

Cinema audiences seemed increasingly uninterested in film adaptations of King's horror output. New Line's *The Mangler* was directed by Tobe Hooper and starred Robert Englund, but the film earned just $1.7 million when the studio released it in March 1995. Although *Child's Play* director Tom Holland scored a minor hit with 1996's *Thinner*, the following year's *The Night Flier*, about a plane-piloting vampire, premiered on HBO. The author's reputation among horror film fans was not helped by Dimension's enthusiasm for releasing straight-to-video sequels of often dubious quality in the King-inspired *Children of the Corn* franchise.

In the '90s, King's horror novels were most successfully adapted as TV miniseries. This manner of tackling the author's stories had been pioneered in 1979, when CBS screened Tobe Hooper's two-part adaptation of the author's vampire novel *'Salems Lot*. In 1990, *Halloween III* director Tommy Lee Wallace also split one of writer's books in two for the ABC miniseries *It*, starring Tim Curry as the clown-monster Pennywise.

In 1994, the King miniseries floodgates opened with the post-apocalypse tale *The Stand*, whose four episodes aired on ABC in May of that year. The series, about a flu epidemic which wipes out nearly all of humanity, was directed by Mick Garris from a screenplay by the author himself. "King was excited about what at the time was being called 'novels for television,'" says Garris. "To be able to adapt an entire novel to television, rather than a two-hour version of, in this case, a 900-page novel." Garris admits to being nervous about making *The Stand*, a project with an epic scope, a $28 million budget, and a cast led by Gary Sinise and Broadway legend Ruby Dee. "For me, my big pic was *Critters 2*," he says. "[On *The Stand*] we shot in six states, it was 100 shooting days, we had 126 speaking parts. Literally, I was away from home for one year making it."

The makeup effects for *The Stand* miniseries were overseen by Steve Johnson, a longtime King reader. "*The Stand* was my favorite book that Stephen King had ever written and he spent a lot on set," says Johnson. "We had to make all the disease makeups, we made tons of dead bodies, we did the old age makeup on Ruby Dee. It was really a dream come true to stand next to Stephen King and he's looking at shit I made that he came up with in his head." *The Stand* was a ratings hit and Johnson would be further rewarded for his efforts with an Emmy.

Johnson won another Emmy for ABC's 1997 miniseries version of King's haunted hotel novel *The Shining*. The show was again directed by Garris from a script by King more faithful to his book than Stanley Kubrick's film. Garris recalls, "When *The Stand* was so successful, ABC asked Steve what he wanted to do, and he said, 'I'd like to do the real *Shining*.'" Garris would adapt more of King's tales for the small screen with 2006's

Desperation and 2011's Pierce Brosnan-starring *Bag of Bones.* "For a while, I wasn't just a horror director, I was a Stephen King horror director," says Garris. "There are a *lot* of worse things than to be a Stephen King director, and I loved it."

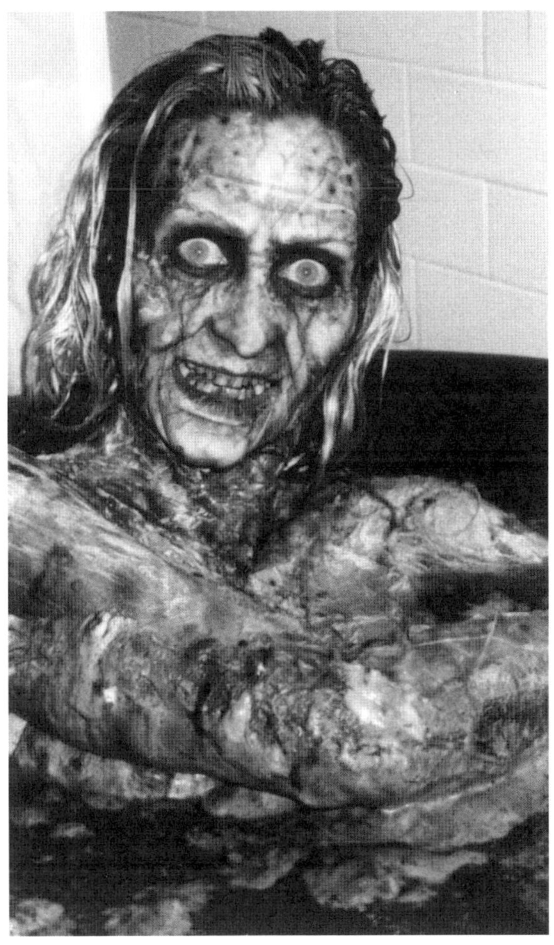

Behind-the-scenes shot of Cynthia Garris in makeup as '217 Woman' in *The Shining* miniseries (1997).

Filmmaker Lawrence Kasdan, whose many credits included directing *The Big Chill* and writing *Raiders of the Lost Ark*, tried to revive King's horror brand on the big screen by adapting his 2001 novel *Dreamcatcher.* The author had written the book not long after he was run over by a truck and was still heavily medicated. The story followed four friends who encounter an alien virus that infects victims and causes 'shit weasels' to erupt from their rectums. *Dreamcatcher* was produced by Castle Rock, which again employed William Goldman to write the screenplay. The reputations of Kasdan and Goldman, together with the project's hefty budget, attracted a quality cast that included Morgan Freeman, Damian Lewis, Donnie Wahlberg, Jason Lee, Timothy Olyphant, and *Deep Blue Sea* star Thomas Jane.

Raised in Washington, D.C., Jane had begun an enduring love affair with the horror genre as a preteen when his parents took him and his younger sister to see *Alien.* "My folks didn't have money for a babysitter, it was cheaper to just haul us along to the movies," he says. "*Alien*, we saw it on opening weekend, downtown D.C., at one of those grand movie houses. The whole audience lost their minds. The chestburster scene happened, and my mother threw her Coke over her shoulder, and it went all over the woman behind her, and I remember that lady didn't get up to clean herself off. She was riveted to the screen and watched the rest of the film soaking wet in Coca-Cola."

Jane landed supporting roles in 1996's *The Crow: City of Angels* and 1997's *Boogie Nights*, graduating to lead status with *Deep Blue Sea*. Director Renny Harlin's movie featured genetically enhanced mako sharks threatening the inhabitants of an underwater scientific facility. While the film was a hit, grossing $73 million in the US during the busy summer of 1999, Jane has mixed feelings about the movie. "I took it because they were going to pay me some money and I was tired of being poor," he says. "I'd been eating out of trash cans and sleeping on sidewalks. The shooting of the film was tough, because you were soaking wet for five months. It gave me a rash that I still have to put Cortisone on today."

Even though the actor was a King reader, he was reluctant to sign on for Kasdan's *Dreamcatcher*. "Stephen King wrote it after his accident, and he was on a lot of pain pills," he says. "There's brilliant stuff in there, [but] I didn't understand the script, nobody did." Jane recalls that he "turned that movie down a few times, but they kept bumping up the money until I was like, 'I'll do the damn movie.'"

Jane's fears about the project were confirmed at a cast reading of the *Dreamcatcher* screenplay. "After we got finished, Morgan Freeman said, 'What the hell was that?!'" the actor remembers. "We all laughed, because we couldn't make head or tails of it." Freeman added to the shoot's surreal nature by wearing outsized fake eyebrows for his performance as an army colonel. "We all made fun of Morgan Freeman," says Jane. "Even Morgan Freeman made fun of his eyebrows. You know, 'Don't let those things escape!' 'We've lost another eyebrow, be on the lookout!'"

Steve Johnson's company Edge FX was responsible for the film's practical effects. One sequence in the movie involved Damian Lewis' character, who has been possessed by an alien, attempting to throw an infected dog into the local water supply. Edge FX constructed a mechanical German Shepherd that appeared to have extraterrestrials squirming in its stomach. "It was the most ridiculously detailed, perfect, animatronic German Shepherd ever," says Johnson. "It was, like, $150,000, maybe more, this thing cost. My most extreme memory of that film is that the dog blew up while it was cabled to Damian. What happened was, ice crystals formed on the electronics. So we cable it all onto Damian, switch on the electronics, the motors heat up, the ice crystals melt—fry, pop, sizzle!—the next thing you know, it explodes while it's cabled to Damian. [The] $150,000 dog puppet, on fire, blowing up on our lead actor." Johnson recalls that the fire was extinguished with "five gallons of Arrowhead water, [we] doused the guy. Then we unhooked him and had to fix it. I think we lost one function, maybe the eyes didn't blink, but you'd never know in the movie. You *would* know if we had killed Damian Lewis, but we didn't."

Released in March 2003, Kasdan's movie was mauled by critics. "*Dreamcatcher* begins as the intriguing story of friends who share a telepathic gift, and ends as a monster movie of stunning awfulness," wrote Roger Ebert. Kasdan's film earned $33 million in the US, less than half of its reported cost.

The next major Stephen King adaptation was 2004's Johnny Depp-starring horror-thriller *Secret Window*. Written and directed by *Stir of Echoes* filmmaker David Koepp, the movie was based on a novella called *Secret Window, Secret Garden*. Published in the 1990 collection *Four Past Midnight*, King's tale concerned a recently divorced novelist, Morton Rainey, who is living

Damian Lewis in *Dreamcatcher* (2003).

alone at a vacation home and trying to overcome a case of writer's block. The author is accused of plagiarism by a stranger named John Shooter, who turns out to be dangerous and also (as Rainey and the reader ultimately discover) a product of the writer's dissociative identity disorder. Koepp was a fan of King and, like so many of his peers, an admirer of Richard Matheson's *I Am Legend.* The writer-director regarded adapting *Secret Window, Secret Garden* as a way to tell his version of Matheson's 'man alone' tale.

Depp was a freshly minted Hollywood superstar following his performance as Captain Jack Sparrow in Gore Verbinski's 2003 blockbuster *Pirates of the Caribbean: The Curse of the Black Pearl,* the director's follow-up to *The Ring. Secret Window* was backed by Sony's Columbia Pictures, which, hoping to attract Depp's teenage fans to the film, insisted that Koepp's movie have a PG-13 rating.

The production was a lavish venture, with a 65-day shoot, which mostly took place in Montreal (doubling for upstate New York), and a supporting cast of John Turturro, Maria Bello, Charles S. Dutton, and Timothy Hutton. Still, many reviewers reacted to the film with a shrug. *Secret Window* was released in March 2004 and grossed $92 million around the world, enough to make the movie a success, but a modest one given its reported $40 million budget.

Koepp's film had a far more extensive theatrical run than the Mick Garris-directed *Riding the Bullet,* which was based on another King novella. The movie starred Jonathan Jackson as an artist hitching home to visit his stroke-stricken mother. Jackson's character is picked up by David Arquette's ghostly antagonist, who asks him to choose between his own survival and that of his relative. The writer-director adapted the tale in part to cathartically deal with tragedies in his own family, including the death of his brother Craig. "I had lost a mother and a brother way before their time, particularly my brother, who was only 39," says Garris. "It's easy to read the story as just a ghost story, but it resonated with me." The film received a limited release in October 2004. "It opened in three cities, and nobody went, and it was really tough," he says. "When you lay your soul open to an audience and it doesn't reach them, it's heartbreaking."

The King story "1408" had originally been released as part of the 1999 audiobook collection *Blood and Smoke.* It detailed the travails of Mike Enslin, an author of books about haunted places whose skepticism is swept away during an overnight stay at a New York hotel called The Dolphin. The rights to the tale were acquired by Warner Bros. executive-turned-producer Lorenzo di Bonaventura, who set Eli Roth to write the screenplay after *Cabin Fever* premiered at the Toronto Film Festival. "That story was so scary," Roth remembers. "I had ways to make it like *Barton Fink* and *Eraserhead*, going inside the walls of the hotel. [But] I never cracked the script in a way that everyone said, 'This is great.'"

In November 2003, *Variety* reported that Dimension had boarded the project with *Halloween H20* co-writer Matt Greenberg hired to come up with the screenplay. *Ed Wood* writers Scott Alexander and Larry Karaszewski later reworked the script for the project, which was directed by Danish filmmaker Mikael Håfström. John Cusack played Mike Enslin and Samuel L. Jackson portrayed Gerald Olin, the manager of The Dolphin Hotel—on the suggestion of Quentin Tarantino.

When *1408* arrived on US cinema screens in June 2007, the horror genre seemed to be falling in popularity for the first time since 1996. The craze for remaking Japanese films had exhausted itself, and the grosses of *The Hills Have Eyes 2*, *Grindhouse*, and *Hostel: Part II*—which came out just two weeks before *1408*—indicated that audiences were losing interest in more extreme material. In mid-June, *Variety* ran a report from the Los Angeles

John Cusack in *1408* (2007).

premiere of *1408*. Writer Bill Higgins began the article by informing readers that it had been a "scary summer for horror movies" and quoted Bob Weinstein about Dimension's limited exposure on the project: "It cost $25 million. Anything over $30 million and we make a profit." *1408* would generate profits aplenty, grossing $71 million at the domestic box office and $132 million in all.

The success of *1408* was particularly pleasing for Weinstein given that his company would be releasing a second King adaptation several months later. In October 2006, *Variety* informed readers that Dimension had signed on to produce Darabont's adaptation of *The Mist*. To play the lead role of David Drayton, the director chose *Dreamcatcher* star Thomas Jane. The actor was familiar with King's novella and was surprised to read Darabont's new conclusion. "I was like, 'This is not the ending of the book, but it's brilliant,'" says Jane. He also saw in the project an opportunity to make up for *Dreamcatcher*. "It was a nice way to redeem myself in the Stephen King world," he says. Darabont picked Marcia Gay Harden to play Mrs. Carmo-

(*Far left*) Laurie Holden and (*right foreground*) Thomas Jane and Nathan Gamble in *The Mist* (2007).

dy, who ultimately calls for a human sacrifice to be made in an attempt to satisfy her deity. The film's supporting cast included Jeffrey DeMunn, William Sadler, and *Silent Hill* actress Laurie Holden.

Bob Weinstein was less thrilled than Jane with Darabont's rewriting of King's story. "He said, 'We will give you double the budget if you don't do that horrible ending,'" recalls the actor. "But myself, and Frank, and all of the people that Frank had brought on board, we all said, 'No, you can't change the ending.' So we took half the money to make the film."

Darabont tapped KNB's Greg Nicotero to oversee the film's practical effects. "Frank Darabont is one of my best friends on the planet, we worked together on *The Green Mile* and *The Majestic*," says Nicotero. "I remember reading the script, and I think my son was the same age as the boy in the movie, and when it got to the end, I threw the script across the room. It was so gut-wrenching."

Visual FX company CafeFX created the computer-generated versions of the monsters that audiences would see on the screen. Nicotero had long embraced the notion that visual effects could work in harmony with the makeups and prosthetics produced by KNB. "In the mid-'90s, when visual effects was starting to find its footing, there were a lot of people that were like, 'That's bullshit, we're just going to double down on doing everything practically,'" he says. "It's like, 'Well, it's not really about what *you* want, it's about what the director wants.'" Nicotero's collaborative attitude was tested on *The Mist*, as KNB created physical models of several monsters with which cast members could interact, even though he was aware that the versions seen in the finished film would be computer-generated. "We knew that a lot of the creature stuff that we spent a tremendous amount of time designing and building—the tentacles, and the flying creatures, and the spiders, all that stuff—was ultimately being used as reference for visual effects," he says. "It's always heartbreaking, because you want your work to be onscreen and it's important. With that movie, it was like, 'Man, no one's ever going to see any of this cool shit that we're making!'"

Darabont decided to adopt a rough and ready style of filmmaking, one influenced by *28 Days Later*. To prepare for the production, the filmmaker directed an episode of the TV show *The Shield* and then hired the show's cinematographer Rohn Schmidt and two of the series' camera operators to work on the movie, which was shot in Shreveport, Louisiana. As someone who had enjoyed Darabont's earlier, more visually composed films, Thomas

Behind-the-scenes shot of KNB-created creature from *The Mist.*

Jane was initially unsure about the director's approach. "I love Frank's work, because his shot designs were so meticulous, right?" explains the actor. "But Frank said, 'I'm not going to do that on this one.' *The Mist* had a little bit of a handheld feeling to it. I was like, 'I don't get that style of shooting.' Frank's like, 'This is how we're doing it.'"

In the film's final shot, the camera moves up from Jane's kneeling, grief-stricken protagonist to show a seemingly endless line of military vehicles arriving to save the day. The actor describes filming the moment as "tough for me, because it was pretty emotional. It was also a huge day, because we had all these military trucks and jeeps coming out of the mist. And then I had to do this emotional reveal where the guy realizes, 'Oh my God, I've just killed my kid, if I had just waited…' I remember going off into the woods and sitting by myself to get ready for that."

Bob Weinstein planned to release the film in the US over 2007's Thanksgiving weekend. Darabont believed people would not want to see a bleak tale of Lovecraftian terror after finishing their turkey dinners, but the director was overruled by the Dimension chief. The filmmaker's fears were justified when *The Mist* placed eighth at the box office over its first week on release and went on to earn just $25 million domestically. "It's the worst possible day of the year to release a film about a family that ends up killing themselves at the end of the movie," says Jane. "You don't need to be a rocket scientist to figure that one out."

The Mist was appreciated by horror connoisseurs, though. In December 2009, Bloody Disgusting ranked Darabont's film as the fourth best horror film of the decade behind *The Descent*, *Shaun of the Dead*, and—at number one—Swedish director Tomas Alfredson's 2008 vampire tale *Let the Right One In*. "It's one of those movies that people really had a reaction to, because of how bleak it was," says Nicotero of *The Mist*. "Now, when people go back and look at it, they have much more appreciation for it."

King himself publicly expressed his own pleasure with both *The Mist* and the way his brand of horror was returning the big screen at a press conference promoting the film. "I think it's good to see my movies back again, too," he said. "They were in rehab for a while, but they're better now."

After finishing work on *Mission: Impossible III*, director J. J. Abrams embarked on an international publicity tour for the film, which led him to Japan in the summer of 2006. During his visit, Abrams went to a toy shop with his eight-year-old son Henry and was fascinated by the abundance of Godzilla toys. The filmmaker began to think about the possibility of an American version of the iconic creature and how it would threaten, and be viewed by, people at street level in the US. This approach was not so different from the one taken by Steven Spielberg on *War of the Worlds*, except that Abrams planned on making his tale of devastation—ultimately named *Cloverfield*—a found footage film, with the action presented as having been captured via a camcorder.

The director-producer approached Drew Goddard, a writer on Abrams' TV shows *Alias* and *Lost*, to help develop the project. The pair put together a five-page treatment detailing the movie's first act, which Goddard turned into a 58-page outline. Abrams pitched the film to Paramount as "a Cameron Crowe movie meets *Godzilla* meets *Blair Witch Project*," and the studio greenlit the film.

To direct the movie, Abrams reached out to Matt Reeves, a seemingly odd choice. Reeves had not made a movie since his directorial debut, 1996's *The Pallbearer*, a commercially unsuccessful romantic comedy starring Gwyneth Paltrow and David Schwimmer. Abrams' confidence in Reeves' abilities came from having known him since they were both teenagers. "So many horror movies we see today are sort of torture porn, ultra-hyperviolent, but there's nothing about them you can relate to," Abrams was quoted as saying in the *Cloverfield* production notes. "I knew that Matt would make us feel for the characters."

Abrams had grown up in Los Angeles, where his father worked as a film producer specializing in made-for-TV movies. Abrams loved fantasy, science fiction, and horror, as evidenced by his fondness for Don Coscarelli's *Phantasm*. Speaking with *Fangoria* to promote the 2001 horror-thriller *Joy Ride*, which he co-wrote, Abrams would recall, "I grew up during that classic late '70s/early '80s horror movies phase, where it was everything from the pure terror of *The Texas Chain Saw Massacre* and the freaky sci-fi of *Scanners* to ridiculous films like *The Beast Within* and *Slumber Party Massacre*."

Abrams started making his own short films with a Eumig sound camera given to him by his grandfather. He wrote fan letters to makeup artists like Rick Baker, Tom Savini, and Dick Smith, who sent him a fake tongue he had used on *The Exorcist*. Abrams became friends with Reeves, another aspiring filmmaker, when they were both just 15 years old.

Abrams attended Sarah Lawrence College and then embarked on a screenwriting career, selling the script for what would become the 1991 Harrison Ford drama *Regarding Henry* and co-writing Michael Bay's *Armageddon*. Reeves studied at USC and co-wrote a spec script that was optioned by Warner Bros. and turned into 1995's Steven Seagal sequel *Under Siege 2: Dark Territory*.

After Abrams directed *Mission: Impossible III*, he signed a first-look deal with Paramount. The initial project announced under the pact was an Abrams-directed reboot of the *Star Trek* franchise. The deal also called for Abrams' company Bad Robot to produce movies with a budget under $25 million. His New York-set monster tale was the first of those to be greenlit.

Abrams hired a designer named Neville Page to create the look of the film's monster. Page had spent much of his early career working in the field of medical products, and had recently broken into the film industry thanks to James Cameron, who liked his portfolio and hired him to create creatures for *Avatar*. The designer was coming to the end of his toils on Cameron's movie when he first met with Abrams. Page recalls that the producer's brief "was very simple. 'I want Godzilla in America—but obviously not Godzilla.'"

Page began to experiment with different designs for this Godzilla-but-not-Godzilla. "J. J. allowed such a broad exploration period," he says. "I was designing giant snake-serpents, flying creatures—flying was a big part of it initially—lizard-like things, humanoid-like things." Page felt that he needed to come up with a motivation for the outsized monster. "If I have an attribute that's beneficial to film, that's different to others, it's my industrial design background of thinking through things as thoroughly as possible," he says. "When somebody says, 'I want big teeth and scary as fuck!', it's like, 'That's going to happen, but we need to understand where it comes from, what it eats, what its motivations are.'" Page and his collaborators settled on the idea that the creature was a baby, terrified by its surroundings. "I thought, Cloverfield is a newborn, and it is scared," says the designer. "I'm from the UK, and my mum and dad were in the circus. My dad told me these stories of when the elephants would get scared and the things they would do. I thought, why not have Cloverfield be like that?"

Page, working with assistant creature designer Tully Summers, was also responsible for the design of the dog-sized parasites that pour off the monster and further menace the film's human protagonists. "The problem with Cloverfield, that J. J. pointed out, was that, because he wanted it to be kaiju-scale, there was nothing terrifying on the ground. Someone said it would be great if there were these smaller creatures on the ground, terrorizing. I started thinking of mites. You know how maggots live in pork, and they don't come out until you let it sit on the counter? It's the same kind of thing. These things are living off sloughing skin. As this flesh is coming off the Cloverfield, and the food source is now on the ground, all these parasitic creatures are running around, and the food source is gone, and so now humans are left."

The visual effects company Double Negative oversaw the images of New York architecture being destroyed, while Tippett Studio was responsible for bringing Page's creature to computer-generated life. "When I heard Phil Tippett was involved, I was just so excited," says the designer. "These are the celebrities that get me all giddy."

Abrams was determined to keep the nature of the film a secret for as long as possible. His agent suggested that they refer to the then-untitled project as 'Cloverfield'—the name of a street near the Bad Robot office in Los Angeles—to throw people off the scent. Many people first became aware of the movie when they saw a mysterious teaser trailer for the film, which screened before Michael Bay's Paramount-backed 2007 summer blockbuster *Transformers*. The clip mostly featured material set at a goodbye party for Michael Stahl-David's character Rob, with attendees witnessing an explosion in another part of the city. The partygoers flee down to the street and see the head of the Statue of Liberty crash to the ground in front of them. The end of the trailer informed viewers that the movie was produced by J. J. Abrams, but the clip revealed little else about the film, not even the movie's title.

The trailer became a viral sensation, with internet users positing theories about the film's plot. Neville Page was astonished by the reaction the footage provoked. "Friends were calling up to say, 'This is the film you were working on with that J. J. Abrams guy? This is amazing!'" says the designer. "I realized I was part of something special."

Cloverfield opened in the US on January 18, 2008, and earned $46 million over the Martin Luther King Day weekend. "*Cloverfield* devours box office" announced a headline in *Variety*. The article itself explained that the mid-budget film could claim to have Paramount's tenth best opening of all time. The movie would stomp its way to a worldwide box office gross of $172 million.

"BECAUSE YOU WERE HOME."

Much like the films M. Night Shyamalan wrote and directed following 1999's *The Sixth Sense*, his career featured plenty of twists and turns in the decade after that movie's release. First, Shyamalan reteamed with Bruce Willis for 2000's *Unbreakable*, a somber superhero tale co-starring Willis' fellow *Pulp Fiction* cast member Samuel L. Jackson. The film was a hit but earned less money than *The Sixth Sense* and was regarded as something of a disappointment compared with the director's breakthrough movie.

For his subsequent release, Shyamalan was determined to make more of an obvious crowd-pleaser. He came up with the idea for a science fiction-horror film called *Signs*, an alien invasion movie which took inspiration from *Night of the Living Dead* in its depiction of a family dealing with a potentially apocalyptic scenario at a remote farm. Shyamalan cast Mel Gibson to play the film's lead character of Graham Hess, a former priest who lost his faith following the death of his wife in a car crash. Rory Culkin and Abigail Breslin portrayed Hess' young children and Joaquin Phoenix his brother.

Shyamalan started shooting *Signs* in Pennsylvania just a few days after the events of 9/11. "I think part of the spirituality of the movie came from its time, where we were at that moment," the director would recall to The Ringer in 2020. Released in the summer of 2002, *Signs* was a blockbuster, earning $408 million worldwide.

Shyamalan stayed close to the horror genre for his next film, *The Village*, which starred Phoenix, William Hurt, and Bryce Dallas Howard. The movie appeared to be a period drama about a remote 19th-century hamlet surrounded by creature-filled woods. Viewers would discover that the movie actually takes place in the present day and the monsters are a fiction invented by the village's founders. The film's creature suit was fabricated at short notice by Edge FX founder Steve Johnson and his collaborators. "My best memory is, I instigated a snowball fight and from, like, fifty yards, I knocked Bill Hurt's wig off his head with an ice ball," he says. "He was

Director M. Night Shyamalan on the set of *Signs* (2002).

not happy." *The Village* was another hit, but a smaller one than *Signs*, with some reviewers arguing that Shyamalan's surprise ending was not such a surprise.

The director had made his last five films for Disney subsidiaries and was keen to continue that relationship with his next project, *Lady in the Water*, a fantasy about a water nymph who visits a Philadelphia apartment complex. Disney executive Nina Jacobson had doubts about numerous aspects of the planned production, including Shyamalan's desire to cast himself in a major supporting role.

The director responded to Jacobson's coolness by making the film at Warner Bros., which agreed to stump up the $70 million budget. Film critics were dumbfounded by the result. *Guardian* critic Peter Bradshaw mused, "Perhaps Shyamalan wanted to be a 21st-century George A. Romero. Instead, I'm afraid he is turning into Ed Wood Jr." *Lady in the Water* was released in the US on July 21, 2006, and earned just $42 million at the domestic box office.

Shyamalan returned to horror basics. The writer-director developed a screenplay he titled *The Green Effect*, in which people commit suicide as the result of a toxin released by plants. In March 2007, *Variety* reported that Fox had picked up the director's spec script, now retitled *The Happening.* The film would have a budget of around $57 million.

Shyamalan planned for *The Happening* to be his first R-rated movie, a decision partly inspired by Guillermo del Toro's *Pan's Labyrinth.* "One of the movies that I was thinking of was *Pan's Labyrinth*, which has some visceral moments of violence juxtaposed against the kind of softer things," he told Movieweb. Shyamalan cast Mark Wahlberg as a science teacher, Zooey Deschanel as his wife, and *Land of the Dead* actor John Leguizamo as a colleague of Wahlberg's character.

Critics were overwhelmingly negative in their assessments of the 2008 film. The A.V. Club writer Nathan Rabin concluded his review by arguing that the gulf between Shyamalan's "lofty ambitions and feeble accomplishments has seldom been wider or more chuckle-inducing." *The Happening* was more popular in terms of ticket sales than *Lady in the Water*, winding up with a global gross of $163 million, but the movie swiftly became a pop culture punchline. Wahlberg himself would trash the film at a press conference to promote his 2010 movie *The Fighter*, in which he starred alongside Christian Bale and Amy Adams. Wahlberg claimed that Adams had been up for Deschanel's part in *The Happening* and said that she had "dodged the bullet" by not doing it. "Fucking trees, man," the actor continued, referencing the plot of *The Happening.* "The plants. Fuck it… At least I wasn't playing a cop or a crook."

Shyamalan followed *The Happening* with *The Last Airbender*, a live-action adaptation of the animated TV show *Avatar: The Last Airbender*, which cost $145 million. Released by Paramount in July 2010, the movie lost its opening weekend to *The Twilight Saga: Eclipse.* The film earned $319 million around the world but was once again excoriated by critics. In his review for the *Chicago Sun-Times*, Roger Ebert described the movie as "an agonizing experience in every category I can think of and others still waiting to be invented."

Further proof that Shyamalan had become a laughing stock to cinemagoers came the same month as the release of *The Last Airbender*, when Universal unveiled the trailer for the studio's horror film *Devil.* A supernatural tale set almost entirely in an elevator, the movie was directed by *Quarantine* filmmaker John Erick Dowdle from a screenplay by *Hard Candy* writer Brian Nelson. The name in the trailer that caught the attention of audiences, though, was that of Shyamalan, who had originated the film's story. In an IndieWire article headlined "*Devil* Trailer Gets Laughs" writer Matt Dentler reported that the appearance of Shyamalan's name onscreen

prompted outright laughter at a packed screening of Christopher Nolan's *Inception* in New York City's Union Square. "After the disgrace of his last few films, most recently *The Last Airbender*, Shyamalan's name is a joke to movie goers," Dentler wrote.

Stephen King gave his assessment of *The Happening* in a column for *Entertainment Weekly* titled "Why Hollywood can't do horror." In the article, the author argued that large budgets were unnecessary to generate scares on the big screen and might actually be counter-productive in the creation of cinematic scares.

King still recommended *The Happening*, despite the film's hefty budget. But he also urged readers to check out another recent release, called *The Strangers*, as an example of a film that did not rely on expensive production values to create moments of true terror. "Horror is the scene in *The Strangers* where Liv Tyler tries to hide beneath the bed… and discovers she can't fit there," he wrote.

King was so enamored with *The Strangers* that he ended his column with another shout-out to the film, which he compared favorably to the upcoming, and much more expensive, *The X-Files: I Want to Believe*. "I can't imagine that anything in *X-Files* will match Liv Tyler's exchange with one of the masked home invaders in one particularly terrifying scene of *The Strangers*," King wrote. "'Why are you doing this to us?' she whispers. To which the woman in the doll-face mask responds, in a dead and affectless voice: 'Because you were home.' In the end, that's all the explanation a good horror film needs."

The movie that had so chilled King's spine was written and—against all the odds—directed by Bryan Bertino. Bertino studied cinematography at the University of Texas film school in Austin and then moved to Los Angeles, where he started working as a gaffer (the film industry's term for an electrician) on low-budget movies and commercials. He also began writing scripts, including the screenplay for *The Strangers*. His story was about a couple, Kristen and James, who stay at the house of James' father after attending a wedding. In the course of the night, the home is invaded by three mask-wearing strangers—identified as Pin-Up Girl, Dollface, and Man in Mask by the finished film's credits—who torment and attempt to kill the pair. The screenplay was notable for the care Bertino took developing the relationship between his two lead characters and the motiveless nature of their assailants' attack.

A masked Gemma Ward and Liv Tyler in *The Strangers* (2008).

In 2004, Bertino submitted his script for a Nicholls Fellowship grant, which the Academy of Motion Picture Arts and Sciences awards to unproduced writers. After reaching the quarterfinals, the script was read by a talent manager, who signed Bertino and set him up with a meeting at Roy Lee's Vertigo Entertainment. "I thought it was amazing," says Lee. "It was a scary-on-the-page script. We were able to get multiple studios wanting to make it."

In November 2004, *The Hollywood Reporter* revealed that Universal had bought the script. *The Strangers* screenplay was developed by filmmaker Mark Romanek, who had directed 2002's Robin Williams thriller *One Hour Photo*. "There were several directors attached," explains Lee. "It was Justin Lin and then, after he dropped off, it was Mark Romanek. He wanted a much higher budget than the studio was willing to [give him]." Bertino, meanwhile, went to work as a writer for producer Jerry Bruckheimer.

The Strangers eventually came under the umbrella of the Universal subsidiary Rogue, whose co-president Andrew Rona requested a meeting with Bertino. Once the sit-down was over, Rona called Bertino's agents to ask if he would be interested in directing *The Strangers* himself. "When he first wrote the script, I don't think he intended on directing it," says Lee. "The studio executive enjoyed meeting Bryan and just suggested him directing the movie. I remember it was a big shock to him. I know he went and got all these books on how to direct movies."

Bertino cast Liv Tyler and *Underworld* star Scott Speedman as Kristen and James. To play the titular killers, he chose Laura Margolis as Pin-Up Girl, Kip Weeks as Man in Mask, and Australian model Gemma Ward as Dollface. Bertino shot the film in South Carolina for a budget of around $9 million. Rogue released *The Strangers* on May 30, 2008, counter-programming the director's debut against the first *Sex and the City* movie. Bertino's film exceeded industry expectations, earning almost $21 million in the US over its initial weekend and winding up with a domestic total of $52 million.

A year after the commercial disappointments of *Grindhouse* and *Hostel: Part II* had prompted hand-wringing about the health of horror, the genre was now being hailed as a box office savior. At the end of June, *Variety* writer Pamela McClintock noted that *The Strangers* and *The Happening* were "helping to fuel a surge at the 2008 domestic box office that virtually no one expected."

Lionsgate's reputation as a friend to the horror genre was dented in the summer of 2008 thanks to the company's unenthusiastic distribution of

The Midnight Meat Train. Directed with brutal bravura by Japanese filmmaker Ryuhei Kitamura, the movie starred a pre-*The Hangover* Bradley Cooper as a photographer who discovers that a murderer played by Vinnie Jones is using the subway system of an unnamed city as his killing zone. The cast also included Sam Raimi's brother Ted, whose character's eyeballs literally shoot out of his head after Jones' character bludgeons the back of his skull with a giant meat-tenderizing mallet. Still, the most notable name attached to the project, at least as far as horror fans were concerned, was Clive Barker, who had written the short story on which the movie was based and produced the film.

The Midnight Meat Train was hyped-up by *Fangoria*, which featured a grimacing Jones on the magazine's cover ahead of the film's planned release. Inside the publication, journalist Ryan Turek teased the gruesome nature of the movie by repeating a story he had been told of how 50 gallons of fake blood were used during a single day's shooting.

Barker was another horror auteur who had endured his fair share of battles with Hollywood studios and had retreated from directing after 1995's Scott Bakula-starring *Lord of Illusions*. But the *Hellraiser* director spoke enthusiastically to Turek about the project and Kitamura's vision. "Christ, he knows how to make movies," said Barker. "The action, the bloody sequences—the way it's choreographed is exceptional, amazing, and brutal."

Despite the movie's pedigree, Lionsgate announced in March 2008 that it was pushing *The Midnight Meat Train* from the film's scheduled May release date. Then, in June, the horror website Shock Till You Drop reported that Lionsgate would only be releasing the movie in 100 cinemas. Barker was irked by this treatment of the film, as he revealed to horror blogger Tom Blunt that month. "The movie is fucking great, and it's not right to stop horror fans who've been looking forward to seeing the picture and seeing it on the big screen," he said.

The Midnight Meat Train was another project championed by Peter Block, but the executive was no longer working at Lionsgate when the film was released. In September 2007, the company had bought Mandate Pictures, whose president, Joe Drake, took over as Lionsgate's co-chief operating officer of the motion picture group. Two months later, *Variety* reported that Block was "ankling his post." "As Lionsgate became bigger, it really became more about non-decision by committee rather than decision by enthusiasm," says Block, explaining why he left the company.

On June 18, 2008, Deadline founder Nikki Finke posted an article suggesting that Lionsgate's revised release plans for *The Midnight Meat Train* had been prompted by a desire not to have Block's name associated with a hit following his departure. "I give TV and movie fans a lot of credit: when they get mad, they scare the crap out of the moguls," Finke wrote. "That's happening at Lionsgate, where the studio's phones and email accounts are jammed with angry fans for the past week. They're making a stink because new Lionsgate topper Joe Drake appears to be dumping all of ex-prez Peter Block's movies. That includes *Midnight Meat Train*, the adaptation of the Barker short story that's a fan fave. Supposedly the trailer tested higher than any film in Lionsgate history. But when Drake took over, he promptly bumped *Midnight Meat Train* from its May 16th release date."

On the day *The Midnight Meat Train* came out at the start of August, Bloody Disgusting founder Brad Miska published an open letter on his website. Miska complained about the film having been "dumped in $1 discount theaters, with no theater listing provided, with no explanation on how to even buy tickets." Miska included a list of cinemas playing the film and urged readers to support the movie, to little avail. Over its opening weekend, *The Midnight Meat Train* grossed a paltry $34,394 at the domestic box office.

In an interview posted by MTV.com following the film's release, Clive Barker insisted that Kitamura "made a fucking great movie, and the politics that are being visited upon it have nothing to do with the movie at all. This is all about ego, and though I mourn the fact that *Midnight Meat Train* was never given its chance in theaters, it's a beautifully stylish, scary movie, and it isn't going anywhere. People will find it, and whether they find it in midnight shows or they find it on DVD, they'll find it, and in the end the Joe Drakes of the world will disappear."

Unsurprisingly, Lionsgate did give a wide release later in the year to *Saw V*, which was directed by David Hackl and opened in over 3,000 cinemas on October 24. The film was kept off the top of the box office chart by a very different sequel, *High School Musical 3: Senior Year*, and the movie's ultimate domestic box office take of $56 million made *Saw V* the least successful entry since Wan's original film. But the franchise continued to be profitable for Lionsgate, with *Saw V* earning a worldwide total of $113 million, around ten times its budget.

While Lionsgate would continue to distribute the *Saw* films, its treatment of *The Midnight Meat Train* confirmed that the company's interest in releasing other movies in a similarly violent and extreme vein was at an end. "Peter Block was the one who gave James Wan his break and produced all the *Saw* movies, so he had that mindset," says *Dracula 2000* director Patrick Lussier. "The new people that were coming in, Joe Drake and his team, were very much not fans of those films."

Still, Lussier would help Lionsgate score another horror hit in early 2009 with *My Bloody Valentine 3D*, a remake of the 1981 slasher film. The original movie had been directed by George Mihalka and depicted a string of killings supposedly being carried out by a miner named Harry Warden in a Canadian town. Executive Block had developed the film before his departure and recalls that his colleagues were keen on the project for two reasons. "One, this was pre-existing IP," he says. "Two, there was the industry's love affair with 3D—which did not reflect my own feelings with 3D—and the movie was crafted to take advantage of that."

Lussier worked with *Jason X* writer Todd Farmer to remodel the remake's screenplay. "The script had already been commissioned [and] was so brutal," says Lussier. "In the first version, the sheriff had kept the real Harry Warden locked in his basement for ten years and was torturing him. Once they told us it was in 3D, we were like, 'Okay, this movie should be fun. I do not want to make a movie like *Hostel*'—that's not saying anything against it—'don't want to make a movie like *Saw*, don't want to make something that's just torture for the sake of it.' I kept saying to Lionsgate, *Scream* is an homage to this era of slasher movies—you know, *Prom Night*, *My Bloody Valentine*, *Happy Birthday to Me*. All those films are murder-mysteries,

Megan Boone in *My Bloody Valentine 3D* (2009).

they're all sort of Agatha Christie-esque. I said, 'What we need to do with *Valentine* is really make it a mystery.'"

Lussier cast *Supernatural* star Jensen Ackles, *Sin City* actor Jaime King, and Kerr Smith from *Final Destination*, as well as horror veteran Tom Atkins. The director shot the movie almost entirely on location in Pennsylvania. "We dragged these cameras the size of refrigerators up the side of hills, we dragged them underground," says Lussier. "We made some cool-looking 3D in a horror movie that had lots of blood and gore but didn't take itself so seriously that you were sick to your stomach."

Lionsgate released *My Bloody Valentine 3D* in January 2009. Lussier's movie earned $27 million during its first week on screens and went on to gross $100 million at the global box office. Prior to the release of the film, activist investor Carl Icahn had embarked on a bid to take over Lionsgate. Icahn's corporate machinations followed the release of several 2008 box office failures, including *Punisher: War Zone* and *The Spirit*, which helped push the company's annual loss to $163 million. Lussier claims that the success of his film helped the company to fend off Icahn's attempted takeover. "If that movie hadn't opened to the numbers it did, they would have lost the company," explains the director. "They said, 'The movie saved the company.' Then they started making different kinds of movies."

Following his departure from Lionsgate, Peter Block formed the company A Bigger Boat, through which he planned to produce genre films and television. In 2008, Block partnered with *Hatchet* director Adam Green and his producer Cory Neal to make *Frozen*, about a trio of skiers who are stranded on a chair lift. Green shot the film that winter in Snow Basin, Utah, 10,000 feet above sea level, in often subzero temperatures. Fittingly, *Frozen* premiered at the Sundance Film Festival in January 2010, but was only given a small release by distributors Anchor Bay.

A Bigger Boat's second project was *The Ward*, director John Carpenter's first film since 2001's *Ghosts of Mars*. The '60s-set horror-thriller starred Amber Heard as an arsonist who is sent to a mental health facility. The production was an at times difficult one for Block. "There was an element of John hating having me there and wanting to make sure that I was far away from the creative process," he says. "He found out early that I'm allergic to cigarette smoke, and he's a chain-smoker. They [had] this room really far away with a monitor that said, like, 'Cigarette-free zone,' and that was where I was to sit." But the producer says he perversely enjoyed those occasions when Carpenter was living up to his reputation for crankiness. "He's a hero of mine," says Block. "Even when he was a curmudgeon, I kind of liked it." *The Ward* premiered at the 2010 Toronto Film Festival, where it underwhelmed critics. The movie was given a belated, and limited, release the following year.

Block's company achieved its first hit with the Jennifer Lawrence horror-thriller *House at the End of the Street*. Released in September 2012, the film claimed second place at the box office over its opening weekend (narrowly beaten by the Jake Gyllenhaal cop movie *End of Watch*) and went on to gross $31 million in the US.

Ghost House Pictures founders Sam Raimi and Robert Tapert had followed *The Grudge* with 2005's *Boogeyman* and 2007's Kristen Stewart-starring *The Messengers*, both supernatural tales and both mid-sized hits. The company enjoyed more success with another 2007 release, *30 Days of Night.* Based on a graphic novel, the film tracked the residents of Barrow, Alaska, as they attempt to survive a month-long vampire rampage in the sunless depths of winter. The movie was directed by *Hard Candy* filmmaker David Slade and starred Josh Hartnett as the town sheriff and Melissa George as his estranged fire-marshal wife.

Slade filmed *30 Days of Night* in New Zealand during the second half of 2006. Raimi was directing *Spider-Man 3* and was unable to visit the set. His absence reflected the filmmaker's hands-off approach to the directors he enlisted to make movies for Ghost House. "I give story and casting notes, but then I try and step out of it," Raimi says. "It's really a director's medium. I don't want to get in the way." The filmmaker was also happy not to be joining Slade as he battled the elements. "Oh yeah, that looked really frigid," he says.

Raimi would be much more hands-on with another Ghost House film. Years previously, the director and his brother Ivan had developed a script about a young bank employee who refuses to loan more money to an elderly Romani woman, meaning that she will lose her house. The Romani curses the bank employee, who comes to believe that she will suffer an extremely unpleasant fate unless she transfers the hex to someone else. As Raimi admits, the screenplay paid obvious homage to Jacques Tourneur's 1957 film *Night of the Demon.* "Once you start stealing the plot, then you want to put in elements so people understand that you're paying tribute to him properly," says the director.

Raimi asked *Shaun of the Dead* filmmaker Edgar Wright to direct the movie, which he and his brother titled *Drag Me to Hell.* Speaking to *The Skinny* in 2013, Wright recalled, "He'd written it, and he wanted me to direct it, but I couldn't really accept, (a) because I was doing *Hot Fuzz* and (b) because it was so obvious to me that it should be Sam Raimi directing it that I said, 'No, you've got to do this. If I did it, it would just feel like karaoke.'"

In December 2007, *Variety* reported that Raimi would indeed direct *Drag Me to Hell.* The movie was the filmmaker's first since wrapping his trilogy of Spider-Man blockbusters. "When one has done three very expensive movies, they get used to eating caviar," Tapert was quoted as saying in the article. "Sam will have to ponder what it means to come down from the mountaintop for a moment."

Tapert was having fun at the expense of his friend, but Raimi did have doubts as to whether he could successfully return to the genre. "I was wor-

Director Sam Raimi on the set of *Drag Me to Hell* (2009).

ried that I might have forgotten how to make a horror film," he says. "But I worry all the time about everything: I was worried that people wouldn't like the screenplay, I was worried that I couldn't get good actors because it's a horror picture."

Raimi cast Elliot Page as the film's lead character, Christine, but Page left the project because of a scheduling conflict. The director then approached Alison Lohman, who had established herself as an actress of note with performances in 2002's *White Oleander* and 2003's Ridley Scott-directed *Matchstick Men*. "Sam had asked me to do *The Grudge* years before," says the actress. "It wasn't my cup of tea to do that type of genre and, frankly, I wasn't interested in the character. Then he approached me again for *Drag Me to Hell*. I had told him that I was not interested in horror movies, and he was telling me on the phone that this one was different, there's a real story behind it. I listened to him tell this story, and it just came to life for me. So I said I would do it."

Raimi cast *Jeepers Creepers* star Justin Long as the boyfriend of Lohman's character and stage veteran Lorna Raver as the curse-giving Mrs. Ganush. The finished film would feature a good deal of computer-generated trickery

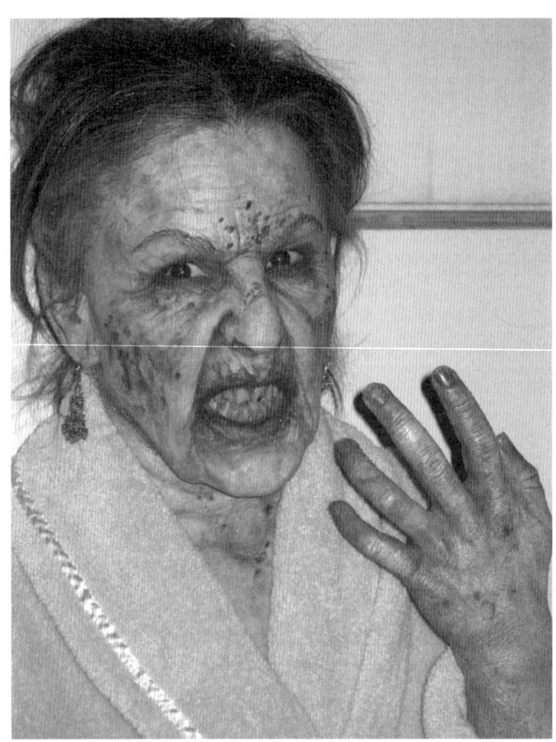

Lorna Raver on the set of *Drag Me to Hell.*

by Tippett Studio, but Raimi was keen to feature prosthetics and practical gags whenever possible and hired KNB to work on the film, too. "*Drag Me to Hell* was a fucking blast," says KNB's Greg Nicotero. "Working with Sam is always a joy; he's such a consummate filmmaker. One of the gags I'm most proud of in that movie is when Christine wakes up and Mrs. Ganush is right over her, and opens her mouth, and vomits [maggots] on her. We did a bunch of tests in the shop, and we cooked different types of pasta in water with food coloring, and one of the girls who worked in the shop was our poor victim, we just blasted her in the face with all this stuff over and over again. I remember showing them to Sam and he couldn't stop laughing. He looked at me and said, 'There's something wrong with you.' I said, 'Sam, this isn't even my idea. This was *your* idea. I'm just the one who's showing you how we'll do it.'"

The Los Angeles shoot was a tough one for Lohman and got harder as the weeks progressed and her character's torments grew. "It became more physical each day," she says. "They tried to film it sequentially, so it really did feel like a ramping up." Having witnessed Raimi physically test Bruce Campbell on *Evil Dead II* and *Army of Darkness*, Nicotero was unsurprised to see the director challenge Lohman in the same way. "When Sam does movies like this, he's torturing the actor," says the makeup effects artist. "He literally tortured Bruce Campbell, especially in *Evil Dead II*. With Bruce, it was different, because they were childhood friends. With Alison, I know for a fact that it was a hard shoot for her."

For Lohman, the most exhausting sequence to shoot featured her character digging up the corpse of Mrs. Ganush during a rainstorm. "Every morning, I had to roll around in mud and they had to hose me down," says the actress. "I truly love Sam, and I don't think he really knew the extent [to which I was suffering]. It was so taxing on me physically. I actually got shingles after this movie. Right after it, I went to the doctor and she was like, 'Whatever you're doing, you need to stop it, because your body is not cooperating.'"

Drag Me to Hell premiered at the Cannes Film Festival in May 2009 and received almost unanimously positive reviews. *Entertainment Weekly* critic Owen Gleiberman enthused to readers, "Raimi has made the most crazy, fun, and terrifying horror movie in years." Universal released *Drag Me to Hell* on May 29, 2009, counter-programming the film against the Pixar film *Up*, which won the weekend with $68 million. Raimi's film placed fourth on the box office chart and its final domestic gross of $42 million was a disappointment given the director's reputation as a terror auteur. *Entertainment Weekly* critic Gleiberman returned to the subject of Raimi's movie following its release and argued that it had underperformed because of its PG-13 rating. "For the folks who swarm to slasher movies, or to holiday torture freakouts like the *Saw* films, horror is heavy metal: it's got to be raw, and brutal, and extreme or it doesn't count," he wrote. "To them, the R rating is a bloody scarlet letter that a horror movie wears like a badge of dishonor [...] In a sane world, the image of a gypsy crone vomiting maggots onto Alison Lohman's face would be sick enough for the room. Make no mistake: The movie is intensely scary. But fear itself may now seem like an almost delicate emotion within the debased universe of hardcore horror films."

After shooting *Drag Me to Hell*, Lohman appeared in 2009's Gerard Butler action film *Gamer*. The actress married the film's co-director Mark Neveldine and put a pause on her acting career to raise their three children. As the years passed, Lohman discovered that *Drag Me to Hell* was becoming one of her most beloved films as her other movies faded in the public consciousness. "It was well-received, but nobody knew me from *Drag Me to Hell*, it was more *Matchstick Men* or *White Oleander*," she says. "[Now] I would say people will recognize me from *Drag Me to Hell* only, and they don't even know *White Oleander*."

In July 2009, *Entertainment Weekly* published an article by Christine Spines headlined "Chicks dig scary movies." The piece explained how women had become important to the continuing success of the horror genre. "Name any recent horror hit and odds are that female moviegoers bought more tickets than men," wrote Spines. "And we're not just talking about psychological spookfests like 2002's *The Ring* (60 percent female), 2004's *The Grudge* (65 percent female), and 2005's *The Exorcism of Emily Rose* (51 percent female). We're also talking about all the slice-and-dice remakes and sequels that Hollywood churns out." Spines went on to describe 2003's *The Texas Chainsaw*

Megan Fox in *Jennifer's Body* (2009).

Massacre as "a female-driven $81 million hit" and quoted producer Brad Fuller about his surprise over the movie's audience make-up. "I don't think there was anyone who expected that women would gravitate toward a movie called *The Texas Chainsaw Massacre*," said the Platinum Dunes co-founder.

Horror movies routinely foregrounded female performers onscreen, but that representation tended to decline sharply behind the camera. The peg for the *Entertainment Weekly* article was the release of *Jennifer's Body*, which joined *American Psycho* in the sparse ranks of genre movies both written and directed by women. The film starred Amanda Seyfried and Megan Fox as high school best friends Anita 'Needy' Lesnicki and Jennifer Check. The pair's bond is tested after Fox disappears for a night with a rock group named Low Shoulder and returns transformed into a student-eating demon succubus. The film featured special effects and blood aplenty, but it also focused on the relationship between its two lead female characters in a manner rarely seen in a major horror movie.

Jennifer's Body was directed by *Girlfight* filmmaker Karyn Kusama and written by Diablo Cody. The collaborators had self-consciously set out to do something different with their horror film. "Karyn Kusama and I are both outspoken feminists," Cody told Reuters ahead of the movie's release. "We wanted to subvert the classic horror model of women being terrorized."

Cody was born Brook Busey and raised in the suburbs of Chicago. She began her writing career with the blog The Pussy Ranch, in which she described her year-long stint as a performer at a Minneapolis strip club, using the nom de plume Diablo Cody. Cody was contacted by Mason Novick, a manager-producer at the Los Angeles production company Benderspink, who encouraged her to write a memoir, 2006's *Candy Girl: A Year in the Life of an Unlikely Stripper*. Novick asked Cody to come up with a screenwriting sample that might encourage a studio to let her write a movie adaptation of the book. Instead, she sent him the script for a comedy named *Juno*, about a teenager who discovers she's pregnant and decides to give the baby up for adoption. The screenplay attracted the attention of filmmaker Jason Reitman, and the director shot the film in Vancouver with Elliot Page playing the lead role. Released in December 2007, *Juno* was a hit, and Cody's script won her the Oscar for Best Original Screenplay.

Tackling the horror genre was a natural move for Cody, who grew up loving *A Nightmare on Elm Street* and *Poltergeist*. The writer had even included a scene in *Juno* where Jason Bateman's character mansplains to Page's titular teenager about the superiority of *Blood Feast* director Herschell Gordon

Lewis to Dario Argento. In October 2007, *The Hollywood Reporter* revealed that Fox Atomic had bought Cody's *Jennifer's Body* script and that Megan Fox was in negotiations to star in the film. The then 21-year-old Fox had become a star with her appearance in that summer's Michael Bay-directed *Transformers*, which depicted the actress in a hyper-sexualized fashion. To play Needy, Kusama and Cody cast *Mean Girls* star Seyfried, after looking at an array of actresses that also included Emma Stone, Amanda Bynes, and *Cloverfield* cast member Lizzy Caplan.

Kusama filmed *Jennifer's Body* in Vancouver during the spring of 2008. KNB's Greg Nicotero worked on the film's bloody mayhem in collaboration with British visual effects company Moving Picture Company. "*Jennifer's Body*, that was a really interesting project, because it was a teen horror-comedy and coming-of-age movie," he says. "I really liked Karyn, and I thought she was a good director. When Jennifer's jaw sort of distends and opens up, we did some makeups that were all digitally augmented, but, for us, [the movie] was [mostly] aftermath dummy bodies."

Fox caused headlines in the lead-up to the film's release for comparing her *Transformers* director Michael Bay to a pair of history's most infamous dictators in an interview with *Wonderland* magazine. "He's like Napoleon and he wants to create this insane, infamous madman reputation," said the actress. "He wants to be like Hitler on his sets, and he is." Fox's quotes turned into a huge media story, with much of the coverage critiquing both her outspokenness and her supposed lack of acting ability.

Cody, too, attracted negative press. After *Jennifer's Body* received its world premiere at the Toronto Film Festival on September 10, 2009, *The Hollywood Reporter* published a review by writer Kirk Honeycutt, which began, "Well, the Diablo Cody mystique sure ended fast." "There was this sort of twin lightning rod of Diablo Cody and Megan Fox," recalls Kusama. "Something about their public persona just inflamed, I want to say, a certain kind of sophomoric male. There was an online chatter around that movie that, in any other circumstance, would have been considered criminal or hate language. I was just shocked at the animus directed toward the movie before it had even come out. To me, it was just a movie about the perils of female friendship when you're young and unformed and what it means to have monstrous tendencies become literalized."

Jennifer's Body was released the week after the film's Toronto premiere. The film placed fifth at the box office over its first weekend in cinemas

and, on the Sunday, Deadline founder Nikki Finke dismissed the film as "DOA," describing the movie's estimated opening weekend takings of $6.8 million as "pathetic."

Cody would claim 20th Century Fox's marketing of the movie hindered its commercial chances. "I know it's so cheap to blame things on external shit—but the movie was marketed all wrong," she said on the podcast *I Think You're Interesting* in 2018. "They said, 'We want to market this movie to boys who like Megan Fox. That's who's going to go see it.' And I was, like, 'No! This movie is for girls!' That audience they did not attempt to reach."

In her Deadline article, Finke told readers that the commercial disappointment of *Jennifer's Body* "shows that screenwriter Diablo Cody may be filmdom's one-hit wonder." The writer would go on to prove Finke wrong with the screenplays for 2011's critically acclaimed *Young Adult* and 2018's *Tully*. Cody also undertook uncredited script revisions on director Fede Álvarez's 2013 franchise continuation *Evil Dead*, a bloody box office hit starring Jane Levy. Karyn Kusama, meanwhile, pivoted to the small screen, directing episodes of the TV show *Halt and Catch Fire*. The filmmaker came back to horror with 2015's slow-burn chiller *The Invitation*, about an increasingly dread-filled dinner party, for which she earned rave reviews.

Jennifer's Body would also rise from the ashes. In November 2017, The Mary Sue writer Princess Weekes posted an article headlined "So... When Are We All Going to Apologize to Megan Fox for What We Let Hollywood Do to Her?" In the piece, Weekes pondered why feminists "didn't commend her for standing up to as well-known and documented a pig as Michael Bay" and also noted that "*Jennifer's Body* is now considered a cult classic by many

Writer Diablo Cody and director Karyn Kusama at San Diego Comic-Con for a *Jennifer's Body* event in 2009.

younger queer girls." This reappraisal of the film coincided with the burgeoning #MeToo movement. In October 2018, the outlet *Vice* published an article titled "Jennifer's Body Would Kill If It Came Out Today," in which writer Frederick Blichert asserted that the film's "themes of abuse, empowerment, and accountability would likely be a winning formula with horror movie critics in the #MeToo era."

The film's elevation from derided box office bomb to horror classic was completed by a couple of 2019 events marking its tenth anniversary. In the first, Cody and Fox reunited for a conversation about the movie for the syndicated show *Entertainment Tonight*. Cody recalled, "There was a time when it was painful for me to talk about *Jennifer's Body*, because that movie was a commercial failure, and I was savaged personally; it wasn't just having a professional failure, and so it was hard. I'd actually gone through therapy because of that experience. And now, ten years later, I genuinely love talking about it."

The movie's creators would be further validated by a screening at Los Angeles' Egyptian Theater, part of that year's Beyond Fest lineup. The film was followed by a Q&A with Fox and Kusama, in which the director offered her own theory to explain the movie's growing popularity. "It's being revisited because it's really fucking good," she said. "That's why it's being revisited."

Diablo Cody and Karyn Kusama at least had the satisfaction of seeing their film open in cinemas. The same was not true for Michael Dougherty, writer and director of another 2009 horror-comedy, *Trick 'r Treat.* Set on Halloween night, the film was made up of five interlinked and twisty tales related in a non-linear manner. Dougherty filled his movie with familiar horror threats, including a serial killer, werewolves, and a busload of zombies. The filmmaker also introduced a new monster creation that he called Sam, a child-sized demonic entity who covers his head in a burlap sack and enforces the laws of Halloween with deadly rigor. *Trick 'r Treat* boasted a healthy $12 million budget and a clutch of well-known actors (Brian Cox, Dylan Baker, Anna Paquin) but was released straight to video by Warner Bros. As pop culture journalist Matt Barone wrote in a 2013 article for Complex, "Dougherty's film is many things in one: a genuinely funny horror-comedy, an ambitious anthology in the vein of Quentin Tarantino's *Pulp Fiction*, an unpredictable and innovative fright flick. Unfortunately, it's also one of Hollywood's countless examples of bad things happening to good movies."

Director Michael Dougherty and Quinn Lord on the set of *Trick 'r Treat* (2007).

Dougherty grew up in Columbus, Ohio, and fell in love with Halloween at an early age. "My next-door neighbor showed up dressed as Darth Vader," says the director. "I remember my parents explaining, 'It's Halloween, that means you're going to dress up, and go out, and get candy.' I knew this was a holiday that I was going to fall in love with."

Dougherty studied film at NYU. His senior thesis project, the animated *Season's Greetings*, showcased Sam. In the course of the short, Dougherty's creation disposes of a much larger character after he fails to give the seemingly helpless Sam a treat. "I really wanted to create an iconic mascot for Halloween," he says. "Sam was my attempt to put a face to the holiday."

Season's Greetings was seen by makeup effects artist Stan Winston, who met with Dougherty and encouraged him to write a feature-length live-action screenplay featuring Sam. Working on the script, Dougherty was inspired by the early *Halloween* movies and particularly John Carpenter and producer Debra Hill's doomed attempt to turn the franchise into an anthology series with *Halloween III: Season of the Witch*. "Audiences at the time did not understand why Michael Myers was not in the movie, but I love that film," he says. "I thought, 'Well, I love that idea, I love horror anthologies, so I'll take that ball and run with it.'"

Winston liked Dougherty's screenplay so much that he agreed to direct one of the movie's chapters and set about recruiting a lineup of legendary horror filmmakers to oversee the others. "It was such an amazing experience, looking back," says Dougherty. "Stan suggested Carpenter, George Romero, and Tobe Hooper. Tobe Hooper said yes. Romero said yes. Carpenter was intrigued but wanted to talk about it in person."

Dougherty met with the *Halloween* director at the Egyptian Theater in Los Angeles. "John was doing a retrospective screening of *The Thing*," he says. "I was told to go meet him in the alley on the side of the theater, which was nerve-racking, because that's like being told God wants you to come

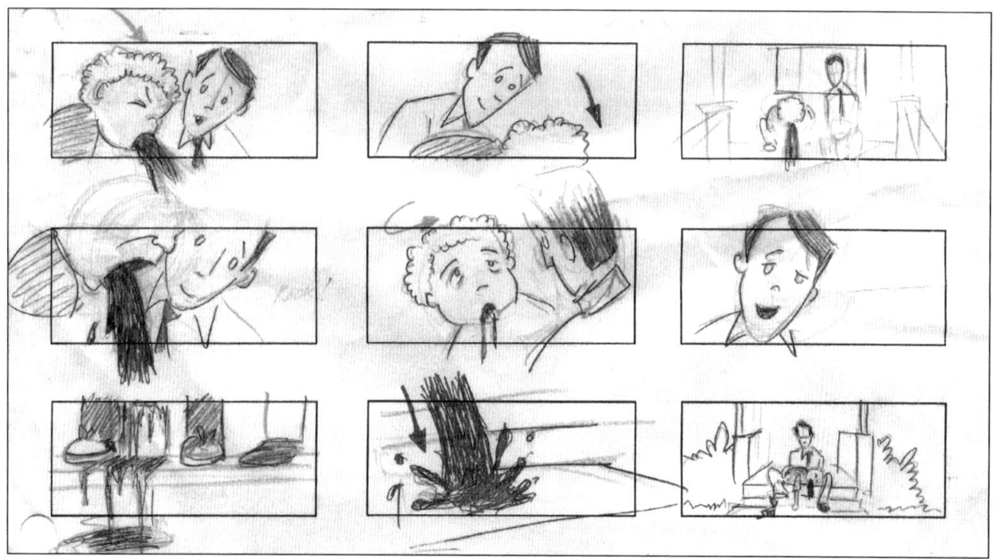

Storyboard for *Trick 'r Treat* by Michael Dougherty.

up to Mount Sinai and have a conversation. He was so gracious, and kind, and warm. Ultimately, he came onboard. He was supposed to do the segment with Dylan Baker."

Having assembled this remarkable group of directing talent, Winston and Dougherty approached studios about backing the project. "Everybody passed," says Dougherty. "Studios love to come up with creative ways to say, 'No.' The one that I did hear multiple times was, 'It's too old-fashioned,' that vampires, zombies, and werewolves were too old-school. *Trick 'r Treat* was sent out to the studios in 2001, roughly. Everybody wanted a *Scream* knock-off." But the quality of Dougherty's script for *Trick 'r Treat* attracted the attention of director Bryan Singer, who hired him to co-write 2003's *X2* and 2006's Gil Adler-produced *Superman Returns*.

Trick 'r Treat would be revived via the enthusiasm of Jon Jashni, an executive at the production company Legendary Entertainment. Founded in the early 2000s by businessman Thomas Tull, Legendary was swiftly establishing itself as a major Hollywood force. In 2005, Tull's company signed a seven-year distribution deal with Warner Bros. to co-finance 40 films. "Jon Jashni saw the potential of it, and Thomas Tull loved the idea, because he is a genre fanboy," says Dougherty. The Legendary executives suggested that the writer make the film his directorial debut. "They knew that I had been working on *Superman* and *X-Men* and knew how to shepherd a movie from pre-production to completion, and asked if I'd be curious about directing it," he says.

Carpenter, who had helped inspire and almost directed a segment of the film, would be represented onscreen in the finished movie thanks to Brian Cox's insistence that his character resemble the famed filmmaker. "That was Brian Cox's idea," says Dougherty. "He wanted a John Carpenter nose and wig. Brian regretted it at the end of the day, only because the process of putting on the makeup was so complex. When we finally called wrap, he ripped the prosthetics off his face, and he was screaming, 'Never again! Never again!'"

Warner Bros. and Legendary tested *Trick 'r Treat* and viewers scored Dougherty's film poorly. "That was a very unpleasant experience," says the director. "The test audience hated it. But in college, I used to run test screenings for the studios, so I knew how the process worked. I noticed the prerequisite to get into the test screening, to qualify to watch *Trick 'r Treat*, they were people who had seen *Saw*, and *Hostel*, and some of the more hardcore torture porn-style movies. I remember saying, 'That's not the audience for this movie.'" He persuaded Legendary to retest the movie using different parameters to choose audience members. "I said, 'You should recruit people

Anna Paquin in *Trick 'r Treat.*

who are more familiar with horror-comedies, people who had seen *Gremlins*, who appreciated *Child's Play*," he says. "We tested again, and the test scores went up. But by then, Warner Bros. had turned their backs on it."

The studio had planned to release *Trick 'r Treat* in October 2007, but first pushed the movie to the following year and then decided not to put it in cinemas at all. Dougherty hoped that if he could build enough buzz around *Trick 'r Treat*, then the company might still give the film a run in theaters. "I asked Thomas Tull, 'What can we do to keep it alive?'" says the director. "Thomas convinced Warner Bros. to let us take two prints to several film festivals." *Trick 'r Treat* received its world premiere at the Butt-Numb-A-Thon in Austin, Texas, an annual event hosted by Ain't It Cool News, where the movie was well-received. "That's when I realized, 'Okay, this movie's not a total piece of shit,'" says Dougherty. The director continued to screen the movie, hauling around the 35mm reels himself. "This is before the days of digital prints," he says. "I had to physically carry these film cans. I remember the handles of the canisters dug into my palms to the point where I was dripping blood from my body onto the film reels. In my mind, I was blessing the film reels with my blood."

The movie began to rack up positive reviews by genre critics. In his assessment for the website Horror Movie a Day, Brian Collins wrote that, "for nearly 20 years I have been looking for something besides a random *Halloween* sequel to join the original film as part of my annual Halloween tradition. I finally have one." Such endorsements did not help *Trick 'r Treat* get a cinema release. "For whatever reason, we couldn't get Warner Bros. to give a crap," Dougherty says.

Warner Home Video finally released *Trick 'r Treat* straight to DVD on October 6, 2009, two years after the movie was initially supposed to debut in theaters. "I don't really hold a grudge against Warner Bros. or the execs who made the decision," says Dougherty. "My gripe is that they never had the courtesy to call me and talk about it like mature adults. If you're going to collaborate with filmmakers, you should have the balls to sit down and have these discussions face to face—and that never happened."

Dougherty (and Sam) would get the last laugh when horror fans began snapping up the film on DVD and Blu-ray. "It was very much a success," says the director. "It was selling out to the point where one of my reps had to call up Warner Bros. and ask, 'Are you guys making more? Because it's sold out everywhere!'"

Dougherty went on to co-write and direct Universal's 2015 Christmas horror movie *Krampus*, which starred *Sixth Sense* actress Toni Collette and did get a theatrical release, grossing $42 million at the US box office. His next film was 2019's *Godzilla: King of the Monsters*, the third movie in the 'Monsterverse' franchise after 2014's *Godzilla* and 2017's *Kong: Skull Island*. Produced by Legendary and distributed by Warner Bros., the film grossed $387 million worldwide.

The reputation of *Trick 'r Treat* as both a Halloween season favorite and a profit center would grow and grow. In 2016, *The Convent* filmmaker Mike Mendez told *Entertainment Weekly* that he regarded Dougherty's movie as the perfect spooky season watch, saying, "I think that is the ultimate Halloween film." The same year, the digital decoration company Atmos FX put on sale a line of products which allowed purchasers to make it seem that Sam was running amok in their home. "It's him murdering people on Halloween—as a decoration!" Dougherty explained to *Entertainment Weekly*. Fans of the movie could buy *Trick 'r Treat* posters, mugs, tee shirts, and even a water bottle from the Legendary online store. In October 2024, the film screened at the Hollywood Forever Cemetery, with many attendees dressed as characters from the film. Dougherty was on hand to introduce the movie and describes the event as "a really big deal. During that dark time when we were shelved, as a coping mechanism I tried to envision a Hollywood Forever Cemetery screening."

The director is delighted at having belatedly fulfilled his ambition of creating a mascot for Halloween. "In my neighborhood, literally around the corner, people put Sam decorations on their front lawn," he says. "I don't think they know I made the movie, but there he is. It's a bit like seeing your kid having snuck out of the house."

The fortunes of *Drag Me to Hell*, *Jennifer's Body*, and *Trick 'r Treat* did little to challenge *Slither* director James Gunn's assessment of the horror-comedy as a tough commercial sell. But the box office drought for films that mixed gore and gags would end, decisively, with the arrival of 2009's *Zombieland*.

When Edgar Wright and Simon Pegg coined the term 'rom-zom-com' to describe *Shaun of the Dead*, they were acknowledging the deliberately preposterous, and unlikely to be repeated, nature of their film. In fact, the romantic-zombie-comedy subgenre would be tackled again almost immediately by writing team Rhett Reese and Paul Wernick, whose *Zombieland* screenplay was about a quartet of survivors bonding in a world full of the sprinting undead.

The film had begun life as a spec script for a TV pilot. "It was pretty mercenary," says Reese. "I mean, we love zombie movies, but we were working in television, and we spied what we thought was a hole in the marketplace. They hadn't really ever explored zombies on television. So we wrote *Zombieland* as a spec television script." The pair had enjoyed *28 Days Later* and knew from the off that their undead would be fast-moving. "*28 Days Later*, we thought, was the most important movie of the time, even more than *Shaun of the Dead*, which we love," says Reese. "Zombie movies have tended to require a horde of zombies to be really threatening, because they're so damn slow. When Alex Garland and Danny Boyle turned that on its head, it really reinvigorated the genre."

The writers' producer Gavin Polone sold the script to CBS, where an executive named Chris Parnell interested John Carpenter in directing the show's pilot. The *Halloween* director agreed to meet with Reese and Wernick, but only if the sit-down occurred late in the day. "He's a true vampire, he's basically a nocturnal man," says Wernick. "They said, 'He can't do any time before four.'" To the writers' delight, Carpenter loved their pilot script. "John said, 'I just want to shoot this word for word,'" recalls Reese. "We thought, you're our new favorite director, because who says that?" CBS ultimately passed on the pilot, though. "It made its way all the way up to Les Moonves," says Wernick, referring to the then network chairman. "He said, 'I can't see zombies on CBS.'"

The two writers reworked the material into the script for what they hoped would become a made-for-TV movie. Polone, who had produced 1999's *Stir of Echoes*, believed that the new *Zombieland* script had cinematic potential. "Gavin Polone said, 'We should make this a *movie* movie,'" Reese remembers. "Thankfully, Sony was very synergistic at the time, and Chris Parnell was willing to let Gavin show it to Columbia Pictures, and they fell in love with it for the big screen."

Zombieland was the directorial debut of Ruben Fleischer, who had begun his career working as a PA on *Dawson's Creek* and later directed music videos for M.I.A. and Dizzee Rascal. Fleischer cast Emma Stone and *Cursed* star Jesse Eisenberg as the movie's romantic couple. Abigail Breslin portrayed the younger sister of Stone's character, and Woody Harrelson signed up for the role of the larger than life, Twinkies-obsessed Tallahassee.

The writers wanted *Zombieland* to feature a cameo appearance by Patrick Swayze, planning for the *Dirty Dancing* star to play a zombified version of himself. Reese recalls, "We had a moment where Tallahassee lifted Patrick Swayze into the air, like [Swayze] had lifted Jennifer Grey in *Dirty Dancing*, and smashed his head into a pillar. That's how he killed Patrick Swayze." The actor became unavailable after he was diagnosed with the pancreatic cancer from which he would pass away in September 2009. "Patrick Swayze got sick, tragically," says Reese. "We were forced to pivot and try to get somebody else in the movie."

The pair fruitlessly approached an array of candidates, including Dwayne Johnson, Mark Hamill, Jean-Claude Van Damme, and Joe Pesci, rewriting the relevant sequence in the screenplay to suit each actor. "We were riffing on their careers," says Reese. "With Mark Hamill, there was a sort of light saber fight. I think Jean-Claude Van Damme did the splits as a zombie. Our pitch to Joe Pesci's agent was, 'We know it's a small part, but it's really fun.' He goes, 'Stop right there. There are no small parts, only small money.'"

The writers still had not found a replacement for Swayze by the start of shooting. Desperate, they asked Harrelson for help. "Woody said, 'Well, I could ask Dustin Hoffman, or I could ask Bill Murray,' because he's buddies with both of them," Reese recalls. "Dustin said no—there was a scheduling issue—so it was down to Bill." The comedy icon warmed to the script, but was unexcited about the nature of the role he was being offered. "He calls Woody back and he says, 'I think this is a hilarious script, but there's not much for me to do here,' because originally Bill was a zombie," says Reese. "We all gathered and thought, 'What could we do to attract to Bill to this?' Someone said, 'What if Bill's alive?' We just banged this thing out, fastest thing we ever wrote, put it in a new draft. By God, two days later, Bill's in the makeup trailer and the rest is history."

Sony released *Zombieland* in the US at the start of October 2009. The film earned $24 million over its opening weekend, slightly more than its budget. Fleischer's movie went on to gross $75 million domestically. "The night it came out, Sony got us all a car, and we were driving around town, popping into theaters," says Wernick. "It was Woody, it was Jesse, it was us, it was Ruben. We popped into a couple of theaters on the early side, and they were near-empty and we're like, 'Oh my God, we have a bomb on our hands.' Then we went to Hollywood and popped into a theater, it was packed. We came in right at the Bill Murray scene, and the crowd was literally rolling in the aisles. We came out and we got a call from the studio saying, 'You're going to open at $25 million'—which made up the budget—'and you're number one.' And it was a huge celebration."

In May 2008, six months before the release of *Saw V*, Bloody Disgusting reported that franchise editor Kevin Greutert was going to direct the next movie in the series. After James Wan's original film became a hit, the distributors of other horror movies had deliberately not competed against the series at the box office. So Lionsgate had good reason to assume that they would own Halloween yet again by releasing *Saw VI* in the second half of October 2009. But the franchise would face serious competition from a movie as free of blood as the *Saw* films were drenched in it.

CHAPTER 13

"GAME OVER."

In the spring of 2008, DreamWorks president of production Adam Goodman called Jason Blum, the Miramax executive who had passed on *The Blair Witch Project.* Blum had left Miramax years earlier to found his own company. He was now trying to convince DreamWorks to release his latest project, *Paranormal Activity*, rather than remake it.

Another found footage film, the movie related the story of a couple, Katie and Micah, who encounter spooky phenomena in their suburban house. Micah uses his video camera to try to find out what is going on, even filming the pair as they sleep. The micro-budgeted movie had no famous actors and was directed by a first-time filmmaker, but DreamWorks co-founder Steven Spielberg had agreed to watch a DVD of the film. Goodman was now calling Blum to tell him what the *Jaws* director thought of the movie. "Jason, I have bad news for you," Goodman told him. "Steven watched the movie and shut it off halfway through."

Producer Jason Blum in 2011.

The DreamWorks executive was joking; Spielberg had stopped watching the film, but not because he thought *Paranormal Activity* was bad. Rather, the director had been too scared to complete the movie. Spielberg did so the next day and then told Stacey Snider, who had left Universal Pictures in 2006 to become co-chairman of DreamWorks, that it deserved a theatrical release. "It was too real to watch in the dark," he later said to *Entertainment Weekly* writer Missy Schwartz. "The next morning, in broad daylight, I watched the whole picture, and it still scared me beyond measure. That's when I called Stacey and said, 'We shouldn't remake this. We should release this.'"

Paranormal Activity was directed by Oren Peli. Born in Israel, Peli enjoyed watching movies like *Star Wars* and Spielberg's *E.T.* but had no ambitions about becoming involved with the movie business. By 1999, he had moved to America and was working as a computer programmer in San Diego, California. One day, Peli attended a preview screening of *The Blair Witch Project*. He was impressed by the original nature of the found footage film and the scares that the movie's directors had managed to create without a big budget or gore effects.

In 2003, Peli moved into a house with his girlfriend, and the couple started to hear strange noises at night. The pair toyed with the idea of buying a video camera to record whatever might be happening in their house. "Then I thought, how absolutely terrifying would it be to watch footage of yourself while you're asleep… and see that there is evidence of something happening that you didn't even know about," Peli recalled in 2017 on the Mick Garris-hosted podcast *Post Mortem*.

The computer programmer spent the next year and a half developing the idea for what would become *Paranormal Activity*, reading about hauntings and possessions and filming test footage for the project. He modeled his proposed project after tense but mostly blood-free films like Spielberg's 1971 movie *Duel* and *The Sixth Sense*.

Peli rented a theater in Los Angeles for $200 to hold auditions and posted ads in *Backstage* and LA Casting. The copy described the untitled film as a "Supernatural thriller/horror; a couple documents their battle with an unknown entity in their home. Not a cheesy teen/slasher (although some bad stuff may happen)." The audition notice elaborated on the proposed nature of the shoot, revealing that, "All dialogue will be ad-libbed" and "Shooting schedule will be mostly overnight. Long hours, little sleep, few breaks."

The ad attracted the attention of Micah Sloat, who had recently arrived in Los Angeles to pursue a career in the arts after studying philosophy at New

York's Skidmore College. "I wanted to go west and be creative, so I followed my heart to LA," he says. "I was auditioning for student films and stuff like that." When Sloat saw the audition notice, he had decided to abandon acting and concentrate on playing guitar. "The only reason I went to the *Paranormal Activity* audition was because the notice was so insane and I saw that it was right down the street," he admits.

Peli styled the casting sessions after those conducted by the *Blair Witch Project* directors. Once he had introduced himself, the aspiring filmmaker asked the auditioner, "What makes you think your house is haunted?" When Sloat entered the audition room, he swiftly responded to Peli's query, explaining that he lived in a creepy house, that he had been hearing strange noises, and that the shutters on his window flapped when there was no wind. Sloat added that he had found his girlfriend unconscious on the bathroom floor "and she doesn't know what happened."

Katie Featherston was another actor who responded to Peli's ad. The Texas native studied theater at the Southern Methodist University in Dallas and then relocated to Los Angeles, where she got a job as a waitress at the Italian restaurant Buca di Beppo on Universal Studios' CityWalk. At her audition, Featherston, like Sloat, began improvising smoothly after being asked by Peli why she thought her house was haunted. "Oh God," she said. "Well, there was this time, it was a couple of weeks ago, and I was sleeping downstairs, instead of upstairs, and I heard this big crash…"

Peli asked Featherston and Sloat to return for a second audition to see how they would improvise together. "We got a callback, and I met Katie for the first time," says Sloat. "Oren said, 'Katie, this is Micah. Micah, this is Katie. Tell us how you first met.' We went right into the backstory, telling how we had met in Europe and stuff. Oren called us back, just to see [if] we could repeat the performance, and then we went on to shoot the movie."

Peli filmed *Paranormal Activity* at his home in San Diego during October 2006. Sloat explains that "the entire movie is improvised. The first day, Oren thought, 'Okay, we'll just turn the camera on, and we'll cut it together.' He soon realized that filming people in their house behaving normally is not entertaining, you have to create scenes which are interesting. So we had to come up with natural dialog on the spot that was believable, and entertaining, and worked for the film."

Peli worked with the tiniest of crews—when he had a crew at all. "It was Oren, and his girlfriend, and his best friend, and a makeup artist, that was the entire crew, and most of the time it was just Oren," Sloat remembers. Peli completed the shoot in just seven days. "It was like, 120-something hours of work in that one week," says Sloat. "It was wild. Definitely not something that the union would be okay with." Peli took a year to edit the film. In all, the director had spent around $12,000 on the project, including $3,000 on a Sony FX1 camera, $400 to rent a cop costume for an ultimately deleted scene, and $100 on Red Bull.

Peli had no useful contacts in the movie industry and no luck finding someone who might help him find distribution. The director decided to attract attention for *Paranormal Activity* via film festivals, but his project was repeatedly rejected by programmers. The movie finally received its world premiere at the Los Angeles-based Screamfest Horror Film Festival in October 2007. "I was jumping out of my seat," says Sloat about seeing the film on the big screen. "The guy next to me says, 'You know you're in the movie, right?' I was like, 'I know, but this thing *works*.'" Featherston won the festival's Best Actress award, and the movie received a glowing review on Dread Central. "Simply put, *Paranormal Activity* is the most frightening ghost story of the year," wrote the website's Debi Moore.

Micah Sloat and Katie Featherston in *Paranormal Activity* (2009).

Peli signed with CAA, which sent out DVDs of the film as a directing sample. Among those who watched the movie was Jason Blum. The executive had left Miramax shortly after beginning to attract the ire of Harvey Weinstein for not acquiring *The Blair Witch Project.* "I had passed on *Blair Witch* when I worked for Miramax," he told Buzzfeed in 2015. "I remember regretting it. And Harvey never let me forget it. And I remember learning a lesson that no one really knows anything—that's what everyone says in Hollywood, but you don't really understand that until you've lived it. I really lived it with *Blair Witch*."

In 2000, Blum founded Blum Israel Productions with another former Miramax executive named Amy Israel, which he would rename Blumhouse Productions after Israel left in 2002. Blum's early producing projects included 2002's Uma Thurman drama *Hysterical Blindness* and the 2007 comedy *The Darwin Awards*. "I had no idea what I was doing," he told the *Chicago Tribune* in 2013. "I spent ten years doing independent movies that nobody saw." After years of failure, he was thinking of throwing in the towel and moving from Los Angeles to New York.

Blum had a production deal at Paramount, where he met Steven Schneider, a producer and horror fan who recommended that he check out *Paranormal Activity*. As a child, Blum had enjoyed dressing up as Frankenstein's Monster or Godzilla for Halloween, but he had no real interest in horror movies. Still, Blum was so impressed by *Paranormal Activity* that he agreed to attach himself as a producer and began to screen Peli's movie at his house. Among the people he invited to watch the film was Ashley Brucks, a production executive at DreamWorks, which had been bought by Paramount in February 2006. Brucks also enjoyed Peli's movie and recommended it to her boss, Adam Goodman.

In the meantime, Blum had gotten his shot at becoming a serious Hollywood player. In February 2008, *Variety* reported that Blumhouse was producing a Dwayne Johnson comedy for 20th Century Fox called *The Tooth Fairy*. The movie was a moderate success at the box office when it was released in January 2010. By then, Blum had soured on the project and on working for a major studio. "I thought it was going to be fun," he later told *Variety*. "Instead, it was very political, with 25 people deciding what the Tooth Fairy costume should look like."

DreamWorks was initially interested in having Peli direct a new version of *Paranormal Activity* with a larger budget and more experienced actors. "There was some discussion about, 'Are we going to remake [it] with J-Lo and Brad Pitt?'" says Sloat. Peli was unhappy about the notion of overseeing a second iteration of his film. Blum convinced the director to sell DreamWorks the remake rights on the condition that the studio test screen the original film. "Jason and Oren said, 'Okay, we'll do whatever you want, but we need a test screening first to see how this film performs,'" says Sloat. "People in the test screening, they were walking out. Adam Goodman was like, 'This is terrible.' They started asking people why they were walking out, and people said, 'Because we're too scared.' DreamWorks went, 'Wait a minute, this is something!'"

After watching the film, Spielberg joined the chorus of voices agitating for Peli's original film to be given a theatrical release. The director told *Entertainment Weekly* that his advocacy of the movie made him sound like a "broken record. I sent more emails and made more phone calls, trying to get everybody to agree with Stacey and me that it should be released."

Spielberg thought the film's original ending was disappointing, however, and Paramount gave Peli $4,000 to shoot a new conclusion. In the first version of the movie, Featherston's character was shot by cops at the climax. The new conclusion, which was again filmed at Peli's house, found Featherston's heroine throwing her boyfriend's body at the camera, then transforming into a demonic being. "Oren calls us up and says, 'We're going to shoot this new ending with the DreamWorks stunt crew,'" says Sloat. "They cut holes in the ceiling, and they had this giant beam suspended from the rafters of Oren's bedroom. I'm wearing the harness that Tom Cruise had worn in a *Mission: Impossible* movie—it was a little small—and I'm suspended from this harness for hours. When you're suspended in a harness, it slowly chokes you out like you're being crucified, so I'm losing consciousness. Eventually, somebody's like, 'Maybe we should take him down, he doesn't look so good.'"

In October 2008, DreamWorks and Paramount announced the companies were ending their partnership, which left *Paranormal Activity* in limbo. "Basically, everything between DreamWorks and Paramount was put on hold, and we didn't know where the movie was going to end up," Peli later recalled to the *Los Angeles Times*. The decision to give *Paranormal Activity* a theatrical release was finally made by Adam Goodman after he became president of Paramount's film group in June, 2009.

Paramount launched *Paranormal Activity* in the last week of September 2009, with midnight screenings at Austin's annual Fantastic Fest and around a dozen college towns across the country. For the first weekend in October, the studio put the film in 33 theaters, including Hollywood's ArcLight cinema, with the movie earning an impressive $532,000 over the weekend. Taking another leaf from the *Blair Witch Project* playbook, Paramount initially kept its two stars away from the press, meaning that the pair were forced to view the crowd going into the ArcLight from afar. "I hid across the street behind a mailbox with Katie, and we were looking at this giant crowd around the movie theater," Sloat recalls. "It was a wild experience."

For the film's third week on release, Paramount expanded distribution to 160 cinemas, which resulted in a gross of $12 million. The movie's fourth week in theaters found it claiming third place on the chart—behind *Where the Wild Things Are* and the Gerard Butler action film *Law Abiding Citizen*—with a seven-day gross of almost $27 million from 760 theaters.

Lionsgate was set to release *Saw VI* on October 23, 2009, when *Paranormal Activity* would be starting its fifth week in cinemas. With Kevin Greutert's movie due to screen in just over 3,000 theaters and Paramount further expanding the release of *Paranormal Activity* to almost 2,000 cinemas, the stage was set for a box office battle royale between Peli's film and the sixth entry in the *Saw* franchise.

The victims in *Saw VI* included predatory lenders and unhelpful health insurance executives, pertinent choices given the ongoing fallout from the 2007–2008 financial crisis. The third entry in the series to be written by Patrick Melton and Marcus Dunstan, the movie was another violent and gory effort, in stark contrast to the bloodless terrors of *Paranormal Activity*. "There's a lot of psychological tactics that were used in *Paranormal Activity* to make it successful," says Micah Sloat. "One of them is to bring the audience into the story by doing the opposite of what *Saw* did—which is to just blast your emotional system over and over again with all this gruesome stuff."

The horror movie head-to-head was covered by media outlets including *Entertainment Weekly*, which ran an article headlined "Box office preview: Will *Paranormal Activity* slaughter *Saw VI*?" That question would be answered in the affirmative. Over the weekend, *Paranormal Activity* grossed $21 million and *Saw VI* earned $14 million. Greutert's film went on to make $68 million around the world, less than half the $164 million grossed by *Saw III*. Its earnings were dwarfed by those of *Paranormal Activity*, which grossed almost $108 million in the US and another $85 million in foreign territories.

This box office triumph of *Paranormal Activity* over *Saw VI* was another indication that many cinemagoers were tiring of gorier material. Even so, there were still plenty of new extreme horror films to be found for those who knew where to look. The same day that *Saw VI* arrived in cinemas, IFC Films released director Lars von Trier's *Antichrist*. A divisive sensation when it had screened at Cannes the previous spring, the film found Charlotte Gainsbourg's grieving mother inflicting physical damage on both her genitals and those of her husband, played by Willem Dafoe. In terms of horrifying grotesquerie, though, *Antichrist* was topped by *A Serbian Film*, which received its world premiere at 2010's SXSW Festival in Austin. Directed by Srđan Spasojević, the movie became instantly infamous among cineastes for including the rape of a newborn baby. For all the outrage they provoked, neither *Antichrist* nor *A Serbian Film* would make a significant impact on mainstream culture. But in the spring of 2010, IFC Films' new genre label IFC Midnight released another hard-to-watch movie whose name, *The Human Centipede*, became known to people who would never dream of watching the actual film.

The Human Centipede (First Sequence)—to give the movie its full, ominous title—was written and directed by Tom Six. The Dutch filmmaker started his career in television and worked as a director on the original version of the reality show *Big Brother*, which premiered in the Netherlands in 1999. When the format was bought by TV networks in other countries, Six acted as an advisor to the producers and directors of these new iterations. "I was one of the Dutch directors who taught about the *Big Brother* process in America," he says, referring to the version that debuted on CBS in 2000. "But I always wanted to make films."

The director was inspired to write the script for *The Human Centipede* after he made a dark joke about a pedophile. "I saw a child molester on television," he recalls. "I said, 'They should stitch this guy with his mouth to the ass of a very fat truck driver. It would be a really good punishment for him.' Then I thought, 'That's a cool idea for a film!'"

In the director's screenplay, a German surgeon named Dr. Heiter kidnaps two women and a man. He stitches them together mouth-to-anus, creating what he describes as "a Siamese triplet, connected via the gastric system." Six and his sister/producer Ilona avoided describing the exact horrors they planned to depict in *The Human Centipede* as they searched for finance. "We made films in Holland before and so we had a group of investors," he says. "We told them, 'We want to make an international horror film and we're going to stitch people together.' If I had mentioned 'ass-to-mouth,' I think they would have said, 'Have a nice day, bye!'"

The director wanted American actresses to play the scientist's two female victims, but filling the roles proved a difficult process. "We were casting in New York, and I made some drawings of the human centipede, and a lot of actresses thought I was crazy and didn't want to work with me," says the filmmaker. Six eventually cast unknowns Ashley C. Williams and Ashlynn Yennie as the American characters and Japanese actor Akihiro Kitamura as the third victim. To play Dr. Heiter, the director hired veteran German actor Dieter Laser.

Six shot the film in the Netherlands, doubling for Germany. His movie mercilessly lingered over the horrific situation Heiter's subjects were enduring. The director's use of lengthy shots was influenced by his experience working on *Big Brother*. "Of course, we were observing those people all the time," he says of the reality show.

The movie was bought by IFC Films after it won Best Horror Feature at Austin's Fantastic Fest in September 2009. The distributor put the film onto a limited number of screens in the spring of 2010, with the movie grossing $180,000. *The Human Centipede* subsequently proved a hit for the company on DVD and Blu-ray, reportedly selling 55,000 units during its first week on sale alone.

The film's macabre premise attracted the interest of the comedy community, which helped spread word about Six's nightmarish concoction. The movie was referenced on several TV shows, including *30 Rock* and *South Park*, whose season 15 premiere was titled "HUMANCENTiPAD." The episode featured a plotline in which the preteen character Kyle fails to read the terms and conditions of an iTunes update and unwittingly allows Apple to make him the middle segment of a human centipede.

The Human Centipede also inspired a sketch on the comedy website Funny Or Die. The skit starred Jon Daly—who wrote the script—Steve Agee, and Rob Huebel as the three segments of a human centipede who have now been separated and are members of a support group. Speaking to *Entertainment Weekly* in May 2011 about why Six's film was so ripe for parody, Daly explained, "It's about eating your friend's poop. It's the ultimate nightmare, especially for the person in the middle, and the ultimate nightmare is always funny. It's really punk-rock. It pushed torture porn just one step further. It kind of took the *Saw* movies and went, 'Oh yeah? Look what I can do. I'm going to sew people together and have them eat poop.'"

Six followed the original film with 2011's *The Human Centipede 2 (Full Sequence)* and 2015's *The Human Centipede 3 (Final Sequence).* The latter's plot found Six, who played himself, giving permission for convicted prisoners at a US prison to be connected together in the manner shown in the two previous films. Just as incredibly, the film's cast included one-time Oscar nominee Eric Roberts.

When Ti West directed his fourth movie, 2009's '80s-set *The House of the Devil,* the filmmaker stayed at the Yankee Pedlar Inn in Torrington, Connecticut. For West, what occurred at the hotel would be as memorable as what took place in front of his cameras. "The whole town thinks it's haunted," he says. "The people that worked there, one had a ghost-hunting website. The phone would ring, and you'd answer, and no one would be there. There's a chair in the lobby that's 'Mrs. Conley's chair,' and if you sit in it, you get cursed." During the course of the shoot, West and his crew started having strange dreams "every night, which was weird. It had a weird vibe."

The eerie events at the hotel echoed the tone of West's film. Born at the start of the '80s, the director was exposed to the decade's so-called 'Satanic panic,' when baseless conspiracy theories about demon-worshipping cults spread across America. That experience informed the script for *The House of the Devil.* The film starred Jocelin Donahue as a cash-poor college student named Sam who signs up for a babysitting job at a remote house where the occupants turn out to be a family of occultists.

Director Ti West on the set of *The House of the Devil* (2009).

West grew up in Wilmington, Delaware. As a child, his favorite movies were *Back to the Future* and *The Karate Kid*, but he also loved *A Nightmare on Elm Street* and *The Monster Squad*. Later, the teenage West checked out more esoteric horror titles, including Larry Fessenden's vampire tale *Habit*. After high school, West attended New York's School of Visual Arts. His tutors included Fessenden's friend and collaborator, the director Kelly Reichardt. "She was like, 'I'll bring him in to talk about movies,' and she didn't," says West. "I nagged her, and she went, 'Nobody cares, here's his phone number.' I called him, and we got along really well."

Fessenden invited West to intern at his company Glass Eye Pix. "He was fantastic," says the *Habit* director. "He would come to my house and talk about movies. My joke is that I started working for Ti, because I had the equipment and would do his dubbing." At the time, Fessenden was newly enthused about continuing to pursue his independent filmmaking model, having witnessed the rise of Peter Jackson from micro-budget horror filmmaker to acclaimed director of the *Lord of the Rings* trilogy. "I never thought,

'Oh, one day that will be me,'" says Fessenden. "I was just excited about the independent project, so to speak. I told Ti, 'Come back when you graduate; if you have a feature, I'll make it.'"

After leaving college, West took Fessenden up on his offer. "He said, 'What if I gave you a little bit of money? Could you just go do it with not a lot of help?'" West recalls. "I probably lied and said 'Yes.' So he gave us $50,000, and we made *The Roost*."

Written and directed by West, and produced by Fessenden, *The Roost* tracked a group of friends who are attacked by zombie bats on the way to attending a wedding. The movie's cast included *The Monster Squad* actor Tom Noonan, who played a TV horror host, and Fessenden, who portrayed a swiftly killed-off truck driver. "We had one take of everything," says West of the shoot. "It was very hard to accomplish even what we accomplished."

The Roost only received a tiny theatrical release in 2005 but became a profit center for Glass Eye Pix through DVD sales and other ancillary markets. "DVD was this blessing," says Fessenden. "Whatever revenue you did from theatrical, that was usually breaking even. But then you'd have the DVD sale, and then you'd have cable, and then you'd have hopefully foreign sales, and then you'd have TV rights. There were all these mechanisms to get your money back. *The Roost* set up this idea that we could be moguls and make these low-budget horror movies." Over the next few years, Glass Eye Pix produced an array of genre titles, including director Glenn McQuaid's period horror-comedy *I Sell the Dead*, Jim Mickle's vampire apocalypse saga *Stake Land*, Fessenden's own *The Last Winter*, and a clutch of further films from West.

Before shooting *The Roost*, West had worked at a Diesel jeans store, and the director returned to the job following the end of production. As he told Ain't It Cool News journalist Eric Vespe shortly after returning from the Sitges Film Festival, "Last week I was in Spain, sitting in a bar talking one-on-one with Tarantino about awesome '80s movies, and this week I am back in the mall selling clothes. It's bizarre." When West started writing the script for *The House of the Devil*, his own financial situation helped inspire the lead character of the desperate-for-money Sam.

Unable to secure a budget for *The House of the Devil*, the director convinced Fessenden to finance another micro-budget movie called *Trigger Man*, about three friends hunting in the woods who are targeted by a sniper (Fessenden once more appeared in the film, and once more his character swiftly perished).

West's growing reputation led to him directing *Cabin Fever 2: Spring Fever*, a high school-set sequel to Eli Roth's debut. He planned the movie to be a black comedy in the vein of John Waters. But the film was re-edited without West's participation and was belatedly released straight to DVD in 2010. "I'm embarrassed to have my name on it," says the director. "The material's not so bad, but the delivery is all messed up."

West returned to his script for *The House of the Devil*, securing a reported $900,000 budget from the recently founded company Dark Sky Films, whose partners on the project included Fessenden's Glass Eye Pix. In addition to Donahue, West cast Noonan and Mary Woronov as a sinister couple in need of a babysitter and A. J. Bowen as their son. Future *Barbie* director and co-writer Greta Gerwig played the best friend of Donahue's heroine.

West was proud of the fact that his slow-paced, period-accurate film was a very different movie from the glut of remakes and sequels which had proved so successful over the previous years. Speaking with *The Washington Post* shortly after the film's release, the director bemoaned the popularity of recent movies that he regarded as generic retreads. "The reality is, last year the only two original horror movies from studios were *Drag Me to Hell*—

Jocelin Donahue in *The House of the Devil.*

the man himself Sam Raimi's return to horror—and *Jennifer's Body*—from fresh-off-the-Oscar-win Diablo Cody," he said. "Neither of those movies were especially successful. I don't know if they were epic fails, but they did not do well. You know what did do well? The *Friday the 13th* remake. Everyone hates it and says it sucks, but it made $40 million in its opening weekend. So it's our fault."

The House of the Devil received its world premiere at the 2009 Tribeca Film Festival and was bought by Magnet Releasing. West's film was made available on VOD at the start of October 2009 and was put into a limited number of cinemas at the end of the month. Reviews were positive, with *New York Times* critic Manohla Dargis gushing, "After years of vivisectionist splatter, here is a horror movie with real shivers." By early 2010, the film had already acquired a following. Interviewed by *The New York Post* to publicize the DVD release, Gerwig was quoted as saying that audiences were "hungry for good, small movies that have some style. That's what Ti provided."

West returned to the Yankee Pedlar for his next film, 2011's *The Innkeepers*. Inspired by the director's experiences during the *House of the Devil* pro-

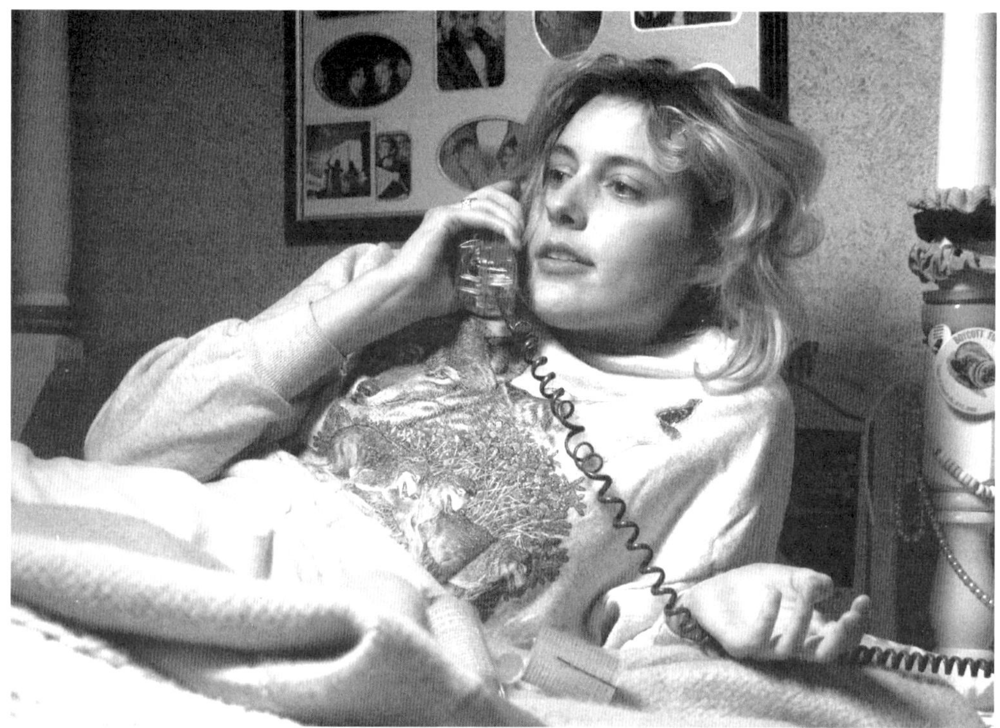

Greta Gerwig on the set of *The House of the Devil.*

duction, the film starred Sara Paxton and Pat Healy as hotel employees who investigate ghostly goings-on at the establishment. West and his team not only stayed at the Pedlar Inn but shot the film there as well. The director was taken aback to discover that he had accidentally chosen the center of the alleged supernatural activities at the hotel as one of the production's main shooting locales. "The room in the movie that's the honeymoon suite, the most haunted room in the movie, I only picked that room because it was on the third floor at the end of the hallway and it was big enough to do a dolly shot," says West. "I found out that is the haunted room in real life. Now, that's just a coincidence. But when you add all of that stuff up, it's a weird coincidence. I don't believe in ghosts, but I believe in the weird Yankee Pedlar."

Paramount and Blumhouse decided to move forward swiftly with a *Paranormal Activity* sequel. Oren Peli was occupied making his second movie, *Area 51*, so Jason Blum recruited the man whose debut had just been beaten at the box office by Peli's film. In January 2010, Paramount announced that *Saw VI* filmmaker Kevin Greutert would direct *Paranormal Activity 2*. The studio gave the sequel a release date of October 22, the same day the seventh *Saw* movie—which was being shot in 3D—would arrive in cinemas.

After *Saw IV*, filmmaker Darren Bousman had continued to work with Twisted Pictures and Lionsgate, directing the 2008 musical *Repo! The Genetic Opera* for the companies. Bousman recalls that this rematch between the two franchises was the talk of Hollywood's horror community. "You've got *Paranormal Activity* going against *Saw* and, oh shit, Kevin Greutert is now attached to direct *Paranormal Activity*!" says the director. "I was on the end of a lot of fucking phone calls about that."

Blum received a blow when Twisted Pictures exercised an option in Greutert's contract to have him direct the seventh *Saw* film, making it impossible for him to oversee *Paranormal Activity 2*. For his part, Greutert was unhappy about being forced to make another *Saw* movie. On January 25, 2010, the filmmaker went public with his dissatisfaction in a blog post headlined "Woo hoo! Lawyers are sending me to Canada tomorrow!" "I just had the task of telling my 83-year-old mother that no, I'm not going to be allowed to direct the movie we were all so excited about when my family last got together, and that I'm being forced to leave town before getting a chance to see her again," he wrote. "Yes, I'll be filming people getting tortured YET AGAIN. So we'll have to put off me making a film she can actually watch for another year."

The *Paranormal Activity* producers scrambled to find a replacement for Greutert. On February 24, the *Los Angeles Times* published an article reporting that the list of candidates included *Session 9* director Brad Anderson, *Wolf Creek* filmmaker Greg McLean, and the legendary Brian De Palma. At one point, Blum and Steven Schneider suggested giving $100,000 to ten different directors, tasking them each with making a *Paranormal Activity 2*, and then releasing the best one. "Thank God Adam shot us down," Blum said in the documentary *Unknown Dimension: The Story of Paranormal Activity*. "That was one of our ideas which was a really bad idea."

Paramount and Blumhouse announced in March that Tod Williams, who had directed the 2004 drama *The Door in the Floor*, had been hired to make the sequel. The film's credited writers would include Christopher Landon, the son of *Little House on the Prairie* actor Michael Landon. "When I was a kid, I developed a fascination with horror films, mega B-movie kind of stuff, and my dad loved that stuff as well," he says. Landon established himself in Hollywood by writing 2007's hit thriller *Disturbia* and was one of the first people Jason Blum had invited to watch the original *Paranormal Activity* at his house. "This was probably a year and a half or two years before [*Paranormal Activity*] came out," says Landon. "He knew I was a crazy horror nut. I don't even know if he had seen it yet. So I went over to his house, and I saw the movie, and it scared the fuck out of me."

Paranormal Activity 2 concerned the supernatural torments visited on the family of Kristi, the sister of Katie Featherston's character. Landon only started working on the film after the production was well underway. "They called and said, 'Hey, we're making the second one, we're kind of struggling with it, will you come to a roundtable with some of the other writers and talk about it?'" he says. "So I got there, and they were trying to make the movie the way they had made it before, which was like, 'We'll just come up with an idea, and shoot stuff, and see what happens.' Everyone in the room was going, 'This is great, this is great.' The head of the studio was watching my body language and finally said, 'What's wrong?' I said, 'This isn't great, you guys are in trouble.'" Landon suggested including a moment that demonstrated the physical power of the film's supernatural entity. "I pitched an idea, which ended up being the scene in the second movie where Kristi gets dragged out of the nursery and down the stairs," he says. "The head of the studio was like, 'Go home and write that scene, we're going to shoot that.' And they did, and they liked it, and I ended up rewriting the entire movie."

Featherston and Micah Sloat both made appearances in *Paranormal Activity 2*. According to Sloat, "Katie and I were treated like actors in a film, where you just show up and read what's on the script, so that was difficult for me to not be as involved. Luckily, the second film works great."

Kevin Greutert, meanwhile, set to work directing the seventh *Saw* movie. Speaking with *Entertainment Weekly* just before the release of the film, he admitted, "Starting with the release of *Saw VI*, and the disappointing box office performance, it's been a dark time for me, no question… There was a lot of crazy turmoil in this production. Frankly, I'm glad it's over. Because there were definitely things that I would have done differently if I had been on the film from the beginning. But at the same time, they wouldn't have brought me on so suddenly and at the last minute if they didn't trust my opinion. It all worked out."

Greutert's film featured the return of Cary Elwes' Dr. Lawrence Gordon, the first time the character had been seen onscreen since he had removed his own foot at the end of the original film. In July 2010, Lionsgate enhanced the box office chances of their franchise's seventh entry, titled *Saw 3D*, by postponing the film's release a week to October 29, thus avoiding a direct head-to-head with *Paranormal Activity 2*. The *Saw* team attempted to pique interest in the upcoming film by insisting that it would be the last entry in the franchise. "It's time to stop," producer Oren Koules said to *USA Today*. "We have told the story we wanted to tell, and this is going to be a great farewell." In the same article, Mark Burg revealed that the film had been submitted six times to the MPAA to bring down the rating from an NC-17 to an R rating. "I'm surprised we got it," said the producer.

Paranormal Activity 2 earned a massive $40 million over its first weekend on release in the US, knocking Paramount's own *Jackass 3D* into second place. The following week, it was *Paranormal Activity 2* that had to settle for the number two slot thanks to the arrival of *Saw 3D*, which grossed $22 million by the end of its initial three days in cinemas. *Paranormal Activity 2* went on to earn $177 million worldwide; *Saw 3D* took in $136 million.

Although the *Saw* franchise remained profitable, the Twisted Pictures producers followed through on their decision to shelve the series. 2011 would be the first year since 2003 not to see the release of a new *Saw* film. "It's crazy to think that an entire generation of teenagers grew up on the *Saw* franchise," says James Wan. "For them, it was like *Harry Potter*. Each year represented another *Saw* movie, and there was seven of them. That's, like, the entire high school career. I don't know why it captured the public imagination the way it did, but it did, and I'm very thankful for it."

As Lionsgate wound down the *Saw* series, Paramount and Blumhouse ploughed on with the *Paranormal Activity* franchise. The companies offered the job of directing the third *Paranormal Activity* film to Henry Joost and Ariel Schulman, the directors of 2010's *Catfish*. Christopher Landon wrote the script for the film, which was set in the '80s and focused on the childhood of siblings Katie and Kristi. "I had a certain random understanding of the format, and I felt we were creating a language for this kind of filmmaking," he says. "It looked easy to people, but it's really hard to make those movies. You don't have traditional coverage, you don't have a score to push things along, you don't have any of the stuff that we get really used to in a traditional movie. So you had to find clever ways to create dread and keep people involved."

Paranormal Activity 3 was released on October 21, 2011, and earned $52 million over its opening weekend, the highest initial gross ever for a horror movie. Speaking the next week to *Entertainment Weekly*, Jason Blum admitted that he had been taken aback by the film's record-breaking success. "I was floored, honestly," he said. "I got an email from Bob Weinstein on Friday: 'Congratulations: 35–40.' And then Saturday he wrote me like, 'Okay, this

Chloe Csengery and Jessica Tyler Brown in *Paranormal Activity 3* (2011).

is disgusting.'" Joost, Schulman, and Landon returned for 2012's *Paranormal Activity 4*. The fourquel was less commercially successful than its predecessor but still grossed $142 million around the globe.

The success of *Cloverfield* and *Paranormal Activity* encouraged filmmakers and executives to look again at the found footage genre as a way of relating horror tales. Platinum Dunes even developed a found footage *Friday the 13th* movie. According to co-founder Brad Fuller, the idea was dropped after fans reacted poorly to it. "There was an outpouring of negative sentiment," he told the website Shock Till You Drop in 2015.

That sentiment was a reaction to the abundance of found footage horror movies that followed the release of the first *Paranormal Activity*. As *Fangoria* writer Michael Gingold noted in an interview with Oren Peli to promote the home entertainment release of *Paranormal Activity 4*, "*The Blair Witch Project* may have popularized the form back in 1999, but it was Peli's movie, a decade later, that lit the fuse that blasted camcorder creepshows—many set in abandoned asylums or other haunted places—all over the genre landscape."

The found footage craze delivered cinematic highs, like Norwegian director André Øvredal's 2011's horror-fantasy *Troll Hunter* and Adam Robitel's 2014 supernatural tale *The Taking of Deborah Logan*. But there were also patience-testing lows. An unnerving trailer propelled 2012's Paramount-distributed exorcism film *The Devil Inside* to a domestic box office gross of $53 million. Yet the actual movie's abrupt ending, which referred audiences to a website "for more information on the ongoing investigation," led viewers to give the film a rare 'F' CinemaScore. As *Empire* critic William Thomas wrote, "Some found footage should really just stay lost."

Although Robert Kirkman had feared that Frank Darabont's promise to make a TV show out of *The Walking Dead* was simply the director "blowing smoke up my ass," Darabont was true to his word. After finishing *The Mist*, the filmmaker partnered on the proposed comic-book adaption with Gale Anne Hurd, producer of *The Terminator* and *Aliens*, and the duo secured a deal with the cable channel AMC.

Darabont wanted Thomas Jane to play the show's lead role, post-apocalyptic survivor Rick Grimes, but the actor was busy shooting the HBO comedy-drama series *Hung*. "HBO were like, 'You can't go star in another show for some other network,'" says Jane. "We tried to convince them to bring [*The Walking Dead*] to HBO. The lady who was running it at the time had done *True Blood* and she basically said, 'We don't want to become the monster channel.' Of course, it turned out to be not a great decision, but that's why I couldn't go along."

Darabont auditioned other candidates for the role, including Andrew Lincoln. The British actor was best known for playing the lovelorn Mark in the 2003 romantic comedy *Love Actually*, a part that had little in common with the tough (and American) Grimes, yet Darabont believed that he had found his man. "He's got this amazing Gary Cooper, Sam Shepard quality," said the director ahead of the show's premiere. "He completely embodies this guy, and I think he's really going to surprise people."

The news that AMC was producing a *Walking Dead* show came as a disappointment to *Phantasm* director Don Coscarelli, who was also interested in adapting the comic. "I reached out to Robert Kirkman, and he came back and said he was a *Bubba Ho-Tep* fan," he recalls. "I said, 'Well, what's happening with the rights to [*The Walking Dead*]?' And he says, 'Oh, we're having a meeting, but it looks like it might just be available.' I said, 'I'll have my manager call.' I guess they made the deal for the rights. Yeah, I was 15 minutes late on that one."

The first, six-episode season of *The Walking Dead* was shot in Atlanta during the hot summer months of 2010. Darabont was determined that the show, like Kirkman's comics, would honor the zombie lore established in George A. Romero's movies. Per the title of the series, the undead would be walking (or at most swiftly stumbling) rather than running. The director decreed that none of the zombies on *The Walking Dead* could move faster than *Night of the Living Dead* actor Bill Hinzman's reanimated corpse in the opening sequence of Romero's movie. "My feeling has always been, let's treat *Night of the Living Dead* as The Book of Genesis," Darabont told *Entertainment Weekly*. "You can run, but it's got to be at the speed [of] the first zombie in *Night of the Living Dead.* It is difficult to explain that to 180 extras in the heat, and God knows how many of them have actually seen that movie. I think most of their understanding comes from more recent films like the *Dawn of the Dead* remake or *28 Days Later*, where they're Olympic sprinters. We're never going to have Olympic sprinter zombies." The show's makeups and gore effects were overseen by Greg Nicotero, who organized a 'zombie school' where extras were coached on how to portray the undead.

Makeup effects artist Greg Nicotero on the set of *The Walking Dead.*

Darabont directed the show's pilot and then handed off the remaining five episodes to others, with Ernest Dickerson hired to make the penultimate show. The *Bones* director was, of course, no stranger to horror and had worked on a slew of TV shows, including *The Wire* and Showtime's serial killer series *Dexter*. "Darabont, he micro-managed everybody but me," says Dickerson. "I pretty much decided, as I was doing the episode, that it was a western, so I was treating it like a western."

The Walking Dead pilot premiered on Sunday, October 31, 2010, and attracted 5.35 million viewers, the most-watched series debut for AMC. The second episode, "Guts," attracted an audience of 4.7 million, which *The Hollywood Reporter* described as "an incredibly high retention of a record rating." The day after "Guts" screened, AMC announced that the cable channel had renewed *The Walking Dead* for a 13-episode second season. "The *Dead* has spread!" AMC president Charlie Collier said in a statement. "No other cable series has ever attracted as many Adults 18–49 as *The Walking Dead*."

Resident Evil director Paul W. S. Anderson's prediction that the zombie film was ripe for a comeback had been proven correct again and again over the previous decade. Now, the undead were shambling around on the small

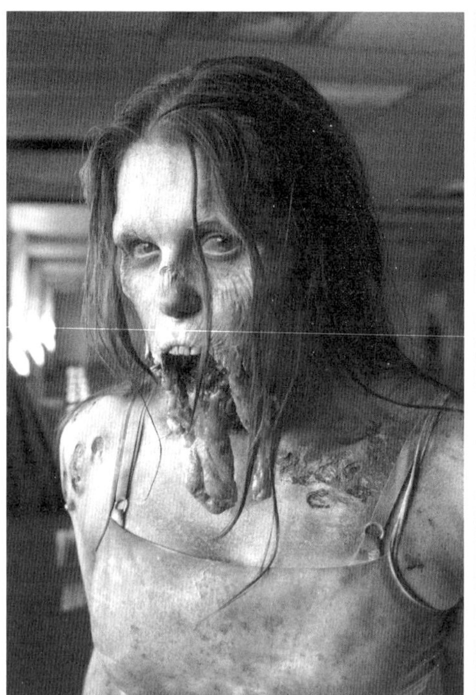
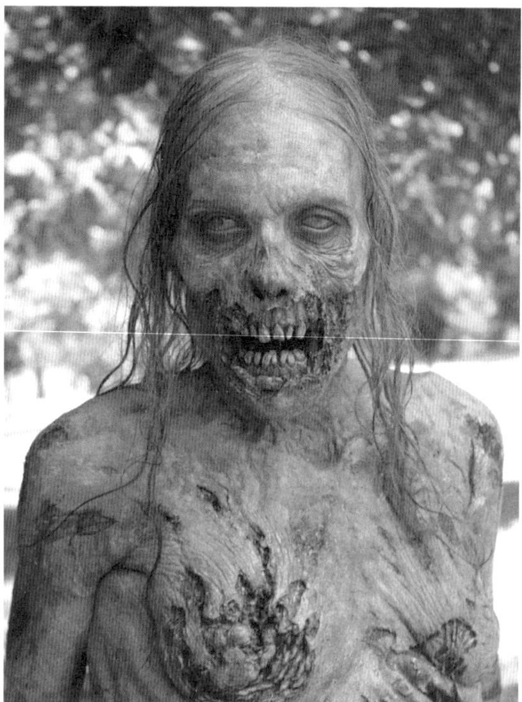

Behind-the-scenes shots of *The Walking Dead* zombies.

screen as well. Looking back, the filmmaker is happy to have played a role in reviving the zombie genre. "*Resident Evil* kind of opened the gates," he admits. "The gates to hell were open, and then the dead got to flood out onto the earth. Yeah, that was really wonderful."

Anderson both wrote and directed the fourth *Resident Evil* film, which he titled *Resident Evil: Afterlife*. The filmmaker decided to shoot the film in 3D after seeing footage from James Cameron's yet-to-be-released *Avatar*. "Cameron had shot *Avatar* when we were thinking of doing a *Resident 4* in 3D," says Anderson. "He gave me a preview. The backgrounds weren't fully rendered, but because he'd shot native 3D, I was really blown away."

The cast for *Resident Evil: Afterlife* included Wentworth Miller, Kim Coates, a returning Ali Larter, and, as always, Milla Jovovich. The film opened in the US on September 10, 2010, and held the number one spot over the weekend. It went on to earn $60 million in North America, more than any previous entry in the franchise. Anderson's movie proved even more popular abroad, grossing $240 million in international markets.

Screen Gems also greenlit a fourth entry in the *Underworld* franchise. After effectively checking out of the series for *Underworld: Rise of the Lycans*, Kate Beckinsale returned as Selene for *Underworld: Awakening*. The movie was co-written by Len Wiseman and directed in Vancouver by Swedish filmmakers Björn Stein and Måns Mårlind. *Underworld: Awakening* opened on January 20, 2012, and matched the $62 million box office take of the second film. As was the case with *Resident Evil*, the *Underworld* franchise had become a bigger deal in foreign territories, with *Underworld: Awakening* earning a total box office gross of $160 million.

Anderson shot a fifth *Resident Evil* film, *Resident Evil: Retribution*, in Toronto during the second half of 2011. In addition to Jovovich, the cast included veteran franchise actors Sienna Guillory, Colin Salmon, Oded Fehr, and Michelle Rodriguez. The film opened on September 14, 2012, snagging the number one spot. *Resident Evil: Retribution* earned $42 million in the US and $197 million elsewhere. Just a few days after the film's release, Sony domestic distribution executive Rory Bruer confirmed to *Variety* that the studio would make a sixth movie in the series. "It ain't ending here," he said.

Jason Blum first met James Wan and Leigh Whannell in November 2009, shortly after the box office face-off between *Paranormal Activity* and *Saw VI*. The encounter took place at Fox Plaza, the skyscraper where Joe Lynch had made his pitch to direct the second *Wrong Turn* film. "I remember it very, very well," says Blum of meeting the *Saw* creators. "I was in post-production on *The Tooth Fairy*, and Fox had given me a closet to work in on the lot. I was so excited to be talking to the two people responsible for *Saw*."

Wan recalls that he and Whannell were thrilled about the location of the meeting. "It was very exciting for Leigh and myself, because we got to meet Jason in what we referred to as 'the Nakatomi building,'" says the director. "We were just geeking out as we were arriving at the front lobby and going, 'Oh my God, this is where Bruce Willis fought terrorists. In this building!'"

Their meeting would be more convivial than the climactic showdown between Willis' John McClane and Alan Rickman's Hans Gruber. While Blum was no horror aficionado, he was happy to further explore a genre that could deliver the kind of profits generated by *Paranormal Activity*. The producer had partnered with Oren Peli and Steven Schneider to develop more low-budget genre films, backed by the Canadian distributor Alliance Films. The trio hoped that Wan and Whannell might have a suitable project for them. They would not be disappointed.

The pair had been developing a movie about astral projection. The film, ultimately titled *Insidious*, would focus on a family whose son falls into a coma. The parents come to believe that their house is haunted, only to later learn that their boy's consciousness is trapped in the Further, a plane of existence occupied by disturbed spirits. "We really wanted to do this independently, because we value creative freedom," Whannell would later tell film journalist Stevie Wong. "And that's when the producers of *Paranormal Activity*… they sat down with us and said, 'Do you guys have an idea? Because we would love to do a horror film with you guys, independently, just like *Saw*.' And James and I just looked at each other, and we were like, 'It just so happens we *do* have an idea.'"

Their pitch was welcomed by Blum and his partners, who were keen to start shooting the film as soon as possible. *Hard Candy* star Patrick Wilson signed on to portray the film's male lead, Josh Lambert, and *28 Weeks Later* actress Rose Byrne agreed to play his wife Renai.

(*Behind*) Joseph Bishara and Patrick Wilson in *Insidious* (2010).

Wan cast Lin Shaye as a psychic named Elise Rainier. The *A Nightmare on Elm Street* actress had met the director and Whannell when the pair worked with her on a 2008 short called *Doggie Heaven*. The film starred Whannell as a man who is shot by Shaye's character after accidentally killing her dog and finds himself in a canine-filled afterlife. *Doggie Heaven* was one of several comedy shorts directed by horror filmmakers and released via the Xbox 360 video game console in 2008. The series of films had been conceived by James Gunn and his manager Peter Safran, who was introduced to Wan by the *Slither* director. Shaye recalls that the script for *Insidious* "scared the daylights out of me. I read it in bed and, when I finished it, I took it downstairs and locked it in the closet." Shaye's terror did not prevent her agreeing to portray Elise.

The film's supporting cast included Barbara Hershey, who played the mother of Wilson's character. Whannell himself portrayed Specs, one of Elise's assistants, and his fellow Australian Angus Sampson was cast as her other helper, Tucker. The budget for *Insidious* was just over $1 million, with the key talent agreeing to accept little money up front in exchange for profit participation.

Before shooting began, Wan enlisted the help of musician, composer, and horror movie devotee Joseph Bishara. In the '90s, Bishara had played guitars and keyboards with the industrial rock band Drown and composed the score for Mike Mendez's film *Killers*. Bishara and Wan were members of a loose grouping of horror-loving creatives known as the Fright Club. "There were a few years where all these people in horror, we'd get together," says Bishara. "I met Darren Bousman that way, I met James through that group. I believe a Fangoria Weekend of Horrors convention was in town, and there were some people hanging at my house, and someone brought him over." Wan asked Bishara to write the music for *Insidious* and also to play the film's supernatural antagonist, the so-called Lipstick-Face Demon. "He mentioned there was this demon character that he wanted to talk to me about playing," says Bishara. "I think it was a combination of him going, 'Well, he's got the right build, he already shaves his head, maybe he can contort his body a little bit.' I just thought, 'Sure, yeah.' When I got the script, it was like, this is the *main* demon."

Wan shot the film at the Herald Examiner Building in downtown Los Angeles. "It was definitely an indie film, no question, but an indie set where you walk in and there's a lot of talent in the room," says Bishara. Patrick Wilson recalls approaching his performance as a genuinely dramatic endeavor.

"When James and I first talked about *Insidious*, in our very early conversations we were thinking about this throwback to the '70s," says the actor. "All the movies that I grew up on, the horror movies that resonated with me, specifically I think of *The Exorcist* and *Poltergeist*, these were dramatic actors."

Wan was determined that *Insidious* should be terrifying but also a far less gruesome affair than *Saw*, believing that his reputation had been harmed by his association with torture porn. "*Saw* was good and bad," he says. "It was good in that it gave me a career start, but it was also negative in that it really marginalized me as a filmmaker. It made a lot of people in Hollywood think that I was 'that guy,' that that was the only kind of movies I made—despite the fact that I only directed the first *Saw* film."

Wan and Whannell disagreed about whether to title the film *Insidious* or *The Further*. "It was a big argument between James and Leigh," Lin Shaye would recall to *Fangoria*. "I said I thought 'insidious' is such a great word. It sounds gnarly with those 's'es, and I was all for it, and I think it helped them to hear another person describe why they thought it was the right name. So *Insidious* stuck, and I still think it's a great title."

Insidious received its world premiere at the Toronto Film Festival in September 2010, six years after *Saw* had played the same event. The film was acquired by FilmDistrict, a new distribution and production company co-

Leigh Whannell and Lin Shaye in *Insidious*.

founded by *The Departed* producer Graham King. "With *Insidious*, James and Leigh are redefining the haunted house genre," FilmDistrict executive Peter Schlessel said in a statement at the time. "By taking well-known horror movie conventions and elevating them to the next level, they've created a film that is fun, suspenseful and very very scary."

Opening on April 1, 2011, the film placed third on the box office chart over its first weekend in theaters, earning $13 million, an impressive return given its low budget. The next weekend, *Insidious* grossed $9 million, and the movie continued to perform well over the ensuing weeks. The film would go on to earn $54 million in the US and $99 million in total.

On June 29, 2011, Deadline journalist Mike Fleming Jr. announced that Blumhouse Productions had struck a three-year first-look deal with Universal Pictures. Fleming's article noted that the first two *Paranormal Activity* films had grossed a combined $370 million and that the Blum-produced *Insidious* was the year's most profitable film. "This guy is minting money," wrote the journalist.

In July 2008, The Weinstein Company and Showtime issued a statement announcing that the two corporate entities had entered into an exclusive seven-year film distribution arrangement. The press release explained that the deal would become effective with the Weinsteins' 2009 slate of releases, which included the Daniel Day-Lewis musical *Nine* and Quentin Tarantino's war movie *Inglourious Basterds*. For horror fans, the big news came near the end of the announcement with the revelation that the company planned on "re-starting the *Scream* franchise with *Scream 4*."

The idea to relaunch the franchise originated with Kevin Williamson. "One day I'm just sitting around, and I go, 'Oh, wait—I think—oh my God, I think I have it,'" Williamson told *Entertainment Weekly* writer Tim Stack in 2011, explaining how he came up with the premise for the film. "I had written this treatment for *Scream 3* that was not what they filmed... So then I always wanted to go back to Woodsboro. Once I figured out where Sidney was today, who dies and who doesn't, I said, 'Okay, maybe now I can have a conversation with Bob [Weinstein].' I called him up and pitched him. Of course, he just heard '*Scream 4*.' Literally, after I pitched the first scene, I think he just stopped listening and was just like, 'Write it, write it, write it.'"

Weinstein's enthusiasm for a new *Scream* was understandable given the poor commercial track record of The Weinstein Company since he and Harvey had founded the independent studio. In August 2009, *The New York Times* published an article detailing the brothers' business woes with the participation of the siblings themselves, who were promoting *Inglourious Basterds*. Writer David Segal included the information that of the 70-odd films released by The Weinstein Company, more than a quarter had failed to break the $1 million box office mark in the US, and 13 of those had taken in less than $100,000. Segal suggested that the brothers had overstretched themselves by investing in businesses like the fashion label Halston and the social networking site ASmallWorld. The article explained that The Weinstein Company was also "coping with the same problems facing every other studio, most notably the grim slowdown of the DVD market." Segal informed readers that the brothers were now returning to their core areas of expertise—and that Bob was "planning three new *Scream* films."

Scream 4 was still in the planning stage when Williamson struck small-screen gold with his TV series *The Vampire Diaries*. The writer had developed the show with Julie Plec, and the teen drama became a hit after its premiere on The CW network in September 2009. The series was on hiatus as *Scream 4* moved toward production, but Williamson's commitment to the show proved a problem when the writer began to butt heads with Bob Weinstein over

Neve Campbell in *Scream 4* (2011).

the horror sequel's script. The writer eventually left the movie, and Kruger was hired to rework the screenplay.

Wes Craven returned to shoot *Scream 4* in Michigan during the summer of 2010. In addition to Neve Campbell, Courteney Cox, and David Arquette, the film featured Emma Roberts, Rory Culkin, Marley Shelton, and Hayden Panettiere. The latter had become a star thanks to her role on the NBC show *Heroes* and was cast as a horror movie-loving high schooler named Kirby Reed. Panettiere describes accepting the role as "one of the best decisions I've ever made in my life and my career. Wes was so warm, and kind, and considerate, and like a father. He was a wonderful human being."

Cox and Arquette would have less pleasant memories of the shoot because of their disintegrating relationship. In October 2010, following the end of principal photography, the couple announced that they were separating after eleven years of marriage. The next January, Arquette checked into rehab, seeking help for depression and alcoholism. In *Entertainment Weekly* writer Tim Stack's 2011 cover story about the film, Craven would say that the pair's relationship issues "never crept into work or made anyone uncomfortable. The only thing that was odd was that when he finished his shooting, he didn't go home. Then we started to wonder what was going on."

Craven's real problem was the film's perpetually changing script. "I always prided myself on coming to the set with a shot list," he told *Entertainment Weekly*. "But quite often we'd literally get pages the night before, sometimes the day of. That part was stressful." Some of those pages were written by Scott Derrickson, who volunteered to remotely assist the production because of his fondness for Craven. "I was in Hawaii, and I got the call from Bob Weinstein," the director says. "I was on the phone with Bob and Wes in the afternoons, and then I would write into the evenings and send them pages. Sometimes the things that I would be writing in Hawaii, they would be faxed to the set, and they would shoot them as they were coming in. It was crazy. I really loved Wes, and I felt terrible for him, being in that kind of a situation. I was like, 'I'm not going to give you anything you don't want, no matter what Bob says.' I was having these sort of side conversations with him, finding out what he liked and really didn't like about Bob Weinstein's ideas."

Scream 4 opened on April 15, 2011, and earned $18 million over its first weekend in cinemas. That figure was twice the amount initially grossed by *Scream* fifteen years previously but much less than the opening figures amassed by the previous two sequels. *Scream 4* ultimately earned a disappointing $59 million in the US.

This comparative failure put The Weinstein Company's plans for more franchise entries on hold. In May 2011, Harvey Weinstein told MTV News that he was "sure" Craven would direct a fifth *Scream*. The following week, the filmmaker declared to *Entertainment Weekly* that he was in no rush to do so. "I'm taking the summer off," said Craven.

In June 2012, TV Line writer Michael Ausiello revealed that MTV was developing a weekly series based on the *Scream* films. Despite Craven being a credited executive producer, he would have little involvement with the show, which premiered in June 2015 and ran for three seasons. "I just put my name on it," he told *The Hollywood Reporter* in an interview published in April 2015.

On Sunday, August 30, 2015, the director's family announced that the 76-year-old director had died at his home in Los Angeles after a battle with brain cancer. "That was a shock in so many ways," says Patrick Lussier. "We hadn't seen a lot of each other in the last three or four years before that, just because I'd been busy doing other movies. I didn't realize he was sick until weeks before he passed, and then reached out to him, and at that point [the family] were really sort of closed ranks. I know his speech had receded with the cancer. For somebody who was always so eloquent and clever, I'm sure that must have been very challenging for him."

A memorial service for Craven was held in Los Angeles later that year. Attendees included Lussier, Matthew Lillard, and Tobe Hooper, who would himself pass away two years later. "So many of these great filmmakers showed up," says Lussier. "But also, there was one of the heads of the Audubon Society, a nature society, who played bird calls as part of the eulogy, which Wes would have loved even more."

CHAPTER 14

"THERE IS SOMETHING HORRIBLE HAPPENING IN MY HOUSE."

Following the release of *Paranormal Activity* and *Insidious*, Jason Blum produced several non-genre projects, including Damien Chazelle's Oscar-winning 2014 drama *Whiplash*. But the producer and his company Blumhouse soon became synonymous with low-budget horror.

In October 2012, Lionsgate released the Blumhouse-produced *Sinister*. The film starred Ethan Hawke as a true crime author named Ellison Oswalt who moves his family into a house where the previous occupants were killed by hanging. Oswalt finds a box of Super 8 films in the attic of his new home that depict those murders and other atrocities, which, the writer learns, have been orchestrated by an entity called Bughuul.

Sinister was directed and co-written by *The Exorcism of Emily Rose* filmmaker Scott Derrickson, and the movie's dark tone echoed his recent professional experiences. Derrickson had not enjoyed the experience of directing his expensive remake of *The Day the Earth Stood Still*, which had been released in December 2008 to poor reviews and mediocre box office. The director was in a bleak place mentally when he visited Guillermo del Toro at the *Hellboy* filmmaker's Los Angeles house. "I had never met him in person until that day," says Derrickson. "I was going to talk to him about something else, but the movie had just come out. I said, 'I'm sorry, I can't even concentrate, I am just bleeding inside.' He was like, 'What's the matter?' I said, 'This movie just came out, this thing is a critical disaster, it's a financial disappointment. We got trapped in the writers' strike, but I still went ahead and did it. I feel like my career is over.'"

Del Toro gave his fellow director some guidance which, he claimed, had the potential to set Derrickson's career back on track. "He stuck his finger in my face, and he said, 'Don't do that again!', which made me laugh, but I've always taken that to heart," says Derrickson. "What he meant was, don't

Ethan Hawke in *Sinister* (2012).

be willing to compromise your vision, it's better to make no movie than a bad one. Every film that I've made since then, my attitude was: if I die on a sword, it's going to be *my* sword."

Sinister was the first movie born from this new attitude. The idea for the film came from C. Robert Cargill, a movie reviewer and Ain't It Cool News contributor, who pitched Derrickson when they properly met for the first time in Las Vegas. "It was at the Mandalay Bay, three in the morning," says Derrickson. "Cargill had had five White Russians—he was like the Dude in *The Big Lebowski*—and he pitched me an idea he had years before, right after seeing *The Ring*. He had a nightmare about a guy going up into his attic and finding a box of Super 8 films that had murders on them. I thought, 'This is an *amazing* idea for a horror film.'"

Derrickson and Cargill developed the screenplay together, and the director struck a deal to make *Sinister* with Blum. "Jason gave me $3 million and final cut," says Derrickson. "I didn't know if the movie was going to succeed or not, but I knew that it was going to be my movie."

Derrickson suggested to Blum that they cast Ethan Hawke in the lead, unaware that the pair were close. "I emailed Jason, and I said, 'I think the perfect actor for Ellison Oswalt is Ethan Hawke. Do you know him?''' says Derrickson. "An email came straight back, and it said, 'He's my dearest friend.'" Hawke was fearful of starring in the movie, however. "He told me, 'I'd like to make a good horror film, but I'm afraid of the experience being too disturbing,'" Derrickson says of the actor. "I was like, 'Oh, Ethan, there's nothing that's more fun to make than a horror film. It's not brutal, it's a blast.'" *Sinister* was a hit, earning $48 million at the domestic box office and another $34 million overseas.

Blum and Hawke swiftly recombined for a second original horror movie, 2013's *The Purge*. Written and directed by James DeMonaco, the film was set in a near-future America where citizens are allowed to commit crimes for one night a year. "We wrote it as an indie," says DeMonaco, who developed the screenplay with his producing partner Sébastien K. Lemercier. "We thought it would play at the Angelika in New York, and that would be it."

Blum liked the script for *The Purge* and believed that the project would appeal to a wide audience. DeMonaco shot the film over 18 days in Los Angeles for just $2.5 million. The budget did not allow for much in the way of luxuries, or even accommodation, with Hawke staying at Blum's home for the duration of the production. "There were no perks," the actor told *The Hollywood Reporter*. "No trailer, no driver, no BS, just a great role, a great director. Hell, on *The Purge*, I slept on his couch the whole shoot."

Masked 'purgers' in *The Purge* (2013).

Distributed by Universal, *The Purge* earned $34 million in the US over its opening weekend in June 2013, going on to gross $89 million worldwide. The original movie would be followed by 2014's *The Purge: Anarchy*, which starred Frank Grillo and earned $22 million more at the global box office than the first film. The Sunday after the release of *The Purge: Anarchy*, Blumhouse and Universal announced that they had struck a ten-year first-look production agreement. The results of that deal would include three more entries in *The Purge* franchise.

Joss Whedon had not enjoyed the wave of extreme horror movies that began with *House of 1000 Corpses* and *Cabin Fever*. The creator of the *Buffy the Vampire Slayer* TV show believed that their creators had confused genuine horror with mere violent mayhem. "We've had a growing disconnect between watching people getting murdered and 'horror,' which is *not* actually about murder," Whedon told *Entertainment Weekly* in 2012. "It can contain murder, but it's not limited to it."

Whedon wanted to make a 'cabin in the woods' movie that channeled the scary but still fun vibes of *Halloween*, *The Evil Dead*, and *A Nightmare on Elm Street*. He reached out to *Cloverfield* co-writer Drew Goddard to help with the project. The pair rented a bungalow at a hotel in Los Angeles and spent three days writing the screenplay, which they titled *The Cabin in the Woods*. The script followed a quintet of deliberately stereotypical college friends (a stoner, a jock, a demure final girl, etc.) who are menaced by a family of zombies during a trip to the country. The group's last two survivors learn that their torments are being overseen by a secret organization that periodically sacrifices groups of young people to prevent the end of the world.

In July 2008, MGM's freshly installed worldwide motion picture group chairman Mary Parent announced that she had greenlit *The Cabin in the Woods*, with Goddard set to direct. The production moved forward under the corporate umbrella of the MGM-owned studio United Artists, which had been resurrected in 2006 by Tom Cruise and Paula Wagner.

MGM executive Dan Kolsrud approached David LeRoy Anderson about overseeing the project's effects, including the movie's many and various monsters. Anderson remembers that he "sat down with Drew and Joss Whedon, and they said, 'Okay, we're doing a movie called *Cabin in the Woods*, and everything has to be practical, and we want every monster to be in this

Zombie carnage in *The Cabin in the Woods* (2012).

movie.' I read the script and my mind exploded. I was saying, 'How the fuck are we going to do this? This is insane!'"

Anderson rented the biggest studio space he could find in Los Angeles and put together a team of around 60 illustrators, designers, and makeup artists. He set them to work conceptualizing and creating the film's murderous monsters, which ranged from a werewolf to zombies to a merman and beyond. "What happened in that room is something that's probably never going to happen in Hollywood again," he says.

Goddard and Whedon assembled a cast which included Richard Jenkins and Bradley Whitford as employees of the secret organization and Kristen Connolly, Fran Kranz, and Chris Hemsworth as members of the film's friend group. Hemsworth was still a somewhat obscure actor when he auditioned, but Goddard immediately knew he was perfect for the part of the jock Curt. "We probably saw over 100 people for that role," he says. "He walked in at the end of that session, and the hair stood up on my arms."

Goddard filmed *The Cabin in the Woods* in Vancouver during the spring of 2009. The director recalls that Anderson's wife and business partner Heather Langenkamp was a hands-on presence during the production. "Heather was on set, in meetings," says the director. "There were definitely days where we would look at each other and go, 'Wait, did the star of *Nightmare on Elm Street* just solve all our problems?'"

In November 2010, MGM filed for Chapter 11 bankruptcy protection and the release of *The Cabin in the Woods* was indefinitely postponed. "It was brutal," says Kranz. "It had two release dates that both got pushed. It got to the point where I was like the crazy person talking about *Cabin in the Woods*. Even my mom [was] like, 'Maybe it just wasn't any good.'"

In July 2011, Lionsgate announced that the company had acquired worldwide distribution rights to *The Cabin in the Woods* and would release the film on April 13, 2012. Ironically, the company whose extreme output had annoyed Whedon would now be releasing his and Goddard's movie.

The film had been on the shelf so long that Hemsworth was now a major star following the release of Marvel's *Thor* in the spring of 2011. By the time *The Cabin in the Woods* was released, Hemsworth would have become more famous

Chris Hemsworth, Jesse Williams, Anna Hutchison, Fran Kranz, and Kristen Connolly in *The Cabin in the Woods*.

still thanks to the publicity campaign for the Joss Whedon-directed *The Avengers*, which arrived in US cinemas just three weeks after Goddard's movie.

The Los Angeles premiere of the film took place on April 10, 2012, three years after the shoot in Vancouver. Guests at the event included Scott Derrickson, Joe Dante, and Wes Craven, who gave his verdict on the film to *The Hollywood Reporter*. "I thought it had a fun, meta feel and a lot of quotes to films of mine and my friends," he said. "But it also went off in its own direction."

When David LeRoy Anderson saw the finished film, he was sad to discover that the monsters were not *all* practical, with Goddard and Whedon having added a giant snake to the bloody climax. "I reacted negatively the very first viewing," he says. "Now I love it, and it wouldn't have been the same movie without things of that scale, but that was a huge surprise when I saw it."

Over its opening weekend in US cinemas, *The Cabin in the Woods* earned $14 million, enough to earn a third place on the box office chart, and the film would gross a satisfying $69 million around the world. But its earnings would be dwarfed by the $1.5 billion earned by Whedon's *The Avengers*, the movie that cemented the dominance of the superhero genre in Hollywood.

You're Next was another horror movie whose theatrical release was endangered by corporate developments beyond the control of its creators. A darkly comedic take on the home invasion subgenre, the film was directed by Adam Wingard and written by Simon Barrett. The pair had previously collaborated on *A Horrible Way to Die*, a grim serial killer drama that Anchor Bay released straight to DVD on 2011. For *You're Next*, Wingard and Barrett found inspiration in the original *Scream*. "We looked a lot at the beginning," says Barrett. "That movie, especially its opening scene, walks a really fine [line] between being intense and scary but also having a pressure release valve, which is a really vicious, fun sense of humor."

You're Next was produced by Keith Calder and Jess Wu of the company Snoot Entertainment. The pair had initially met up with Wingard and Barrett on the suggestion of Colin Geddes, who programmed the Midnight Madness section of the Toronto Film Festival. "We talked about how we were getting frustrated with the home invasion genre being so torture-y and not fun," says Calder. "Simon's like, 'Well, I have this thing I've been kicking around.' By the end of that year, Simon had the first draft of *You're Next*, and we loved it."

You're Next starred Australian Sharni Vinson, *House of the Devil* actor A. J. Bowen, Amy Seimetz, and a clutch of indie filmmakers: Joe Swanberg, Ti West, and Larry Fessenden. "It was a real honor for me to actually have Larry in the movie, because *Habit* was a huge influence on me," says Wingard. The cast also featured Barbara Crampton, playing the matriarch of a family under attack from animal mask-wearing killers. The actress had starred in a clutch of beloved '80s horror films, including 1985's Stuart Gordon-directed *Re-Animator* and the following year's *Chopping Mall.* Crampton was open to the idea of acting again after taking several years off to raise her children. "I got a call from my agent, and I said, 'Oh, Mike, you haven't lost my number!'" the actress recalls. "He said, 'No. In fact, I have an offer for you to be the matriarch-mom in a horror movie.'"

You're Next received its world premiere at the Toronto Film Festival in September 2011. Before the end of the month, Lionsgate announced that the company had acquired the US rights to the film. Producer Calder recalls that Lionsgate was "so passionate, and they were making a wide release offer. Jason Constantine really understands genre movies, and is on the executive side but is not a total shithead. It was intended to be a pretty fast rush into release off the momentum of Toronto."

Barbara Crampton in *You're Next* (2013).

Following the sale of the film to Lionsgate, Wingard reshot the start of the movie, in which characters played by Kate Lyn Sheil and a towel-wearing Fessenden are killed. "They wanted to pump up the opening, so I went to Hollywood to refilm," says Fessenden. "It was stressful, because I was naked with my towel, and all the Lionsgate executives were there. I remember this very nice female executive saying, 'I just loved *Habit*.' I'm sitting there, practically naked, going, 'Wonderful, yes, yes. We really *must* talk.'"

The plan to give *You're Next* a speedy theatrical release was derailed by Lionsgate's acquisition of Summit Entertainment, which was announced in January 2012. Summit was best known as the home of the *Twilight* franchise, whose fifth entry, *The Twilight Saga: Breaking Dawn—Part 2*, was set for release in November 2012. Aside from *Twilight*, the production and distribution company had a healthy slate of upcoming films, including Scott Derrickson's *Sinister* and yet another 'rom-zom-com,' this one titled *Warm Bodies*. "We got this sad call from Jason," says Calder. "He's like, 'I don't know what's going to happen. These two companies have merged together, they have two companies-worth of movies already in the pipeline.' We kept thinking *You're Next* was going to just disappear."

Around the time they were working on *You're Next,* Wingard and Barrett also helped create the found footage anthology horror film *V/H/S*. The project was the brainchild of Bloody Disgusting founder Brad Miska, who produced it with aspiring filmmaker Roxanne Benjamin. "I had this idea for doing a modern *Tales from the Crypt* with a bunch of kids finding some old tapes and each week watch a new tape," says Miska. "It became this weird, experimental project where I used my Bloody Disgusting relationships to bring in different filmmakers."

Wingard and Barrett created the movie's framing story, and Barrett also wrote a segment directed by Joe Swanberg. Other contributors included Ti West and the filmmaking collective Radio Silence. *V/H/S* first screened in 2012 at the Sundance Film Festival, where, just a year later, the film's sequel, *V/H/S 2*, would also receive its world premiere.

In September 2012, Lionsgate announced that *You're Next* would be getting a theatrical release in August of the following year. "We finally got a call from Jason saying, 'It is going to be a wide release but it's not going to be until 2013,'" says Calder. The delay meant that *You're Next* followed Blumhouse's home invasion film *The Purge*, which was released two months prior to Wingard's movie. "The only thing I was annoyed about was, I went

Lane Hughes in *You're Next*.

to see [Fede Álvarez's] *Evil Dead* and they played the *You're Next* trailer after *The Purge* trailer," says Wingard, "which just made us look like assholes."

Lionsgate marketed the movie with posters that showed the film's killers seemingly reflected in ads for other releases, including the Tyler Perry-directed *Temptation: Confessions of a Marriage Counselor*. "That was Tim Palen and his team, and it was brilliant," says Calder. The company also attempted to entice cinemagoers with a trailer soundtracked by Lou Reed's "Perfect Day." "Honestly, I think that trailer cost almost as much as the film," says Wingard.

You're Next came out on August 23, 2013. The same week saw the release of the fantasy film *The Mortal Instruments: City of Bones* and director Edgar Wright's science fiction comedy *The World's End*. The website Box Office Mojo had predicted that *You're Next* could be the weekend's number one movie. In fact, Wingard's film finished in sixth place, grossing $7 million over its first three days on release. *You're Next* would go on to earn a robust $18 million at the domestic box office, but media outlets routinely wrote up the long-delayed movie as a commercial disappointment. "I regard *You're Next* as a huge success," says Keith Calder. "It was an under-$1 million movie that sat on the shelf for two years, it's grossing 18 times its budget. What else do you *want* from a movie?"

Calder could also find satisfaction in *You're Next* having reignited Barbara Crampton's interest in acting and horror. "I knew that I wanted to come back to the genre because of the experience that I had on that film," says the actress. "I said to my agent, 'I want to get back into the business, could you please look for some roles for me?'"

Lionsgate continued to release horror movies after *You're Next*. In 2014, the company rebooted the Leprechaun franchise with *Leprechaun: Origins*, for which Warwick Davis was replaced by the wrestler Dylan Postl (a.k.a. 'Hornswoggle'). Two years later, Lionsgate released *Blair Witch*, another franchise revamp, this one from *You're Next* creators Adam Wingard and Simon Barrett. However, Tim Palen admits that the company's interest in horror waned after the arrival of Joe Drake and the departure of Peter Block. "It became less of a focus," he says. "It's just the way the company evolved. Nobody was like, 'We should abandon horror.' It's just the players on the board and what their skill sets were. It never seemed like there was a plan. The *plan* was not to go out of business."

Lionsgate had found success in the young adult space that had already birthed the blockbuster *Harry Potter* and *Twilight* franchises. In March 2009, the company announced that it had acquired worldwide distribution rights to the film adaptation of Suzanne Collins' *The Hunger Games*, about a televised contest in which teenage contestants kill each other. Despite the book's high death count, Collins' tale was aimed at young readers, and Palen recalls the author being wary of getting into business with a studio so associated with horror. "I was sort of branded as 'the horror guy' and I was constantly put in a position to defend myself," he says. "I remember when Suzanne Collins was shopping *The Hunger Games* book, her first question was, 'You're the *Saw* guy, don't you think that's a problem?' [I basically said] 'If I can do that, I can do this. That's hard, this is easy.'" Released in March 2012, *The Hunger Games* was a blockbuster, earning $695 million around the world. Three successful sequels would swiftly follow.

Lionsgate thrived in other genres, too, launching a lucrative action franchise with 2014's Keanu Reeves-starring *John Wick* and scoring a critically acclaimed hit with the 2016 musical *La La Land*. Lionsgate's reputation as a house of horror would become a memory, albeit one fondly recalled by those responsible for the company's genre product. "The whole thing is a fever dream, candidly," says Palen, who left Lionsgate in 2019. "I think, one year, we did 28 movies. That's 28 media plans, 28 filmmakers screaming and yelling at you, it was insane. The studio brought you *The Hunger Games*, and *The Expendables*, and *La La Land*. We did a lot of things. We just did horror really well."

Barbara Crampton's *Re-Animator* director Stuart Gordon had begun his career directing experimental stage productions while a student at the University of Wisconsin, once putting on a version of *Peter Pan* with naked actors. He later moved to Chicago, where his Organic Theater Company presented the world premiere of David Mamet's play *Sexual Perversity in Chicago* in 1974. Gordon established his reputation as a horror auteur with 1985's *Re-Animator* and 1986's *From Beyond*, a pair of H. P. Lovecraft adaptations starring Crampton and Jeffrey Combs. Gordon mined Lovecraft again for 1995's *Castle Freak* and then 2001's *Dagon*, about a village with half-human, half-piscine residents. An adaptation of the author's novella *The Shadow Over Innsmouth*, *Dagon* had been a difficult film to get off the ground. "It was frustrating," Gordon told Crampton in a 2011 interview that the actress conducted with the director for *Fangoria*. "We even had one studio tell us that if they turned into werewolves, they would finance it." Lionsgate released the film straight to DVD in 2002.

Outside of his work with the *Masters of Horror* and *Fear Itself* TV shows, Gordon spent most of the 2000s directing admired but little seen films, including 2007's horror-thriller *Stuck*, starring Mena Suvari. Following the limited release of the latter project, Gordon returned to the stage. First, he directed Jeffrey Combs in the one-man show *Nevermore… An Evening with Edgar Allan Poe*, written by the filmmaker's frequent collaborator Dennis Paoli. Then he revived his greatest genre success by both directing and co-writing the book for *Re-Animator: The Musical*, one of the most unlikely takes on Lovecraft ever produced. "I just saw it in my head, how you could do this as a musical," Gordon said. "All of the effects we did in the movie were done practically, so we could do them all live in front of the audiences."

The show's cast included George Wendt, Rachel Avery, Jesse Merlin (who was decapitated, and reanimated, onstage nightly as the villainous Dr. Hill), and Graham Skipper, playing the scientist Herbert West. "There was a lot of time spent making sure the magic tricks worked," says Skipper. "I would behead Hill behind the lab table, and then do the switcheroo with the head, and people loved it. You could always tell when you got it just right, because people would gasp." Skipper befriended the show's stage manager Joe Begos, a fellow horror fan. "My final song, I'm wrestling with the bloody intestine, and within the intestine is a hose that is spraying blood," says the actor. "Joe was the guy underneath the stage pumping blood while I'm singing, and at the end, when the intestine drags me back under the stage, I'm literally crawling on top of him. We got very close very fast."

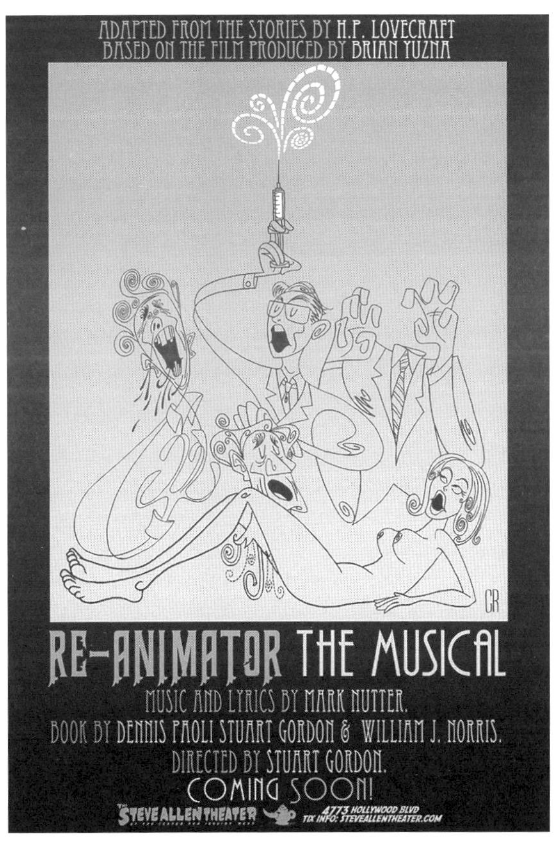

Gordon initially staged *Re-Animator: The Musical* at Los Angeles' Steve Allen Theater in March 2011. *Variety* critic Bob Verini enthused that, "Not since *Little Shop of Horrors* has a screamfest tuner so deftly balanced seriousness and camp." The show attracted an array of genre notables. "So many people from the horror film industry came," says Skipper. "Eli Roth. Wes Craven. Whenever the show was flagging, Barbara Crampton would sign autographs as a way to drive sales." The play was later staged as part of the New York Musical Festival in July 2012 and the Edinburgh Fringe Festival the following month. "Stuart cared so deeply," says Skipper. "Even on the last show, he had a note for me. I said, 'Stuart, this is literally the last show.' He said, 'This is the last time we have to get it right.' That really stuck with me."

Several of Gordon's younger collaborators would embark on horror movie careers of their own. Stage manager Begos directed 2014's alien invasion movie *Almost Human* and the following year's *Scanners*-homaging *The Mind's Eye*. The films starred Graham Skipper, who would himself direct the 2017 horror tale *Sequence Break*. Skipper also played one of the leads in 2016's possessed VCR board game movie *Beyond the Gates*, which was directed by Gordon's former assistant Jackson Stewart.

Gordon passed away at the age of 72 in March 2020 without making another film. "Truthfully, that part of Stuart's career, that was sort of his coda," says Skipper. "That was his returning to theater and acknowledging the end of his run as a film director. That's how he wanted to wrap it up—and he did."

British filmmakers, meanwhile, had continued to explore the horror genre following *Dog Soldiers*, *28 Days Later*, *Shaun of the Dead*, and *The Descent*. Michael Fassbender and Kelly Reilly played a couple menaced by locals during a weekend away in James Watkins' 2008 survival-thriller *Eden Lake*; Ben Wheatley enmeshed hit men portrayed by Neil Maskell and Michael Smiley in a cultist conspiracy with 2011's *Kill List*; and Joe Cornish introduced the world to future *Star Wars* franchise actor John Boyega in the same year's alien invasion saga *Attack the Block*. However, the era's biggest success would come from a long-slumbering giant of British horror cinema: Hammer Films.

Hammer's vintage output may have proven an enduring influence on directors like Tim Burton and James Wan, but the British company had not produced a movie since the late '70s. After Hammer's heyday in the '50s and '60s, the studio's brand of gothic horror had seemed outdated in the era of *The Exorcist* and *The Texas Chain Saw Massacre*, and the company entered liquidation in 1979. With the horror genre having enjoyed a decade of huge success, by the mid-2000s a resurrection made commercial sense. In May 2007, Dutch media tycoon John de Mol Jr. announced that his company Cyrte Investments had acquired the rights to Hammer's library and would revive the studio as a production unit.

The relaunched company's early films included 2010's *Let Me In*—an English-language version of *Let the Right One In* directed by Matt Reeves—and 2011's thriller *The Resident*, which starred Hilary Swank and Hammer legend Christopher Lee. *Let Me In* was surprisingly well reviewed for a remake but performed poorly at the box office; despite its noteworthy cast, *The Resident* was released straight to video in the US.

Hammer finally recaptured the company's box office success of the '60s with 2012's gothic tale *The Woman in Black*. Directed by *Eden Lake* filmmaker James Watkins, the film starred *Harry Potter* franchise actor Daniel Radcliffe as a London lawyer who encounters unhelpful locals and unquiet spirits in a remote English village. The movie was based on a 1983 novel by Susan Hill

Daniel Radcliffe in *The Woman in Black* (2012).

that had previously been adapted into a 1989 TV film and a long-running West End play.

The screenplay for the new version of the tale was by Jane Goldman, whose credits included the superhero movies *Kick-Ass* and *X-Men: First Class.* "I always was passionate about science fiction and horror, and I was fortunate that my parents enjoyed that as well," she says. "I know there's some home video footage of my tenth birthday, and my dad comes in the room brandishing a copy of *Eraserhead* and going, 'Look what we've got for tonight!'"

CBS Films released *The Woman in Black* in the US on February 3, 2012. The film was narrowly beaten to the number one position on the box office chart by another new release, the found footage superhero movie *Chronicle*, but went on to gross $54 million domestically. In the UK, where the film was released a week later, *The Woman in Black* was the most popular movie in the country for three weeks in a row. On February 28, *The Hollywood Reporter* noted that Hammer was claiming that the movie had become the highest grossing British horror film since records began.

Guillermo del Toro had followed *Pan's Labyrinth* with 2008's *Hellboy II: The Golden Army*. The sequel was a bigger hit than the first Hellboy adventure and further burnished the reputation of the filmmaker, seemingly putting him in the position to direct almost anything he wanted. Del Toro would in fact spend a frustrating half-decade not directing any movies at all.

In April 2008, Peter Jackson and the *Lord of the Rings* production team announced that the Mexican had agreed to direct a two-movie adaptation of J. R. R. Tolkien's *The Hobbit.* The filmmaker relocated to New Zealand and began prepping the duology. After two years and repeated delays (caused in part by the financial problems of MGM), the director left the project, which would later be brought to the screen as a trilogy by Jackson himself. Del Toro also developed an R-rated 3D film version of H. P. Lovecraft's Antarctica-set horror novella *At the Mountains of Madness* for Universal. Tom Cruise was interested in starring in the film, but the studio never greenlit the film. Del Toro finally returned to directing with 2013's *Pacific Rim*, a commercially successful tale of kaiju and giant robots produced by Legendary Entertainment.

When not occupied trying to get his own projects off the ground, del Toro was helping other filmmakers bring their respective visions to the screen.

He executive produced *Cube* director Vincenzo Natali's 2009 science fiction-horror tale *Splice* and produced Troy Nixey's 2011 remake *Don't Be Afraid of the Dark*. Del Toro also helped produce J. A. Bayona's 2007 tale *El orfanato* (a.k.a. *The Orphanage*), about a child's mysterious disappearance. The movie premiered at the 2007 Cannes Film Festival and won seven trophies at Spain's Goya Awards.

Del Toro developed an English-language version of *The Orphanage* with Larry Fessenden for New Line. The plan was for the *Habit* filmmaker to direct the movie, and Fessenden even spoke with Kate Winslet about appearing in the project. "I met Kate Winslet in London, the most incredible, fun experience," he says. "She agreed to do the film and then, three weeks later, I got an email saying she didn't want to [appear in] another downer of a movie, because she'd made *The Reader*. It all fell through."

Acting as executive producer, del Toro enjoyed one of his biggest hits to date with the 2013 ghost story *Mama*. The feature debut of Argentinian filmmaker Andy Muschietti, the movie starred Jessica Chastain as a musician attempting to raise two young girls who have spent years in the care of the titular supernatural entity. Del Toro agreed to help produce the film after seeing Muschietti's short, also called *Mama*. "It was really elegant, very well done, had a real style," he told JoBlo. "But more importantly, it was scary as fuck."

In the feature version, the character of Mama was portrayed by Spanish actor Javier Botet. As a child, Botet was diagnosed with Marfan syndrome, a genetic disorder that elongates limbs and extremities. Six feet seven inches tall as an adult, the actor was cast by director Brian Yuzna as a water-dwelling monster in his 2005 film *Beneath Still Waters* and then played a dramatically transformed young girl in 2007's *Rec*.

Muschietti shot *Mama* on a budget of around $15 million at Pinewood Toronto Studios, where del Toro was in pre-production on *Pacific Rim*. The shoot was a physically demanding one for Botet. To give the character a suitably supernatural demeanor, he spent his shoot days hanging from a rig while his arms and legs were pulled in different directions with monofilament wires. Botet's discomfort was increased by Muschietti's perfectionism. "He makes always 30, sometimes 40 takes," says the actor. "*Sometimes* ten, but he never does it in two or three takes. [You think] 'Okay, we're here, and if you think it's going to go better, let's do it 1,000 times, no matter.'"

Botet's suffering would be rewarded: when Universal released *Mama* in January 2013, Muschietti's film won the weekend, pushing Kathryn Bigelow's *Zero Dark Thirty*—which also starred Chastain—into second position. The movie went on to gross $146 million worldwide.

Identical twins Jen and Sylvia Soska were teenagers when Mary Harron's *American Psycho* was released in their native Canada. "Mary Harron was on the Canadian news for 'promoting violence against women,'" says Sylvia. "She kept explaining, 'It's a satire, it's not real, it's based on a book.' I remember watching her and I was like, 'A Canadian woman is directing a horror movie?' It's one of the first times I had ever seen anything like that." The film became a huge inspiration to the Soskas. Years later, the pair became friendly with Harron and told her that they had named their own second feature, 2013's *American Mary*, after the Christian Bale movie and its creator. It was like, 'Well, it's American because of [*American*] *Psycho*, and it's Mary because of you!'" says Jen. "She was so touched."

(*Left to right*) Director Jen Soska, actress Katharine Isabelle, and director Sylvia Soska attend a preview screening for *American Mary* in 2012.

American Mary starred *Ginger Snaps* actress Katharine Isabelle as a surgical student who is drugged and raped by one of her teachers, David Lovgren's Dr. Grant, at a party. Mary leaves her trainee position and begins performing illegal operations on members of the body modification community. Isabelle's character also kidnaps her rapist and, while keeping him alive, enacts her revenge by amputating all four of his limbs. In addition to *American Psycho*, the movie was influenced by the films of David Cronenberg, Takashi Miike's *Audition*, and the Soskas' own struggles trying to gain a foothold in the male-dominated film industry. "It was very reflective of our own experience," says Sylvia.

The sisters inherited their love of horror from their mother. "My mom loved Stephen King, she loved horror movies," says Jen. "She tricked us into reading at an early age. She said, 'If you can read the novel, you can watch the movie.' So you're sitting there reading these Bible-sized Stephen King [books] being like, 'What does 'fuck' mean?' Mom's like, 'That's a sentence-enhancer.'"

While attending film school, the Soskas saw the just-released *Grindhouse*. The pair loved the fake trailers and were particularly inspired by the clip for *Hobo with a Shotgun*. Jen suggested that, as the pair's graduating project, they make their own fake trailer for an action-thriller called *Dead Hooker in a Trunk*. "The school had a list of everything that was inappropriate to put in projects," says Sylvia. "We were like, 'Let's put everything in there.' We played it last at graduation. Half the audience got up and walked out, and the other half was cheering so loud you couldn't hear all the disgusting dialog."

Encouraged, the twins directed a micro-budgeted feature version of *Dead Hooker in a Trunk* starring themselves. "The actors were crew, the crew were actors," says Sylvia. "Sometimes all of us were in the shot, so we just put the camera on a log." The sisters had sent their fake trailer to the directors involved with *Grindhouse* and received a positive response from Eli Roth. "He watched the movie, he gave us great compliments, and he gave us a huge amount of notes," says Sylvia. "We took half of them, and he was totally fine with it." Despite costing just $2,500 Canadian, *Dead Hooker in a Trunk* was picked up for distribution by IFC Midnight, which released the film to VOD in the spring of 2009.

The Soskas credit Roth with suggesting that they pursue their idea for a rape-revenge movie about a surgeon as their second film. Sylvia recalls that, when they were trying to get *Dead Hooker in a Trunk* accepted at film festivals, the *Hostel* director told them to start thinking about their next movie. "We didn't know we needed a *next* movie," says Sylvia. "We lied and we were like, 'Eli, we have so many movies we might be making, which one do you think we should do?' We listed off a bunch, and he was like, 'Ooh, that one sounds interesting.'"

When the sisters went looking for money, they discovered that potential financiers were often interested in meeting with them for reasons that had little to do with their screenplay. "It was constantly like, 'Oh, I want to make this movie,' and they were like, 'But do you want to be my girlfriend?'" says Sylvia. "It's like, 'No! I'm a filmmaker, I want to be taken seriously.' I found it really shocking. That [experience] went into the script." The pair eventually found seed money for the project close to home. "It was our 27th birthday," says Sylvia. "Our parents had finally paid off their house, and my dad said, 'Girls, we've decided to remortgage the house to be the first investors so the movie can get made.' I'm forever grateful for that."

The sisters hired Todd Masters to create the film's makeup effects, including a puppet version of the limbless Dr. Grant. The finished article was realistic enough to lastingly unnerve star Katharine Isabelle. "Katy is not a horror movie fan," says Sylvia. "The situations we put her in were terrifying for her. I remember after she wrapped, she talked about the storage locker scene with the puppet of Grant, all mutilated. She said that took a really long time to get over."

American Mary was given a limited release in the US during the early summer of 2013 by the recently founded XLrator Media but in the UK was picked up for distribution by Universal. Sylvia remembers, "Being a filmmaker and seeing the Universal logo before your film—Jennifer, and me, and Katy were all teared up in the theater."

The Soskas would go on to direct 2015's Lionsgate-distributed vigilante film *Vendetta*, 2019's *Rabid*, a remake of Cronenberg's body-horror classic, and 2024's George A. Romero-inspired *Festival of the Dead*. The sisters also became familiar figures on the growing horror convention circuit, where they discovered that *American Mary* had a large and growing fanbase. "Every time I go to a convention, I see, like, three or four girls dressed up as Mary," says Sylvia. "It always makes me so happy.

In July 2009, *Variety* reported that 20th Century Fox was "resuscitating" the *Alien* franchise with a prequel to Ridley Scott's original 1979 film. Scott himself was attached to direct the movie from a script by Jon Spaihts. In, January 2011, Deadline revealed that the project had morphed into something "more original," with *Lost* showrunner Damon Lindelof having re-written Spaihts' screenplay. "While *Alien* was indeed the jumping point for this project, out of the creative process evolved a new, grand mythology and universe in which this original movie takes place," Scott was quoted as saying in the article. "The keen fan will recognize strands of *Alien*'s DNA, so to speak, but the ideas tackled in this film are unique, large, and provocative."

Alien aficionados would have to wait until the film, titled *Prometheus* and starring Noomi Rapace, Michael Fassbender, and Charlize Theron, was released in the summer of 2012 to find out exactly how much *Alien* DNA featured in the film.

The series was in need of resuscitating. Paul W. S. Anderson's 2004 *Alien vs. Predator* was poorly received by critics but earned a satisfactory $80 million in the US. 2007's *Aliens vs. Predator: Requiem*, directed by The Brothers Strause, was even more negatively reviewed than its predecessor. "The door is left open for a sequel," The A.V. Club critic Scott Tobias wrote. "If someone would shut it and board it up, that would be much appreciated." Tobias got his wish. After *Aliens vs. Predator: Requiem* earned around half as much as Anderson's movie domestically, Fox decided not to go forward with another *AvP* film, instead backing Ridley Scott to reboot the franchise.

The director split the difference between making a prequel to *Alien* and creating an entirely new universe. Set 29 years before the original film, *Prometheus* followed the misadventures of an expedition attempting to discover the origins of humanity on a remote planet. Although Scott made clear that the movie was set in the *Alien* universe, he fulfilled his promise to introduce a new mythology hinged around the so-called 'Engineers,' tall, hairless humanoids responsible for creating intelligent life on earth.

Daniel James in *Prometheus* (2012).

The final appearance of the Engineers was the responsibility of *Cloverfield* designer Neville Page, who describes perfecting the look of the characters as "quite the journey. There were other artists before me working on it. I remember seeing the artwork, going, 'Well, you're done.' Ridley felt, 'No, we're not quite there yet.'" The director surprised Page by suggesting that the Engineer be a fusion of two American icons. "He said, 'It's kind of like the Statue of Liberty, but mixed with Elvis,'" recalls the designer. "I thought, 'Elvis?! Okay, now you've lost me.' Then I looked at Elvis, and the shape of his lips, and his eyes, and I looked at the Statue of Liberty, and I thought, 'Oh, I can see the relationship.' I started to combine the two."

Made for a reported budget of around $130 million, *Prometheus* opened on June 8, 2012. The film earned an encouraging $51 million over its first weekend of release and went on to gross $403 million worldwide. In April 2016, Scott began shooting a sequel, titled *Alien: Covenant.* That film would feature more of the franchise's signature xenomorphs than *Prometheus* but earned much less than its predecessor when released in 2017, forcing Scott to abandon plans for a third prequel movie.

The *Alien* saga was, of course, not the only example of a horror series proceeding in fits and starts. All long-running genre franchises, from the Universal Classic Monsters to *Scream*, had suffered from varying commercial fortunes. But the year after the release of *Prometheus* witnessed the arrival of a new horror film that would kick off a record-breaking string of profitable sequels and spin-offs. The movie would also cement its director's reputation as a modern-day master of horror, capable of summoning up big scares and outsized box office. The film was originally titled *The Warren Files* but was ultimately gifted a much more evocative name: *The Conjuring.*

James Wan had enjoyed enormous success working with independent companies on *Saw* and *Insidious* and had suffered a miserable experience making *Dead Silence* at Universal. Still, the Australian yearned to direct another horror film for a major studio. "I wanted to make the kind of studio horror movies that we grew up loving, like *The Exorcist* or *Jaws*," he says. "I love that kind of filmmaking, because they were made by respectable directors with a real budget. It wasn't trying to make a horror film for $1 million or less."

Wan got his chance by partnering with Peter Safran, for whom the filmmaker had directed the *Doggie Heaven* short. The manager had begun producing films, including the 2008 comedy *Disaster Movie* and the 2010 Ryan Reynolds thriller *Buried.* When the first *Insidious* arrived on screens, Safran was looking for someone to direct a horror movie. The film, inspired by purportedly real events, centered on Ed and Lorraine Warren, a pair of supernatural investigators, and their involvement in an alleged haunting which afflicted the Perron family in Harrisville, Rhode Island, during the 1970s. "I always wanted to make a supernatural thriller, because I loved those movies, and I just thought this story was a particularly great one," says Safran. The producer was drawn to the plight of the Perron paterfamilias Roger, who agreed to have the Warrens investigate the phenomena taking place in the home that he and his wife Carolyn shared with their five daughters, Andrea, Nancy, Christine, Cindy, and April. "I was a relatively new father at the time, and it's a story about what a father will do to save the women in his life, his wife and daughters," Safran explains. "It really resonated with me."

The producer developed what would eventually become *The Conjuring* at New Line, which in 2008 had merged with Warner Bros., resulting in the departure of Robert Shaye. Safran believed that Wan was the right man to bring the story to the screen. "*Insidious* had just come out, and we all loved it," the producer recalls.

The real Annabelle doll at the Warrens' occult museum in Monroe, Connecticut.

The lives of Ed and Lorraine Warren offered plenty of material for a horror filmmaker. Lorraine claimed to be a clairvoyant and medium, while Ed was a self-declared expert in the supernatural, or 'demonologist.' The couple married in 1945 and investigated many paranormal incidents over the ensuing decades, including the famous haunting in Amityville. The Warrens collected artifacts from their cases and kept them in an 'occult museum' in the basement of their house in Connecticut. These curios included a Raggedy Ann doll named Annabelle, which had supposedly tormented several student nurses in the early '70s.

The couple's career was detailed in author Gerald Brittle's 1980 book *The Demonologist*. The Warrens were also portrayed in a 1991 TV movie called *The Haunted*. While Ed Warren foregrounded the supposedly science-based nature of the couple's investigations, others found the proof they offered of supernatural happenings to be wanting. In 1997, the Warrens were investigated by the New England Skeptical Society (a.k.a. NESS), a non-profit educational organization founded to promote "science and reason." NESS co-founders Steven Novella and Perry DeAngelis published their findings in an article titled "Hunting the Ghost Hunters." "In the final analysis, the field of research into spiritual and ghostly phenomena lacks any scientific rigor," the pair wrote. "The field is fully and unreservedly a pseudoscience."

The haunting of the Perron family began on the day in January 1971 when the clan moved into their new house in Harrisville. According to the eldest daughter, Andrea, the Perrons were still unloading their possessions when several of the children saw a man, a figure they came to believe was a supernatural apparition, watching the previous owner pack up. The Perron family would claim that, over the next few years, they were visited by an array of entities, some friendly, some terrifying. "There was one we used to call 'The Kitchen Witch,' and then we stopped doing that so as not to be rude to her," says Andrea. "Then there was one that had what appeared to be a desiccated hornet's nest for a head." The Warrens attempted to help the Perrons but, according to Andrea, were ultimately unsuccessful. "Mrs. Warren insisted [that] not only did we have numerous spirits in the house, she claimed that there was a demonic presence in the house," Andrea continues. "Lorraine said that she and Ed, with the assistance of a medium and a priest, would be able to clear the house, and that was not the case." In 1980, the Perrons moved out of the farmhouse and relocated to Georgia.

Ed Warren became convinced that the Perron case could be turned into a film. The Warrens were befriended by a producer named Tony DeRosa-Grund, who agreed. After Ed Warren passed away in 2006, DeRosa-Grund continued to pursue the project, which attracted the attention of Safran. To work on the script, Safran hired twin brothers Chad and Carey Hayes, who had written 2005's *House of Wax* remake.

By the end of 2009, Safran had struck a deal with New Line to develop the film. Independently, Wan expressed interest to his representation about depicting the Warrens onscreen. "When you're dealing in this world, it's hard not to have heard of the Warrens," explains the director. "I've always said, someone needs to make a movie about these guys. I remember saying to my agent, 'I'm curious if there's anyone in town who's potentially doing a real-life biopic on the two of them.' My agent got back to me and said, 'Yes, the property is actually at New Line with Peter Safran and Tony DeRosa-Grund on it.'"

Wan believed a film about the Warrens would be an ideal follow-up to *Insidious*. "It's in the same world as *Insidious*, but it's a big step up, with more money," he says. "I didn't want to rehash myself with stuff that I'd already done, so I felt that the real-life aspect would be a challenge and something interesting for me to tackle." Safran was delighted by Wan's interest in the project. "He was the only guy we ever spoke to about the movie," says the producer. In June 2011, *Variety* reported that Wan was in final negotiations to direct the film.

The finished movie would feature a more crowd-pleasing conclusion to the Warrens' involvement with the Perrons than had happened in real life,

Director James Wan on the set of *The Conjuring* (2013).

with Ed and Lorraine defeating the demonic spirit which has been haunting the family. But Wan was determined to recreate the rest of the story with as much accuracy as possible. "James fought for it to be the period that it was, he fought for it to have all the kids," says Rob Cowan, another of the film's producers. "Because your first instinct is, 'Let's get rid of all those kids!' And his feeling was, he really wanted to tell the real story."

Wan remains open-minded as to whether the supernatural events described by the Perrons actually occurred. "I haven't really had things [like that] that have happened to me," he says. "But I like to give things the benefit of the doubt, especially things in the spiritual world that we don't understand." He did, however, decline the opportunity to visit the Perrons' former home in Rhode Island. "Just because I make movies in the scary world doesn't mean I want to visit scary worlds," says the director. "I am such a chickenshit."

Wan thought Patrick Wilson and *The Departed* actress Vera Farmiga would be the perfect pair to portray Ed and Lorraine Warren but assumed that his *Insidious* star would be reluctant to appear in another horror project. "In the back of my mind, I felt like, 'Oh, Patrick's not going to want to do the same movie again,'" says Wan. "Funnily enough, the two actors that we went out to first were Andrew Lincoln and Michelle Monaghan. But they didn't want to do it. I was like, 'Okay, you know what? I really wanted Patrick and Vera, and I'm going to stop second-guessing myself, and I'm going to reach out to those guys.'"

Wan was right to be worried about Wilson's reluctance to play Ed Warren. The actor knew that he would likely star in an *Insidious* sequel and had qualms about signing on for a second horror movie with franchise potential. But Wan convinced him that Warren was a very different character to the one he had played in *Insidious*. "It always comes down to the character," says Wilson. "I didn't know a lot about Ed and Lorraine Warren. Once James won me over on that, then it became a totally different beast. This was a real character. He's got to step up, and I loved that."

Farmiga, too, was no stranger to horror. The actress had appeared in 2009's *Orphan*, which starred Isabelle Fuhrman as an adult serial killer who masquerades as a child. Produced by Dark Castle, the film was a hit, earning $78 million worldwide. Even so, Farmiga was freaked out by *The Conjuring*'s script and recalls "chucking it multiple times across the room and then refusing to read it within the sanctity of my own home." Farmiga was ultimately convinced to sign on to the project by the thought of partnering onscreen with Wilson. "I texted him and said that I would be in if he was in," she says.

Patrick Wilson and Vera Farmiga in *The Conjuring*.

As part of their preparation to portray the Warrens, Farmiga and Wilson visited the now octogenarian Lorraine at her house in Connecticut. "I tried to ask the really difficult questions, the intimate and embarrassing ones," says Farmiga. "Like, 'What was your sex life like?' What I was really mining for was: 'What toll did witnessing that depravity, that darkness, take on your relationship?' But honestly, this was one of the most positive, cheerful, charming women I've ever met."

During the pair's visit, Wilson went down to the house's basement and inspected the collection of artifacts, including the Annabelle doll. Farmiga had read *The Demonologist* and was too alarmed by its contents to follow suit. "I did not want to go downstairs," she admits. "Patrick went downstairs. But he's just like Ed, he's the more practical of us two."

Wan filmed *The Conjuring* in Wilmington, North Carolina, on a reported budget of $20 million. The film's cast also included Ron Livingston and Lili Taylor as Roger and Carolyn Perron. "I felt like, with all these actors, I could potentially have a really good movie here," says Wan. "I've just got to tell the best character-driven story I can."

Lili Taylor in *The Conjuring.*

The Annabelle doll that appeared in the film looked different from the one in the Warrens' occult collection. "I could not use the actual Annabelle doll because it's a Raggedy Ann doll, right?" says Wan. "And I'm pretty sure that the company that owns the rights to that are not gonna want us to say that the doll which they make is possibly possessed. So when I knew that I had to change the look of the doll anyway, I thought, 'I'm going to use this opportunity to just create a doll which is more human-like.'"

Wan once again asked Joseph Bishara to compose the film's score *and* play the movie's supernatural antagonist, this time the spirit of a long-dead woman named Bathsheba. "This was most definitely *not* an indie movie," says the musician. "Yeah, that was a whole different level. The house was built on a soundstage. Patrick's always amazing to work with, and then Vera as well. James always surrounds himself with a very high level of talent. When you're in that fold, on a set with all of that, you can't help but get swept up in it."

Following the end of the shoot, Warner Bros. and New Line announced that they were delaying the release of *The Conjuring* from January 2013 to the following July. This switch was noted by *Variety* in an article headlined "*Conjuring* test screenings scare up B.O. potential." The piece detailed how the reaction of audiences at test screenings had prompted the studios to risk a summer opening for the movie. "For the first time in recent memory, a straight-up horror film [...] will bow during the heart of summer, a result of scary-good test screening results," wrote reporters Marc Graser and Andrew Stewart. Producer Peter Safran recalls, "When we tested it for the first time, we knew James Wan had captured lightning in a bottle. I mean, it scored through the roof."

Wan had made a movie that contained little in the way of gore, nudity, or bad language. Yet the film received an R rating regardless. When New Line asked what they needed to cut to release the movie as a PG-13, the ratings board could not give specific notes. "They said there isn't a moment, there isn't a scene, there's not an image, there's nothing we can point to," New Line production executive Walter Hamada told The Wrap. "It's the totality of the film; it's just too scary."

Wan received the best notices of his career up to that point for *The Conjuring*. *New York Times* critic Manohla Dargis began her review by describing the film as a "fantastically effective haunted-house movie" and ended by hailing it as "the next great shocker." *New York* magazine writer Bilge Ebiri was equally enthusiastic. "The damned thing works you so well that you may even consider leaving halfway through, for fear you'll have a heart attack," he warned.

The public's interest in horror had been reaffirmed in the months leading up to the July release of *The Conjuring*. In January, Lionsgate distributed a *Texas Chainsaw Massacre* reboot-sequel titled *Texas Chainsaw 3D*, which starred Alexandra Daddario and earned $34 million in the US. (The franchise would be rebooted again with 2017's *Leatherface* and *again* with 2022's *Texas Chainsaw Massacre*.) April's Fede Álvarez-directed *Evil Dead* earned $54 million at the domestic box office, and June's *The Purge* performed even better. James DeMonaco's home invasion tale was followed into cinemas two weeks later by *World War Z*. Director Marc Foster's expensive adaptation of Max Brooks' book had had a tortured production history, with the filmmaker reshooting the movie's entire final act, but the Brad Pitt-starring result still grossed $540 million worldwide.

The Conjuring had neither the brand recognition of the *Evil Dead* franchise nor the lavish budget and star power of *World War Z*. The movie also faced stiff competition at the box office. *The Conjuring* shared its July 19 release date with Lionsgate's Bruce Willis action sequel *Red 2* and Universal's supernatural action film *R.I.P.D.*, which starred Ryan Reynolds and Jeff Bridges. Safran admits that he had fears about his movie's commercial fortunes. "It was a busy weekend," he says. "It was in the summer. *The Conjuring* was a brand that nobody knew."

But Wan's film won the weekend in a manner that exceeded Safran's wildest expectations. "We were tracking, going into the weekend, to do $20 million," he says. "By the way, everyone would have been thrilled with that, based on the cost of the movie. Over the course of the weekend, we were getting calls saying, 'It's going to be 22,' 'It's going to be 24.' And by the end of the weekend, it's $40 million."

The Conjuring ultimately grossed $137 million in the US and $319 million in all. When *Entertainment Weekly* rounded up the summer's box office winners and losers, Wan's film was included in the former category. "Thanks to an uber-creepy trailer, James Wan's $20 million fright-fest pummeled its pricey competition on opening weekend with $41.9 million," wrote Grady Smith. "And thanks to great word-of-mouth, the film didn't nosedive the way most horror films do."

The Conjuring was still playing on hundreds of screens when Blumhouse and distributors FilmDistrict released the summer's second Wan-directed horror hit, *Insidious: Chapter 2*. The movie reunited the director with Wilson, Rose Byrne, Lin Shaye, and actor-screenwriter Leigh Whannell. *Insidious: Chapter 2* was a direct sequel to the first film, whose conclusion had left the body of Wilson's character possessed by a murderous spirit. The movie was even more successful than its predecessor, grossing $161 million worldwide.

In November 2013, Bloody Disgusting revealed that Warner Bros. and New Line had plans for three *Conjuring* spin-offs, the first of which would showcase Annabelle. "When we made the first *Conjuring*, we always kind of quietly, jokingly, felt that the world of the Warrens, and all the interesting artifacts they have in their haunted room, could spawn movies," says Wan. "We had hopes and aspirations, but we never thought in our wildest dreams that we could actually go on and do it."

Annabelle was set before the events of *The Conjuring* and starred Ward Norton and Annabelle Wallis as a couple whose lives are plagued by paranormal events after they take possession of the doll. The movie was produced by Wan and Safran, and the duo would shepherd the *Conjuring* universe going forward. *Annabelle* was directed by Wan's long-time cinematographer John R. Leonetti, who had worked as an assistant cameraman on Wan's beloved *Poltergeist*. "I love picking his brains about all the *Poltergeist* stories," the filmmaker says.

Annabelle was written by Gary Dauberman, who had toiled on a handful of low-budget horror movies for the Syfy network, including 2007's *In the Spider's Web*, a tale of venomous arachnids and organ-harvesting. "They'd be like, 'We have a title, we have a cast, we have a location—the thing we don't have is a script. We need one in, like, a week. Can you give us one?'" says Dauberman. The writer entered Wan's orbit after working uncredited on the scripts for *Final Destination 5* and the *A Nightmare on Elm Street* remake. "When *Conjuring* came out, and it did so well, I got a call saying, 'Hey, would you consider writing a movie for *Annabelle*?'" Dauberman recalls. "That was an easy yes. You know, changed my life, that call." *Annabelle* cost just $6 million and grossed an astonishing $257 million worldwide.

In April 2013, Deadline announced that Universal was in negotiations with Wan to direct the seventh installment of the *Fast & Furious* franchise. The result of those negotiations, 2015's *Furious 7*, grossed $1.5 billion worldwide, a new record for the series. But the production was a particularly testing one for the director because of actor Paul Walker's death in a car crash before the end of principal photography.

In October 2014, Deadline reported that Wan's newly founded company Atomic Monster had struck a first-look producing deal with New Line. The article revealed that the filmmaker would direct *The Conjuring 2* after completing his promotional duties on *Furious 7*. "I just knew that I wanted to go back to something I felt very comfortable with and I was familiar with," says the director.

The second *Conjuring* concerned the so-called 'Enfield poltergeist,' which tormented the Hodgson family in London during the late '70s. The director wanted to feature two new frightful apparitions in the film. The first was the Crooked Man, a ghoul played by *Mama* actor Javier Botet. Wan planned the film's second antagonist to be a winged demon portrayed by Joseph Bishara. Makeup effects designer Justin Raleigh constructed an animatronic suit, footage of which Wan filmed on set, with the wings to be digitally added later. "It was many days of shooting," says Bishara. "Again, very cool, very interesting. But it was about 1,000 degrees inside the suit, so there was that."

Wan had a change of heart about Bishara's demon following the end of principal photography. "When I got into post-production, it just felt too much," says the director. He replaced Bishara's character with a different supernatural antagonist that he called the Demon Nun. "I remember Lorraine saying that a lot of her close friends were nuns or people from the church," recalls the director about Warren, who would pass away in 2019. "I thought, if a demon were to try and attack her, it would take on the image of something that is close to her, to sort of corrupt her faith." To play the character, Wan cast Bonnie Aarons, who had appeared, briefly but memorably, as a terrifying figure in David Lynch's *Mulholland Drive*. Released in June 2016, Wan's sequel would beat the worldwide gross of *The Conjuring*, earning $321 million.

Studios had continued raiding the ranks of filmmakers with horror credentials to direct the growing number of superhero films. Zack Snyder inaugurated Warner Bros.' DC Extended Universe with 2013's *Man of Steel* and followed that with 2016's *Batman v Superman: Dawn of Justice*. James Gunn directed Marvel's 2014 film *Guardians of the Galaxy* and later oversaw two sequels, as well as the 2021 DCEU film *The Suicide Squad*. In the summer of 2015, Wan signed on to direct *Aquaman*, another DCEU movie, with Jason Momoa in the title role and Patrick Wilson portraying his villainous half-brother Orm. Released in 2018, the film was the DCEU's biggest hit at the global box office, earning $1.1 billion.

Meanwhile, Wan and Safran hired Swedish filmmaker David F. Sandberg to direct a second Annabelle film, 2017's *Annabelle: Creation*. Written by Gary Dauberman, the movie earned $306 million around the globe, making the *Conjuring* series just the third horror franchise to gross more than $1 billion, after the *Alien* series and the *Resident Evil* films.

The next *Conjuring* universe film would center around Aarons' breakout character, the Demon Nun. "We really, at the time, felt that the Crooked

Man was going to be the one," says Safran. "But it just turned out that the audience had such a fascination with the Nun that we felt that was the origin story we had to tell." Dauberman once again wrote the script for the film, which he and Wan wanted to have a different flavor from the *Conjuring* movies. The pair concocted a tale set in the early 1950s that concerned a priest and a novitiate nun investigating a demonic presence at a Romanian monastery. "We wanted to give a little bit of an action-adventure flavor to it, rather than just someone moving into a house and something creepy happens," says Dauberman.

The Nun was directed by British director Corin Hardy, whose low-budget horror movie *The Hallow* had played the Sundance Film Festival in 2015. "I said to Corin, 'Bro, I really would love to do a horror film very much in the spirit of the old Hammer horror films,'" says Wan. "He was like, 'Say no more!'" Demián Bichir was cast as the film's priest, Father Burke, and Taissa Farmiga, the younger sibling of Vera, played the movie's heroine, Sister Irene.

Hardy began shooting *The Nun* in May 2017 at Bucharest's Castel Film Studios and then relocated to Transylvania. Following the end of principal photography, Hardy filmed more footage in Los Angeles, with Wan acting as his second unit director. "James is a hands-on guy, and he was like, 'Anything I can do [to be] of service,'" says Hardy. "[I] was like, 'I really want to take you up on that.' So there were nights when he was shooting a section in the forest and I was shooting interiors." Released in September 2018, *The Nun* grossed $365 million worldwide, making Hardy's film the most successful entry in the *Conjuring* franchise to date.

Like the original *Scream*, *The Conjuring* meant a lot not just for its creators but for horror as a whole. By the time of the film's arrival in 2013, the release schedules were becoming clogged with superhero films and big-budget ventures based on established IP. Another clutch of once-thriving big-screen genres seemed to be following the western and the musical into effective redundancy. People who wanted to see thrillers, or adult dramas, or romantic comedies—or indeed comedies of any sort—would increasingly do so via streaming services like Netflix and Hulu rather than theatrically. Wan's R-rated chiller proved that original horror could not only be wildly profitable but could carve out real estate at the center of an increasingly fragmented and siloed pop culture. As *Hostel* director Eli Roth recalls of the film's success, "I thought, 'Man, this is amazing.' I was like, this is great for all of us. This is ground-breaking. This is R-rated horror now as mainstream as it gets. This is a new level."

While reminding executives and financiers that the remained a good investment, *The Conjuring* showed creatives that operating within horror was one of the few ways left to get their visions onto the big screen. As the *Conjuring* universe flourished, so, too, would the genre, with Wan's film helping to usher in a new golden age of cinematic terror that would feature frights both familiar and thrillingly strange.

EPILOGUE. "WHO GIVES A FUCK ABOUT THE MOVIES?!"

The world premiere of *Scream VI* took place on March 6, 2023, at AMC Lincoln Square in New York City. Like the event held in Los Angeles for Wes Craven's original film, the evening was a starry affair thanks to the presence of cast members Courteney Cox, Jenna Ortega, Melissa Barrera, Hayden Panettiere, Jack Quaid, and Skeet Ulrich, whose deceased *Scream* character Billy Loomis made a surprise appearance in the movie. Also echoing events from 27 years before, there were doubts about the movie's box office potential, given the onscreen absence, for the first time in the film franchise's history, of David Arquette and Neve Campbell.

The now venerable series had been rebooted the year before with 2022's *Scream*. That film was directed by Matt Bettinelli-Olpin and Tyler Gillett from the Radio Silence collective, whose third member, Chad Villella, was among the movie's executive producers. The fifth *Scream* film was set in Woodsboro and centered around a group of young protagonists played by Ortega, Barrera, Mason Gooding, Jasmin Savoy Brown, and Mikey Madison, among others. The movie also featured the return of Campbell's Sidney Prescott, Cox's Gale Weathers, and Arquette's Dewey Riley, who is killed by Ghostface in the course of the movie. Made for $24 million, *Scream* was positively received by critics and fans and grossed $137 million worldwide.

Spyglass Media Group, which had produced the film, and distributor Paramount Pictures, swiftly began prepping another installment. The sixth movie would again be directed by Bettinelli-Olpin and Gillett from a screenplay by James Vanderbilt and Guy Busick, who had written the 2022 *Scream*. Kevin Williamson signed on as executive producer, the same role he had played on the first of the new films.

In May 2022, Spyglass and Paramount announced that Ortega, Barrera, Brown, and Gooding were all set to come back for the sixth *Scream* film. On June 6, *Variety* published an interview with Cox, in which she revealed that Gale Weathers, too, would be seen in the movie. "Gale's pretty strong," she said. "She may not ever [die], but who knows!" The same day that the *Variety* interview was published, Campbell issued a statement announcing she had left the franchise because of a pay dispute. "As a woman, I have had to work extremely hard in my career to establish my value, especially when it comes to *Scream*," the actress said in the statement. "I felt the offer that was presented to me did not equate to the value I have brought to the franchise."

With Campbell out of the picture, the film's behind-the-scenes team pivoted to focus more fully on the characters played by the younger cast members, in particular the sisters portrayed by Ortega and Barrera. Shot in Montreal, Canada, but set in New York, the finished film revealed that Ortega's Tara Carpenter is studying at the fictitious Blackmore University, with Barrera's Sam Carpenter living close by so she can protect her younger sister from Ghostface. As co-director Gillett said ahead of the film's release, "We love

Ghostface in *Scream VI* (2023).

Neve, and we're huge fans of Sidney Prescott, but it felt like there's an opportunity to really dig into this new crop of characters."

Scream VI was released on March 10, 2023, and comfortably won its opening weekend with a gross of $44 million. In April, the film overtook the $103 million domestic gross of Wes Craven's original *Scream*.

The movie's commercial triumph was helped by the fame of Ortega, whose hit show *Wednesday* had premiered on Netflix the previous November. However, the success of the new *Scream* movies would not have surprised anyone who had tracked the genre's continuing appeal over the previous decade. As *Variety* journalist Rebecca Rubin wrote in an article about the movie hitting the $100 million mark in the US, *Scream VI* benefited from "horror's enduring box office popularity." In fact, during a period of unprecedented turmoil for the film industry, the genre had definitively emerged as the closest thing Hollywood could call a sure bet.

Many of the horror films released over the previous decade had arrived on screen with the help of Jason Blum and his company. In addition to shepherding the *Paranormal Activity*, *Insidious*, and *Purge* franchises, Blumhouse produced Rob Zombie's film *The Lords of Salem*, which was released in April 2013. The movie starred Sheri Moon Zombie as a DJ who discovers that she has a link to the Salem Witch Trials. The director enjoyed collaborating with Blum after spending the previous few years working for Dimension. "With the Weinstein *Halloween* movies, I had control, but I didn't contractually have control," Zombie told *Fangoria*. "So I was always fighting, and it was draining. With [*The Lords of Salem*], I didn't need to run anything past anyone." Other Blumhouse releases included Bryan Bertino's 2014 found footage movie *Mockingbird* and Greg McLean's 2016 supernatural tale *The Darkness*, which starred Kevin Bacon and Radha Mitchell.

Blum continued to follow the business model with which he had found success on *Insidious* and *Sinister*, keeping budgets low so that filmmakers could have greater creative freedom. As he explained during a 2015 appearance on the *Geek's Guide to the Galaxy* podcast, "When you do a movie for a low budget, the pressure to be a financial success goes down exponentially; it's hard to make a movie that's very expensive and not be thinking about the results all the time."

Blum's approach resonated with M. Night Shyamalan. The filmmaker felt that he had become creatively lost directing *The Last Airbender* and then

2013's *After Earth*, a big-budget science fiction movie starring Will Smith and his son Jaden. "I started to get away from a sense of agency and started to give more and more power to everything around me," says the director. Inspired by the Blum-produced *Paranormal Activity,* Shyamalan raised $5 million, using his 125-acre Philadelphia estate as collateral, and made *The Visit.* A darkly humorous found footage horror film, the movie tracked two young siblings whose visit with their grandparents turns nightmarish.

Shyamalan was unable to sell the movie when he screened an early cut for potential buyers. "I just finished shooting it, and I showed it to all of them, and said, 'It's a funny, scary movie. Get it? Get it?'" he recalls. "And they were like, 'No, we don't get it. People don't know how to laugh and scream at the same time.'" Shyamalan approached Blum, who signed on to produce the film and helped the director tweak his movie. Distributed by Universal and released in the late summer of 2015, the low budget film earned $98 million worldwide.

Shyamalan and Blum partnered again on 2017's horror-thriller *Split*, which starred James McAvoy as a killer with 23 distinct personalities. In the movie's closing seconds, *Split* was revealed to be a surprise sequel to 2000's *Unbreakable.* The new film earned $278 million worldwide. Shyamalan concluded the trilogy with 2019's *Glass*, another Blumhouse-produced success.

Blum's company oversaw a clutch of films by up-and-coming horror director Mike Flanagan, including 2016's *Hush*, about a deaf woman played by Kate Siegel who is terrorized by a masked killer, which debuted on Netflix. Fans of Flanagan's movie included Stephen King, who hailed *Hush* as "White knuckle time." Blumhouse also produced the Flanagan-directed 2016 prequel *Ouija: Origin of Evil.* The film's cast included Doug Jones, who had appeared in Flanagan's micro-budgeted 2011 movie *Absentia.* "He created *Absentia* for zero money almost," says Jones. "For locations, he used his own apartment and a tunnel across the street from his apartment. Who knows if we had permits or not. I don't want to ask!"

Blumhouse continued to nurture the filmmaking career of *Paranormal Activity* franchise writer Christopher Landon, who directed 2014's spin-off *Paranormal Activity: The Marked Ones* and 2017's horror-comedy *Happy Death Day* for the company. The latter movie fused together the slasher genre with *Groundhog Day* for a tale in which Jessica Rothe's heroine is repeatedly murdered by a killer wearing a baby mask, created in real-life by makeup designer Tony Gardner. "I pitched Tony Gardner a baby and I pitched him a pig," says Landon. "When I received the prototype for the baby, I knew that was it. It struck the perfect balance of being weird, slightly funny, but ultimately scary." *Happy Death Day* earned $125 million at the global box office.

Blum bet on another new talent, at least when it came to directing films, with Jordan Peele. The comedian was well known for provoking laughter with Keegan-Michael Key on the TV sketch show *Key & Peele*. When Peele tried to sell his script for a horror film about a Black photographer whose weekend away with his white girlfriend goes terrifyingly awry, few people took the project seriously. He finally struck a deal to write and direct the tale, titled *Get Out*, for Blumhouse and Universal on a budget of $4.5 million. The first-time filmmaker cast Daniel Kaluuya as the movie's hero Chris and Allison Williams as his girlfriend Rose, part of an organization that transplants the minds of rich white people into the bodies of Black men and women. "Before I left to film it, I told my publicist that I thought it would be nominated for Oscars," says Williams. "She was like, 'This girl is delusional. Who says that?' Then, much to her shock, I happened to be right."

Released in 2017, *Get Out* made $255 million worldwide and earned Oscar nominations in the categories of Best Picture, Best Actor, Best Director, and Best Original Screenplay. Speaking to *Entertainment Weekly* on the day the nominations were announced, Peele described horror as "my favorite genre. It's not always respected, I think mainly because you either like horror or you don't, and there are some people that just won't see it. So the fact that the word of mouth on this film has pushed people who wouldn't dabble into this genre—which I think just really takes tremendous precision and artistry—is a real point of pride." On the night of the Academy Awards ceremony in March 2018, Peele won the Oscar for Best Original Screenplay, the first African-American to do so.

Guillermo del Toro was another horror filmmaker who left the 2018 Academy Awards a happy man. The director had followed *Pacific Rim* with 2015's beautiful, brutal, gothic ghost story *Crimson Peak* and stuck with horror for his next film, 2017's *The Shape of Water*. Written by del Toro and Vanessa Taylor, the film starred Sally Hawkins as a mute janitor at a government laboratory who falls in love—and lust—with an amphibian creature played by Doug Jones. "Guillermo said to me, 'I want to make sure you're going to be okay with this one scene, it's a fuck scene in a bathtub,'" recalls Jones. "I'm like, 'Guillermo, start at the beginning and get me to the bathtub.' So he tells me the entire story. It was so beautiful, what he was telling me, and I could picture all of it. I said to him, 'This is your next trip to the Oscars.'"

Set in 1962, *The Shape of Water* was a full-throated plea for open-mindedness and acceptance. Del Toro believed that the film had gained extra resonance following the political rise of Donald Trump, who was elected President the year before its release. "When America says, 'Let's make America great again,' they are dreaming of 1962," the director told *GQ*. "But it was only ideal if you were a WASP—a white Anglo-Saxon Protestant. If you were anybody else, it was not that great, which is very similar to what we are experiencing today."

The Shape of Water was a commercial and critical hit, nominated for 13 Academy Awards. On Oscar night, the film triumphed in four categories, including Best Director and Best Picture. "Growing up in Mexico, I thought this could never happen. It happens," del Toro said, accepting the Best Picture trophy. "And I want to tell you, everyone that is dreaming of a parable, of using genre and fantasy to tell the stories about the things that are real in the world today, you can do this." The director looked at the Oscar and then continued: "This is a door, kick it open and come in."

Andy Muschietti had already kicked in the door with his del Toro-assisted debut *Mama*. The filmmaker enjoyed an even greater success directing a two-part New Line-produced adaptation of Stephen King's *It*. The first half of the tale received a boost ahead of its release when King wrote on Twitter that the movie "succeeds beyond my expectations." "After a year and a half, I felt like I could finally exhale," Gary Dauberman, who co-wrote the film's screenplay, told *Entertainment Weekly* about King's compliment. Released in

Bill Skarsgård in *It* (2017).

September 2017, *It* grossed $701 million worldwide. *It Chapter Two* arrived in cinemas a couple of years later and earned $473 million.

2019 was a banner year for Stephen King adaptations. In addition to *It Chapter Two*, horror fans were treated to a remake of *Pet Sematary* from filmmakers Kevin Kölsch and Dennis Widmyer and a sequel to *The Shining* called *Doctor Sleep*, which was adapted from King's novel of the same name by Mike Flanagan. "The first time I ever met Stephen King in my life, I brought *Doctor Sleep* to Bangor and watched the movie with him," the director says. "The film ended, and he leaned over, and he said, 'You did a beautiful job.' I kind of died."

Jason Blum produced *The Purge* movies in partnership with Platinum Dunes. The company's co-founder Andrew Form had noticed Blum's hit rate with low-budget horror and sent him an email asking to meet. "It said something along the lines of, 'Now that you've stolen our business, what you can do is buy me a cup of coffee,'" Form would recall to *Variety*. "He responded right away, saying, 'Any time, any place.'"

Platinum Dunes also produced 2018's *A Quiet Place*, about a family attempting to survive in a world ravaged by alien creatures that cannot see but have an acute sense of hearing. To play the father of the family in the film, Fuller and Form approached John Krasinski, the star of Platinum Dunes' upcoming thriller show *Jack Ryan*. Krasinski signed on to both appear in and direct the movie, casting his wife Emily Blunt as his character's spouse. Made for $17 million, *A Quiet Place* grossed $188 million at the domestic box office. In August 2018, the film's distributors Paramount announced that a sequel would be released in May 2020.

The last movies in the *Resident Evil* and *Underworld* film franchises—at least the iterations respectively overseen by Paul W. S. Anderson and Len Wiseman—debuted in the US within a month of each other at the start of 2017.

The Kate Beckinsale-starring *Underworld: Blood Wars* was released on January 6, 2017. The film opened fourth at the box office with a three-day take of $13 million, the worst start by an *Underworld* to date. *Resident Evil: The Final Chapter* was released three weeks later. The film would gross just $26 million in the US but racked up global earnings of $312 million. "I wanted to go out on a high, and that's exactly what we did," says Anderson.

The *Resident Evil* franchise would return in new forms, although none fully clicked with audiences. A film, titled *Resident Evil: Welcome to Raccoon City* and directed by Johannes Roberts, was released in 2021. The movie grossed $41 million worldwide, roughly an eighth of that earned by the last film in Anderson's series. The following year, Netflix premiered a *Resident Evil* TV show starring Lance Reddick but then decided not to order a second season. Anderson tracked the franchise's faltering fortunes with sadness. "I feel like, when we walked away from it, it was definitely the right time to do that," says the director, speaking in 2024. "But a substantial amount of time has passed and *Resident Evil* has seemingly gone nowhere. It's a reboot that didn't work and a TV show that got cancelled. Which doesn't make me feel good."

On August 22, 2017, a crowd of horror fans arrived at Hollywood's ArcLight Cinema to attend what director Adam Green had advertised as a '10th

Anniversary Celebration' of *Hatchet.* Instead of watching a decade-old film, though, the audience was treated to the world premiere of *Victor Crowley*, the fourth movie in the *Hatchet* franchise, which the director had filmed in secret.

Green was inspired to make *Victory Crowley* after interviewing George A. Romero onstage at Massachusetts' Rock and Shock Festival in October 2015. The *Hatchet* creator had fallen into a depression prompted by the breakdown of his marriage, the fatal 2014 overdose of his friend, GWAR frontman Dave Brockie, and the recent passing of Wes Craven. Green's mood was lifted by a comment Romero made to him at the end of the panel discussion. "George said, 'I know you've been going through a rough time—you have to get over that and get back on your feet,'" recalls Green. "And as part of his pep talk, he said, 'So, where's the next Crowley picture?' And I said, 'There isn't going to be one, I'm done with that.' And he pointed to this standing ovation in the audience, and he said, 'You've got to understand, 'til they say it's over, it isn't.' 48 hours later, I'm back in LA, and I'm sitting at my desk, and I'm typing: 'Ext. Honey Island Swamp. Night.'"

That 2015 Rock and Shock panel was among the last public appearances made by Romero, who died from lung cancer in July 2017. The previous year, he had been selected to receive a star on the Hollywood Walk of Fame, and the director's widow Suzanne accepted the honor on his behalf several months after his passing. She was joined at the ceremony by Tom Savini, Greg Nicotero, and Edgar Wright, who that summer had scored his biggest hit to date with the action-comedy *Baby Driver.* "I'm not sure I would be working in Hollywood right now if it wasn't for George," the *Shaun of the Dead* filmmaker said in his speech praising the late director. "A lot of people owe George a huge debt of gratitude for his inspiration, and I'm just one of many."

The zombie subgenre that George Romero had pioneered continued to be popular with filmmakers. *World War Z* was followed onto screens by a host of undead tales, including the Christopher Landon-directed *Scouts Guide to the Zombie Apocalypse*, *Pride and Prejudice and Zombies*, *Life After Beth*, *Zombeavers*, *Train to Busan*, *The Girl with All the Gifts*, *The Battery*, *One Cut of the Dead*, the musical *Anna and the Apocalypse*, Joe Dante's *Burying the Ex*, Jim Jarmusch's *The Dead Don't Die*, and the Arnold Schwarzenegger-starring *Maggie.*

A decade after the release of *Zombieland*, Sony put out a sequel, 2019's *Zombieland: Double Tap.* The film reunited director Ruben Fleischer, screenwriters

Rhett Reese and Paul Wernick, and the original movie's four stars. "Now the joke is, we'll make one every ten years!" says Reese.

Romero's most successful spiritual progeny was AMC's *The Walking Dead.* Showrunner Frank Darabont left the series during the production of its second season and would later launch a lawsuit seeking $300 million in profit participation payments, but the series went on to become a ratings juggernaut. *The Walking Dead* achieved an audience peak in 2014 with its Nicotero-directed season 5 premiere "No Sanctuary," which was watched by a record-breaking 17.3 million viewers in the US. The original show finally concluded in 2021 after eleven seasons, but its universe continued via several spin-off shows.

In the years following the successful launch of *The Walking Dead*, TV executives sought to attract viewers with a slew of horror shows like *American Horror Story*, *Black Mirror*, *The Strain*, co-created by Guillermo del Toro, executive producer M. Night Shyamalan's *Wayward Pines*, Netflix's Mike Flanagan-directed *The Haunting of Hill House*, and the same streaming service's wildly successful *Stranger Things.* Netflix scored another global hit in 2021 with *Squid Game*, a South Korean show created by director Hwang Dong-hyuk, whose plot about people being murdered for the pleasure of the rich had echoes of Eli Roth's *Hostel* films. "I met Dong, and he told me he was watching *Hostel I* and *II* while he was writing it," says Roth. "I told him, 'South Korean cinema is what made me make *Hostel*, and *Hostel* is what made you make *Squid Game.*' There's this beautiful symbiosis." In the summer of 2024, *The Hollywood Reporter* revealed that Roth was himself developing a *Hostel* TV show, which would star Paul Giamatti.

Meanwhile, a clutch of existing horror film franchises found a second life on the small screen. Bruce Campbell reprised his *Evil Dead* character on Starz's *Ash vs Evil Dead*, which premiered in 2015 and ran for three seasons. And in 2019, Greg Nicotero resurrected George Romero's horror anthology franchise *Creepshow* as a TV series for the horror streaming service Shudder.

Shudder revived another movie franchise (of sorts) by screening *The Last Drive-in with Joe Bob Briggs.* The titular horror host was the stage name of journalist John Bloom, who had previously portrayed the character on The Movie Channel's *Joe Bob's Drive-In Theater* and TNT's *MonsterVision.* When Bloom-as-Briggs hosted a movie marathon for Shudder in July 2018, the experiment proved so popular that the streamer's servers broke. "I kept get-

Game guards in *Squid Game.*

ting these messages from people saying, 'You sons of bitches, I can't get this fucking show! I paid for this! You assholes!'" he says. "Then, after about an hour, I started getting these very favorable messages, these congratulatory messages, like, 'Joe Bob, did you know that you just broke the internet?'" The first season of *The Last Drive-in* premiered in 2019 and the show rapidly became essential viewing for dedicated horror fans. Over time, the films introduced by Briggs and his onscreen partner Diana 'Darcy the Mail Girl' Prince ranged from vintage fare such as the original 1922 *Nosferatu* and *The Changeling* to more recent films like the 2013 cult hit *Sharknado*, André Øvredal's 2016 scare machine *The Autopsy of Jane Doe*, and Joe Lynch's 2017 virus movie *Mayhem.*

Following *Seed of Chucky*, Don Mancini continued the *Child's Play* franchise with 2013's *Curse of Chucky* and 2017's *Cult of Chucky*, both straight-to-DVD releases. Mancini also worked as a writer on *Hannibal*, NBC's TV version of the Hannibal Lecter saga, which premiered in 2013. The experience inspired him to think about how his homicidal doll franchise might transfer to the small screen. The resulting show, *Chucky*, began airing on Syfy and USA Network in October 2021, with Zackary Arthur playing the lead role of a queer teenager named Jake Wheeler. "Each iteration of *Chucky* has gotten a lot more personal and autobiographical for me," Mancini told *Entertainment Weekly* in 2022. "I'm able to use the character of Jake Wheeler as a figure for dealing with a lot of the things that I had to deal with as a young gay kid." Arthur's co-stars included *Final Destination* actor Devon Sawa, who played an assortment of different doomed characters before the series was canceled after three seasons. "I absolutely love *Chucky*," Sawa said in 2021. "I think my managers and agents were a little nervous bringing *Chucky* to me. They probably didn't know what I would think. But when it came through my emails, I was like, 'Oh my God, *Chucky*!'"

As these older franchises got another chance, so, too, did the horror anthology film. Following the release of *Trick 'r Treat* and *V/H/S*, New Zealand producer Ant Timpson and Alamo Drafthouse Cinema founder Tim League unleashed 2013's 26-segment film *The ABCs of Death* and its follow-ups; Neil Marshall, Darren Bousman, and Mike Mendez, among others, combined for 2015's *Tales of Halloween*; *V/H/S* creators Brad Miska and Roxanne Benjamin produced 2016's *Southbound*; and Benjamin directed one of the tales in 2017's *XX*, whose all-female filmmaking roster also boasted Karyn Kusama.

Masters of Horror executive producer Mick Garris returned to the horror anthology fray with the 2019 film *Nightmare Cinema*. "The intention was to do a [TV] series, each [episode] shot in a different country with a genre filmmaker from that country," he says. "That was a little too ambitious. People were afraid of globe-hopping." *Nightmare Cinema* featured stories from Garris, Joe Dante, David Slade, Ryuhei Kitamura, and Alejandro Brugués, director of the 2012 zombie film *Juan of the Dead*. Brugués and Mike Mendez later joined forces for 2023's *Satanic Hispanics*. "Alejandro jokingly said, 'When are we making *Satanic Hispanics*, the all-Latino horror anthology?'" Mendez recalls. "We gathered some of our favorite Latino indie-horror filmmakers we felt were kick-ass, and we said, 'Come join us!'"

Meanwhile, the *V/H/S* franchise continued to grow, attracting both new and established talent. Scott Derrickson and his writing partner C. Robert Cargill came up with a segment for 2023's sixth franchise entry *V/H/S/85*, while Mike Flanagan wrote a tale for 2024's *V/H/S/Beyond* that was directed by *Hush* actress Kate Siegel.

"I would like to think that *Trick 'r Treat* had something to do with the resurgence of horror anthologies," says that film's writer-director Michael Dougherty. "I do wish the studios would re-embrace the anthology as a format. The *V/H/S* films and some of the other horror anthologies are very much scrappy independent movies—which is great, because we need those, too—but it seems like the studios haven't quite grown the balls to get behind a proper anthology."

Most of the horror franchises that had emerged in the post-*Scream* years continued in one form or another. Filmmakers the Spierig Brothers oversaw an eighth *Saw* movie, 2017's *Jigsaw*, while Rob Zombie unleashed a third tale featuring the homicidal Firefly clan, 2019's *3 From Hell*. *Wrong Turn* writer Alan B. McElroy returned to the franchise for a 2021 reboot, also called *Wrong Turn*, about an Appalachian cult named the Foundation. This new entry was the seventh *Wrong Turn* movie, but McElroy is interested in making still more. "I had planned two more films," he says. "I'd love to finish it and see it all come out the way I wanted."

Victor Salva, too, came back to the franchise he had created, writing and directing 2017's *Jeepers Creepers 3*. The film sparked controversy after IGN reviewer Adam Dileo noted that some dialog in the film discussed child abuse. Dileo's review prompted IndieWire to post an article headlined "Jeepers Creepers 3 Director Victor Salva, A Convicted Pedophile, Wrote Molestation Into the Film." The movie was given a limited release, with the offending dialog removed, and grossed $2 million. A fourth film in the franchise, 2022's *Jeepers Creepers: Reborn*, was made without Salva's creative participation. "He's not involved in any way," the movie's director Timo Vuorensola told the outlet Cinefied. "I wouldn't have worked on this any other way."

The J-horror remake craze of the 2000s was revisited with 2017's *Rings* and 2020's *The Grudge*, starring Lin Shaye. The latest chapter in the *Ju-On* saga was once again produced by Ghost House Pictures. Sam Raimi and Rob Tapert's company had continued to develop horror movies in the years following *Drag Me to Hell*, producing 2012's haunted Jewish wine-cabinet tale *The Possession* and Fede Álvarez's *Evil Dead*. Ghost House was also responsible for Álvarez's 2016's hit *Don't Breathe*, which starred Stephen Lang as a blind man with grotesque designs on Jane Levy's burglar.

The Strangers spawned a belated sequel, 2018's *The Strangers: Prey at Night*, and then an entire trilogy of films, whose first entry, *The Strangers: Chapter 1*, was released in 2024. The three movies were directed by Renny Harlin, who shot them simultaneously in Slovakia. "On Monday morning, I could be shooting the second chapter, and Monday afternoon I could be shooting the first chapter, and Tuesday morning I could be shooting the third chapter," Harlin explains. "It just kept all of our juices pumping all the time." Critics were unimpressed by the return of Pin-Up Girl, Dollface, and Man in Mask, but *The Strangers: Chapter 1* earned a respectable $35 million in the US.

Vin Diesel and director David Twohy revived the *Pitch Black* franchise with 2013's *Riddick* and began developing a fourth entry, *Riddick: Furya*. "I think it was Vin who had the vision that it could continue [beyond *Pitch Black*] and he had that collaboration with David Twohy," says actress Radha Mitchell. Of her own absence from the franchise's sequels, she adds, "I don't think about it, but it would have been better to stay alive. Maybe that's the advice for any young actors: don't get your character killed in the action movie! But to be perfectly honest, I haven't seen the other ones."

Long-time *Conjuring* universe writer Gary Dauberman made his directorial debut with *Annabelle Comes Home*. His script focused on the Warrens' young daughter Judy and the many dangers of the couple's artifact room. Released in the summer of 2019, *Annabelle Comes Home* earned $231 million at the global box office.

A third *Conjuring* movie, *The Conjuring: The Devil Made Me Do It*, detailed the trial of a Connecticut resident named Arne Cheyenne Johnson, who claimed he had been possessed by a demon when he killed his landlord in November 1981. Directed by Michael Chaves and released in June 2021, *The Conjuring: The Devil Made Me Do It* grossed $65 million at the US box office and $206 million in all. The month after the movie debuted in cinemas, New Line issued a press release announcing that the gross revenues of Wan and Safran's franchise had now surpassed $2 billion, an unprecedented feat for a horror series.

Hammer Films was unable to capitalize on the success of *The Woman in Black* and only produced a handful of movies in the decade after that tale's release. But over the same period, several other companies emerged as prolific producers of genre product.

In the early 2000s, *The Faculty* actor Elijah Wood became famous around the world for portraying Frodo Baggins in Peter Jackson's *The Lord of the Rings* trilogy. Wood subsequently co-founded the horror-focused production company SpectreVision. Among the label's first releases were director Ana Lily Amirpour's 2014 vampire film *A Girl Walks Home Alone at Night* and 2015's *Cooties*, in which Wood and co-writer Leigh Whannell played teachers menaced by violent, virus-stricken children. SpectreVision later attracted the attention of adventurous horror fans with 2018's hallucinogenic Panos Cosmatos-directed *Mandy*, starring Nicolas Cage as a vengeful lumberjack named Red.

A24 was another new production house whose horror movies were as likely to be screened in arthouses as multiplexes. The company's early releases included Jonathan Glazer's 2014 film *Under the Skin* and Robert Eggers' acclaimed 2016 period tale *The Witch*, the breakthrough movie of Anya Taylor-Joy. A24's reputation as a house of horror was confirmed with writer-director Ari Aster's 2018 directorial debut *Hereditary*, which starred Toni Collette as a parent whose life harrowingly disintegrates. Prior to signing on for the film, *The Sixth Sense* star had told her representatives that she was sick of dramatic, emotional roles and only wanted to appear in comedies. Collette was won over by the quality of Aster's script. "One of my agents called me and said, 'Listen, I think you need to read this,'" says the actress. "It was so perfectly written. I was like, 'Fuck you!' Because how do you say no to that?" Aster followed *Hereditary* with another A24-produced movie, 2019's *Midsommar*, a fresh twist on folk horror with a cast led by Florence Pugh.

Florence Pugh in *Midsommar* (2019).

Distributors IFC Midnight also proved a firm friend to horror. After introducing America to *The Human Centipede*, the label released the Elijah Wood-starring slasher remake *Maniac*,

Nicholas McCarthy's supernatural chiller *At the Devil's Door*, and 2014's *The Babadook*. Written and directed by Australian filmmaker Jennifer Kent, the latter movie starred Essie Davis as an exhausted single mother named Amelia whose family is threatened by the top hat-wearing supernatural creature of the film's title. "Women understand fear very well, we live with it on a day-to-day basis," Kent said ahead of the film's US release. "I don't look down on horror, never have." Kent's movie was ecstatically reviewed by critics and received a thumbs-up from *The Exorcist* director William Friedkin, who wrote on Twitter that he had "never seen a more terrifying film than *The Babadook*."

Larry Fessenden continued to direct his own horror movies, including 2019's *Frankenstein* retelling *Depraved* (whose cast included *The Blair Witch Project* star Joshua Leonard), and to help new filmmakers. His Glass Eye Pix company produced Adrián García Bogliano's 2015 werewolf tale *Late Phases*, Mickey Keating's 2016 psychological thriller *Darling*, and Jenn Wexler's 2018 slasher film *The Ranger*. Fessenden also leant his onscreen presence to an array of low-budget terror tales, such as Ted Geoghegan's 2015 ghost story *We Are Still Here* and Travis Stevens' 2021 vampire film *Jakob's Wife*. Both of those films co-starred Barbara Crampton, who, following *You're Next*, became one of horror's most active and well-known supporters. The actress appeared in, and on occasion produced, a slew of genre movies, from Jackson Stewart's *Beyond the Gates* to 2023's Joe Lynch-directed *Suitable Flesh*. An adaptation of H. P. Lovecraft's short story "The Thing on the Doorstep," Lynch's film had originally been developed by Stuart Gordon and featured several of the late director's collaborators, including *Re-Animator: The Musical* star Graham Skipper. "We wanted to tip our hat to Stuart," says Crampton.

In the years after the release of *Scream 4*, Bob Weinstein's Dimension continued to pump out sequels like 2011's *Hellraiser: Revelations*, 2012's *Piranha 3DD*, and 2013's *Scary Movie 5*. But several of the Weinsteins' notable genre films of the period were distributed by a different wing of the siblings' empire. In 2012, The Weinstein Company launched Radius-TWC, a multiplatform boutique label overseen by executives Jason Janego and Tom Quinn. Radius-TWC was responsible for distributing Alexandre Aja's 2014 horror-comedy *Horns*—which starred Daniel Radcliffe and was adapted from a novel by Stephen King's son Joe Hill—Bong Joon-ho's *Snowpiercer*, and 2015's *Goodnight Mommy*.

Radius-TWC's most outstanding genre release, certainly in terms of its reputation as an instant horror classic, was *It Follows*. Written and directed by David Robert Mitchell, the film starred Maika Monroe as a teenager who, after a sexual encounter, finds herself pursued by a slow-moving but relentless entity. Writing for outlet The Dissolve, critic Scott Tobias described Mitchell's creepfest as "the best American horror film since *The Blair Witch Project*," while Vox reviewer Emily St. James told readers that *It Follows* "is a movie you need to see right now." The film cost a reported $1.3 million and opened on just four US screens in March 2015. Within a month, the movie was playing in more than a thousand cinemas, and went on to gross $14 million at the domestic box office. "It was supposed to be a small release and then, all of a sudden, it's doing incredibly well," Monroe told *Entertainment Weekly* a couple of weeks after the film came out. "People on Twitter are like, 'It's not playing here! I'm driving two hours to a movie theater to see it!'" Few would have predicted that this latest horror release from the Weinstein brothers would also be one of their last.

The new *Scream* films were not produced by Dimension Films, because Bob Weinstein's company effectively no longer existed thanks to his brother's criminal behavior. In October 2017, *New York Times* journalists Jodi Kantor and Megan Twohey and *New Yorker* writer Ronan Farrow published articles detailing multiple accusations of sexual misconduct against Harvey Weinstein over the previous three decades. In *The New York Times* article, Kantor and Twohey revealed that Weinstein had reached a settlement with *Scream* actress Rose McGowan in 1997 after an episode during that year's Sundance Film Festival. In her 2018 autobiography *Brave*, McGowan would recount how Weinstein had sexually assaulted her in his hotel suite.

Weinstein denied the allegations of criminality but was fired from The Weinstein Company by its board of directors. On May 25, 2018, the producer was arrested in New York and charged with rape, criminal sex acts, sex abuse, and sexual misconduct for incidents involving two separate women. In February 2020, he was found guilty of forcing oral sex on a production assistant, Miriam Haley, and of raping another woman, and was later sentenced to 23 years in jail. In 2024, Weinstein's convictions were overturned because the trial judge had admitted testimony concerning uncharged sex acts. He would remain in jail, however, having been sentenced to a further 16 years behind bars for rape and sexual assault following another trial in Los Angeles.

On March 19, 2018, The Weinstein Company filed for Chapter 11 bankruptcy. Four months later, equity firm Lantern Capital Partners bought the company's assets for $289 million. Lantern partnered with film executive Gary Barber to produce movie and TV projects based on The Weinstein Company titles via Barber's revived Spyglass corporate brand. In addition to resurrecting the *Scream* franchise, Spyglass also produced 2022's *Hellraiser*, which debuted on Hulu. Directed by *V/H/S* filmmaker David Bruckner, this reboot of the Clive Barker-created franchise starred Jamie Clayton as the new leader of the Cenobites. The film was better received by critics and fans than the many sequels produced by Dimension.

Harvey Weinstein was one of many men involved in the entertainment business to be accused of rape, assault, or otherwise toxic behavior during this period. Members of that group with strong links to the horror community included Ain't It Cool News website founder Harry Knowles and *The Cabin in the Woods* co-writer Joss Whedon.

In September 2017, IndieWire reported that an Austin area woman named Jasmine Baker claimed she had been sexually assaulted by Knowles two decades previously. Three days after the initial article was posted, IndieWire published another piece revealing that four more women had come forward accusing him of sexual assault or harassment. On September 29, Knowles announced via social media that he was stepping away from Ain't It Cool News to spend time on "therapy, detox, and getting to a better place."

Knowles was a comparatively fringe figure whose postings could display a thick vein of misogyny. The revelations about Joss Whedon took more people by surprise, partly because of his greater fame and partly because he tended to center strong female characters in his work. On February 10, 2021, actress Charisma Carpenter posted a statement to Twitter recalling how Whedon had "abused his power on numerous occasions" on both *Buffy the Vampire Slayer* and the spin-off series *Angel*. Carpenter alleged that, after learning she was pregnant, Whedon "proceeded to attack my character and my religious beliefs, accuse me of sabotaging the show, and then unceremoniously fired me [from *Angel*] the following season once I gave birth." Two days after Carpenter posted her statement, Michelle Trachtenberg wrote on Instagram that, when she had worked on *Buffy the Vampire Slayer* as a teenager, Whedon was not allowed to be alone in a room with the young actress. In a later interview with *New York* magazine, Whedon would deny knowledge of any such rule, but his reputation as a creator would be lastingly eclipsed by his newfound infamy.

In May 2016, Blumhouse announced that the company would co-finance a new *Halloween* movie and that John Carpenter had signed on as executive producer. In February of the following year, Carpenter revealed on his Facebook page that the film would be directed by David Gordon Green from a script by Green and *Eastbound & Down* star Danny McBride (not to be confused with the *Underworld* co-creator of the same name). Green had previously developed a remake of Dario Argento's *Suspiria*—a project finally brought to the screen in 2018 by Luca Guadagnino—and was a fan of Carpenter. "I'd always wanted to make a horror film," he says. "I was obsessed with John Carpenter as a kid."

Green, McBride, and co-writer Jeff Fradley delivered a script which acted as a direct sequel to Carpenter's first movie. In September 2017, Jamie Lee Curtis confirmed that she would reprise the role of Laurie Strode in the film. Curtis was surprised at how emotionally demanding she found returning to the part she had first played four decades before. "I started crying the day I arrived," she says. "I didn't stop crying until the day I left."

Carpenter himself was more creatively involved with the project than he had been with the remakes of *The Fog* and *Assault on Precinct 13* or Rob Zombie's *Halloween* films. "Jason Blum came to me and said, 'Instead of sitting on the sidelines, criticizing these people, why don't you jump in and help?'" explains the director. "So I decided to help try to get it as good as I could." In the years since the release of *The Ward*, Carpenter had concentrated on music, releasing the albums *Lost Themes* and *Lost Themes II* in 2015 and 2016 and touring with his band. The director agreed to provide the score for Green's *Halloween*, working with his son Cody Carpenter and family friend Daniel Davies, the son of Kinks guitarist Dave Davies. "The movie was cut together, and we had a spotting session with David," says Carpenter. "David's a real smart guy, and he knew exactly the feel [he wanted]. And that's all I care about. 'What feeling do you want to hear, man?'" The finished soundtrack would feature both new music and reworked material from the original *Halloween*. "It was just a blast," says Carpenter. "It was fun!"

Universal released Green's *Halloween* on October 19, 2018. The film earned $159 million at the domestic box office and another $96 million abroad. In

Jamie Lee Curtis in a promotional shot for *Halloween* (2018).

July 2019, Carpenter posted a video on social media announcing that the movie would be followed by two sequels, *Halloween Kills* and *Halloween Ends*.

While promoting his company's *Halloween*, Jason Blum spoke to Polygon writer Matt Patches. The journalist asked Blum why Blumhouse had not produced a theatrically released horror film directed by a woman. "There are not a lot of female directors period, and even less who are inclined to do horror," he replied. Blum went on to explain that he had offered projects to *Babadook* director Jennifer Kent, who had turned them down, but his assertion about the paucity of female horror filmmakers provoked outrage. "If you want a list of female horror or genre filmmakers… that list is LONG AS FUCK," *V/H/S* producer Roxanne Benjamin wrote on Twitter. The day before the release of *Halloween*, Blum tweeted out a statement apologizing for his comments. "We have not done a good enough job working with female directors, and it is not because they don't exist," he said. "I will do better." The following June, the company announced that filmmaker Sophia Takal was set to direct a new remake of *Black Christmas*.

Away from Blumhouse, female directors repeatedly proved that they could terrify—and gross out—viewers just as well as their male counterparts. The list of notable releases from female filmmakers began, but certainly did not end, with Julia Ducournau's cannibal film *Raw* and subsequent Cannes sensation *Titane*, Rose Glass' *Saint Maud*, Issa López's *Tigers Are Not Afraid*, Leigh Janiak's *Honeymoon*, Brea Grant's *12 Hour Shift*, Rebekah McKendry's *Glorious*, and Alice Lowe's *Prevenge*. "I think that it is more likely [now] for a woman to be given a chance," says *American Mary* co-director Jen Soska. "I do know, back when I was really starting, they would interview us just so they could check off [a box]. Like, 'We talked with *two* women, and we hired our buddy. What's the problem?' People were like, 'Ugh, I don't care about the horrors of what it's like to be a woman.' I'm like, 'But I do! 51 [percent] of the population, we do!'"

Horror filmmakers continued to be courted by studios keen for them to apply their skills in the superhero genre. Scott Derrickson directed 2016's *Doctor Strange* for Marvel, and *Annabelle: Creation* filmmaker David F. Sandberg oversaw the 2019 hit *Shazam!* for DC and Warner Bros. Jon Watts made his debut with the 2016 horror movie *Clown*, which was produced by Eli Roth, and went on to direct a trilogy of Spider-Man blockbusters starting with 2017's *Spider-Man: Homecoming*. Filmmaking duo Justin Benson and Aaron Moorhead wrote and directed 2015's Lovecraftian romance *Spring*, which Guillermo del Toro described on Twitter as "one of the best horror films of this decade." Marvel later hired the pair to work on the TV shows *Moon Knight* and *Loki*.

Following their success with *Zombieland*, Rhett Reese and Paul Wernick also entered the superhero realm. The pair co-wrote the Deadpool movies including the 2024 blockbuster *Deadpool & Wolverine*, which saw Wesley Snipes reprise the role of Blade. Reese is unsurprised that so many filmmakers with experience in the horror genre have overseen superhero tales.

"Horror is very much a visual medium," he says. "Something can be scary on the page, [but] if it's not shot right, it's going to be terrible. Sam Raimi, Zack Snyder, those guys are masters visually, so I think it does make sense that there is a connection there."

The same thinking was being applied to films that lay outside the superhero arena but still within the realm of valuable IP, leading to Adam Wingard being handed the reins of the MonsterVerse. The *You're Next* filmmaker would direct 2021's *Godzilla vs. Kong* and 2024's *Godzilla x Kong: The New Empire.*

In May 2017, Universal announced that its upcoming remake of *The Mummy* would be the first in a series of interconnected films set in what the studio called the 'Dark Universe.' In addition to *The Mummy* stars Tom Cruise, Sofia Boutella, and Russell Crowe, Universal promised that the Dark Universe movies would feature Javier Bardem as Frankenstein's Monster and Johnny Depp, who would appear in a remake of *The Invisible Man.*

Universal had sporadically attempted to exploit its gallery of monsters in the years since 2008's *The Mummy: Tomb of the Dragon Emperor*, with limited success. In 2010, the studio released *The Wolfman* starring Benicio del Toro, Anthony Hopkins, and Emily Blunt, a big budget venture which underwhelmed at the box office. Rick Baker would win his seventh Oscar for designing the movie's werewolf effects but was disappointed by how little of his practical work wound up onscreen. "The whole transformation was done on computers," he told The Playlist in 2011. Universal followed *The Wolfman* with 2014's *Dracula Untold*, which starred Luke Evans. The film was cheaper than *The Wolfman* and earned more at the global box office but again failed to repeat the blockbuster success of Stephen Sommers' *The Mummy.*

The 2017 iteration of *The Mummy* was directed by Alex Kurtzman, best known as a writer on the *Transformers* and *Star Trek* franchises. Kurtzman's film was reviled by critics and did not excite audiences. On June 19, 2017, shortly after the film's release, Deadline published an article estimating that the movie would lose $95 million. As part of the Dark Universe announcement, Universal had teased that the second entry in the franchise would be director Bill Condon's *The Bride of Frankenstein*, which was scheduled for release in February 2019. The box office failure of *The Mummy* caused the studio to shelve Condon's film and the Dark Universe concept as a whole.

Universal's lineup of monsters was more successfully raided by someone with little more directing experience than Kurtzman but a longer track record of scaring cinemagoers. *Saw* screenwriter Leigh Whannell made his directorial debut with 2015's *Insidious: Chapter 3* and followed that with 2018's science fiction action-thriller *Upgrade*. In 2019, *Variety* revealed that the Australian would write and direct a new version of *The Invisible Man* for Universal, to be produced by Jason Blum. Whannell's film starred *Mad Men* actress Elisabeth Moss as a woman who is terrorized by her ex-boyfriend, a scientist played by Oliver Jackson-Cohen with the power to make himself invisible. Universal released the movie on February 28, 2020, and Whannell's film—a much more modestly budgeted venture than Kurtzman's *The Mummy*—comfortably won its opening three-day frame, earning $28 million.

The Invisible Man would be the last movie many horror fans saw in the cinema for a long time. On January 4, 2020, the World Health Organization warned about a cluster of pneumonia cases in Wuhan, China. On January 30, the WHO issued a situation report revealing that there were now 7,818 confirmed cases worldwide of a novel coronavirus, 82 of them in countries outside China. Within just a few months, the world was plunged into a tragic nightmare, unprecedented in the modern era, as COVID-19 progressed around the globe. Citizens self-isolated at home and non-essential industries, including the theatrical film distribution business, were shuttered. Interviewed by *Entertainment Weekly* at the end of 2020, Whannell admitted that many people had told him that *The Invisible Man* was the final film they had seen in cinemas before the lockdown began. "I was thinking, 'God, if theaters never open again, it will always be this footnote in history,'" he said. "The last film! That's not a mantle I want to carry."

The big-screen experience seemed under genuine threat following the start of the COVID outbreak, as studios pushed the release dates of their respective films. One of 2020's most talked-about horror movies, British director Rob Savage's *Host*, premiered not in cinemas but on Shudder. Shot over Zoom at the start of the lockdown, the film depicted a virtual séance whose geographically distant participants are attacked by an unquiet spirit. "We didn't have a script, our pitch was basically, 'It's going to be scary, you've got to trust us,'" says Savage. "Shudder totally got on board, and we just figured it out as we went along."

In December 2020, Warner Bros. announced that the company's entire 2021 slate of films would be available to watch on the streaming service HBO Max at the same time that they arrived in cinemas. The list of projects affected by this decision included James Wan's deliriously grotesque *Malignant*, about a woman who has a homicidal tumor living in her head. "Right after *Aquaman 1*, I knew I was jumping into *Aquaman 2* at some point, but I needed to take a little break, I needed a palette cleanser," said Wan ahead of the film's release. "There's only so many PG-13 movies I can make before I get bored of that." Given Warner Bros.' release strategy, *Malignant* earned an unsurprisingly slight $13 million at the domestic box office.

The once all-conquering *Paranormal Activity* franchise had lost much of its box office mojo even before COVID, with 2015's *Paranormal Activity: The Ghost Dimension* grossing a comparatively meager $18 million in the US. As the real-world crisis continued, Paramount decided to premiere a seventh entry, *Paranormal Activity: Next of Kin*, on its streaming service Paramount+ in October 2021.

Zack Snyder's stewardship of the DC Extended Universe ended during the production of 2017's *Justice League*. The director left the project following the death of his daughter, Autumn, and was replaced by a pre-scandal Joss Whedon. Snyder returned to filmmaking, and to horror, with the 2021 Netflix movie *Army of the Dead*, a heist tale set in a Las Vegas overrun by zombies. The streaming service subsequently announced that the film had been watched in 75 million households during its first 28 days of release.

Thankfully, with COVID vaccines starting to become widely available, audiences were returning to cinemas, and horror movies proved a popular distraction from the real-life terrors of the pandemic.

Paramount had held the world premiere of *A Quiet Place Part II* in New York on March 8, 2020, but delayed the film's release as incidents of COVID increased. When John Krasinski's sequel finally appeared in May 2021, it earned $297 million worldwide. The year's other horror releases included *Halloween Kills*, a new *Candyman* film, *The Forever Purge*, and the Edgar Wright-directed *Last Night in Soho*.

2021 also saw the release of a new *Saw* film called *Spiral*. The movie was conceived by Chris Rock and starred the comedian as a cop investigating a Jigsaw-inspired copycat killer. *Spiral* co-starred Samuel L. Jackson and was directed by Darren Bousman, but it did not feature Tobin Bell and was a commercial letdown. Still, the ninth *Saw* film earned enough to push the franchise's cumulative box office grosses over the $1 billion mark.

Horror movies continued to attract audiences in 2022. Box office successes included *Smile*, Jordan Peele's *Nope*, *Halloween Ends*, the prequel *Orphan: First Kill*, *Terrifier 2*, and *Barbarian*. Written and directed by former sketch comedian Zach Cregger, the twisty *Barbarian* starred Georgina Campbell and Bill Skarsgård as strangers who stay at the same Airbnb accommodation and Justin Long as a canceled actor who owns the house. The trio are unaware that the abode's basement is home to a feral creature obsessed with mothering, and feeding milk to, visitors. Produced by Roy Lee, *Barbarian* cost $4.5 million and earned $40 million in the US after it was released in September 2022. "I went, like, ten times to see it in a theater," says Matthew Patrick Davis, who played the film's 'Mother.' "It was fun hearing the audience go, 'What the fuck?!'" In March 2025, Deadline announced that Sony would release a Cregger-directed *Resident Evil* film in September 2026. "I've been a rabid fan of these games for decades, and to be able to bring this amazing title to life is a true honor," the filmmaker told the outlet.

After directing *Doctor Strange*, Scott Derrickson made 2022's horror film *The Black Phone*. The movie was adapted from a short story by Joe Hill, with a script by Derrickson and C. Robert Cargill. The Blumhouse-produced tale of a teenager attempting to escape the clutches of a masked maniac played by Ethan Hawke was a personal project for the filmmaker. "I had been in therapy, really dealing with trauma from my own childhood and violence from my own childhood, for about three years," he says. "I thought: 'What if I combined my childhood memories with that story that Joe wrote?' And that's really what the movie is." The film was a hit, and, in November 2023,

Deadline reported that Hawke, Derrickson, and Cargill would reunite for a sequel.

Ti West directed not one but two A24-backed horror movies released in 2022: *X* and *Pearl.* The '70s-set *X* starred Mia Goth as both an adult film actress and an older killer; *Pearl* took place decades earlier and found Goth playing a young version of her aged character from the first movie. West would conclude the trilogy with a 2024 sequel to *X* called *MaXXXine.* That film's cast included Goth, Kevin Bacon, and Larry Fessenden, whose character, for once, did not perish onscreen.

2023 would also see a raft of successful horror releases, from *Scream VI* to *Evil Dead Rise* to A24's *Talk to Me* to the Jeff Katz-produced *The Pope's Exorcist* to M. Night Shyamalan's *Knock at the Cabin* to Eli Roth's Sony-distributed *Thanksgiving.* Roth spent much of the previous decade directing films outside the horror genre, including the 2018 fantasy tale *The House with a Clock in Its Walls*, but had finally turned his fake *Grindhouse* trailer into a real movie. The film was a bloody affair, albeit one not as grotesque as Roth had planned. "Nobody knows this, but on *Thanksgiving*, first I filmed the cheerleader with the knife the way it was in the trailer," he says. "The

Mia Goth in *Pearl* (2022).

footage went all the way through Sony, and they were so outraged they shut the movie down. They said, 'You have to reshoot this.' It wasn't screaming fights, it was just like, 'You're *not* in 2007 anymore.'" *Thanksgiving* earned a Sony-satisfying $31 million at the US box office, and Roth set to work writing a sequel.

Remarkably, 2023 featured the release of three new entries in horror franchises inaugurated by James Wan. Filmmaker Kevin Greutert's *Saw X* was a Jigsaw origin story that returned Tobin Bell and Shawnee Smith to the franchise and grossed $53 million in the US. Patrick Wilson both starred in and directed *Insidious: The Red Door*, which earned $189 million at the global box office. The Blumhouse film was distributed by Screen Gems, whose parent company Sony later confirmed plans for another *Insidious* movie in addition to a previously announced spin-off, *Thread: An Insidious Tale. The Nun II* was an even bigger hit, grossing $269 million around the world. The film was directed by Michael Chaves, who would go on to make the supernatural universe's next movie, 2025's *The Conjuring: Last Rites.*

Wan's company Atomic Monster also produced 2023's much-memeified killer robot movie *M3GAN*. "We thought it would be fun to do a movie that

M3GAN in *M3GAN* (2023).

is basically *Annabelle* meets *The Terminator*," he says. Directed by Gerard Johnstone from a script by Akela Cooper, *M3GAN* earned $180 million worldwide.

Wan produced *M3GAN* with Jason Blum, whose roster of 2023 horror films would include both a notorious misstep and one of his biggest hits to date. In July 2021, *The New York Times* reported that Universal and the streaming service Peacock had closed what journalist Brooks Barnes described as "a $400 million-plus megadeal to buy a new *Exorcist* trilogy." The first fruit of that deal, *The Exorcist: Believer*, was produced by Blumhouse and directed by David Gordon Green. Released on October 6, 2023, the movie garnered bad reviews and, given the cost of the project, poor box office. Blum's reputation as a commercial force would be restored just three weeks later with the release of the Josh Hutcherson-starring *Five Nights at Freddy's*. The film was adapted from the popular video game franchise and directed by Emma Tammi, who had impressed Blum with her 2018 horror-western *The Wind*. *Five Nights at Freddy's* grossed $80 million over its opening weekend and would go on to become the year's most successful horror film, eventually earning $291 million worldwide.

Five Nights at Freddy's co-starred *Scream* killer Matthew Lillard, who played the movie's villain. In July 2023, the actors' union SAG-AFTRA had gone on strike in an industrial action that would not end until early November. Unable to undertake promotional activities, Lillard watched *Five Nights at Freddy's* over its opening weekend at a local cinema, where his fellow cinemagoers were surprised to find the one-time Ghostface in their midst. "Look, nobody really cares that you're an actor unless you're in a big hit movie *and* in the theater to see your movie," the actor says, with a laugh. "I was standing out like a sore thumb, but it was very sweet. The audience responded in an incredible way, and as they walked out everyone was saying congratulations. My kids were mortified, which is exactly what you want." In October 2024, Blumhouse revealed that *Five Nights at Freddy's 2* would be released in December of the following year.

Jason Blum and James Wan would cement their professional relationship in January 2024 by merging Atomic Monster and Blumhouse. "It's official!" declared a message on Blumhouse's Instagram page announcing the completion of the deal. "The pre-eminent homes for horror are now under one roof."

As horror thrived in the post-pandemic years, the superhero genre faltered. Andy Muschietti's *The Flash* and David F. Sandberg's *Shazam! Fury of the Gods* were a pair of DCEU bombs distributed by Warner Bros. in 2023. Shortly after the release of his *Shazam!* sequel, Sandberg put out a statement on social media explaining that he was "very eager to go back to horror (as well as trying some new things). After six years of *Shazam*, I'm definitely done with superheroes for now." The director's next project would be *Until Dawn*, his adaptation of a 2015 horror video game co-written by Larry Fessenden and Graham Reznick. Marvel's 2023 release *The Marvels* was another commercial disappointment, and the studio seemed unable to get its long-planned, Mahershala Ali-starring *Blade* movie off the ground.

Slither and *American Mary* special makeup designer Todd Masters does not shed any tears over the travails of the superhero genre. "I try to watch all those damn movies, but it's a bunch of bullshit," he says. "I'm surprised people fell for it. I want to see something that I can actually believe in, and that's why I like making movies with practical effects. I think people agree. We don't have to make a lot of AI bullshit and lose art forever."

In October 2022, Warner Bros. announced that Masters' *Slither* director James Gunn and *Conjuring* universe producer Peter Safran had been hired as co-chairs of the newly formed DC Studios. The pair would later make clear their intention to start afresh, with Gunn writing and directing a new Superman film, set to arrive in 2025. The last movie to come out under the banner of the old DCEU was Wan's now-orphaned *Aquaman and the Lost Kingdom*. The film debuted in December 2023 and earned $439 million, less than half of the original *Aquaman*. Eli Roth recalls commiserating with Wan following the release of the film and the subsequent box office failure of Roth's own big-budget 2024 video game adaptation *Borderlands*. "We just start laughing about what troubles he went through on *Aquaman* and what I went through on *Borderlands*," says the *Hostel* director. "Both of us are rolling our eyes like, 'Oh my God, we're back to horror, fuck these projects!'" In August 2024, *Variety* reported that Wan was developing a remake of *Creature from the Black Lagoon* for Universal.

The box office returns of 2023's *Scream VI* made a seventh movie in the franchise an inevitability. Spyglass hired Christopher Landon to direct the film, with Melissa Barrera among the *Scream VI* cast members expected to return for the new movie. Then, in November 2023, the actress reposted a social media message accusing Israel of "genocide and ethnic cleansing" in its response to the attack by Hamas the previous month. Spyglass swiftly fired Barrera from the film, issuing a statement that the production company had "zero tolerance for antisemitism or the incitement of hate in any form." The next day, Deadline reported that Jenna Ortega would also not be returning to the franchise, purportedly because of the actress' commitment to shooting the second season of *Wednesday*. On December 23, Landon announced on social media that he, too, had exited the project. "It was a dream job that turned into a nightmare," wrote the filmmaker. "And my heart did break for everyone involved. Everyone. But it's time to move on."

Spyglass moved on by moving back, hiring Kevin Williamson to direct the seventh *Scream* film and striking a deal with Neve Campbell for the actress' return to the franchise. Campbell would be joined in the cast by fellow franchise veterans Courteney Cox, David Arquette, and Matthew Lillard. On January 8, 2025, Williamson posted a message on Instagram to mark the start of shooting. "What an extraordinary day I had working with an amazing and talented cast and crew," he wrote. "They brought their 'A' game and

Neve Campbell, Courteney Cox, and Kevin Williamson on the set of *Scream* (2022).

had my back every step of the way. I'm so very grateful for this opportunity and to Wes Craven, who was on my mind through it all."

Julie Plec was thrilled to learn that Williamson was directing the film. "I think that's a beautiful way to come full circle on the franchise," she says, speaking in October 2024. "I know he's got lots of surprises and goodies lined up. I was sad when *Scream 3* continued without him, I thought that was sad. So there was a bittersweet era for me for a while. This kind of rights that wrong, and I'm excited about it."

If horror movies teach us anything, it is that the future is unknowable. One moment, a character is enjoying a pleasant stroll in the woods. The next, they are being hacked to pieces by a masked, knife-wielding maniac or bitten by one of the walking (or sprinting) undead. The success of horror in the decades since the release of Wes Craven's *Scream* does not guarantee a similarly blockbuster-filled future. In the spring of 2024, several films, including the prequel *The First Omen* and Radio Silence's vampire movie *Abigail*, sputtered at the box office, prompting concerns about the genre. As the outlet Comic Book Resources asked in a headline, "The 2024 Box Office Is Burying Its Dead With the Horror Genre—What Happened?" What happened, as it turned out, was nothing to keep horror fans awake at night. In the following months, fears about the robustness of the genre were swept away by the successes of *A Quiet Place: Day One*, *Smile 2*, *Heretic*, *Alien: Romulus*, *Longlegs*, *Terrifier 3*, *The Substance*, and Robert Eggers' *Nosferatu*. Like the Demi Moore body-horror film, Eggers' period vampire tale was both a box office hit, earning $95 million in the US, and multiple Oscar nominee.

The sleepless nights of horror junkies would be caused not by worries over the future of the genre but by the terrors contained in the films coming their way. Many of those movies were made by talents who had gotten their breaks in the years after the release of Craven's *Scream*, and many were continuations of franchises created during the same period.

In January 2022, New Line announced that a sixth *Final Destination* film was in the works, based on a treatment from *Spider-Man* franchise director Jon Watts. "Jon Watts, who is huge *FD* fan, came to us and said, 'I have an idea,'" says series producer Craig Perry. "I was like, 'I like that!'" The movie, titled *Final Destination Bloodlines*, was originally set to premiere on HBO Max but would later be rerouted into theaters in 2025.

In January 2023, Deadline reported that Sony was developing a sequel to *I Know What You Did Last Summer*. In January 2024, *The Hollywood Reporter* revealed that Danny Boyle and Alex Garland were reuniting for *28 Years Later*. In April 2024, Lionsgate announced that the company was partnering with Blumhouse to reboot the *Blair Witch* franchise (news which prompted the three stars of the original film to ask for increased retroactive compensation). In October 2024, Deadline reported that Luca Guadagnino was in talks with Lionsgate to direct a new version of *American Psycho*. The same month, Paramount and the now Weinstein-less Miramax announced that the *Scary Movie* creative team of Marlon, Shawn, and Keenen Ivory Wayans were working on a new film in the parody series. In December, 2024, *The Hollywood Reporter* told readers that "horror powerhouses" Atomic Monster and Blumhouse were producing a new take on *The Mummy* from *Evil Dead Rise* filmmaker Lee Cronin. "This will be unlike any *Mummy* movie you ever laid eyeballs on before," Cronin said in a statement. "I'm digging deep into the earth to raise something very ancient and very frightening."

Resident Evil star Milla Jovovich would continue to battle zombies. On November 1, 2024, Deadline revealed that she was set to star in *Twilight of the Dead*, the script for which was based on a treatment George Romero had written before his passing. The film was being directed by *Session 9* auteur Brad Anderson and would feature makeup effects created by Greg Nicotero.

The day before the announcement of Jovovich's casting, Deadline revealed that her *Resident Evil* franchise director and husband Paul W. S. Anderson had been hired to write and direct a new film based on the *House of the Dead* video game series. Anderson is keen to point out that his new project is technically not a zombie film. "They're bio-engineered monsters, they're created in a lab, they're cloned, so they're not zombies," he says of the movie's creatures. "When we started *Resident Evil*, no one had seen zombies for fifteen years, now everyone's seen zombies *for* fifteen years. There's a bit of zombie fatigue going on. We're going to give the audience something they can't get from a traditional zombie movie."

The Deadline article failed to mention Uwe Boll's 2003 *House of the Dead* adaptation. But the earlier film's co-writer Mark A. Altman insists that even that much-maligned movie has its diehard fans. "I've been a guest at a lot of conventions, and I've been talking a little more about *House of the Dead*," he says. "A lot of people come up and want me to sign it. I go, 'Ugh, *that* one?' And they're like, 'Why are you making that face? It's great! I love it!' Some people love it because it's terrible, other people genuinely think it's a wonderful movie. It's not that way for me, but if that's their truth, more power to them!"

"People go to the movies to feel things," says *Sinister* and *The Black Phone* filmmaker Scott Derrickson. "There's no more powerful feeling than fear, and young audiences especially love to experience fear vicariously. They go to horror films for the same reason they go to amusement parks and ride rollercoasters in the summer, because it's a heart-pounding experience that is safe, even though it doesn't feel safe in the moment. People like to go to a theater and experience a scary movie communally with an audience. That's not going to change."

Decades after the dark days he experienced in the early '90s, *Phantasm* and *Bubba Ho-Tep* director Don Coscarelli is similarly bullish about the future of the genre. "Listen, horror has never been more popular," he says. "It's visceral, and people love the thrill ride experience of it. I think all of us, when we go into a movie theater, you pay your $20 now and it's like, 'Show me, make me feel something.' It's hard to do with a comedy and harder with a drama, but a little easier with a horror film. If you do it right, you can shoot them out of their seats!"

As of the spring of 2025, the imminent future (of horror, at least) looks blood-red rosy. Cinemagoers, many of whom had not been born when Wes Craven's original *Scream* was released, are still watching horror films, finding new answers to the question that Ghostface asked Drew Barrymore's doomed Casey Becker all those years ago:

What's your favorite scary movie?

ACKNOWLEDGMENTS

Writing this book reminded me on an hourly basis that making a movie is an extraordinarily difficult thing to do. Thank you to the many people who worked on the projects covered in *Screaming and Conjuring* and particularly to those who spoke with me about their toils. I've long believed that horror filmmakers are, for the most part, among the nicest people you could ever meet and the interviews I conducted only reinforced that notion. Thank you, as well, to the folks who helped arrange those interviews and sourced the images included here.

Screaming and Conjuring would not exist without two magazines: *Entertainment Weekly* and *Fangoria*. I spent almost two decades working as a senior writer at *Entertainment Weekly* where I was allowed to indulge my love for horror and had the opportunity to speak with a huge amount of genre creators (and even got to see Jamie Lee Curtis play Laurie Strode *in the flesh*). While I have yet to contribute to *Fangoria* (give me a call, Phil!), the magazine fueled and informed my love for genre when I was growing up and proved an incredible resource for this book. I must also thank London's BFI Reuben Library, where I spent many a happy day perusing vintage copies of *Fango* in the name of research while everyone else was reading books about Godard and Tarkovsky.

Thank you to my publisher Matthew Chojnacki, who was enthusiastic about my original pitch and helped turn it into something less cockamamie. Thank you also to this book's cover artist Gary Pullin, layout designer Arkadii Pankevich, proofreader Dan Lockwood, and indexer Nick de Somogyi. I apologize again to the latter for introducing him to *The Human Centipede*.

Thank you to my friends and family. I hope to see more of you all, now I've finished this book.

Finally, thank you to Emma, for your love and patience, and to our cat Coco, for keeping office hours with me.

IMAGE CREDITS

Photos and illustrations (with corresponding page numbers) are courtesy of the following:

Michael Dougherty: 361, 362
Mick Garris: 279
Adam Green: 307
Steve Johnson: 66, 77, 243 (*both*), 329
Greg Nicotero / KNB EFX Group: 70, 141 (*both*), 235 (*both*), 272, 283 (*both*), 300, 336, 354, 389, 390 (*both*)
Tim Palen: 253, 312 (*right*)
Graham Reznick / Dark Sky Films: 379, 382
Eli Roth: 211, 215 (*left*), 258, 302, 313

Alamy and:

Dimension / Everett Collection: 16; Falcon International / Album: 22; Paramount / AJ Pics: 24; New Line / Mike Ditz / AJ Pics: 28; New Line / Album: 29; Dimension / Cinematic: 34; Dimension / Maximum Film: 38; Dimension / AJ Pics: 40; Dimension / Photo 12: 41; Victoria Jones / PA Images: 42; Columbia / AJ Pics: 47; Dimension / Kimberly Wright / Masheter Movie Archive: 49; Dimension / TCD-Prod.DB: 54; Universal / RGR Collection: 55; New Line / BFA: 60; New Line / AJ Pics: 67; Trimark / Cinematic: 73; Universal / Maximum Film: 79 and 82; Hollywood Pictures / PictureLux / Hollywood Archive: 86; Artisan / Maximum Film: 88; Artisan / RGR Collection: 92; HBO / 20th Century Fox / AJ Pics: 94; Paramount / Archives du 7e Art / Photo 12: 99; Columbia / Everett Collection: 106; Dimension / Cinematic: 110; Universal / Moviestore Collection: 111; Universal / IFA Film / United Archives GmbH: 113; New Line / AJ Pics: 118; New Line / Everett Collection: 119; Dimension / Everett Collection: 122; Columbia / Stephen Vaughn / Photo 12: 124 (*top*); Columbia / American Pictorial Collection / PictureLux / Hollywood Archive: 124 (*bottom*); Dimension / AJ Pics: 126; MGM / AJ Pics: 130; Dimension / Pictorial Press: 132; United Artists / Maximum Film: 137; New Line / Album: 139; Toho / Ringu-Rasen / Moviestore Collection: 142; DreamWorks / Cinematic: 143; Columbia / Entertainment Pictures: 146; Warner Bros. / Cinematic: 150; Warner Bros. / RGR Collection: 151; Paramount / Moviestore Collection: 155; Paramount

/ AJ Pics: 156; Sony / PictureLux / Hollywood Archive: 158; Sony / TCD-Prod. DB: 160; 20th Century Fox / RGR Collection: 167; Artisan / Maximum Film: 170; 20th Century Fox / Pathe / Cinematic: 174; Vitagraph / A7A Collection / Photo 12: 179; New Line / PictureLux / Hollywood Archive: 181; New Line / AJ Pics: 185 and 186; Lakeshore Entertainment / Maximum Film: 190 and 191; Focus Features / Cinematic: 194; Michael Germana / Everett Collection: 197; Universal / AJ Pics: 201; Lions Gate / Moviestore Collection: 203; Lions Gate / Album: 206; Lions Gate / Everett Collection: 208 and 213; Lions Gate / Tonic Films / Photo 12: 215 (*right*); Lions Gate / Greg Gayne / Everett Collection; 218; Lions Gate / BFA: 221; Universal / AJ Pics: 225; Universal / TCD-Prod.DB: 226; Universal / A7A Collection / Photo 12: 230; Universal / AJ Pics: 231; Dimension / Maximum Film: 233; Universal / RGR Collection: 239; Universal / kpa Publicity Stills / United Archives GmbH: 240; Paramount / Photo 12: 241; Screen Gems / Album: 248; Lionsgate / Twisted Pictures / Collection Christophel: 249 and 252; Lionsgate / Twisted Pictures / BFA: 254 (*left*); Lionsgate / Twisted Pictures / TCD-Prod.DB: 254 (*right*); Lionsgate / Hostel LLC / Photo 12: 257; Lionsgate / Hostel LLC / RGR Collection: 259; Gene Blevins / ZUMA Press: 261; Celador Films / AJ Pics: 264; Dimension / mrk / Universal Images Group North America: 268 (*top left*); Sony / Cinematic: 268 (*top right*); Screen Gems / Everett Collection: 268 (*bottom left*); Warner Bros. / Album: 268 (*bottom right*); Dimension Films / AJ Pics: 269; 20th Century Fox / Dune Entertainment / Cinematic: 271; Universal / Gold Circle Films / Maximum Film: 276; Universal / Gold Circle Films / Cinematic: 277; Showtime / A7A Collection / Photo 12: 284; TriStar Pictures / Album: 287; TriStar Pictures / Maximum Film: 289; Warner Bros. / Cinematic: 292 (*top*); Phil McCarten / UPI: 292 (*bottom*); Lionsgate / A7A Collection / Photo 12: 295; Universal / Everett Collection: 297; Dimension / Cinematic: 298; Dimension / Maximum Film: 299; 20th Century Fox / Everett Collection: 304; Magnolia Pictures / Cinematic: 310; Lionsgate / Screen Gems / Raw Nerve / Album: 311 and 312 (*left*); Warner Bros. / kpa Publicity Stills / United Archives GmbH: 319; Third Rail Releasing / Collection Christophel: 321; Filmax / A7A Collection / Photo 12: 323 (*left*); Screen Gems / Cinematic: 323 (*right*); Warner Bros. / Maximum Film: 326; Castle Rock / Cinematic: 331; Dimension / AJ Pics: 333; MGM / Dimension / Pictorial Press: 334; Paramount / FlixPix: 340; Walt Disney / Cinematic: 342 and 344 (*left*); 20th Century Fox / Blinding Edge / Album: 344 (*right*); Universal / Rogue / Intrepid / Vertigo / Album: 345; Lionsgate / Everett Collection: 348; Lionsgate / Album: 350; Universal / Cinematic: 353; Universal / Everett Collection: 355; 20th Century Fox / Maximum Film: 356; 20th Century Fox / Photo 12: 359; Nikki Nelson / WENN Rights Ltd: 360; Warner Bros. / Cinematic: 364; Columbia / AJ Pics: 368; Steve Mack: 369; Blumhouse / Paramount / Archives du 7e Art / Photo 12: 372; IFC Films / Everett Collection: 377; MPI Media Group / Glass Eye Pix / Moviestore Collection: 381; Blumhouse / Paramount / Pictorial Press: 386; Blumhouse / Sony / TCD-Prod.DB: 392; Blumhouse / Sony / AJ Pics: 394; Dimension / Cinematic: 396; Dimension / Photo 12: 398; Alliance Films / Moviestore Collection: 400;

Universal / AJ Pics: 401; MGM / Lionsgate / Pictorial Press: 403; MGM / Lionsgate / Moviestore Collection: 404; Lionsgate / Icon / HanWay / Snoot / TCD-Prod.DB: 406; Lionsgate / Icon / HanWay / Snoot / Cinematic: 408; CBS / Momentum / PictureLux / Hollywood Archive: 413; Julie Edwards / JEP Celebrity Photos: 416; 20th Century Fox / AJ Pics: 419; AmityPhotos: 421; Warner Bros. / New Line / PictureLux / Hollywood Archive: 423; Warner Bros. / New Line / WENN US: 425; Warner Bros. / New Line / AJ Pics: 426; Warner Bros. / New Line / BFA: 429; Warner Bros. / New Line / Collection Christophel: 431; Paramount / Album: 434; Universal / BFA: 437; New Line / Brooke Palmer / Photo 12: 439; Netflix / Siren Pictures / FlixPix: 443; A24 / B-REEL Films / Album: 447; Miramax / Blumhouse / Universal / Entertainment Pictures: 452; 20th Century Studios / BoulderLight / Album: 457; A24 / Little Lamb / Album: 458; Universal / BFA: 459; Paramount / Album: 462; Mubi / TCD-Prod.DB: 464 (*left*); Focus Features / FlixPix: 464 (*right*).

Special thanks:

Glass Eye Pix: 58; Richard Matheson / Bantam: 318; Dean Schramm / Stuart Gordon: 411.

INDEX OF TITLES

INDEX OF NAMES

ABOUT THE AUTHOR

Clark Collis is a veteran entertainment journalist who has contributed to *The Guardian*, *Empire* magazine, and *Entertainment Weekly*, where he was a senior writer for 18 years. He studied history at Cambridge University, and is the author of the 2021 book *You've Got Red on You: How Shaun of the Dead Was Brought to Life*. His favorite horror movie is John Carpenter's *The Thing*.